From Hugo Walter
Princeton University
Class of 1981

Magnificent Houses in Twentieth Century European Literature

Studies on Themes and Motifs in Literature

Horst S. Daemmrich
General Editor

Vol. 115

PETER LANG
New York • Washington, D.C./Baltimore • Bern
Frankfurt • Berlin • Brussels • Vienna • Oxford

Hugo G. Walter

Magnificent Houses in Twentieth Century European Literature

PETER LANG
New York • Washington, D.C./Baltimore • Bern
Frankfurt • Berlin • Brussels • Vienna • Oxford

Library of Congress Cataloging-in-Publication Data
Walter, Hugo.
Magnificent houses in twentieth century European literature / Hugo G. Walter.
p. cm. — (Studies on themes and motifs in literature; v. 115)
Includes bibliographical references and index.
1. Architecture in literature. 2. Dwellings in literature. 3. Landscape in literature.
4. Setting (Literature). 5. Mann, Thomas, 1875–1955. Buddenbrooks.
6. Waugh, Evelyn, 1903–1966. Brideshead revisited. 7. Tolkien, J. R. R. (John
Ronald Reuel), 1892–1973. Lord of the rings. 8. Lenz, Siegfried, 1926– Deutschstunde.
9. European literature—20th century—History and criticism. I. Title.
PN56.A73W35   809'.93357—dc23   2012002736
ISBN 978-1-4331-1847-0 (hardcover)
ISBN 978-1-4539-0575-3 (e-book)
ISSN 1056-3970

Bibliographic information published by **Die Deutsche Nationalbibliothek.**
Die Deutsche Nationalbibliothek lists this publication in the "Deutsche
Nationalbibliografie"; detailed bibliographic data is available
on the Internet at http://dnb.d-nb.de/.

The paper in this book meets the guidelines for permanence and durability
of the Committee on Production Guidelines for Book Longevity
of the Council of Library Resources.

© 2012 Peter Lang Publishing, Inc., New York
29 Broadway, 18th floor, New York, NY 10006
www.peterlang.com

Printed in Germany

This book is dedicated to all individuals who have
an appreciation of magnificent and beautiful houses.

Contents

Preface

In my two previous monographs, *Sanctuaries of Light in Nineteenth Century European Literature* and *Beautiful Sanctuaries in Nineteenth- and Early-Twentieth- Century European Literature,* I explored the themes of sanctuaries of light, serenity, harmony, and natural beauty in selected works of William Wordsworth, Percy Shelley, E. T. A. Hoffmann, Joseph von Eichendorff, Charlotte Brontë, Henrik Ibsen, and James Hilton.

In this new monograph I discuss the depiction and the representation of magnificent houses and lovely architectural creations in twentieth century European literature, focusing especially on the works of Thomas Mann, Evelyn Waugh, J. R. R. Tolkien, and Siegfried Lenz. The chapter on Thomas Mann is a revised version of my essay on Mann in *Space and Time on the Magic Mountain.*

I would also like to add a personal note here which is relevant to my discussion of the notion of sanctuaries of light. I have been interested in literary studies and in the theme of beautiful places (places of natural loveliness as well as places of gorgeous and interesting aesthetic vitality) in literature for many years, dating back to my youth growing up in Princeton, New Jersey. The natural beauty, the architectural magnificence and splendor, the luminescence, and the tranquility of the town of Princeton and of Princeton University have always attracted and appealed to me and have been consistently inspirational for me aesthetically, emotionally, and spiritually. The sense of a lovely sanctuary or refuge which I have felt in Princeton and in various other places in the United States, in Europe, in Great Britain, in Canada, and in Asia is infused with the aura of the "healing Paradise" (355) of rejuvenating vitality which culminates Percy Shelley's "Lines Written among the Euganean Hills" and with the spirit of the "sense sublime" of which William Wordsworth speaks in "Tintern Abbey":

And I have felt
A presence that disturbs me with the joy
Of elevated thoughts; a sense sublime
Of something far more deeply interfused,
Whose dwelling is the light of setting suns,
And the round ocean, and the living air,
And the blue sky, and in the mind of man;
A motion and a spirit, that impels
All thinking things, all objects of all thought,
And rolls through all things. (93–102)

I have been fortunate to experience various lovely architectural creations and places of sanctuary (as aesthetically interesting interiors and as scenic and picturesque natural spaces) over the years (especially in beautiful areas of the United States, Europe, Great Britain, Canada, and Asia). College libraries, university libraries, beautiful gardens, historic houses, churches, and museums in beautiful natural settings especially exemplify for me sanctuaries of luminescence, harmony, and serenity in the spirit of the statement of Prometheus in Act III, Scene iii of Percy Shelley's *Prometheus Unbound*. For these are extraordinary places where "lovely apparitions.../ Then radiant—as the mind, arising bright / From the embrace of beauty" (III. iii. 49–51) will inspire "the progeny immortal / Of Painting, Sculpture, and rapt Poesy / And arts, though unimagined, yet to be" (III.iii.54–56). These are beautiful places which have the capacity, in the sense of Wordsworth's statement in the "Ode: Intimations of Immortality from Recollections of Early Childhood," to signify "the fountain-light of all our day" (151) and the "master-light of all our seeing" (152) and to preserve perpetually the "power to make / Our noisy years seem moments in the being / Of the eternal Silence: truths that wake, / To perish never" (153–56).

Hugo Walter, Ph.D.
hgw@berkeleycollege.edu

Acknowledgments

I would like to thank my literature and humanities professors at Princeton University, Yale University, Old Dominion University, and Drew University for their guidance and supportiveness over the years. In my previous book I mentioned the names of several of my graduate school professors. In this book I would like to thank several of my undergraduate professors at Princeton whose teaching and whose writings have been inspirational for me: Theodore Ziolkowski, Michael Curschmann, Sandra Bermann, Carl Schorske, Walter Hinderer, Victor Lange, John Fleming, Claudia L. Johnson, Victor Brombert, John R. Martin, David Coffin, and William G. Moulton.

I would also like to thank Professor Horst Daemmrich of the University of Pennsylvania and Dr. Heidi Burns of Peter Lang Publishing for their insightful and thoughtful comments regarding my manuscript.

I would like to express my gratitude to my many colleagues at Berkeley College (Online, New Jersey, and New York) for their kindness, encouragement, and supportiveness.

Finally, I would like to thank the Production Department of Peter Lang for their helpful assistance and patience in the production of the manuscript.

I would like to acknowledge the following institutions for permission to reprint from the following works:

From *Space and Time on the Magic Mountain: Studies in Nineteenth- and Early-Twentieth-Century European Literature*, by Hugo G. Walter, Copyright © 1999, Peter Lang Publishing, reprinted with the permission of the publisher.

From *Sanctuaries of Light in Nineteenth Century European Literature*, by Hugo G. Walter, Copyright © 2010, Peter Lang Publishing, reprinted with the permission of the publisher.

Introduction

One of the most magnificent houses in the history of European literature, and even in the history of world literature, is the splendid home of the Archivarius Lindhorst and his family in E. T. A. Hoffmann's *Der goldne Topf, The golden Pot* (1814). This great house is characterized by a luminescence, a vital sense of inner space and spatial expansiveness, an aura of architectural beauty, an atmosphere of aesthetic splendor affirmed in the presence of various extraordinary and lovely objects, and a serene elegance. The splendor of Lindhorst's house is derived not only from its potent capacity for creating and generating light and for suffusing diverse gorgeous objects in its domain such as the golden pot in an exquisite radiance but also from its existence as a dynamic effulgent space which counters the presence of forces of darkness in the surrounding environment and in contemporary society.

Another of the most splendid and extraordinary mansions in the history of European literature and world literature is Pemberley in Jane Austen's *Pride and Prejudice* (1813). Pemberley House, the home of the Darcy family, represents a quintessential sanctuary of architectural loveliness, peacefulness, natural beauty, and serenity in Derbyshire. Pemberley House, "a large, handsome, stone building, standing well on rising ground" (159), is beautiful and offers picturesque views of the delightful natural environment from its perspective of security. The majestic property surrounding Pemberley House is also noteworthy because of its spatial expansiveness. The interior of the mansion is praised as possessing and signifying an atmosphere of genuine elegance, decorum, and taste.

In this book I will discuss magnificent houses and mansions in twentieth century European literature which represent and exemplify the spirit of the architectural beauty, aesthetic splendor, luminescence, serenity, and vitality of Lindhorst's extraordinary house in Hoffmann's *Der goldne Topf* and of Darcy's lovely mansion in Austen's *Pride and Prejudice*. In chapter one I will discuss the depiction of magnificent houses in various works of Thomas Mann, especially focusing on *Buddenbrooks* (1901), *Tonio Kröger, Tristan,* and *Der Zauberberg, The Magic Mountain* (1924). In chapter two I will analyze the importance and the representation of the beautiful Brideshead Castle for the protagonists in Evelyn Waugh's *Brideshead Revisited*. In chapter three I will examine the depiction of lovely houses and exceptional architectural creations in J. R. R. Tolkien's *The Lord of the Rings*. In chapter four I will discuss the description of important and aesthetically interesting houses in Siegfried Lenz's *Deutschstunde, The German Lesson* (1968). I will show that the protagonists in these works develop an attachment to and a love for certain gorgeous architectural spaces which they will strive to maintain and preserve throughout their lives. In works such as *Buddenbrooks, Tonio Kröger, Brideshead Revisited,* and *The Lord of the Rings* some of the protagonists develop a lifelong love for and devotion to their beautiful childhood homes; in other works such as *Deutschstunde* one of the protagonists, Max Nansen, nurtures a deep admiration for a lovely house acquired later in life. If a character is temporarily distanced from or even more permanently separated from an admired and cherished house or mansion, he or she will internalize a vision of this magnificent place so that it will perpetually signify an important and an inspirational part of his or her life. Such a lovely vision has the capacity to consistently revitalize the individual emotionally, intellectually, aesthetically, and spiritually when there is no longer a direct or immediate connection to the splendid house or mansion which generated and motivated the vision.

In a world characterized by and often permeated by change and transformation, the power of the imagination and the capacity to internalize the beauty of magnificent houses, which are, as all other mortal creations, typically subject to the ravages and vicissitudes of time, is important for individuals who wish to remain spiritually connected to such lovely spaces, to remember the beauty and the congenial times which they enjoyed there, and to preserve their emotional integrity and vitality. An individual who is very emotionally and aesthetically attached to a house or architectural space will attempt to preserve such an attachment, literally or symbolically, for the duration of his or her life. Tony Buddenbrook in Mann's *Buddenbrooks,* Tonio Kröger in Mann's *Tonio Kröger,* Sebastian Flyte in Waugh's *Brideshead Revisited,* Bilbo Baggins, Elrond, Galadriel, Frodo, and Sam in Tolkien's *The Lord of the Rings,* and Max Nansen in Lenz's *Deutschstunde* are all very attached to and devoted to such environments which one might describe as the central architectural experience of their lives. In the case of Tony Buddenbrook, Tonio Kröger, and Sebastian Flyte such places have been of vital importance since childhood—these three individuals remember with great fondness and longing their magnificent childhood homes and yearn to revitalize at least to some extent in their present lives the spirit of happiness and delight which they enjoyed or recall enjoying in the recent or in the distant past. For

Max Nansen the most important architectural space of his life was first experienced in adulthood. One might say that he has nurtured the image and the hope of finding such a place in his heart—reality has manifested and affirmed what his imagination had desired. For Nansen the house and studio in which he lives in close connectedness to the lovely surrounding natural environment represents an ultimate aesthetic experience. It is as if the house and nature are reflections or extensions of one another—the presence of the exuberant colors and lovely flowers in the studio and in the surrounding environment reaffirm this intimate association.

Tony Buddenbrook, Tonio Kröger, Sebastian Flyte, Frodo, and Galadriel are ultimately separated by everyday mortality and its vicissitudes from the house, the architectural space, which they love best—the rest of their lives represents an attempt to restore and revitalize the spirit of this beautiful space in their hearts and souls. They know instinctively, as does the persona in Wordsworth's "I Wandered Lonely as a Cloud" and the persona in Eichendorff's "Abschied," that even if they are distant from or separated from such a magnificent space, or even if they are compelled by circumstances never to be able to experience such a space in person or directly again, as long as they are able to reflect on the beauty and loveliness of such a place and on the congenial memories associated with it, they will be able to preserve a sense of happiness and contentment in their lives. By internalizing the aesthetic, emotional, and spiritual beauty and magnificence of such a vitally important architectural space each of these individuals is able to modify and to transform the anguish and the transience of mortality into a lovely, pleasant, and sustained vision of a luminescent and peaceful sanctuary which will guide and motivate the future and comfort the heart and soul.

In this introduction I will now discuss several significant examples of the heritage of magnificent houses, interesting architectural creations, and lovely natural spaces which have the aura of an effulgent architectural ambience in nineteenth century European literature, focusing on seminal works of such authors as E. T. A. Hoffmann, Joseph von Eichendorff, Jane Austen, William Wordsworth, Percy Shelley, Wilhelm Grimm, Jacob Grimm, Victor Hugo, Charlotte Brontë, Emily Brontë, Charles Dickens, George Eliot, Thomas Hardy, Leo Tolstoy, Theodor Storm, August Strindberg, Henrik Ibsen, and Oscar Wilde.

In E. T. A. Hoffmann's *Der goldne Topf* (1814) the house of the Archivarius Lindhorst is a lovely sanctuary of light and an extraordinary architectural creation which celebrates the importance of the light. Anselmus is destined to fall in love with Serpentina, one of Lindhorst's daughters, and to work for him copying manuscripts in his magnificent house. It is noteworthy that Lindhorst's house is not easily accessible, even to someone like Anselmus who is fated to become part of his family. For the narrative represents the struggle between good and evil, light and darkness even at the threshold of Lindhorst's domain. Anselmus has to be given a special liquid to put on the door-knocker of Lindhorst's house, which somehow manifests itself as the face of the evil woman from the Black Gate, so that he may enter. This woman is Lindhorst's nemesis and is trying to prevent Anselmus from establishing his destined connection with the family of Lindhorst and Serpentina.

At the beginning of the Third Vigil of *Der goldne Topf* the Archivist Lindhorst tells a story about his ancestry which is infused with and permeated by light and love. In the story, for example, when the youth Phosphorus enters a vale, his presence is described as a brilliant and vital light. And when Phosphorus kisses the lily, she becomes a flame and seems filled with an effusively radiant light. At the end of Lindhorst's story when the lily is freed, Phosphorus embraces her, and she becomes the queen of the vale. This vale represents a sanctuary of considerable radiance. Most of the other individuals who are at the narrative presentation by Lindhorst laugh at the distinctive and seemingly incredible details in disbelief. However, Anselmus responds differently and more thoughtfully, suggesting that he, unlike the others, has a poetic and a sensitive soul as well as an instinctive appreciation of the unusual circumstances which the Archivist Lindhorst relates. At the end of the Third Vigil Anselmus is officially introduced to the Archivist Lindhorst as the individual who would be willing to copy his rare manuscripts.

In the Sixth Vigil Anselmus begins his important work with the Archivist Lindhorst. It is noteworthy that Anselmus feels instinctively that if he performs his work proficiently for Lindhorst then he will be rewarded with the love of Lindhorst's daughter, Serpentina. Horst Daemmrich argues very effectively in *The Shattered Self: E. T. A. Hoffmann's Tragic Vision* that Serpentina assists Anselmus in realizing and appreciating "the true significance of the myth of creation" (29) and ultimately "helps him mature into a true poet who understands the voices of nature" (29).

After Anselmus enters the house of Lindhorst he is taken to a gorgeous conservatory which has an aura of spatial expansiveness and sensory exuberance about it. Moreover, the conservatory is filled with a lovely radiance. The magical light of this beautiful sanctuary seems to arise from this extraordinary space for there is no window present which can allow the entrance of light from the outside. Anselmus experiences a sense of spatial expansiveness in this environment when he observes the bushes and trees, for "long avenues appeared to open into remote distance" (31). The sensory abundance of the moment is manifest in the fact that Anselmus not only views beautiful objects (from marble fountains to the fire lilies) and listens to delightful murmurs of unusual voices but also is enchanted by exotic fragrances.

The house of the Archivist Lindhorst is a paradise of gorgeous flowers, plants, objects, fragrances, and melodies. One might say that the house itself is characterized by an inner sense or aura of spatial expansiveness. For when the Archivist Lindhorst shows Anselmus more of the house after the sojourn in the conservatory, he is described as going through many more rooms with exquisite and aesthetically interesting and stimulating colors and decorations. In one distinctive room, in particular, there were "gold-bronze trunks of high palm-trees" (32) rising from the walls and weaving "their colossal leaves, glittering like bright emeralds" (32) towards the ceiling. In the middle of this room is the golden pot.

The golden pot, "ein einfacher goldener Topf," which rests on a porphyry plate on three bronze Egyptian lions, is an extraordinarily beautiful and luminescent object which seems to contain on its surface of polished gold "a thousand gleaming reflections" (32) of various shapes. Anselmus is entranced by the presence of this lovely object and even believes that he observes Serpentina in the radiant reflections gazing at him. However, Lindhorst appears to deflect such intensive observation by saying that Serpentina is actually in another part of the house practicing on the harpsichord.

The Archivist Lindhorst then proceeds to take Anselmus to a library in the house where he will copy the precious manuscripts. As Anselmus works on the manuscript which the Archivist gives him to copy he feels increasingly more at home in the isolated room. The diligence and careful work of Anselmus is motivated by his love for Serpentina and by her faith in him. For as Anselmus copies the manuscript he believes that he hears a crystal murmuring in the room which encourages him to be steadfast and to believe that he is being assisted in his labors by the spiritual presence of Serpentina.

When Lindhorst addresses Anselmus at the end of the Sixth Vigil he speaks of the love which Serpentina has for Anselmus, of the destiny which he and Serpentina appear to share and which will be fulfilled in the future, and of his ultimate reception of the golden pot, which is her dowry. The Archivist also emphasizes that Anselmus is confronted by evil forces and can only survive if he believes in his own inner strength and in the love which he shares with Serpentina. One of the most important concluding points which Lindhorst makes is that if Anselmus carries the love and spirit of Serpentina within his heart and soul, he will overcome all of the negative forces around him and will ultimately achieve eternal happiness. The Archivist also asserts that Anselmus will experience the wonders of the golden pot if he develops and strengthens his love for Serpentina. As Anselmus leaves the house of Lindhorst at the end of the day he admits to himself that he has the most profound love for Serpentina and will do everything he can to fulfill his commitment and devotion to her.

There are interesting parallels between the experience of Anselmus in *Der goldne Topf* and the adventures and life-philosophy of the protagonist in Joseph von Eichendorff's *Aus dem Leben eines Taugenichts, The Memoirs of a Good-for-Nothing* (1826). Both individuals have similarly innocent and virtuous characters, are motivated by a devotion to light, love, and luminescence, and are typically undervalued and devalued by the contemporary society in which they live. Both of these narratives contain an abundance of references to luminescent spaces and to sanctuaries of light, whether transient or more permanent. In Section One of the Eichendorff narrative, for example, the estate in Vienna (or near Vienna, depending on one's interpretation of the text) where the protagonist works as a gardener represents a sanctuary of light and tranquility, especially in the morning. The park of the estate is particularly beautiful; various features of the natural landscape have a golden hue in the morning sunlight. The aesthetic vitality and sanctuary-like atmosphere of this scene is reinforced in the delineation of the silent and solemn atmosphere of the avenues of tall beeches.

Both Anselmus and the Taugenichts work in an atmosphere of luminescence. As Anselmus works to copy the manuscripts in Lindhorst's house without excessive pressure while admiring the beauty around him, so the Taugenichts savors the relatively minimal responsibilities of his new position as the tollkeeper as well as the beautiful landscape of the estate where he is employed. Moreover, he develops his creativity and establishes a flower garden from which he takes various bouquets to the young lady at the palace. The natural beauty of this environment is poignantly described in the following passage about the vitality of the evening light on the estate: "The sun was just setting, covering the countryside with a carpet of glowing color, and the Danube, like a ribbon of fiery gold, meandered off into the distance" (German Romantic Stories 199). A rich golden light suffuses the atmosphere of Lindhorst's house as well as the Vienna estate where the Taugenichts is working.

Later in Section Two of *Aus dem Leben eines Taugenichts* the protagonist, in the process of picking special flowers for the woman he reveres, portrays the natural scene around him as a sanctuary of beauty and light: not only is it a tranquil and lovely evening but the softly soothing and pleasant murmuring of the Danube can be heard in the distance. One could claim that the love which the protagonist feels for the young lady strongly influences his perception of the surrounding natural environment. And yet, there is an essential natural loveliness to the estate and the park encompassing the palace which would be delightful even if the scene were not being depicted through the eyes of an admirer or lover. A further passage which offers the aura of a sanctuary is presented as the protagonist carries his basket with the lovely flowers into the park. In the moonlight he walks across white bridges beneath which swans were sleeping, and continues further past gorgeous arbors. Such an atmosphere reveals precisely the same salient aspects as are seen in the description of the experience of Anselmus at the house of Lindhorst. For the house of Lindhorst with its refulgent interior spaces represents a sanctuary of beauty and aesthetic richness, which is observed, appreciated, and delighted in by Anselmus as he nurtures his love for Serpentina.

Even though the sanctuary presented in this part of *Der goldne Topf* is an interior and not a palace with immediately surrounding parkland which are so brilliantly illuminated during the nocturnal festivities that the garden is suffused by a radiantly golden aura of exceptional vitality, this is an interior of extraordinary beauty and spatial expansiveness. Both the house of Lindhorst and the palace estate in Vienna epitomize the profound golden light of a special sanctuary which is beyond the vicissitudes of everyday mortality. The vibrant luminescence of both of these golden spaces is further reinforced by the fact that the environment surrounding each of these is depicted as being dark, either literally or symbolically.

At the beginning of the Eighth Vigil the considerable happiness and bliss of Anselmus is described. Anselmus admits that the several days during which he has been working on manuscripts at the house of the Archivist Lindhorst and during which he has consistently heard the consoling words of Serpentina and occasionally felt her gentle breath have been the happiest of his entire life. Anselmus even feels as if he does not have any notable concerns or worries in his everyday life. Moreover, he senses that a new life is beginning for him, a new life which is characterized by an aura of "serene sunny splendour" (42) and which reveals to him the secrets of a higher world.

It is interesting that the Archivist Lindhorst appears just at the moment when Anselmus finishes the final character of a manuscript so that he may give him another to copy. This event could suggest an instinctive connectedness between Lindhorst and Anselmus; it could even imply that Lindhorst is always aware of the progress which Anselmus makes in copying the manuscripts and is perhaps even actively guiding the process. It is noteworthy that Lindhorst typically wears a dressing-gown filled with images of brilliant flowers, so that he becomes a symbol of vernal dynamism and colorful energy.

On one particular day the Archivist takes Anselmus once again through the halls and chambers which he had seen on his first visit. As before Anselmus is amazed at the great beauty of the garden and of various objects and images in this lovely place. The themes of visual clarity, of visual integrity, and of visual illusion are all important in this scenario for Anselmus now observes that many of the objects which he thought were flowers are actually insects gleaming with glorious colors. Moreover, Anselmus also observes that some of the beings which he thought were birds are actually beautiful flowers spreading their lovely fragrances over the entire space and inspiring in him an insatiable longing. The Archivist then takes Anselmus into the azure chamber which now contains, instead of the golden pot and its porphyry stand, a special table in velvet where Anselmus will work on a new manuscript. The Archivist Lindhorst praises the work which Anselmus has done so far and now gives him a new and even more demanding challenge. The new work for Anselmus deals with the "transcribing or rather painting of certain works, written in a peculiar character" (43).

Serpentina proceeds to tell the story of her father and of the race of salamanders from which he is descended. In her narrative Serpentina articulates the importance of the kind of character of her beloved which Prince Phosphorus proclaimed should be a condition of marriage to her and to both of her sisters. Serpentina describes this special individual as having a "child-like poetic character" (47), a noble heart, a capacity to understand her romantic song, and a capacity to appreciate the extraordinary and the uncommon in everyday life. The ultimate reward for the individual who has these qualities and who loves Serpentina will be a life of sustained happiness and bliss in Atlantis. Serpentina also warns Anselmus against the treacherousness and maliciousness of the woman from the Black Gate who is a hostile spirit and the nemesis of the Archivist Lindhorst and who is trying to gain possession of the golden pot. It is noteworthy that Serpentina emphasizes to Anselmus that his commitment to their love and his child-like poetic character will sustain him against the destructive and evil tendencies of the Frau Rauerin.

Anselmus is enraptured by the delightful, melodious presence of Serpentina. Whether Anselmus actually experiences the presence of Serpentina in this episode or merely dreams vitally and exuberantly of her presence is not clear. For when Anselmus awakes as if from a dream, Serpentina is no longer there. Anselmus is especially anxious because he suddenly realizes that he has not copied a single character on this occasion. The emotional and spiritual closeness of Anselmus to Serpentina and to Lindhorst is exemplified by the fact that even though Anselmus has not copied anything (or feels that he has not copied anything) on this occasion the manuscript has been completely finished. The manuscript which Anselmus had to copy was the story which Serpentina related about her father, her mother, herself, and her sisters. By listening so attentively, so sensitively, and so thoughtfully and by loving Serpentina and by believing so devotedly in his love for her Anselmus has completed the necessary work.

At the beginning of the Twelfth Vigil the narrator acknowledges the difficulty of articulating the wonderful experiences and the shared happiness of Anselmus and Serpentina. The narrator does not feel that he can adequately describe in words the joyous new life of Anselmus and Serpentina in Atlantis. In a state of emotional turmoil and uncertainty about how to complete his work, the narrator receives a note from the Archivist Lindhorst who says that he can assist him in the final stages of his literary endeavor. When the narrator meets with Lindhorst he is given a special elixir after which he develops a heightened sensitivity for the various objects and colors in the room and experiences a radiant vision.

The narrator believes that the emerald leaves of the palm trees in the room are whispering of wonders which are also expressed in the distant melodies of a harp. The narrator also perceives the dynamic azure of the walls mingling with and interspersed by glorious rays of light which ultimately reveals a grove in which one sees Anselmus. The beautiful flowers (hyacinths, tulips, and roses), bushes, and trees are effulgently vital. Serpentina appears carrying the golden pot "from which a bright lily has sprung" (68–69). As Serpentina and Anselmus embrace lovingly, they are enveloped by a dynamic luminescence which permeates all of the surrounding natural environment. This moment is a sanctuary of glorious radiance and effulgent light which energizes and enlivens various aspects of the natural environment: for example, the leaves of the trees rustle more vigorously and the brooks babble more melodically. This is a sanctuary of luminescent vitality, harmony, and peacefulness.

Armand de Loecker asserts in *Zwischen Atlantis und Frankfurt: Märchendichtung und Goldenes Zeitalter bei E. T. A. Hoffmann* that the inner development of Anselmus and the array of his experiences lead ultimately "zu einer Apotheose"(62). De Loecker proclaims that the end of the narrative represents "die eigentliche Erfüllung der Sehnsucht, das Zusammensein von Anselmus und Serpentina in Atlantis" (66). The end of the story signifies the fulfillment of the longing which Anselmus and Serpentina reveal and affirms their eternal union in Atlantis. The "goldenes Zeitalter" (66) is discovered in "dem poetischen Erleben dieser Welt als kosmische Harmonie" (66). The poetic and imaginative conception of the world affirms the presence of a golden age of existence permeated by a sense of luminescent vitality and cosmic harmony.

K. Deterding describes in *Hoffmanns Erzählungen: Eine Einführung in das Werk E. T. A. Hoffmanns* the narrator's observation of Anselmus in this blissful paradise very thoughtfully: "In einer rauschhaften Synästhesie von Farben, Duften, Pflanzen, Tieren, Sonne, und Wasser spricht die Natur nun mit dem, der sie durchwandelt: mit Anselmus" (59). Deterding proceeds to make the following interesting observation about the ending of the narrative: "Im Einswerden der Töne (als Farben und als Klänge), der Pflanzen, Dinge, und Wesen in dem wundersamen Garten von Atlantis werden auch die Liebenden eins.... Das steigert sich bis zur 'Verklärung' des Anselmus im 'Strahlenglanz'" (80). The existence which Anselmus and Serpentina enjoy in Atlantis is in the spirit of a Garden of Eden. There is a golden atmosphere, an atmosphere of golden light, here which suffuses this blissful domain and perpetually revitalizes the spirit of love and faith.

In addressing Serpentina at this moment of colorful and sensory exuberance, Anselmus expresses the depth of his love for her: "Belief in you, love of you has unfolded to my soul the inmost spirit of nature" (69). Anselmus proceeds to say that Serpentina brought him the lily "which sprang from gold, from the primeval force of the world" (69) which represents "knowledge of the sacred harmony of all beings" (69). In proclaiming his ardent love for Serpentina, Anselmus also asserts the importance of the knowledge which the lily brings and which the presence of the lily enables him to achieve. Anselmus even states that his eternal happiness will be motivated by the knowledge which the lily brings. Such an awareness signifies a sensitive appreciation and understanding of the beautiful natural environment. This condition of love and knowledge is presented as a perpetual sanctuary of light for Anselmus proclaims that the golden blossoms of the lily will never fade.

After such a blissful vision of the eternal happiness of Anselmus and Serpentina and of the lovely natural surroundings of their life together on their estate in Atlantis, the narrator returns to a sense of reality and laments that he will now have to confront the tribulations of everyday life. Lindhorst tries to give the narrator some encouraging advice by saying that as he has just been in Atlantis he should feel that he too has a piece of land there as the poetic property of his mind. The final statement of the narrative reaffirms that the happiness of Anselmus exists in poetry, in the power of the imagination which reveals the sacred harmony of all things as a secret of nature. The radiant beauty and eternal loveliness of the estate of Serpentina and Anselmus is not diminished at all by the fact that it could be interpreted as a landscape of the mind. Atlantis is a sanctuary of light and love beyond the ravages and vicissitudes of everyday mortality and an inspirational and a suitable place for sensitive, artistic, poetic, and thoughtful souls.

The ending of Eichendorff's *Aus dem Leben eines Taugenichts* is strikingly similar to the presentation of Atlantis in the final section of *Der goldne Topf*. In Section Nine of the Eichendorff narrative the perception by the Taugenichts of his beloved Austrian landscape after travelling from Italy is comparable to the experience of viewing Atlantis: this is a moment infused with joy and wonder. Section Ten reinforces the bliss which the protagonist feels about being in the beautiful environment of Vienna and of the palace again. The protagonist is here in an ebullient state of mind and even feels that the golden trees, the trees suffused with a golden light, are inclining their branches towards him in a gesture of welcome. Shortly thereafter the Taugenichts finally sees his beloved, the lovely lady whom he esteems, near the lake imbued with the golden rays of the evening sun.

The very endings of *Der goldne Topf* and *Aus dem Leben eines Taugenichts* are also similar because both stories celebrate a vision of paradise, a brilliant sanctuary of permanently vital luminescence. In *Der goldne Topf* the life of Anselmus and Serpentina in Atlantis signifies their blissful companionship and love in a beautiful natural environment of extraordinary radiance. In *Aus dem Leben eines Taugenichts* the protagonist and his beloved are given a pleasant villa with vineyards in a lovely natural setting near the palace. The last paragraph of the narrative reinforces the gorgeous atmosphere of the moment. The sound of congenial music and the flares lighting up the night sky mingle gently with the nearby murmurs of the Danube to create an epiphanic moment of luminescent harmony and serenity. This moment represents the culmination of various similar and similarly orchestrated scenarios in the narrative which are characterized by an inner radiance within the darkness or by a light which is generated and strengthened by the delightful moonlight which permeates the natural landscape and the soul of the protagonist as well as of other individuals who possess a comparably sensitive nature-sensibility.

Egon Schwarz describes the significance of the ending of *Aus dem Leben eines Taugenichts* effectively as follows: "The ending brings for the Taugenichts the inevitable consequences of his decision to forgo the urge to lose himself in nature and to wander. He has been tamed; love has harmonized the two worlds in his soul" (148). Schwarz also asserts insightfully that a steadfastness (motivated considerably by the protagonist's faith and trust in God) is "the only virtue required in Eichendorff's world in order to attain heavenly and earthly bliss" (148). Such a steadfastness is an essential feature of the life-philosophy of both the Taugenichts and Anselmus.

Through a consistent devotion to the light, to nurturing and appreciating sanctuaries of light, and through a vital dedication to love, to the preservation of their love despite the temptations and vicissitudes of everyday mortality, both Anselmus and the Taugenichts attain a vital sense of happiness and mortal bliss.

E. T. A. Hoffmann's *Nußknacker und Mausekönig, The Nutcracker and the King of Mice* (completed in November, 1816 and published in the autumn of 1816 in a collection of fairy tales by Fouqué, Hoffmann, and Contessa, and then published in *Die Serapionsbrüder*, Volume 1), is another narrative with interesting and important architectural spaces.

At the beginning of Hoffmann's *Nußknacker und Mausekönig* it is Christmas eve at the home of the Stahlbaum family. The children of the family are not allowed to enter certain drawing-rooms in the house because of the festive preparations which are occurring there. In addition to the family members, Dr. Stahlbaum, his wife, and three children (Marie, Fritz, and Louise), Godpapa Drosselmeier is present for the holiday celebration. One of the first references in the narrative to a special place of light and natural beauty is Marie's statement on page 2 that Godpapa Drosselmeier told her about such a place. Marie says that he described "a beautiful garden with a great lake in it, and beautiful swans swimming about with great gold collars, singing lovely music" (72). There is also a lovely little girl in the scene who walks through the garden to the lake and feeds the swans. Marie's more realistic older brother, Fritz, tries to discourage her from thinking that the little girl in the story would have fed the swans cake and shortbread. However, Marie has a special innocence about her which nurtures a delightful imagination and enables her to believe such tales about the swans. At the end of the first section, entitled "Christmas Eve," silvery bells clang and the drawing-room doors are opened as a brilliant light shines from the room. This is the moment when the Stahlbaum children are invited to see their presents.

In the second section, "Christmas Presents," the beautiful Christmas tree is described as bearing "many apples of silver and gold" (73) as well as many other delightful items to eat and to admire. This splendid tree is presented as a tree of radiance, for "in all the recesses of its spreading branches hundreds of little tapers glittered like stars" (73). The gorgeous tree signifies a sanctuary of light which creates and sustains an atmosphere of festive illumination reaffirming the sense of sanctuary in the lovely Stahlbaum home.

Godpapa Drosselmeier's Christmas present is also soon displayed. When a curtain is drawn, a lovely castle with many radiant windows and impressive towers is revealed. In addition to the chime of bells which is heard, another notable feature is the considerable luminescence in the central hall. There are many small figures walking around in the castle environment. The scenario also contains a miniature version of Godpapa Drosselmeier.

In the next section, "Marie's Pet and Protégé," Marie notices the presence of a little man who seems very kind and benevolent and is dressed in the same manner as

Godpapa Drosselmeier. It is explained to Marie that this little man beside the tree is "the Nutcracker." Marie seems especially interested in the Nutcracker and even addresses him as if he were an animate being. When the Nutcracker loses several teeth as he is trying to crack a very hard nut and looks at Marie mournfully, she shows genuine affection and concern for him and wants to protect him from further activity.

In the section, "Toyland," the nutcracker shows Marie a lovely, luminescent meadow called 'Candy Mead.' He then proceeds to take her to various other lovely, colorful, deliciously radiant spaces such as 'Almond and Raisin Gate,' 'Christmas Wood,' 'Orange Brook,' 'River Lemonade,' 'Honey River,' and even a beautiful lake where "the loveliest swans were floating, white as silver, with collars of gold" (113). Marie remembers at this moment that Godpapa Drosselmeier had once told her that she would be the girl to play with the swans. All of the lakes and waters in Toyland are especially beautiful, vital, and luminescent. And the 'Christmas Wood' represents a distinctive sanctuary of light and color, characterized by glittering and sparkling fruits in the trees. The gold and silver fruits chime softly in an effusion of light. As in other episodes in this and other Hoffmann stories such as *Der goldne Topf* the fusion of radiant light and soft chimes creates a sanctuary away from the vicissitudes of everyday mortality.

In the next section, "Metropolis," which is also the second-to-last part of the narrative, Marie again experiences epiphanies and sanctuaries of light and color. For example, in "Comfit Grove" many objects glitter, glisten, and sparkle and their colors are very beautiful. In the metropolis Marie is amazed by the splendor of the entire ambience. Not only are there shining towers and gorgeous walls in the metropolis but there is an aesthetic sensibility here which manifests itself in various sculptured and artistically crafted nuances and subtleties. There is even a group of individuals who are portrayed as worshippers of the sun and of light.

At the end of "Metropolis" Marie is taken by the nutcracker to the Marzipan Castle, "a castle shining in roseate radiance, with a hundred beautiful towers" (117). The luminescent atmosphere of the castle is reinforced by the fact that the "great dome of the central building, as well as the pyramidal roofs of the towers, were all set over with thousands of sparkling gold and silver stars" (117). Such a radiant castle is reminiscent of the effulgent castle and architectural paradise which K. Schinkel created in several of his Romantic paintings such as *Castle along a River*. Other important images of light at the castle, this beautiful sanctuary of light and serenity, are the little pages with their "lighted clove-sticks" (117), the brilliantly attired ladies of the court, a hall "whose walls were composed of a sparkling crystal" (118), and the profusion of golden flowers in and around the exquisite furniture. Gradually, a silver mist appears to permeate these images and the experience of Marie at the Marzipan Castle and she feels as if she, the nutcracker, and other individuals at the castle were floating and rising ever higher on a succession of waves.

In the "Conclusion" Marie suddenly awakens in broad daylight with her mother standing next to her bed. Her mother assures Marie that she has had an extraordinary dream and should now put all of those images out of her head. Her father also encourages her to stop what he considers to be foolish fancies. However, Marie continues dreaming in solitude of the beautiful and magnificent fairy realm. One day Marie even says to the wooden doll, the nutcracker, that she would not act as Princess Pirlipat had done and despise him if he were not handsome because he had had to suffer a physical transformation for her sake. Soon after this Godpapa Drosselmeier brings his young nephew to the Stahlbaum house and introduces him to Marie.

When young Drosselmeier and Marie are alone he thanks Marie for having rescued him from his enchantment. For when Marie said that she would not have despised him, as the princess had done, if he had been compelled to become physically unattractive for her sake, he ceased to be the wooden nutcracker and was transformed into his normal self. Marie is enraptured by the aura and ambience of the Marzipan Castle. She is enchanted by the radiant colors, luminescent forms, and delightful images. This is a realm of extraordinary beauty and imaginative vitality. The story ends with the assertion that Marie is "to this day the queen of a realm where all kinds of sparkling Christmas Woods, and transparent Marzipan Castles… are to be seen by those who have the eyes to see them" (123). This narrative is permeated and generated by various vital moments of light and radiance, culminating in a moment of supreme luminescence. For Marie, whether in reality or in the realm of her imagination, is the queen of a realm where beautiful and gorgeous objects exist, glisten, and sparkle. Marie is the queen of a realm which signifies a lovely sanctuary of light where peace and beauty reign supreme.

In *The Shattered Self: E. T. A. Hoffmann's Tragic Vision* Horst Daemmrich interprets the ending of this narrative insightfully as offering through Marie's behavior "a specific solution for man in his search for existential commitment" (62). Daemmrich concludes his argument effectively by saying of Marie that "by conquering her fear, retaining faith in her vision, and unselfishly helping another person, she transforms the nutcracker and succeeds in transcending the limitations of the world" (62).

In the novels of Jane Austen there are various splendid mansions, sanctuaries of light and tranquility, which offer a sense of secure refuge from the clamor and turmoil of everyday mortality. In *Pride and Prejudice*, Pemberley House, the home of the Darcy family, is a quintessential sanctuary of luminescence, peacefulness, natural beauty, and serenity in Derbyshire. The estate is also vitally important in the course of the novel because it represents the special location where Darcy and Elizabeth begin, though with understandable awkwardness after what had occurred during Elizabeth's visit to Charlotte, their enduring friendship which eventually blossoms into a vital relationship. Pemberley also signifies a sanctuary of truth, for it is here that Elizabeth, while visiting the estate with her aunt and uncle, hears the glowing account which Mrs. Reynolds gives of Mr. Darcy. Eventually, Elizabeth will realize that the very positive description of Mr. Darcy and his nobility of character which Mrs. Reynolds offers is the correct one. This is a refuge of natural beauty, truth, and tranquility which would reasonably distance itself from deceitful individuals such as Mr. Wickham. The depiction of the interior of Pemberley House during the tour which Elizabeth is given with Mr. and Mrs. Gardiner is also noteworthy for it celebrates the genuine elegance and lofty atmosphere of the mansion.

While there are other architecturally interesting houses in *Pride and Prejudice* such as Longbourn (with its library sanctuary), Netherfield, Rosings (the splendid mansion and the surrounding park), Lucas Lodge, and the estate which Mr. Bingley and Jane eventually purchase in a county adjacent to Derbyshire, the most magnificent and naturally beautiful house and estate is Pemberley. In Volume III, Chapter I of *Pride and Prejudice*, for example, Elizabeth observes on her tour of the estate with her aunt and uncle that the ambience of the interior of the mansion, including the furniture, is characterized and pervaded by a spirit of genuine elegance, which is to be distinguished from the aura of seemingly gaudy wealth which is manifest at Rosings. At the end of the novel there is the sense that the naturally lovely ambience of Pemberley will be perpetually affirmed and enhanced not only by the fact that such noble-spirited individuals as Darcy and Elizabeth live in the mansion after their marriage but also by the fact that Georgiana, Darcy's quietly aristocratic sister, will maintain a continuous presence there in the future.

It has been argued by several writers, including Nigel Nicolson in *The World of Jane Austen*, that the model or original for Pemberley in *Pride and Prejudice* was Godmersham, the home of Edward Austen, one of Jane's brothers. It is known that Jane visited Godmersham more frequently than any other country house. Edward Austen was adopted as a teenager by Thomas and Catherine Knight of Godmersham (the Austens shared a common ancestor, John Austen III, with the Knights) and assumed the name of Knight when his adoptive mother passed away in 1812. Nigel Nicolson writes in *The World of Jane Austen* that "Godmersham became for Jane the central architectural experience of her life" (61) for she was very fortunate to be able to visit this house for many years.

In Austen's *Sense and Sensibility* (1811) there are various architecturally interesting houses and mansions, including Norland Park, Barton Park, Barton Cottage, Allenham, Combe Magna, Cleveland, the house of Mrs. Jennings in London, and Delaford. While Norland Park, Barton Park, and Cleveland, in particular, are depicted as houses of notable splendor and spaciousness, perhaps the most beautiful mansion in the novel is Delaford, not only because of its natural architectural loveliness but also because of the important characters who ultimately settle down on the estate. The architectural beauty of Delaford and the spaciousness of the surrounding property is alluded to by John Dashwood in Chapter 14 of the novel when he says of Colonel Brandon: "His property here, his place, his house, every thing in such respectable and excellent condition!—and his woods!—I have not seen such timber anywhere in Dorsetshire" (380). For Colonel Brandon and Marianne, Delaford will represent a lovely sanctuary of happiness and serenity. Likewise, the Parsonage on the estate at Delaford where Edward and Elinor will live signifies an equally delightful space of blissful peacefulness.

In Austen's novel *Emma* (1816) the homes of Emma Woodhouse and her father, of Mr. Knightley, and of Mr. and Mrs. Weston all represent sanctuaries of relatively peaceful stability and secure tranquility beyond the exigencies and vicissitudes of everyday mortality. In the home of Emma Woodhouse, Hartfield, there is the sense that the difficulties and tensions of everyday life can be soothed, sublimated, transformed, or forgotten in this lovely ambience. Mr. Knightley's estate, Donwell Abbey, possesses an extraordinary and noteworthy natural beauty and spatial expansiveness. Each of these mansions has an aura of serenity and stability which reinforces and reaffirms the ambience of tranquility and security in the other two mansions of this group because of the personal connectedness and abiding friendship between the individuals who are the respective owners of these estates.

In diverse fairy tales of Wilhelm and Jacob Grimm, *Kinder- und Hausmärchen, Children's and Household Stories* (first published in two volumes, in 1812 and 1815) there are also sanctuaries of light and serenity. Typically, in these fairy tales the sense of sanctuary emerges at the end of the narrative as a peaceful and delightfully splendid refuge where the prince or princess, king and queen, or coupled protagonists can reside in harmony, bliss, and congenial security for the rest of their lives. For example, in "Snow-White and the Seven Dwarfs" the prince says to Snow-White when she awakens after the poison-apple is dislodged from her mouth that she is safe with him. This sense of sanctuary is reaffirmed forever in their happy wedding at the end of the story. In "Briar Rose" the palace around which the almost impenetrable hedge of briars grows signifies a sanctuary. The prince who is destined to walk easily through this potentially perilous hedge as the hundred years' sleep which encompasses the palace world is ending is enchanted by the beauty of Briar Rose. The end of the narrative implies a sense of sanctuary in the proclamation that after the wedding the prince and Briar Rose lived happily until the end of their lives.

One might say that the arduously difficult and often dangerous course of the protagonist's life for much of the fairy tale makes the sense of sanctuary which one at least sometimes finds at the end of the narrative more satisfying. The physical hardship and emotional suffering which Snow-White, Briar Rose, Cinderella, and Rapunzel, to name several such fairy tale protagonists, have to endure in their lives before they can achieve a semblance of happiness is extraordinary. As Snow-White and Briar Rose, Rapunzel suffers greatly before fortuitously meeting her beloved, blind and despairing, in the wilderness. After their happy reunion, which is initiated by the prince's recognition of her lovely voice, they travel to his kingdom where they are fortunate in being able to live long and contented lives. The ending of "Cinderella," while not specifically addressing the issue of the duration of the relationship of

Cinderella and the prince, does suggest that their eventual marriage will be characterized by a very congenial and exemplary longevity. Characters such as Cinderella are also rewarded for their goodness and virtue with the prospect of a congenial future in a beautiful house or spacious mansion.

Various poems by William Wordsworth and Percy Shelley also describe sanctuaries of light, natural beauty, luminescent magnificence, and architectural vitality (whether presented as special architectural spaces or as lovely natural places which have an architectural aura and ambience).

William Wordsworth's "Tintern Abbey" (1798) celebrates a lovely natural sanctuary and emphasizes the importance of a sense of space in this beautiful environment.In the first ten to fifteen lines Wordsworth speaks of the significance of the "steep and lofty cliffs" (5) which not only inspire profound thoughts, but also represent the link between the earth and "the quiet of the sky" (8). The aura of heavenly tranquility is subsequently applied to the repose which the persona experiences under the dark sycamore. Wordsworth views with admiration various features of his immediate natural environment, including the "orchard-tufts" (11) and the "hedge-rows" (15). He asserts that although he has not seen "these beauteous forms" (22) directly for several years, these lovely images of nature have influenced his mind and heart powerfully from a distance. These images have given him not only "sensations sweet" (27), but they have also infused his soul with a semblance of the tranquillity which characterizes "the quiet of the sky" (8).

The sensitive contemplation of the beautiful forms of nature creates a mood of profound serenity in which the individual experiences a psychic suspension of corporeal existence and becomes a living soul. In attaining this existential condition the persona prepares himself (as lines 46–48 suggest) to achieve a diastolic sense of space and time. At this epiphanic moment of harmony and joy the persona sees "into the life of things" (49). This vision or visionary capacity seems to be a precursor of and perhaps even comparable to the "faith that looks through death" (185) of the Immortality Ode. Such a visionary capability coupled with an exceptional sensitivity for nature is also seen in Samuel Palmer's *The Magic Apple Tree*. The persona in Wordsworth's poem and the primary individual in Palmer's painting achieve a similarly vital epiphanic moment of harmony and a sense of a serene sanctuary.

In the section of the poem starting with line 49 the persona claims that he has often turned to the sense and spirit of the "sylvan Wye" (56) and its surroundings to help and guide him through his present existence. The persona declares that reflecting on this beautiful natural environment often illuminated his mind and spirit and gave him a sense of hope when he was experiencing spiritual or physical darkness. The sense of spatial fluidity which was established in the first fifteen lines of the poem is reinforced by the image of the "sylvan Wye" (56) wandering through the forest. Although the Wye represents an image of water and not of earth (in contrast to the previously foregrounded images of nature) all of the dominant features of nature described so far in the poem possess an inner energy. The "orchard-tufts" (11) and "hedge-rows" (15), like the "sylvan Wye" (56), are infused with a dynamic motion which affirms the vitality of nature and perhaps even enhances the capacity of the living soul to see into the life of things. This vital energy in nature encourages the persona to feel that his present observations of this lovely environment will generate a host of congenial images and reflections for many years to come and will provide an inner illumination of the soul in the future.

The return to this inspirational place is important not only for the present revitalization of the individual, but also for his future development. Although the persona is able to revive some of the past spirit of this space and of his feeling for nature, he realizes the noticeable difference between his earlier and his current experience of nature. The emotional passion which the persona felt as a youth in the presence of nature has been toned down to a more serene awareness of and feeling for nature. Yet, there is still a unity of past and present through the power of memory which sustains and will continue to preserve the poet's faith in the vitality of the present. Moreover, change is not seen necessarily as a negative dimension of life; rather, it produces "abundant recompense" (88), perhaps most of all in the increasing development of a more mature and insightful creative vision.

The persona, in becoming a more mature and profound observer of and participant in nature, feels a presence that disturbs him "with the joy / Of elevated thoughts" (94–95). This "sense sublime" (95) is characterized above all by a spatial expansiveness—the motion and the spirit which the persona senses as the source of nature's creative energy and sublimity is a diastolic spatiality that encompasses not only sky, earth, and water, but also the mind of man.

Wordsworth's persona asserts that because he feels vitally this spatially generated energy, light, and vitality which "impels / All thinking things" (100–01) and "rolls through all things" (102) he is a nature-lover, a lover of the spatial expansiveness of nature. This awareness of the diastolic power of nature inspires the persona to proclaim that nature (and the language of the sense) represents the guide and the guardian of his heart, soul, and moral being.

The spatial metaphor is reaffirmed in the last section of the poem, lines 111–159, where the persona speaks, for example, of the importance of the mind, which through the benevolent and pervasive influence of nature "shall be a mansion for all lovely forms" (140) and of the significance of the memory which shall "be as a dwelling-place / For all sweet sounds and harmonies" (141–42). The structural framework of this spatial metaphor reinforces the sense of space established by the initial experience of the sycamore. The poet grounds or establishes himself in a particular space from where he envisions the beauteous forms of nature and the motion and spirit that vitalizes those forms. From this secure, or seemingly secure, space the persona perceives and conceives the diastolic spatiality of his natural environment. The aura of spatial expansiveness possesses and reveals dynamic healing qualities. The individual who is aware of and sensitive to the beauteous forms of nature and who develops a profound feeling for nature may achieve this sense of a spatial expansiveness of the soul.

In "Hymn to Intellectual Beauty" Percy Shelley creates a sanctuary of light and suggests that the light of intellectual beauty has the capacity to challenge and counterbalance mortality. In asserting that the light of intellectual beauty "Gives grace and truth to life's unquiet dream" (36), the persona implies the capacity of the individual who is sensitively aware of such beauty to distance himself from the vicissitudes of mortality, whether temporarily or more permanently. In the first stanza of the "Hymn to Intellectual Beauty" the persona laments that the power of such nonmaterial beauty is transient; in the second stanza the persona continues this concern, praising the vitality of the spirit of beauty to illuminate the surrounding environment while at the same time expressing a sadness that such beauty does not last.

In the third stanza the persona praises the spirit of such beauty as offering the only light and radiance which can comfort and inspire in the world of mortality:

> Thy light alone—like mist o'er mountains driven,
>   Or music by the night wind sent
>   Through strings of some still instrument,
>   Or moonlight on a midnight stream,
> Gives grace and truth to life's unquiet dream. (32–36)

One might describe these five lines as a sanctuary of light within the poem, a refuge of potent light which not only affirms the importance of the light and the spirit of intellectual beauty but which also illuminates the rest of the poem, the emotional and spiritual existence of the poet, and the world of everyday mortality surrounding and encroaching upon the verbal domain of the poem.

Shelley's "Lines written among the Euganean Hills" offers an approach to mortality similar to that expressed in "Hymn to Intellectual Beauty." This poem was written, as Shelley says in the advertisement to the *Rosalind and Helen* volume, "after a day's excursion among those lovely mountains which surround what was once the retreat, and where is now the sepulchre, of Petrarch" (Reiman, *Percy Bysshe Shelley* 69). In wandering across the sea of mortality the persona finds flowering isles, temporary epiphanies of light and happiness, which revitalize not only the individual but also the potential of the earth to renew itself. One such sanctuary of light and serenity is a place among the Euganean Hills near Padua where the persona observes the majestic sunrise and the dynamic effusion of light across the landscape. As the poem proceeds the persona reflects upon the inevitability of change and the concomitant loss of glory and prominence.

The atmosphere and the tone of the poem from line 285 through the end are reminiscent of stanza seven, the final stanza, of "Hymn to Intellectual Beauty." In both contexts the magical vitality of the luminescence of an autumn afternoon is delineated. This is a special light which has the capacity not only to illuminate the world around it but also to create an aura of harmony in this environment. In the last stanza of "Lines written among the Euganean Hills" the persona speaks of creating a sanctuary of exquisite light and tranquility:

> Far from passion, pain, and guilt,
> In a dell 'mid lawny hills,
> Which the wild sea-murmur fills,
> And soft sunshine, and the sound
> Of old forests echoing round,
> And the light and smell divine
> Of all flowers that breathe and shine. (345–51)

This is a sanctuary which encompasses in its blossoming vitality various salient aspects of the natural environment representing earth, sea, and sky and appreciates the historical dynamism of important features of nature. For example, this is a place which values and reveres the sounds and melodies of the old forests, fusing past and present, as well as the beauty of the flowers which exist primarily in the present. In the final section of the "Epipsychidion" there is a parallel "flowering isle," an island Eden, a profoundly tranquil place of natural beauty and radiantly blossoming flowers and plants permeated by an aura of immortality. In this section of the "Epipsychidion" the hope of the poet is that he and Emily can become the "living soul of this Elysian isle" (539). The ending of the "Epipsychidion" in its conviction that human language cannot adequately capture the vision and the vitality of the union of the poet and Emily is noticeably less positive and affirmative than that of "Lines written among the Euganean Hills" which delineates a paradise of light, calm, and melodic resonances which will nurture a new and vernal world of humanity.

The persona proceeds to proclaim that this lovely refuge, this space of beautiful "natural architecture," is so special and unique that even if the spirits of the air would, out of envy, send to this locus amoenus many strangers and many people of varying characters and inclinations, the divine and serene atmosphere of this sanctuary would transform them and their emotional turbulence and violence into a community of kindness. Such a luminescent place is not only inspirational but also creates its own inner musicality. Another of the most prominent qualities of this sanctuary is the spirit of love which pervades and nurtures it. Through this atmosphere of love the envious spirits would also be transformed and realize the exemplary uniqueness of this radiant sanctuary. The poem concludes with a hopeful vision of a bright future which will revitalize the earth. The emphasis on a powerful light, a calm atmosphere, the importance of an appreciation of self, and the significance of a transformational and rejuvenating love are conspicuously present both in the last three stanzas of "Lines written among the Euganean Hills" (from line 285–373) and in stanza seven of "Hymn to Intellectual Beauty."

The notion of the epiphanic moment of luminescent vitality which is so important in Shelley's "Hymn to Intellectual Beauty" and "Lines written among the

Euganean Hills" is also manifest in Wordsworth's "Ode: Intimations of Immortality from Recollections of Early Childhood" (1807). In stanza nine of the Immortality Ode Wordsworth's persona glorifies "those first affections" (148) which represent the sources of our creative and visionary capacity. Moreover, such affections, such "shadowy recollections" (149), have the power to transform the boisterous flux of mortality into epiphanically serene moments of eternal truth. By achieving a continuity of such dynamic moments, the creative self shapes a meaningful, worthwhile life. The conception of eternity expressed in this stanza by Wordsworth's persona anticipates that of Hermann Hesse's Steppenwolf, who claims that "eternity was nothing else than the redemption of time, its return to innocence, so to speak, and its transformation again into space" (176). For Shelley and for Wordsworth mortality is redeemed in the eternity of spatial permanences of pristine vitality and luminescent tranquility.

Stanza ten of Wordsworth's Immortality Ode is also very similar in spirit and reflection to Shelley's "Hymn to Intellectual Beauty" and "Lines written among the Euganean Hills." In stanza ten of the Immortality Ode the persona wishes once again to revel in the effusive dynamism of nature—yet, this is not an ingenuous activity, but rather one infused with an awareness of mortality, a consciousness informed and shaped by consistently assiduous questionings. Unlike the earlier phase of the persona in stanza three who overcomes his thought of grief merely by expressing it and exhorting the "Child of Joy" (34) to shout merrily to distance any morose or mournful thoughts, the persona of stanza ten admits a poignant awareness of evanescence. By this point in the development of the poem such a consciousness of the inevitable passing of animate life no longer links with grief. The persona has achieved an emotional and an intellectual acceptance not only of the necessity or inevitability of mortality, but also of his capacity to participate in the dynamic cyclicality of nature to transform or transcend such transience.

In the last lines of stanza ten the persona responds to his poignant and thoughtful awareness of mortality by asserting that he will find hope and comfort in what remains behind after the splendor of the past is gone. He will find strength in a "timeless" present of things past, things present, and things future. In fusing these qualities in the "faith that looks through death" (185), the persona implies his capacity to participate in and to shape an expansive sense of time. In stanza ten especially Wordsworth's persona attains intimations of immortality not only through the joy of nature, by participating instinctively and vitally in the eternal beauty and dynamic joyousness of nature, but also through his experience of "the primal sympathy" (181) and "the philosophic mind" (186) and through his own creative endeavor.

In articulating the notion of "the primal sympathy" (181), the poet implies that he is an integral part of the harmonious whole which is the universe. He uses the language of that universe (tangible objects and specific aspects of nature) to describe his place in it and even to suggest a sense of transcendence. Wordsworth's philoso-

phy of nature and his belief in the harmonious wholeness of the universe is reminiscent of the belief of the idealistic philosopher Friedrich Wilhelm Schelling that the
universe is an organic, living whole permeated by a unified, vital spirit and that the
natural environment represents visible spirit, a manifestation of the spirit of the universe. In "Hymn to Intellectual Beauty" and "Lines written among the Euganean
Hills" Shelley is also presenting a persona who signifies an integral dimension of the
universe, who experiences a primal sympathy, and who envisions, in the spirit of the
philosophic mind, a future existential condition motivated by love and shaped by
humanitarian vitality.

In Victor Hugo's *Notre-Dame de Paris, The Hunchback of Notre-Dame* (1831), a
romance of medieval times, the themes of architectural space and sanctuary are
extremely important. The original French title of the novel, *Notre-Dame de Paris*,
affirms that the cathedral is the thematic focus of the novel for almost all of the
actions and events in the narrative occur in the cathedral, in the vicinity of the cathedral, or from the perspective of the cathedral (either within the sacred building or on
or along its exterior). One of Hugo's primary semantic concerns in the novel is an
emphasis on the idea that the Gothic cathedral and architecture (especially medieval
and late medieval) in general as a means of artistic expression will be replaced or displaced by the written word and by the invention of the printing press. The aesthetic
vitality and creative passion which produced these "thoughts in stone" which the
cathedral displays so eloquently in their medieval exuberance will be channeled and
developed in other artistic directions and proclivities as the Renaissance emerges and
blossoms. Hugo suggests that the sense of freedom of architectural expression which
the medieval and late medieval periods appreciated and valued is comparable to the
freedom of the press and of literary expression in his own lifetime. In *Notre-Dame de
Paris* the life and death of such main characters as Quasimodo, the hunchbacked
bell-ringer of Notre Dame, Esmeralda, the compassionate, lovely gypsy, and Frollo,
the Archdeacon of Notre Dame are intimately and inextricably connected to and
intertwined with the grand presence and sanctuary-like aura of the impressive cathedral. Esmeralda finds a temporary sense of sanctuary from the rapacious mob in the
belfry of the cathedral; Quasimodo also experiences a sense of sanctuary in the architectural heights of the great cathedral. It is noteworthy that the popularity of this
novel in France inspired a renewed interest in pre-Renaissance architecture, including considerable and creative renovations of the Notre-Dame Cathedral in Paris by
the architect Eugène Viollet-le-Duc.

Another literary work from the first half of the nineteenth century which depicts
interesting architectural creations and sanctuaries and which contains an abundance
of images of light and luminescence is Charlotte Brontë's *Jane Eyre* (1847). The idea
of and experience of a sanctuary is important to Jane from the beginning of *Jane Eyre*,
for she is treated as an outsider and needs to have a place where she can recover from
the mistreatment which she receives in the world of everyday mortality. The suffer-

ing which Jane endures in her early youth encourages her to a considerable extent to develop and to strengthen a sense of imaginative vitality to compensate for and to transcend the anguish of her emotionally painful environment. This capacity for imaginative vitality is present at the beginning of the novel, as W. A. Craik argues in *The Brontë Novels*: "At the beginning of *Jane Eyre* what Jane thinks is not fact, but an imaginative heightening and distortion" (77).

In Chapter 2 of *Jane Eyre*, Jane experiences the extreme isolation of the red room, a spare room which is rarely used by the Reed family. Theoretically, the red room is a kind of sanctuary characterized by opulent furnishings. Even though the red room is one of the most lavish and exuberantly decorated rooms in the house, it has a chill atmosphere, in part because this is where Mr. Reed had died. One interesting moment in the red-room experience for Jane is her observation of herself in the looking-glass: "…the strange little figure there gazing at me, with a white face and arms specking the gloom, and glittering eyes of fear moving where all else was still, had the effect of a real spirit" (16). As Jane looks at herself thoughtfully, she is reminded of the fairy-like creatures who emerge abruptly from the lonely dells and other isolated natural environments. Such an elfish quality and strong nature-sensibility which Jane appears to observe in herself will also be apparent at Lowood and at Thornfield, where Rochester makes a similar observation about Jane. Even though the red room sojourn is not an essentially congenial experience for Jane, this hauntingly eerie chamber could be said to represent "a sanctuary" of light which stimulates the visionary imagination.

When Jane is at Lowood School, she experiences several sanctuaries of light. Perhaps the most important and the most vital is the meal which Jane shares with Miss Temple and Helen at the end of Chapter 8. This moment is characterized by an abundance of light. Not only "the brilliant fire" (75) in the room but also the generosity and kindness of Miss Temple, the delightful meal, and the vibrant conversation help to create a sanctuary of glorious light. Jane says that she feasted "as on nectar and ambrosia" (75), noteworthy features of any "divine" repast. The luminescent vitality of the scenario is reflected in and reinforced by the glow of vitality within Helen, whom Jane describes with considerable admiration. Jane says that the powers within Helen "glowed in the bright tint of her cheek…then they shone in the liquid luster of her eyes, which had suddenly acquired a beauty more singular than that of Miss Temple's—a beauty…of meaning, of movement, of radiance" (75).

Jane is inspired that evening by the wondrously clever and thoughtful conversation of Miss Temple and Helen to work more diligently and assiduously and to nurture her imaginative potential more vitally. At the end of this chapter Jane conceives various ideal images which she would like to draw and to explore artistically. She imagines "picturesque rocks and ruins, Cuyp-like groups of cattle, sweet paintings of butterflies" (77) in addition to other images of the natural environment. The mention of Cuyp, the Dutch landscape artist, is noteworthy because his paintings of natural harmony and stability suffused with a golden light signify an ambience of refuge implicitly reinforcing the sanctuary-like atmosphere of Jane's experience with Miss Temple and Helen, while also offering a conspicuous thematic contrast with some of Jane's darker and more tempestuous present and future artistic conceptions. This luminescent moment of sanctuary which Jane shares with Miss Temple and Helen is extremely important for it inspires Jane to greater creativity, imaginative vitality, and intellectual curiosity. This congenial meal also represents a turning point for Jane at Lowood as it is a prelude to the announcement several days later by Miss Temple in front of the whole school that Jane has been cleared of the negative charges which had been made against her.

Chapter 11 of *Jane Eyre* marks the beginning of a new phase in Jane's life. As the new governess at Thornfield Hall, Jane is pleased with the kindness of Mrs. Fairfax and enchanted by the material beauty of her surroundings. Jane appears to feel very much at home in Thornfield Hall and in its aura of spatial expansiveness, which is an appropriate location for her to develop her imaginative capacity. When Jane awakens in her own room on the morning after her arrival, the sun is shining brightly into the room. Jane also appreciates the abundance of light and sunshine over the groves and fields around the mansion. This is an aesthetically vital ambience which reveals various sanctuaries of light both within the mansion and in the surrounding natural environment. There is even a pleasant drawing-room in the impressive house which seems to Jane like "a fairy-place" with its rich furniture, carpets, mirrors, and luminescent atmosphere.

Jane's initial conversation with Rochester in Chapter 13 is presented in the ambience of an enclosed place or sanctuary of light. When Jane enters the room to meet Mr. Rochester there are two lighted wax candles on the table and two on the mantelpiece—and there is a brilliant fire in the fireplace. This conversation between Jane and Rochester represents a sanctuary of radiance, aesthetic, physical, and intellectual. The primary features of this sanctuary of light and conversational vitality are repeated and reinforced in Chapter 14. On another occasion, several days after the initial conversation, Rochester and Jane are talking in the dining-room, which is permeated by and with an abundance of light not only from the luster which spreads "a festal breadth of light" (133) around the room, but also from a large fire in the fireplace.

In Chapter 23 Jane reveals her interest in and her appreciation of the beauty of a self-enclosed, gorgeous space (comparable to her earlier appreciation of the lovely interior spaces of Thornfield), which fulfills the aesthetic aspirations and desires of her imaginative vitality. In wandering into the orchard, Jane describes it as "sheltered" (250) and "Eden-like" (250), a delightful place of blossoming exuberance protected and sheltered from the outside world. Jane chooses to walk alone in this place of sacred and blooming tranquility so that she can wander with carefree ease and so that she may strengthen an inner expansiveness of soul which revels in such a sheltered, lovely space.

As Chapter 23 develops, Jane and Rochester declare their love for one another in a sanctuary setting. The sunset-moonrise meeting is symbolic of the emotional connection between Rochester and Jane. When Rochester teases Jane rather excessively about the prospect of having to depart from Thornfield, she responds with considerable sadness that she would be very sorry to leave because she has enjoyed her life here so much. Finally, Rochester admits his love for Jane and desires her to accept his marriage proposal. The aura of sanctuary which Rochester and Jane experience in each other's presence is reinforced by the fact that Rochester proclaims that Jane is his equal. The sense of an emotional and intellectual equality existing between Rochester and Jane sustains and strengthens the atmosphere of a sanctuary which they feel when they are together. Jane accepts Rochester's proposal gladly when he affirms that he truly loves her and that he will take an oath to that effect. This statement by Rochester is directly connected to one which he makes several paragraphs later, saying that he does not care about the world's judgement and that he defies popular opinion. That Rochester would make such a statement, which exemplifies the individualistic strain in Romanticism, shows that he has a strong capacity to appreciate the importance of a sanctuary away from the world of everyday mortality.

The loss of the feeling of sanctuary which had been so important to Jane at Thornfield culminates in her personal anguish at the beginning of Chapter 28. When Jane is left by the coach at Whitcross, a stone pillar at the juncture of several roads, she experiences extreme despair and an atmosphere which is the antithesis of a sense of sanctuary. When Jane leaves the coach at Whitcross, emotionally distraught after the cataclysmic "wedding day," and destitute, having forgotten her parcel, she epitomizes the lonely individual wandering hopelessly through an unknown landscape. Surrounded by great moors and mountains Jane experiences the primordial tension of the universe, as if she were the thematic and formal focus of John Martin's painting of the last bard or of Joseph Turner's painting *Shade and Darkness—the Evening of the Deluge*.

Jane frees herself from the imminence of the abyss which her arrival at Whitcross represents and gains emotional sustenance from the natural environment and spiritual support from her belief in the divine. In moving upon the heath Jane is able to overcome her feeling of despair which had threatened to overwhelm her at Whitcross by attaining a profound connection to the dynamically silent and tranquil spatiality of nature and by the conviction that nature loves her even as an outcast from society. It is the enclosed space of the tranquil natural environment with its calming silences, not a space of human construction, which comforts Jane here. As Jane reveals that she is tormented by melancholy thoughts of Rochester, she asserts that she is comforted not only by nature but also by God. Jane is especially soothed by the sense of infinite space which the conception of the divine offers, symbolized by "the unclouded night-sky, where His worlds wheel their silent course" (326). In observing the Milky Way and reflecting on its diastolic spatiality Jane says that she soothes her sadness by feeling the might and the strength of God. Jane's longing for the infinitude of the horizon in Chapter 12, which finds a visual analogue in a Romantic painting such as Caspar David Friedrich's *Der Mönch am Meer (Monk by the Seashore)*, which articulates a similar yearning for the eternity of the horizon, culminates in Chapter 28 in her appreciation of God's infinity and omnipresence in the night-sky.

As Chapter 28 of the novel continues Jane's vision is drawn towards a light in the distant twilight. This light of hermetic vitality is the light of Moor House which guides Jane out of the wilderness. At a moment of profound despair Jane is very fortunate to be taken in by the family at Moor House. The friendship which Jane develops here with Diana and Mary Rivers is very important to her and to her emotional and aesthetic development. Helene Moglen describes this burgeoning friendship very effectively: "She shares with them their love of nature. She admires and respects their superior learning, their fine minds. She listens to them talk as she had once listened to Miss Temple and Helen Burns, as Charlotte had listened to Emily and Anne" (Modern Critical Interpretations 50). Jane, Diana, and Mary appear to be kindred spirits, for not only do they have similar characters and motivations in life, but they also share various interests.

Through her imaginative vitality and through her emotional and spiritual affection for nature Jane affirms the beauty of the Moor House landscape and its aura of sanctuary. Moor House represents a delightful sanctuary of serenity and natural beauty which Diana and Mary Rivers and Jane all appreciate. Jane says that she felt "the consecration of its loneliness" (352) and that the various interesting features of the landscape were "so many pure and sweet sources of pleasure" (352). Jane's profound nature-sensibility values diverse spatial and temporal aspects of this natural sanctuary and she says that she felt enraptured by its spell.

The sense of sanctuary which Moor House offers is suspended at the end of Chapter 30, for Mr. Rivers goes to the parsonage, Diana and Mary Rivers proceed to their positions as governesses, and Jane accepts the position of schoolmistress in Morton which St. John had offered her. As Jane observes the simplicity of her life and the austerity of her material surroundings in her new cottage, she thinks about Rochester. While admitting to herself that no one will ever love her as Rochester did, Jane also proclaims that she made the right decision according to moral and legal principle—she is grateful to God for having guided her in this important decision.

In Chapter 35 at the moment when Jane seems almost on the verge of accepting St. John's persistent proposal, she hears the distant and familiar voice of Rochester which was anguished and urgent. This voice appears to be as much a part of Jane as it is a call from beyond her present existential context. Ernst Knies describes this voice effectively: "The mysterious call from Rochester—the voice which seems to Jane to be in her, not in the external world—comes just in time" (134).

The ambience of this extraordinary experience is one of abundant light, for the room in which Jane and St. John are conversing is described as being "full of moonlight" (422). The atmosphere is reminiscent of the nocturnal aura in Eichendorff's "Sehnsucht." In both contexts the individual expresses a sense of longing and yearning for a distant being. In both situations there is a stream of moonlight which permeates and enlivens the scene. The primary difference between the two contexts is that whereas Eichendorff's persona is inspired to follow the magical possibilities of longing imaginatively, Jane is motivated to leave her new home and seek Rochester directly and in person.

Because Jane does not receive an external affirmation of Rochester's existence, although she thinks about him consistently, she searches within her soul, which is, presumably, where the answer could be found all along. Jane's capacity for an imaginative expansiveness of soul is revitalized in her prayer that night, which leads her to the aura of a Mighty Spirit—that she is able to elevate her soul to such an extent implies an emotional and a spiritual expansiveness of renewed intensity and vitality. This moment of solitary and thoughtful prayer represents a sanctuary of inner light for Jane, for in her solitude she even describes herself as being "enlightened" (423).

After Jane hears the distant call of Rochester in Chapter 35, she leaves to seek him. Although shocked and dismayed to see Thornfield in ruins and to hear about the current condition of Rochester as a blind cripple, Jane is determined to go to Ferndean to see him. Jane, as Gulliver in one of her formerly favorite readings, has been accustomed to being a "desolate wanderer" and has always been fascinated by "forlorn regions of dreary space." When Jane returns to this scene she is no longer the desolate traveler she was when she said farewell after the disrupted wedding ceremony, for she now has a strong inner hope to fulfill what was undermined before.

Helene Moglen makes an interesting parallel between Jane Eyre and Little Brier Rose, suggesting that Jane's seeking Rochester at Ferndean is reminiscent "of the Prince who comes to awaken the sleeping Beauty with a kiss" (Modern Critical Interpretations 58). The gloom of Rochester's isolated life at Ferndean is immediately transformed with the arrival of Jane into an aura of enchantment. Rochester says that the return of his beloved is for him a dream. Rochester emphasizes the importance of Jane's return to him, saying that all the melody on earth is generated by the presence of Jane's voice and that all of the light and sunshine which he can feel and sense is in her being near him.

Of the setting of Ferndean, Sandra Gilbert and Susan Gubar write: "As a dramatic setting, Ferndean is notably...asocial, so that the physical isolation of the lovers suggests their spiritual isolation in a world where such egalitarian marriages as theirs are rare, if not impossible" (Modern Critical Interpretations 93). Through Jane's love and affection, Ferndean is transformed from a lonely place to a sanctuary of light and serenity for herself and Rochester. In becoming Rochester's eyes and vision as she describes to him various aspects of the beautiful natural environment around them, in loving Rochester deeply and in encouraging him in his debilitated state to feel youthful, and in rejuvenating his forlorn spirit, Jane transforms her mythological vitality into a stream of present-focussed energies. The aura of sanctuary for Jane and Rochester at Ferndean is reinforced by their spiritual connectedness and by their mutual belief in a divine realm and in a divine being. One indication of the profound spiritual relation of Jane and Rochester is the moment when Rochester in his despair called out to Jane and she, although many miles away, heard his voice and felt that she needed to be with him. The shared life of Jane and Rochester, which exemplifies the depth and the intensity of the love expressed in Elizabeth Barrett Browning's poem "How Do I Love Thee," represents a sanctuary of light, love, and mutual appreciation and understanding.

Jane ultimately reveals herself to be a character of Promethean vitality, for she creates harmony, serenity, and love out of disorder and misery in the spirit of Demogorgon's monologue at the end of Percy Shelley's *Prometheus Unbound*. Jane signifies the power of love of which Demogorgon speaks at the end of Act 4:

> Love from its awful throne of patient power
> In the wise heart, from the last giddy hour
> Of dread endurance, from the slippery, steep,
> And narrow verge of crag-like Agony, springs
> And folds over the world its healing wings. (IV. 557–61)

Jane, having emerged from the "last giddy hour / Of dread endurance" (IV.558–59), has saved herself from the abyss to heal Rochester's life and make her own whole and delightful as well. Jane has suffered "woes which Hope thinks infinite" (IV. 570) and yet she has still, through her indomitable spirit, creative vision, imaginative vitality, and noble heart, sought "To love, and bear; to hope, till Hope creates / From its own wreck the thing it contemplates" (IV. 573–74).

In the post-Romantic period, in the second half of the nineteenth century and in the early twentieth century, when a realistic life-philosophy and a realistic aesthetics are more conspicuously present and in the ascendancy, the sense and spirit of sanctuary appears less prominent in European literature, perhaps in part because the creation of a sanctuary or a lovely, secluded, and serene architectural space seems less viable in the world of everyday mortality and perhaps in part because of the existence of various deceitful and malicious individuals in the narrative realms who challenge or undermine the aura of a sanctuary. Yet, there are attempts in the works of several writers in the mid-nineteenth century and in the second half of the nineteenth century to create an aura or a spirit of sanctuary in an aesthetically interesting architectural space. In the Victorian novel, for example, sanctuaries are occasionally developed and articulated which may be manifested in a particular location or even in a character of noble presence and generous heart.

For example, in Charles Dickens' *David Copperfield* (1849–50) the home of David's aunt represents a temporary sanctuary for David as he tries to revitalize his youthful life after fleeing from the baleful influence of the Murdstones. In chapter 14 of the novel Miss Trotwood, David's aunt, and Mr. Dick decide to allow the child to stay with them and liberate him from the malignant influence of the Murdstones. In chapter 15 Miss Trotwood takes David, newly renamed Trotwood Copperfield to signify a new phase of his life, to Canterbury so that he can go to school. Their first stop is at the house of Mr. Wickfield, the lawyer—this very old house has an old-fashioned and serene aura which is affirmed by the two portraits in the parlour of Mr. Wickfield and his wife, now deceased. Miss Trotwood wants to send her nephew to the best school in Canterbury—and it is decided that David will board with the Wickfields. It is noteworthy that Mr. Wickfield and Agnes, his young daughter, seem immediately to develop a liking for Trotwood. When saying to Miss Trotwood that she can leave her nephew to stay in his house Mr. Wickfield describes it as an excellent domicile for study because of its profound quiet, as if it were a monastery, and its spacious serenity. The room in which David will be permitted to stay is described as "glorious" (280), has an antiquated aura with its "oak beams" (280) and "diamond panes" (280), and is reached by ascending the lovely old staircase, which reinforces the ambience of spaciousness in the house. The presence of Agnes, Mr. Wickfield's daughter, in the house immeasurably enhances the aura of sanctuary and tranquility which it offers. For Agnes exemplifies by her very nature a sanctuary of light and peacefulness. Agnes Wickfield is the kind of noble-hearted individual who carries an aura of sanctuary with her throughout her life. David Copperfield comes to realize, and perhaps he senses it instinctively from the very first moments of meeting Agnes, that she is his good angel. At the end of the novel David describes the seraphic countenance of Agnes, his kindred spirit, in glowing terms: "But one face, shining on me like a Heavenly light by which I see all other objects, is above them and beyond them all" (950). The presence of Agnes not only generates and sustains the aura of a serene sanctuary in David Copperfield's life, but also inspires him creatively and provides him with supreme emotional and spiritual comfort.

In Thomas Hardy's *The Return of the Native* (1878), Thomasin Yeobright bears, like Agnes Wickfield in *David Copperfield*, an aura of sanctuary in her everyday presence. The Yeobright home on Egdon Heath, Blooms-End, at least until the death of Mrs. Yeobright, represents a sanctuary for Clym, who appreciates with great sensitivity the natural beauty of this isolated environment. The interior of Blooms-End is depicted as being pleasant and comfortable; the house itself appears to have the aura of a Frank Lloyd Wright creation in its aesthetic unity with the surrounding natural environment.

The house of Bathsheba Everdene in Thomas Hardy's *Far from the Madding Crowd* (1874) is also very interesting architecturally. An example of "the early stage of Classic Renaissance" (59) this house "had once been the manorial hall upon a small estate around it" (59) and was now "merged in the vast tract of a non-resident landlord" (59). This house is further described as follows: "Fluted pilasters, worked from the solid stone, decorated its front, and above the roof the chimneys were paneled or columnar, some coped gables with finials and like features still retaining traces of their Gothic extraction" (59). The antiquated atmosphere of the building is enhanced by the presence of moss on the stone tiling. The house of Boldwood, Little Weatherbury Farm, is also noteworthy because he is the single individual in the world of the novel who represents an aura of aristocracy. It is implied that the house, "recessed from the road" (95) has an atmosphere of quiet dignity.

The description of the great barn in *Far from the Madding Crowd* is especially interesting because Hardy praises it for its immutability and its simple grandeur: "The dusky, filmed, chestnut roof, braced and tied in by huge collars, curves, and diagonals, was far nobler in design, because more wealthy in material, than nine-tenths of those in our modern churches" (113). Through the passage of four centuries this great barn, unlike various other architectural creations, retained its original purpose and a spirit of constancy. It is even suggested that the threshing-floor of the barn with the passage of time "had grown as slippery and as rich in hue as the state-room floors of an Elizabethan mansion" (114).

In George Eliot's *Middlemarch* (1871–2) the sense of sanctuary and attractiveness of Lowick Manor which Dorothea feels on her visit in Chapter 9 (in anticipation of her impending marriage) is not sustained when she returns with Mr. Casaubon in the middle of January from their wedding journey to Rome. In Chapter 9 Dorothea is impressed by the house and the property—she is especially pleased with the "dark book-shelves in the long library, the carpets and curtains with colours subdued by time, the curious old maps and bird's-eye views on the walls of the corridor, with here and there an old vase below" (65). The atmosphere of antiquity at Lowick which attracts Dorothea initially is definitely diminished after the rather uncongenial wedding journey. In Chapter 28 when Dorothea and Mr. Casaubon return from the wedding trip to Rome the aura of the house is less appealing. As Dorothea moves from her dressing-room into the blue-green boudoir, she observes that "...the furniture in the room seemed to have shrunk since she saw it before: the stag in the tapestry looked more like a ghost in his ghostly blue-green world; the volumes of polite literature in the bookcase looked more like immovable imitations of books" (248). Although there is no house in the course of the novel which signifies or symbolizes the vitality of Dorothea's character, one could claim that Dorothea, as other great nineteenth-century literary heroines such as Elizabeth Bennet, Jane Eyre, Agnes Wickfield, Thomasin Yeobright, and Natasha Rostova, represents a sanctuary of goodness and light in her own right. The "finely-touched spirit" (766) of Dorothea, whose noble existence motivated the "growing good of the world" (766) around her, epitomizes a sanctuary of luminescence which generously influences and shapes the progress of humanity.

In Leo Tolstoy's *Voina i mir, War and Peace* (1864–69), the houses and estates of the Bolkonsky and the Bezukhov families are extensive, lovely, and spacious. In Part One, Chapter XXII the Bolkonsky's country estate, Bleak Hills, represents a theoretical haven from the world of everyday mortality. Prince Nikolay Bolkonsky is depicted as living in splendid isolation at Bleak Hills with his daughter, Princess Marya, and her companion. Having no interest in journeying into Moscow Prince Nikolay occupies himself with his memoirs, studying higher mathematics, working in his garden, or planning the development of farm buildings on the estate. That his meals are served at a definite time every day could suggest his interest in a thoroughly and regularly organized life or even an inclination to transcend mortality by controlling the flux of time. That the aura of potential sanctuary in this mansion is not sustained and is even diminished is made evident by various events in Chapters XXII through XXV. For example, Prince Nikolay's rigidity of demeanor and his undervaluation of his daughter and her abilities undermines the ambience of harmony and serenity which such an isolated estate might typically offer. Despite the beauty of the house there is an underlying tension because Princess Marya's piety—manifest in her statement to Andrey that in God alone is truth and peace—contrasts with the life-philosophy of her father. The less than completely blissful marriage of Prince Andrey and his wife and the fact that the wife of Prince Andrey does not really feel comfortable in this ambience also undermine the potential for an aura of sanctuary in this isolated country estate.

Prince Andrey's arrival at Bleak Hills with his pregnant wife in Chapter XXIII of Part One creates a temporarily congenial atmosphere at the Bolkonsky estate, which from the perspective of at least one character is a palace. The aura of magnificence of the mansion's interior is reinforced in Chapter XXIV by the declaration that the dining-room, as all of the other rooms in the house, was "immensely lofty" (106). Prince Andrey tries at least to some extent to free himself from the isolationist approach of his father, whose high standards separate him from society and restrain him from associating with various individuals of less than exemplary ethical vitality. Prince Andrey achieves a thoughtful and critical awareness of society while trying to participate directly in the world of everyday mortality.

While the houses of the wealthy Bezukhov family are richly adorned with an abundance of material possessions, various personal conflicts and tragedies such as the failure of the marriage of Pierre diminish the potential of such residences to represent a sense of sanctuary. In Part One, Chapter XIX Pierre goes with Anna Mihalovna to visit his dying father, Count Bezukhov. The count's reception room is impressive, opening into the conservatory, with the large bust and full-length portrait of Catherine the Great. In Part One, Chapter XX the spacious bedroom where the dying Count Bezukhov is surrounded by doctors, princesses, family members, servants is divided into parts by columns and an arch and displays Persian rugs. The section of the bedroom behind the columns contains a high silk-curtained mahogany bed and a large case of illuminated icons and holy images. At the end of Part One, Chapter XXI the Count passes away and Pierre inherits great wealth.

While Natasha Rostova's family is not as wealthy as that of Pierre Bezukhov, there is an ambience of congenial material comfort in their mansion in the city, until the devastation of the war impacts its existence. The turbulence of the historical background of the novel, the first two decades of the nineteenth century with such major events as Napoleon's invasion of Russia and the Russian resistance to this invasion, makes it difficult to attain a sense of sanctuary or to preserve a place of serene architectural beauty. However, the major characters such as Natasha Rostova, Prince Andrey Bolkonsky, and Pierre Bezukhov are all able in their personal lives to achieve and sustain, at least for a time, a sense of sanctuary. For example, in Part Five, Chapter II, Pierre, travelling towards Petersburg in melancholy despair about having married a dissolute woman whom he never really loved, is addressed by a stranger who is a freemason. In the ensuing conversation Pierre admits that he hates his life—the freemason criticizes the dissipated and idle life which Pierre has been leading and emphasizes to him the importance of purifying and renewing the inner self with the presence of the light of God, the individual conscience. This conversation initiates a new phase in Pierre's life, during which he develops an inner luminescent sanctuary which helps to guide him towards a more virtuous and productive existence.

In Part Twelve, Chapter XVI Prince Andrey, aware that he is dying, proclaims that love is life, that love can hinder death, and that everything is associated with the presence of love, culminating in his belief that "Love is God, and dying means for me a particle of love, to go back to the universal and eternal source of love" (1120). After the dream which Prince Andrey has of death, he exclaims that death represents an awakening. As this idea illuminated his soul, Prince Andrey "felt, as it were, set free from some force that held him in bondage, and was aware of that strange lightness of being that had not left him since" (1121). This is an inner sanctuary of light which comforts and soothes his soul. As Prince Andrey is watched over in his final days and hours by Princess Marya and Natasha, his physical being slowly fades away and returns to "the eternal source of love."

In several of the Novellen of Theodor Storm architectural spaces have a special importance. In *Immensee* (1849) the gabled house in which the protagonist lives contains an aura of past splendor. The elderly man, after entering the house, makes his way through the wide hallway into another hall which displays sizeable oak chests with porcelain vases. Passing through this hall he walks to a small corridor from which a staircase leads to the rooms upstairs. His room, located at the back of the house, is congenial and quiet. Along one wall there are bookshelves and closets; along the other are pictures of places and people. As the elderly man sits reflecting for a moment after his afternoon walk, his gaze rests upon a picture which had been illuminated by a strand of early moonlight. The sight of this picture of Elizabeth, his childhood love, inspires reflections about his past, and especially about his youth. As the protagonist, Reinhard, reminisces about his past, he thinks about the lovely days spent with Elizabeth during his childhood and youth, about their separation, and about her eventual marriage to someone else. Reinhard also reflects on his visit to the mansion of Elizabeth and her husband on a lake, Immensee. His visit there is a fusion of pleasure and pain, for while he is happy to see Elizabeth, he also becomes aware that he can never revitalize the past love which they shared—his parting from Elizabeth is not very warm or congenial. One poignant symbol of this is his failed attempt to reach the water lily in the middle of the lake. The elusive and unattainable water lily could symbolize the fact that none of the major characters in the story achieve a real sense of happiness in their lives. When the darkness finally overwhelms the atmosphere of the room in his gabled house in the present, the elderly man's final reflection from his past is of a water lily floating alone in the distance. At the end of the narrative the elderly man devotes himself once again to those studies which are the focus of his life.

In Theodor Storm's *Der Schimmelreiter, The Rider on the White Horse* (1888), the story within the larger narrative tells of Hauke and Elke Haien and of their devotion to each other and to their home landscape. The dikemaster, Elke's father, in the story comes from a long line of dikemasters and lives in a very respectable house which can be seen from the distance as it is located on a hill and is adjacent to an ash tree, the tallest in the region. Hauke, who does various jobs for the dikemaster, Tede Volkerts, including revealing to him various observations he makes about violations which occur with respect to the dike, falls in love with Elke, the dikemaster's daughter. Hauke is devoted to the protection and preservation of the dike against the tempestuousness of the sea and gradually does most of the work of the dikemaster. After the deaths of his father and of Elke's father, Hauke is chosen as the new dikemaster, with Elke's supportive assistance. After Hauke and Elke are married they work extremely hard, although they are relatively wealthy and could enjoy a more relaxed lifestyle. Hauke even plans to build a new dike to reclaim some land and provide a protection for future generations living in this area. Several years after Hauke's very devoted efforts to create a new dike, the reclaimed fields are prospering. However, as often happens with reformers such as Hauke, despite a strong commitment to the well-being of the community, he loses friends along the way because his mission of creating a new dike seems more important than obliging local idiosyncrasies and whims. Sadly but inevitably, there are also various individuals in the community who are jealous of Hauke's heroic and well-intentioned efforts. As the years pass, Hauke and Elke are alone in the community, alone with their own concerns and struggles and with their pleasant and somewhat handicapped child. Hauke feels as if he were waging a perpetual struggle as he tries to protect his community against "God's sea." One year in late October just before All Saints' Day there is a terrible storm. Hauke is such a devoted dikemaster that he feels compelled to mount his white horse and travel along the dike to watch for any damage or deterioration during the tempest. Tragically, Hauke, Elke, and their child are all killed during the ferocious storm as parts of his village are inundated. At the end of this narrative Hauke can see the light shining from his window but it offers no comfort before he plunges into the seething waves. The narrator of this inner narrative within the larger framework of the story makes an interesting parallel at the end between Hauke, Socrates, and Jesus, suggesting that they all suffered for the sake of a community and a world which did not appreciate and value their contributions.

The quest for transcendent spaces and for a sense of architectural sanctuary is also prominent in several dramas of Henrik Ibsen. In some dramas such a quest for liberation or transcendence is the primary thematic focus. In other dramas, such as *The Master Builder*, the quest for liberation or transcendence is intimately connected to the theme of creativity. In various works by Ibsen the notion of a sanctuary exists or is developed at a threshold moment, the threshold of day and night or the threshold of life and death. That the sense of sanctuary is in a threshold context perhaps ensures its fragility and uncertainty. In post-Romantic European literature places of sanctuary, sanctuaries of light and serenity, can be very beautiful. However, they are typically as fragile and transient as they are beautiful. In the literary landscape of European realism it is difficult to preserve and sustain such sanctuaries of light and tranquility.

In *The Master Builder* (1892) the notion of absolute commitment to his professional work is of the utmost importance to Solness as the master builder. Solness speaks in Act 3 of the drama about the development of his creativity and sense of commitment. Solness states that in his youth he was reared in an atmosphere which respected the divine and religious faith. So as Solness began his career as an architect, he thought that building churches was the most significant goal one could have as a creative individual. Solness proceeds to explain to Hilde, with whom he is discussing this issue, that he built various churches in a spirit of such sincerity and dedication that he thought God would have been delighted with him. Solness sadly acknowledges that instead of receiving a positive reaction, he initially had the feeling that God was not pleased with him and wanted to make him suffer. The master builder even declares that he believed that the divine being allowed the old house to burn down as a sign of this displeasure.

However, as Solness tries to understand God's motivation for such a seemingly negative reaction and for making him and those around him suffer, he believes that he discovers a plausible reason. Solness proclaims that he experienced an epiphanic moment of awareness when he built the church tower at Lysanger. During this venture the master builder realized that God made him suffer so inexorably because he wanted to encourage him to become a thorough master of his craft. Solness interprets the loss of his children as a further indication of God's ultimate purpose—namely, to encourage the master builder to be a creator first and foremost, without any personal distractions. Solness comes to believe that the divine being wanted him to create architectural structures for Him and in His honor. There should be no personal life which might distract Solness from his endeavors; there should be no interference from personal concerns in his divinely appointed task.

Solness is here symbolic of many creative artists (painters, sculptors, architects, writers) through the centuries who have dedicated themselves completely to their work and have not allowed a "personal" life to interfere with and encroach upon such dedication. This notion that a genuine and a genuinely vital creator should devote himself completely and exclusively to his work has an established tradition in the history of world civilization. Rainer Maria Rilke speaks similarly of the devotion which an artist should show in and to his work—this devotion should be absolute, allowing for no personal intervention from the world of everyday mortality.

A turning point in the career of Solness occurred when he climbed the tower of the completed church in Hilde's home town to hang the wreath on the weathercock and signify the successful completion of the project. As the conversation with Hilde in Act 3 continues, Solness admits that he had always been afraid of heights but on that particular day in Lysanger he seemed to be impelled by an inner force to climb up to the heights. Yet, this was not merely a physically exhilarating exercise. Even more importantly Solness asserts that when he reached the top of the building, he spoke to God and proclaimed his independence as a master builder. One could describe this scenario as Solness's declaration of independence from his career as a builder of churches.

Solness, perhaps inspired or stimulated by the accomplishment of what had before seemed to him an impossible task (namely, climbing to the top), declares to God that from now on he will only build homes for people. This passage is also interesting because Solness creates an analogy between himself and the divine, claiming to God that he is a "master builder free in his own field, as you are in yours" (349). It is noteworthy that Hilde, with glistening eyes, says with apparent admiration at this point that such an exchange between Solness and the divine was the song which she heard in the air. One might wonder whether Hilde's statement is positive and in a spirit of genuine respect for Solness or whether her statement has a more negative motivation in the sense that she is trying to lead Solness on, to lure him to the symbolic "depths" which he experiences at the end of the drama.

The sense of absolute commitment which Solness shows in and to his work evolves into his quest for transcendence. Once Solness has achieved what he aimed to accomplish in the sphere of everyday reality and mortality, then he aspires to attain something greater and more elusive. In *Ibsen the Romantic* Errol Durbach describes this aspiration of Solness effectively as follows: "He commits himself, in soul-camradeship with Hilde Wangel, to that most Romantic of impulses: the lure of the impossible, the temptation to transcend not only his own physical infirmity in high places but the mortal and temporal limitations of mankind" (127). The ultimate plan of Solness is to embark on a new architectural venture which will represent a culmination of his career. His aim is to construct the only buildings which he believes can contain human happiness—castles in the air.

Happiness is an important issue for Solness the master builder. In Act 2, for example, Solness argues that everything he has achieved has had to be paid for in human happiness, not only his own, but especially the happiness of others such as that of his wife. Solness declares especially that he succeeded as a master builder through the suffering of his wife, Aline. He believes that her capacity for nurturing and developing children's souls had to be undermined for his talent as a builder to thrive. Moreover, the burning of Aline's spacious family home helped to promote the career of Solness, for it gave him the opportunity to build various houses. Although Solness presumably was not responsible for the conflagration in any way, he is continually tormented by the sense that he may have been the cause of everything destructive that happened in his recent family history, or he may be completely innocent. Such a persistent inner conflict helps to motivate Solness in seeking a sense of sanctuary, a place of transcendence which can liberate him from the travails and tribulations of everyday mortality.

That Solness, who has spent his entire professional life building real structures with real foundations, would claim at the end of the drama that the only constructions which really matter are "castles in the air" represents an ironic and critical commentary on contemporary society. Ibsen seems to imply here that there is little genuine happiness in the world of everyday reality and mortality—the only source of true happiness is found in the ideal and in the world of the imagination (and of dream). For Ibsen, as for some of his European romantic predecessors, this world of dream and of the ideal is subtly and sometimes even more directly connected to death and eternity. In several poems by Novalis and by Clemens Brentano, for example, there is a "Sehnsucht nach dem Tode," a longing for death to liberate the spirit from the hardship and the suffering which are being endured in or which are imposed by the world of everyday reality. Death is viewed as a pleasant and a congenial realm which can offer solace for the soul overwhelmed by the frailties, the inadequacies, and the vicissitudes of mortal existence.

Solness seems mesmerized by Hilde at the end, for in his final conversation with her he even revives parts of the narrative of the past encounter which they had (that is, according to Hilde's version of the event) in Hilde's home town ten years ago. Perhaps the final act does represent Solness fulfilling his dream of creating "a castle in the air." As this phrase refers to the realm of the ideal one might interpret Solness and Ibsen as suggesting that castles in the air have no tangible place in the world of everyday mortality among the hardships and struggles of reality. The castle in the air of Solness, as the exceptional space of Atlantis which Anselmus and Serpentina inhabit in their blissful love, is perhaps only truly viable and vital in the world of the ideal and in the realm of the imagination.

Errol Durbach asserts in *Ibsen the Romantic* that the castles in the air, as well as the Kingdom of Orangia are "symbols of reality but not reality itself" (135). The inherent problem in the quest for such romantic structures, says Durbach, is that it signifies "an ascent into the no man's land of stasis, from which all human vitality has been purged and drained away" (135). Or perhaps one could say that the vitality has already been achieved and demonstrated by Solness in his career as a preparation for the final romantic quest of creating a "castle in the air."

Durbach and other critics have thoughtfully discussed the "tragedy of Solness's and Hilde's romanticism" (136) in connection with the presence of the empty nurseries and the houses which are and remain uninhabited. The empty nurseries and the houses which are uninhabitable or appear to be so certainly reinforce the aura of melancholy and tragedy in the drama. However, I would say that the "castle in the air" represents a more positive structure, a more emotionally and spiritually vital entity. The castle in the air signifies for Solness the creation of the ideal and of an ideal image and place which transcends the limitations and sufferings inherent in and perceptible in everyday mortality. As Solness declares in Act 3 that up to that point of his career he has not really accomplished anything, the opportunity to create a castle in the air could also suggest the possibility of a strategy of self-revitalization. Solness might view the challenge to create such an extraordinary structure as an occasion to renew his creative energies and capacities.

The final statement of Nathaniel Hawthorne's "The Artist of the Beautiful" offers an interesting parallel to the situation of Solness in Act 3 of *The Master Builder*: "When the artist rose high enough to achieve the beautiful, the symbol by which he made it perceptible to mortal senses became of little value in his eyes while his spirit possessed itself in the enjoyment of the reality" (Hawthorne 95). The grandson and spiritual heir of the arch-realist Peter Hovenden has just destroyed the beautiful and magical butterfly which the romantic Owen Warland created. Hawthorne, in the final sentence of the story, suggests that what really matters to this artist of the beautiful is the achievement of the ideal. Even though the real manifestation of his art work has been ruined, the ideal, once achieved, is eternal.

One could argue that Solness has risen to achieve the beautiful, his "castle in the air," and now the "real" construction of his structure to the top of which he has climbed is not as important or vital. In speaking to the divine being or realm, the spirit of Solness is possessing and reenergizing itself "in the enjoyment of the reality" as Owen Warland does in the Hawthorne narrative. Unlike Solness, of course, Owen Warland does physically survive his immediate contact with the deleterious realism symbolized by Peter Hovenden and the blacksmith Robert Danforth. However, just as Solness has died to life so presumably will Owen. Solness has removed himself literally from the tribulations and vicissitudes of everyday mortality. Owen Warland in "The Artist of the Beautiful" will presumably separate himself literally and symbolically from the encroachments and machinations of everyday reality by isolating himself further after this painful contact with the doubting and unsupportive world around him.

In Ibsen's *A Doll's House* (1879) Nora is a devoted and self-sacrificial wife and mother who tries to create an aura of sanctuary in her domestic environment. Nora aspires to create a home which is characterized by an atmosphere of serenity and tranquility. She plays along with Helmer's undervaluation and devaluation of her because she does not want to challenge this sense of serenity. Moreover, Nora saves Helmer's life by taking out a loan to enable him to travel for his health. Sadly, she feels that she cannot reveal her role in this effort to him because it would undermine his self-pride and because she senses that he would react in an irrational manner to such news.

Act 2 of *A Doll's House* offers an ironic reversal of Nora's quest for a sanctuary. One of the central issues of Act 2 is that Helmer does not take Nora and her concerns seriously. When Nora pleads with Helmer to consider her request regarding Krogstad, he treats her with callous indifference and ignores the anxiety and fear which she expresses. Helmer's indifference towards Nora culminates when he encourages her to practice her dance for the upcoming party while he proceeds into his study, shutting both doors, thus literally and symbolically ignoring her actions and feelings. Helmer lives in a pleasant "refuge" of domestic bliss which Nora has endeavored diligently to create for him and for the family. Yet, he is not content with this. For at this point in the drama he feels the need to retreat even further into his own inner space which distances him from the family atmosphere and its tribulations.

Nora's awareness and consciousness of Rank's profound emotional attachment to her represents an inner sanctuary in her life, a sanctuary of heart and soul, which helps to sustain her in the problematic and painful circumstances which occur throughout the rest of the drama. Knowing inwardly that she is so valued by someone is very important to Nora, especially considering the sense of despair which she feels and expresses at the end of Act 2 and the verbal abuse from Helmer which she suffers in Act 3.

The notion that Nora, by virtue of her kindness, generosity, and emotional luminescence, all qualities which Rank in particular appreciates, signifies a sanctuary of goodness and light in everyday life is reinforced in an important conversation in Act 3. In this conversation we see clearly that Helmer and Rank have distinctly different views of Nora. Helmer still treats Nora as an object in the spirit of his earlier claim that she is his "most treasured possession" (69) and doubts that Nora could find a costume to represent Lady Luck. Rank, on the other hand, asserts that Nora just has to wear her everyday clothes to symbolize Lady Luck. This exchange is very revealing for it shows clearly Helmer's undervaluation of Nora in contrast to Rank's appreciation of Nora and her radiant qualities. For Rank's statement suggests that Nora is such a positive force in the world of mortality and has such an affirmative presence in everyday life that she merely has to be herself to exemplify Lady Luck.

Any remaining semblance of sanctuary in the domestic environment of this household is obliterated in Act 3 by Helmer's harshly abusive criticism of Nora after he reads Krogstad's letter. The selfish and self-oriented response of Helmer in this situation contrasts sharply with Nora's typically family-directed and family-motivated aims and ambitions which have been evident from the beginning of the drama. At the end of the drama Nora decides to liberate herself from the doll house to create a new and a more congenial life for herself. Nora proclaims that her first duty will now be to herself, to develop and to educate herself more vitally for an uncertain future. The dramatic narrative which began with the attempt to create and sustain a sanctuary of domestic felicity and tranquility during the day concludes during the night with the destruction of any potential for the creation of a sanctuary.

Yet, Nora is, as Rank so appropriately and sensitively described her, the embodiment of Lady Luck. She will take her luminescent presence with her into the world of everyday mortality. Although her immediate future will presumably be challenging and difficult, Nora carries within her heart and soul a sanctuary of goodness and radiance which will guide, nurture, and sustain her. As Jane in Charlotte Brontë's novel *Jane Eyre*, Nora has a special resilience, a capacity to illuminate the world around her with her thoughtfulness which will presumably triumph eventually against various obstacles.

In Ibsen's *When We Dead Awaken* (1899) there are, as in *The Master Builder*, important architectural features. The Rubek mansion, the villa, and the small farmhouse are three such notable places. The farmhouse, although no longer existent, signifies a special space for Irene, for she believed that Rubek and she could have enjoyed a pleasant existence here. Rubek, the famous sculptor, returns to his homeland, apparently Norway, after a lengthy absence. At a seaside resort he meets, after a long interval of separation, Irene, who was the model for his masterpiece, "Resurrection Day." Irene had been very disappointed in the past when she discovered that Rubek did not truly love her, but was only using her for his art work. As Solness, Rubek has sacrificed a desire and an inclination for human happiness by absolute devotion to his art. In "Resurrection Day" Rubek had wanted to create an image of a "pure young woman, untainted by the world, waking to light and glory" (Durbach 140).

In *When We Dead Awaken* Irene tries to inspire Rubek to reenergize himself and their mutual existence. In climbing to the top of the mountain, they hope to achieve a spiritual revitalization. In ascending the mountain Rubek, who has left his wife Maja behind to join with Ulfhejm, the bear-hunter, implicitly aims to achieve the luminescent spirit of a resurrection. This ascent, or ascension, is similar to that of Solness in *The Master Builder*. Both artists have already created their masterpieces—they are searching for something new and vital in their lives, something to renew their artistic dynamism.

Rubek and Irene attain a spiritual union and revitalization in a luminescent sanctuary. For the peak to which they ascend is bathed in light, in a glorious radiance. Durbach describes the ascension of Rubek and Irene effectively in *Ibsen the Romantic*:

"They enter the world of metaphor, not 'poetically,' as Keats enters the Urn-world or Yeats Byzantium, but by moving physically into Paradise, by enacting literally the mythical scenario shaped by the artistic vision out of the realities of experience" (148). Durbach proceeds to argue thoughtfully that Rubek and Irene "become the art-work, 'Resurrection Day,'" (148).

In *When We Dead Awaken* the most salient sanctuary is the image of the mountain peak where Rubek and Irene will achieve their spiritual revitalization. Yet, this "sanctuary" is, as various other special places of architectural or natural refuge in Ibsen's dramas, as beautiful as it is fragile, as nurturing as it is destructive. The context of this sublime sanctuary cannot be sustained and Rubek and Irene are killed on the mountain in an avalanche. Yet, in death they might be said to achieve a spiritual revitalization, a liberation of the soul from the sufferings and vicissitudes of everyday mortality.

In Ibsen's *Peer Gynt* (1867) the most important, vital, and sustainable sanctuary-like ambience is that of the mountain hut where Solveig waits so patiently and lovingly for Peer for so many years. This space represents a sanctuary in the sense that it is the place of the spiritual reunion of Solveig and Peer and of Peer's redemption after his numerous adventures and experiences in the world of everyday mortality.

In the dramatic works of Henrik Ibsen sanctuaries of light and luminescent vitality are often as beautiful as they are fragile. One might even say that their beauty is defined and signified by their fragility, by their transient radiance. Yet, these distinctive architectural spaces and sanctuaries of light are very important for the individuals who have aspired to achieve them and who cherish them.

The interrelation or interconnectedness of architectural beauty and fragility or transience is exemplified in other nineteenth century literary works as well. For example, in E. T. A. Hoffmann's *Das Majorat, The Entail* (1817), there is Castle R., the ancestral seat of Baron Roderich von R., a gloomy, isolated structure not far from the Baltic coast with a splendid interior, an impressive baronial hall containing many paintings and carvings, though somewhat faded with the passage of time, and an observatory with telescopes for the scientific and personal interests of the reclusive owner. Baron Roderich also shows a fascination with and an affection for the sea, even seeming to people as if he is addressing the waves as a kindred spirit. The castle and its owner enjoy this secluded environment of splendid isolation. At the end of the narrative, after the tragic events which oppressed the Baron and his family, the castle lay in ruins, but various stones from it were used to build the lighthouse which looks over the shore of the Baltic. In this instance the demise of one structure enables the foundation of a new building to be created in a similar spirit and on a contiguous site. In E. A. Poe's "The Fall of the House of Usher" there is the sense of an incipient fissure or weakness which foreshadows the doom of the house and its residents, Roderick and Madeline Usher. The aura of closure and finality in this narrative becomes increasingly more inevitable and inescapable, ensuring the degeneration of the house.

Two other houses in nineteenth century literature which show, as in Hoffmann's *Das Majorat*, the profound consanguinity of a special architectural creation and the surrounding isolated natural environment as well as the negative effects of the flux of time on aesthetically distinctive dwellings are Thrushcross Grange and Wuthering Heights in Emily Brontë's *Wuthering Heights* (1847). Emily, as Catherine Earnshaw in this novel, felt very isolated from the harsh world of everyday mortality and found considerable comfort in the world of nature and especially in roaming over the austere, solitary beauty of the Yorkshire moors. Heathcliff, Catherine's kindred spirit, exemplifies in his personality the passionate and turbulent dynamism of the natural environment. High Withens, Haworth Moor, is thought to have inspired the house Wuthering Heights; and Shibden Hall, in the proximity of which Emily was briefly a governess at Law Hill, a girls' boarding school, is believed to represent the model for Thrushcross Grange. The home of the Linton family, Thrushcross Grange, appears to have an aura of splendor, security, and stability which is sadly diminished and undermined by the passage of time and by several tragic personal events in the narrative.

Thornfield, the home of the Rochester family for generations and a lovely mansion with delightful and aesthetically interesting interiors which is embraced and enclosed by a spacious property, has already been mentioned in the discussion of Charlotte Brontë's *Jane Eyre*. The beauty of this mansion is tragically fleeting for it is completely destroyed in the conflagration initiated by Rochester's "isolated" first wife. Yet, this unfortunate destruction leads to the revitalization of Ferndean, a manor house owned by Rochester and not often used in the past, which also represents the central architectural space of the rejuvenated love of Rochester and Jane at the end of the narrative. Another house in nineteenth century British literature which is undermined by a painful and problematic love experience is Satis House, the home of Miss Havisham in Charles Dickens' *Great Expectations* (1860–61). The interior of Satis House when Pip visits it to socialize with Miss Havisham possesses a dark and melancholy ambience. The interior gloom, which has the aura of a relative timelessness, is affirmed by the fact that the clocks in the house are all stopped at the time of the betrayal of Miss Havisham by her lover. In educating Estella to preserve a coldhearted attitude towards men as a consequence of her personal mistreatment, Miss Havisham creates an emotional wasteland in Satis House. Miss Havisham's wealth does not comfort her—the tragic fire later in the narrative leads to her death. Yet, there is a spirit of hope which rises from the ashes of this ruined space—the friendship of Pip and Estella, despite past conflicts and misunderstandings, will seemingly persevere.

In other narratives, for example, in several stories by Nathaniel Hawthorne, an architectural space is infused with an aura of ambiguity and duality. In "The

Birthmark" (1843) the outer part of Aylmer's lab is characterized as a place of enchantment, for the scientist had converted these dark rooms "into a series of beautiful apartments, not unfit to be the secluded abode of a lovely woman" (266). The resplendent curtains on the walls create an atmosphere of "grandeur and grace" (266). The heavenly ambience of this architectural space contrasts sharply with Aylmer's laboratory, which is depicted as a hellish domain of intense heat, fire, and soot. This duality within an architectural space, with contiguous parts of an architectural realm representing antithetical visions or philosophies, is symbolized by images of heaven and hell. One might even say that such a duality is reflected in Georgiana's presence, for while she is described as exceptionally beautiful, she also possesses a "problematic" birthmark. Yet, the issue of perspective is important here, for although Aylmer and those who are jealous of Georgiana's beauty dislike the birthmark, it is admired by many others as a feature of seemingly mythical origins contributing to her physical attractiveness. The journal of Aylmer's experiments also reinforces the theme of duality in the narrative by displaying a combination of successes and failures.

In Nathaniel Hawthorne's "Rappaccini's Daughter" (1844), Giovanni lodges in "a high and gloomy chamber of an old edifice" (388) which had been the palace of a Paduan nobleman. It is even mentioned that one of the ancestors of this now extinct family, who might have resided in this dwelling, had been portrayed by Dante in "The Inferno." From the window of his apartment Giovanni can see an intriguing garden, which could be a botanic garden and might once have been the pleasure-garden of a wealthy family. The remnant of a marble fountain in the center of the garden implies an original aesthetic vitality, despite its shattered current condition. Yet, the water continues to flow and gush from the fountain, as if affirming the eternal cyclicality of nature. This apparent refuge of lovely and rare flowers and plants is immeasurably enhanced by the beautiful presence of Beatrice, Rappaccini's daughter, who seems to signify a lovely flower in her own right. However, as Giovanni observes, the flowers in this scientifically arranged garden, as Beatrice, are as beautiful as they are deadly. As Georgiana in "The Birthmark," so Beatrice in "Rappaccini's Daughter" is a noble-spirited, ethereal being who is a passive victim of the plans and machinations of those around her. The vision of Beatrice, a being very superior to the world of everyday mortality, is that in dying her spirit will ascend beyond the touch of the evil which has assailed her into an Eden-like existence. The pain, frailty, and suffering of mortal life are transcended for Beatrice, as for Solness, in a vision of an architectural Eden, in an aspiration to participate in a spiritual realm of aesthetic beauty.

There are several interesting parallels between Henrik Ibsen's *The Master Builder* and August Strindberg's *Miss Julie* (1888) with respect to the issues of architectural space, time, and character. Miss Julie in Strindberg's *Miss Julie* yearns, as does Solness in Ibsen's *The Master Builder*, for a sense of sanctuary, for an architectural Eden, and for a better, more congenial, and more humane existential condition. The characters of Miss Julie and Solness reveal various interesting parallels. Both Solness and Miss

Julie are discontented and dissatisfied with their present lives and long for a more beautiful and a more vital existence. The "kingdom of Orangia" which Solness has imagined for Hilde, and, by implication, for himself, is similar in spirit to Miss Julie's dream or vision of a paradise along a southern European lake. It is noteworthy that the visions of Solness and Miss Julie are both characterized in part by the image and idea of orange, a vibrant, dynamic color and aura.

Both Solness and Miss Julie have a dream or a vision relating to heights or an experience of climbing. Solness climbed to the top of the church tower in Hilde's home town to lay the wreath at the conclusion of the architectural work. Solness mentions the danger which he felt during this endeavor, especially because a "little devil in white" (291), who was Hilde, was shouting at him so vociferously.

Solness says that he almost grew dizzy at the sight of her waving her flag. The peril which Solness senses in this instance culminates in the final act of the drama when he falls to his death. The experience of Solness at the end of *The Master Builder* is strikingly similar to the dream which Miss Julie has of climbing up a pillar. As Solness, Miss Julie speaks of the fear of climbing down, of getting dizzy when she looks down, of longing to fall, of longing to reach the ground. One might claim that Miss Julie's dream foreshadows death, for she talks of desiring to reach the ground, to get to the ground, so she can be under the earth. Both Miss Julie and Solness could be said to have suicidal motivations.

As Miss Julie and Jean are contemplating the possibility of leaving together for a distant destination, Jean suggests that they travel to the Italian lakes where there is an eternal summer characterized by "oranges growing everywhere, laurel trees, always green" (Allison 416). This image of an earthly paradise, of a sanctuary beyond the exigencies and tribulations of everyday reality, is comparable in scope to Hilde's sense of the kingdom of Orangia, which she anticipates receiving from Solness. The dream of a happy future which Jean began to inspire Miss Julie to create and develop is short-lived, for he soon criticizes her severely.

One of the most important and profound similarities between Miss Julie and Solness is that they are both instinctively romantic and idealistic characters. For example, Julie wishes to take her greenfinch with her on the proposed trip with Jean which she momentarily contemplates. In claiming that the greenfinch is the only living being that loves her, Julie pleads with Jean to allow her to take the bird along with them. In response, Jean, the coldhearted realist, kills the bird because of the problem of carrying a birdcage on the journey. Miss Julie is thoroughly horrified by Jean's brutal action and curses the moment when she first saw him.

Another example of Miss Julie's romanticism is revealed in her ensuing conversation with Kristine. Miss Julie informs Kristine of the plan to travel to Switzerland with Jean so that the three of them can open a hotel. It is noteworthy that Miss Julie mentions that along the way to Switzerland and the Alps they can visit the castles of King Ludwig, another quintessentially romantic and creatively vital character who was consistently misunderstood and undervalued by his contemporary society. Miss Julie's statement to Kristine that Ludwig's castles are "like castles in fairy tales" (Allison 424) is as much an attempt to persuade Kristine of the value and vitality of the journey as it is to affirm to herself that the ideal beauty of which these castles are an exquisite earthly embodiment truly does exist.

Miss Julie is trying desperately to create a beautiful and a viable vision and to nurture the dream of a lovely sanctuary of light, color, and harmony to elevate her life above the sordidness and anguish of everyday reality. Sadly, Kristine's question, after Miss Julie's description of this picturesque vision, whether she really believes what she has just said, challenges and undermines Julie's fragile dream. Miss Julie's interest in visiting the beautiful castles of King Ludwig as symbols of an earthly paradise and sanctuary is analogous to the commitment of Solness to the creation of a castle in the air. A castle in the air signifies a vision of extraordinary beauty and symbolizes the triumph of the ideal over the real—such an image of an ethereal sanctuary represents a tribute to the power of creativity and the imagination.

Whether one interprets the ascent of Solness at the end of the drama as a visionary creation of a transcendent space, or as a "Sehnsucht nach dem Tode," a fulfillment of his longing for death, or as an attempt to revitalize himself emotionally and aesthetically, or as a venture to prove to himself and to Hilde that he still has the power and the potency to be the master builder, or as an enterprise to prove to his architectural peers and to contemporary society that he is still publicly worthy of being considered the master builder, this is a moment of transient grace and ultimate despair. For Solness falls from the spire and plunges to his death. Solness may have achieved his "castle in the air," the only place on earth which he believes can contain happiness and peacefulness. Yet, despite Hilde's creative claim that she heard "harps in the air" (355), this moment of apparent sanctuary, as the ending of Strindberg's *Miss Julie*, is one of profound sadness. Hilde is the only character who appears to interpret the fatal descent of Solness in a positive light. Perhaps Hilde's effusive assertion as she energetically waves her shawl in a spirit of moderate triumph, which signifies the end of the drama, suggests that Solness, the master builder, has ultimately attained his "castle in the air," his creative vision of a congenial and a transcendent space beyond everyday mortality.

Finally, I would like to discuss the importance of architectural space in two dramas by Oscar Wilde. In Oscar Wilde's *The Importance of Being Earnest* (1895) the two especially lovely architectural spaces are the apartment of Algernon Moncrieff which is described as luxurious and artistically furnished and the Manor House at Woolton where John (Jack) Worthing lives along with his ward Cecily Cardew. During the conversation between Jack and Lady Bracknell in which she is trying to ascertain whether he is an appropriate suitor for her daughter he explains that he has a country house as well as a house in town which he rents to an elderly lady. Although the interior of the Manor House at Woolton is not depicted in considerable detail, there is the sense that it is a beautiful place. For the garden which surrounds it is depicted as lovely with an old-fashioned, congenial aura and an abundance of roses. In this drama, as in Wilde's *An Ideal Husband*, the beautiful house is the propitious location of the thoroughly happy ending, as John Worthing discovers that his name is really Earnest and is able to marry Gwendolen and as Algernon and Cecily are also allowed to get married. It is also noteworthy that various characters, especially John, Cecily, and Algernon, seem perfectly at home in the ambience of the Manor House at Woolton. One might even describe Cecily as the embodiment of the spirit of the house and the property for her presence is as lovely and as pristine as the beautiful and radiantly colorful garden which creates the appropriate romantic atmosphere for the congenial denouement.

In Wilde's *An Ideal Husband* (1895) the home of Sir Robert and Lady Chiltern in London's Grosvenor Square is architecturally impressive, delightful, fashionable, and spacious. Lord Goring's home is also depicted as an aesthetically interesting, elaborate, and well-furnished space. A considerable portion of the drama occurs in the lovely home of Sir Robert and Lady Chiltern. As in Wilde's *The Importance of Being Earnest*, a beautiful house is the congenial final location where various conflicts are resolved and reconciled—Sir Robert and Lady Chiltern revitalize their happy relationship and Lord Goring and Mabel, seemingly well-suited for one another through their consistently playful banter, decide to get married. As beauty, whether architectural, natural, personal, or physical beauty, is such an important theme and motivation for Wilde, one could make the argument that the lovely ambience of the splendid and architecturally interesting houses in these two dramas, *The Importance of Being Earnest* and *An Ideal Husband*, contributes significantly to the blissful and congenial conclusion. The aesthetically beautiful rooms where these dramas achieve their thoroughly happy endings represent, as the similarly gorgeous interior of Lindhorst's house in Hoffmann's *Der goldne Topf* and of Pemberley House in Austen's *Pride and Prejudice*, exquisite architectural spaces of luminescent vitality which inspire and affirm the revitalization of the spirit.

CHAPTER I

Thomas Mann

Buddenbrooks—The Rise and Fall
of a Prominent Family and Its Aura of Sanctuary

Buddenbrooks (1901), one of the greatest novels of the twentieth century, is a narrative by Thomas Mann which focuses on a patrician family and on its fortunes, misfortunes, motivations, and inclinations. While concentrating on the lives of four generations of the Buddenbrooks, the novel focuses especially on the third generation of the family, that of Thomas and Tony Buddenbrook. Even though the subtitle of the novel is "Verfall einer Familie," the narrative presents much more than just a precipitous decline, offering instead a rich tapestry of characters and themes in the presentation of the apparent rise and fall of the family fortunes, as Inge Diersen effectively points out in *Thomas Mann: Episches Werk, Weltanschauung, Leben*: "Doch die Verfallsgeschichte entpuppt sich als ein kompliziertes Ineinander von Verlust und Gewinn, das keine einfachen Wertungen, keine einfachen Ursache-Wirkung-Beziehungen herzustellen erlaubt" (23).

Helmut Koopmann writes effectively in "*Buddenbrooks*: Die Ambivalenz im Problem des Verfalls" that the notion of "Verfall" represents and encompasses both a sense of biological decline and a sense of intellectual and spiritual heightening: "Die wachsende biologische Dekadenz der Familie Buddenbrook wird zugleich eine geistige Verfeinerung und eine Sublimation des Seelischen zeitigen, die ihren Zenit am

Ende des Romans haben wird" (41). Koopmann also suggests insightfully that there are indications of an inner decline already at the beginning of the novel when the family is enjoying its exuberant celebration (42). For even in the description of this resplendent celebration there are signs of incipient conflicts and differences within the aura of the family (42). Koopmann states that "Der Brief Gottholds, die Charakteristiken der beiden Söhne durch Hoffstede, die verborgene Selbstcharakteristik Christians, beginnende Differenzen zwischen Köppen und dem Konsul, vor allem aber Hinweise auf das Schicksal der früheren Bewohner des Hauses in der Mengstraße" (42) imply or indicate "die beginnende Morbidität dieser äußerlich so gefestigten Familie" (42). Moreover, the conflicts and differences in the family circle which are presented initially develop and intensify over time.

The socioeconomic ambience and cultural aura of the Buddenbrooks family and their houses is effectively characterized by Herbert Lehnert in *Thomas Mann: Fiktion, Mythos, Religion* as Biedermeier: "Die Buddenbrooks erweisen sich als eine Biedermeierfamilie. Thomas Buddenbrook hilft zwar, die neue Zeit herbeizuführen, erweist sich in ihr aber als nicht heimisch. Sein ästhetischer Versuch, die Bürgertradition zu spielen, ist auf biedermeierliche Enge bezogen" (84). Lehnert asserts that the need of Thomas to achieve fame and a superior position in society "steht damit in Widerspruch" (84). Lehnert also emphasizes the importance of a sense of domestic felicity and groundedness for some members of the Buddenbrook family: "die 'selbstverständlichen' Orientierungen der noch unreflektierten, echten, das heißt nicht ästhetischen, Existenzen der beiden ersten Buddenbrooks werden äußerlich durch ihre Bindung an das Haus in der Mengstraße spürbar" (85). In contrast to Christian who leaves the home environment to explore the world, Tony Buddenbrook "hat diese Bindung behalten, sie kehrt immer wieder gern in ihr Elternhaus zurück" (85).

Part One of *Buddenbrooks* begins with a housewarming party given by the Buddenbrooks family in October, 1835 to celebrate the new house, a personal, family-motivated accomplishment as well as an architectural achievement. In chapter one of Part One the landscape-room of the family mansion on Meng Strasse is described as containing lovely tapestries which are typically illuminated by a pale yellow sunset. The landscape-room tapestries contain idyllic pastoral images and depictions which are important not only as aspects of the beauty of the mansion but also as features of the aesthetic spirit of this extensive house. The luminescent atmosphere of this scene is enhanced by the fact that the yellow sunset in the tapestries fits well with the yellow coverings of the furniture and with the yellow silk curtains in the room. One might even say that the tapestries in the landscape-room on the first floor of the house on Meng Strasse with their delightful representations of idyllic harmony and serenity signify the inner spirit, or a vital dimension of the inner spirit, of the house.

These landscape-room tapestries instinctively possess an Arcadian aura and con-
fer upon the surrounding house an atmosphere of peacefulness, paradise, serenity,
and harmony. Carl F. Schröer makes the important point in his essay "Gardens—
Models of a better world" that "the Arcadian ideal of an ancient, pastoral world was…
taken up and promoted at royal courts with aristocratic extravagance" (12). Carl F.
Schröer asserts, for example, that the court of the Medici in Florence became "a work
of art set in an ideal classical landscape" (12). And several "hundred years later,
Frederick the Great, an enlightened ruler, transformed sandy moraine in Brandenburg
into an 'Arcadia in the Brandenburg Marches'" (12). The Buddenbrook mansion on
Meng Strasse contains and reveals an Arcadian atmosphere in its aspiration to achieve
a nobility of stature of aristocratic vitality reaffirming the importance of the family
in its socioeconomic context.

It is noteworthy that the Buddenbrook mansion on Meng Strasse is based on
and modeled after an important house on the Meng Strasse in central Lübeck which
was owned by Mann's grandparents and which now contains a museum devoted to
the Mann family. Thomas Mann visited and knew his grandparents' house on Meng
Strasse very well for he spent time here in his childhood and youth. In the novel he
transformed this home into a house of literary significance: "Thomas Manns
Botschaft lautet: Das Buddenbrookhaus hat keine primär biographisch begründete
Aura, sondern eine literarische. Nicht so sehr die in ihm lebenden Personen interes-
sieren, sondern vor allem die vom Autor im Roman 'Buddenbrooks' erfundenen literarischen Figuren" (B. Dittman 8). In *Buddenbrooks* the details of the
'Landschaftszimmer', as well as those of other rooms, are preserved and also given a
new significance in their depiction in the narrative.

In the third chapter of Part One as the celebration continues the family members and guests move into the bright dining-room which, like the landscape-room,
contains tapestries but has a more somber and heavy atmosphere. The tapestries in
the dining-room possess figures of gods and goddesses with a blue background. Both
rooms have an aura of aesthetic unity for the colors of the various material objects fit
well with one another. The dining-room, as the landscape-room, is a luminescent
space, a sanctuary of light separated from the world of everyday mortality. The aura
of sanctuary and of solidity and security which permeates the dining-room is to some
extent created and sustained by the red damask window-curtains and the large sofas
in red damask.The radiance of the dining-room derives from the presence of a gilt
candelabrum with eight candles in each corner as well as from the presence of silver
sconces with candles on the table. The painting of an Italian bay in the dining-room
also represents part of the spirit of classical grace and mythological vitality which is
an essential dimension of this splendid house. The tapestries and exquisite art objects
in the dining-room also signify an essential dimension of the aesthetic spirit of this
great building.

The presence of the figures of gods and goddesses in these tapestries is especially significant—such images participate in and reaffirm a tradition of mythological representation which dates back to the Renaissance. The figures of gods and goddesses displayed in the artistic expression of the Renaissance are often derived from such important works as Ovid's *Metamorphoses* and Virgil's *Eclogues*. In his essay "Gardens—Models of a better world" Carl F. Schröer argues that during the Renaissance it "was believed that the secret, lost knowledge of the ancients was hidden in myth" (14). By developing a profound appreciation for such mythological characters one could gain a more insightful understanding of the natural world, of natural laws, and of the human condition. The presence of the figures of gods and goddesses in the Buddenbrook dining-room suggests not only that they are at home here, that they belong in this context as part of the natural order of life, but also that they are bathed in a light of effulgent appreciation. One might even claim that the presence of such images of gods and goddesses in these tapestries implies that they signify an essential dimension of the heritage of the Buddenbrook family—they are the symbolic portraits of ancestors, perhaps now lost and forgotten in the genealogical annals, but nevertheless spiritually accessible through their artistic representation in this luminescent dining-room. The ambience of the dining-room and its distinctive tapestries in the Buddenbrook mansion, as the landscape-room and its special tapestries, generates and affirms a world permeated by beauty, harmony, order, serenity, and mythological potency.

At the end of Chapter VI the town poet Hoffstede reads a poem to celebrate the housewarming party. Several of the lines of his poem reinforce the importance of this house as a sanctuary of personal joy and blessings away from the potential storms of the outside world. The last stanza of his lyrical offering also emphasizes the solidity of the walls of this mansion as establishing an aura of security in which happiness may be achieved. The sense of sanctuary is suggested in chapter nine as well when Consul Buddenbrook, after saying goodbye to the guests, views the motto carved over the entrance, Dominus providebit ("The Lord will provide"), which is an essential feature of the work-ethic of several family members. Jochen Vogt discusses this effectively in *Thomas Mann: Buddenbrooks*: " In diesem Sinn ist das 'Dominus providebit' über dem Buddenbrookschen Portal ein Fundamentalsatz protestantischer Ethik—und keiner nimmt ihn im Roman so ernst und versucht ihn so ungebrochen zum Fundament seines 'Handelns' zu machen wie Johann Buddenbrook der Jüngere" (43). Vogt also makes the interesting observation that 'Dominus providebit' could suggest on the one hand that God or a divine being will provide for the family which is devoted to integrity and to its religious faith and could imply on the other hand that "Der Herr wird voraussehen" (25), raising the question "was sieht er in der Zukunft, die den Menschen noch verborgen ist?" (25).

It is also noteworthy that Hoffstede speaks in the previous chapter of the various beautiful places which he visited during his Italian journey years ago. Such places, as, for example, the Villa Borghese, can be seen as a parallel to the aesthetically interesting Buddenbrooks house. In this context Johann, Consul Buddenbrook, praises the natural beauty and openness of the landscape in the Buddenbrooks garden outside the Castle Gate, saying that he enjoys the sense of freedom in such an environment.

The Buddenbrook family is so prominent and important that it is delineated by Jürg Zimmermann as representing a "Fürstenfamilie" (15). There are various indications that this family appears to be a noble or an aristocratic family. For example, even as a girl Tony, Antonie, Buddenbrook is described as a little queen who has an appreciation for the nobility. At least several members of the Buddenbrook family view themselves as representatives of a dynasty—the presence of numerous members of the family at the housewarming celebration would seem to affirm this. Of the Buddenbrook family Todd Kontje writes in *The Cambridge Introduction to Thomas Mann*: "Like the Manns, on whose family history the novel is based, the fictional Buddenbrooks are a prominent family in the city and the owners of a thriving export business" (25). One of the reasons why the Buddenbrooks possess the aura of a dynasty is because Jean Buddenbrook consistently devotes himself to his company and his family. These are the two motivating features of his existence. Todd Kontje describes Johann Buddenbrook, the grandfather of Thomas and Tony, effectively as "a jovial gentleman who exudes the combination of local patriotism and cosmopolitanism typical of Hanseatic Lübeck" (26). Kontje also depicts Consul Johann (Jean) Buddenbrook, his son, as "a zealous Christian who takes the family business seriously and is an advocate of modern progress" (26).

The house in Meng Strasse and the other houses of the Buddenbrooks family in the novel have an aesthetic and spiritual precursor in the house of the Archivarius Lindhorst in Hoffmann's *Der goldne Topf.* For these are houses in an urban setting that are characterized by a luminescence, a vital sense of inner space and spatial expansiveness, an aura of architectural beauty, an atmosphere of aesthetic splendor signified by several extraordinarily beautiful art objects, and a serene elegance. The Buddenbrooks houses, as the Kröger house in *Tonio Kröger*, have the solidity, security, and patrician elegance which various important mansions in cities such as Bremen and Lübeck had during the golden age of their mercantile activity when the merchant-class dominated the socioeconomic environment.

In Chapter VIII the expansiveness of the house on Meng Strasse is implied as the Consul leads several members of the dinner-party to the billiard-room. One of the guests, Herr Köppen, even declares how exhausting it was walking through the meandering passageways. Yet, already in Chapter X there are signs that the sense of sanctuary is not as solid as appearances would suggest. The letter from Gotthold, Consul Buddenbrook's elder brother, requesting more funds has the potential to dampen the joy of the family celebration for Johann Buddenbrook Senior and for Johann, the Consul. Consul Buddenbrook even says to his father, the family patriarch, in this chapter that the conflict with Gotthold is like a crack in the family edifice—such a crack is strikingly reminiscent of the flaw in the building in E. A. Poe's story "The Fall of the House of Usher." However, it is decided not to yield to Gotthold's financial demands. The last paragraph of the chapter, which is also the final paragraph of Part One of the novel, suggests that the stability and architectural stature of the house will protect the family from the problems and challenges which may arise as it shelters the family members from the rain and the wind outside on this autumn evening. However, one might also interpret the last paragraph as implying that the fears of possible future problems remain even though the hopes for a bright future are very vital.

In *Thomas Mann: Buddenbrooks*, Jochen Vogt stresses the historical depth of the house of the Buddenbrooks: "Das stattliche Gebäude, das ihr Grossvater im Jahre 1835 erwirbt, so erfährt der Leser bald, stammt ja aus dem Jahre 1682" (31). Vogt proceeds to discuss the all-encompassing nature of such a prominent house: "Es ist ein Haus für das 'ganze Haus,' für Familie und Firma, umschließt den Wohnraum der Familie (und Räumlichkeiten für den großzügigen Empfang ihrer Freunde) ebenso wie die Geschäftsräume (Kontor, Speicher) für den Getreidehandel grösseren Umfangs, den die Firma Buddenbrook betreibt" (31). With the passage of time and the deaths and departures of various family members the house itself seems too large and sprawling so that parts of it remain empty for extended periods and other parts are even used by non-family members.

At the beginning of Part Two of the novel Consul Johann Buddenbrook, inspired by the birth of his daughter Clara, reflects on the development of his own life. He thinks especially about various narrow escapes with death (the small-pox in his youth, the time when a vat of beer fell upon him and had injured him severely, and the time when he was almost drowned) which he has experienced, events which might suggest a life guided by fate. As Consul Buddenbrook reflects on his own life and on the history of his family, he shows a strong appreciation for the importance of a sense of family tradition and continuity. In these reflections is also the implication that a spiritual, non-commercial dimension will blossom in subtle ways in his children. The gilt-edged notebook which contains various personal reflections and the leather portfolio with family documents represent, as the images in the landscape-room and in the dining-room, an integral dimension of the spirit, of the aesthetic and spiritual essence, of the house. These are features which create, generate, and affirm the inner vitality, the symbolic heart, of the house and its capacity for future existence.

The gilt-edged notebook in which Consul Buddenbrook writes or inscribes important family events is not only a crucial facet of the spirit of this magnificent house. It also offers a sense of an inner sanctum, of a sanctuary which is the heart and soul of the mansion. This aura of sanctuary is somewhat enhanced by the awareness of family history and tradition. For example, the passing down of the Wittenberg Bible from one generation to the next creates an ambience of sanctuary and continuity. There is also the sense that the family had socially prominent ancestors: for example, the first documented Buddenbrook is described as living in Parchim around the end of the sixteenth century, and his son had been a senator of Grabau. That an earlier family member was a businessman in Rostock is also mentioned because one of his descendants eventually founded the family's grain business in Lübeck. However, such an awareness of family history, while explicitly proclaiming the vitality of a sense of family continuity in the series of births and favorable events, also inevitably implies the encroachment of mortality by its emphasis on deaths and difficult circumstances. The gilt-edged notebook exists physically in the inner sanctum of the mansion. However, the capacity of the notebook, in conjunction with the portfolio containing other family documents, to represent a perpetual sanctuary is challenged by the chime which is heard from above the secretary. This sign of the inevitable passage of time, the flux of mortality, appears to be reinforced by the image of the church-tower in the painting of the old market-square.

The autobiographical dimension of *Buddenbrooks* is evident here. Thomas Mann was born into "ein altes und angesehenes Kaufmannsgeschlecht" (7), as Inge Diersen so appropriately states in *Untersuchungen zu Thomas Mann*. Thomas Mann was the second son of the Lübeck businessman and senator Thomas Johann Heinrich Mann. His father played a prominent role in the public affairs of the city. However, as in various literary works by Thomas Mann, the children of the commercially and financially successful father were not conspicuously interested in the family business. Heinrich Mann, the eldest son, and Thomas Mann both became writers and liberated themselves in a sense from the commercial and mercantile heritage of the family.

In Chapter II of Part Two Tony Buddenbrook's visit to her grandparents is described. This visit, which typically occurs in the early part of the summer, is to the house of the grandparents outside the Castle Gate. The grand villa in which the grandparents live represents a sanctuary for Tony. The expansiveness of the villa is affirmed by the extensive parterres, orchards, and kitchen-gardens which surround it going down to the river Trave. One of the aspects of this experience which Tony especially values is waking up every morning in a spacious bedroom with lovely tapestries. There is also a carefree atmosphere here so that Tony is free from various duties and responsibilities. Tony also shows a playfully haughty demeanor on occasion for she acts like a little queen.

The prominence and prestige of the Buddenbrook family which had seemed so exemplary in Part One of the novel appears to decline somewhat as Part Two progresses. In Chapter IV of Part Two the imminence of death and then the presence of death, the death of Madame Antoinette Buddenbrook, undermines the aura of sanctuary in the house on Meng Strasse. This atmosphere of decline is produced not only by the death of prominent family members such as Johann Buddenbrook and his wife, but also by the direct statements of the Consul that the firm is not as financially vibrant as it used to be so that he cannot afford an extra servant. This sense of decline reflects a difference in the life-philosophies of old Johann Buddenbrook and his son. Johann Buddenbrook Senior, who was the head of the well-established family firm for years and who purchased the sizeable house on Meng Strasse, shows himself to be a strong and successful businessman, loves life, and feels very much at home in the world of everyday reality. His son, Johann, Consul Buddenbrook, although a successful businessman in his own right, is less instinctively devoted to the world of business and develops a religious sensibility. Of the two sons of Johann, the Consul, and Elisabeth Buddenbrook, Thomas shows himself to be a diligent worker in the family business, while Christian is unable to apply himself as effectively to the rigors of everyday life and is more artistically inclined. The occasionally erratic behavior of Christian could also be interpreted as a sign of potential decline in the stability of this prominent family.

Hugh Ridley argues in *Thomas Mann—Buddenbrooks* that the sense of decay comes from within the family: "The novel repeatedly emphasises the continuity of the Buddenbrooks' marriages, and shows decline to lie within a tradition, rather than in deviation from it" (33). Ridley proceeds to assert that "Tony's marriages…most prominently display the Buddenbrooks' inability to continue their success and prestige" (35). And yet, one might say that even though outwardly Tony Buddenbrook does not appear to be successful, whether in her marriages or in her position in society, at least according to the public and common definition of "success," inwardly, in her own sense of self she is successful. For she preserves a consistency of goodness, sensitivity, and thoughtfulness throughout the course of the novel and throughout her life.

The economic dimension of the family's decline is addressed effectively by Inge Diersen in *Thomas Mann* who asserts that at the death of old Johann Buddenbrook the wealth of the family was greater than before and would subsequently decline: "Von da an geht das Vermögen zurück, nicht ununterbrochen…doch die Bilanz beim Tod der folgenden Firmenchefs, des Konsuls Johann Buddenbrook und des Senators Thomas Buddenbrook, ergibt jeweils eine beträchtlich niedrigere Summe" (23). Diersen also argues thoughtfully that the "Unternehmungsgeist" (23) of old Johann Buddenbrook "wird zu einer Art Familienmythos" (23). One might even say that the mythical vitality of old Johann Buddenbrook is symbolically captured in the aura of divine figures in the tapestries.

The intimation of a financial decline in the Buddenbrook company is temporarily sublimated by a focus on the vital life of Tony who enters Therese Weichbrodt's boarding school which includes the daughters of some other prominent families. The happy childhood and youth of Tony Buddenbrook is reinforced by the delineation at the end of Part Two of her spending most enjoyable times at home and visiting her grandparents just outside the town as well as travelling to the Mecklenburg estates of two of her friends. Such places are all sanctuaries of congenial vitality and dynamic repose for Tony—the buoyant happiness of this phase of her life contributes positively to the aura of success of the Buddenbrook family.

In the first several chapters of Part Three Tony's sense of serenity and sanctuary is upset by the marriage proposal of Herr Grünlich, which she rejects. In Chapter I of Part Three Tony senses the superficiality of Herr Grünlich as he encroaches ingratiatingly upon the Buddenbrooks family circle. Grünlich's comment about the sunshine playing in Tony Buddenbrooks's hair is reminiscent of the image in *Tristan* of the crown in Gabrielle's hair which Spinell notices or claims that he notices. For a respite from this personal crisis and to escape the attentions of Grünlich, Tony goes to Travemünde. The conversation between Tony and Thomas on the way to Travemünde is very revealing. Tony admits to her brother that she despises the society and the world of the Hagenströms and similar families which are motivated primarily by commercial aggressiveness and socioeconomic gain.

Tony feels a sense of liberation during her stay at Travemünde and is emotionally and spiritually renewed by the ambience of the sea and by Morten's presence. As Tony walks down to the beach with Morten Schwarzkopf she says that she desires to have a sense of peacefulness and quiet. Although Tony disagrees with Morten's criticism of the nobility and his intense political ideas, she feels revitalized by the ambience in Travemünde. In fact, although Tony has been to Travemünde often before, her relatively brief visit on this occasion is the most pleasant ever. One of the main reasons for this is the fact that she takes congenial walks with Morten. Walking along the beach with Morten and listening to the whispering waves, Tony cherishes the profound peacefulness of this environment. Perhaps Tony even feels that such pristine, Arcadian serenity is reminiscent of the ambience of her family's mansion in town.

On one stroll along the beach, Tony and Morten walk to a round pavilion, called the temple, which is a sheltered milieu. The quiet of the natural ambience is somewhat undermined by Morten's tirade against the nobility. And yet, such critical statements could also be viewed in a positive light as a moment of personal revelation of Morten's innermost thoughts and feelings which he feels comfortable mentioning to and sharing with Tony. In the last sentence of Chapter VIII Tony and Morten are quietly sitting together enjoying the enchantment of the sea. This moment is so poignant for Tony that she even feels a sense of communion with Morten in his yearning for a sense of freedom. Perhaps one reason why Tony feels a sense of harmony with Morten is because she also longs for a spirit of freedom from some of the pressures and responsibilities in her life. The vitality of this moment is comparable to the spiritual union which Spinell and Gabriele Klöterjahn experience in the musical episode of "Tristan."

Sadly, Tony is encouraged to disregard her feelings for Morten and to marry someone else. In Chapter XIII when Tony returns to Lübeck with her brother she appreciates the old and traditional gables and images which she has not seen during her summer vacation. Later in Chapter XIII as Tony glances at the book which chronicles the life and development of the Buddenbrook family her spirit is obsessed and swept away by a sense of tradition. Tony notices the meticulous representation of facts regarding individual family members and cannot resist an inner impulse to participate constructively as a link in the chain of her family's development. The sense of importance about being a part of this family motivates her to conclude by writing in the blank space next to her name that she is betrothed to Herr Grünlich of Hamburg. In her heart Tony feels more attached to Morten; but for the sake of the family she feels a compulsion to marry Grünlich.

Inge Diersen proclaims in *Thomas Mann: Episches Werk, Weltanschauung, Leben* that Consul Buddenbrook initiated Tony Buddenbrook's social decline by encouraging her to marry Grünlich: "Er zwingt Tony zur Ehe mit Herrn Grünlich, dem hoffnungsvoll aufstrebenden jungen Kaufmann, der sich binnen kurzem als Betrüger entpuppt" (25). Herbert Lehnert writes in *Thomas Mann: Fiktion, Mythos, Religion* of the self-sacrificial demeanor which Tony Buddenbrook shows, for "ihre Liebe zu Morten Schwarzkopf wird zum Opfer auf dem Altar des Familiengötzen" (66). Lehnert views Tony's self-sacrifice as a noteworthy feature and sign of the family's aura of decline: "die Buddenbrooks schließen die Liebe aus ihren Beziehungen aus, teils durch Konventionen veranlaßt, teils auch aus eigener innerer Notwendigkeit..."(66).

The issue of language and of linguistic correctness is important in a consideration of Tony's relationship with Grünlich, as it is also with regard to Tony's later relationship with Permaneder. Ernest M. Wolf argues effectively in "Scheidung und Mischung: Sprache und Gesellschaft in Thomas Manns *Buddenbrooks*" that the standard form of High German represents "das alltäglich-gewöhnliche Ausdrucks- und Verständigungsmittel der oberen Bürgerschicht Lübecks" (77). Wolf proceeds to say that "Die Hauptvertreter der Familie Buddenbrook sprechen und schreiben eine sehr gepflegte Form des Hochdeutschen, die grammatisch und lautlich korrekt ist" (77) and that such linguistic correctness und purity "kennzeichnen diese Sprecher in den Augen ihrer Umgebung unverkennbar als Mitglieder der gebildeten Elitegruppe" (77). Tony has a sensitive awareness of the standard form of "das Hochdeutsche" and is disturbed by Grünlich's artificiality and by his linguistic errors. Tony is also concerned about Permaneder's linguistic mistakes and idiosyncrasies such as his confusion of the dative and accusative pronouns. Although Tony does proceed with her consecutive marriages for the sake of the family, to fulfill her sense of commitment to the prestige and advancement of the family, she does not allow her appreciation of "das Hochdeutsche" to be diminished, for she can admit to her brother after the failure of her marriage to Permaneder that the society of which he is a part speaks a false and incorrect German.

In the opening chapters of Part Four we learn that Tony has given birth to a daughter, although she does not seem perfectly happy in her new life. Tony's letter at the beginning of Chapter I of Part Four provides details about her material existence but does not offer many positive revelations about her emotional state of mind.

Yet, that Grünlich does not seem to like to go into society with her and that she signs the letter as "your dutiful daughter" implies that Tony is not really happy in her married life. We also learn that Thomas is not as vibrantly healthy in his new position in Amsterdam as he seemed to be previously. The year is 1848 and there is a spirit of rebellion in the air. The spirit of rebellion interferes with the meeting of the assembly and undermines any potential for the experience of a refuge in these difficult times. The tension and emotional turmoil of this encroachment on the assembly even causes the death of Lebrecht Kröger, a relative of the Buddenbrooks.

In Chapter V of Part Four Herr and Frau Grünlich have a very tense conversation in which Tony says that Grünlich is trying to isolate her and also expresses her interest in having a governess for their daughter. He responds rather indifferently and harshly that they cannot afford a governess. The house of Herr and Frau Grünlich is not a sanctuary at all because of the emotional and intellectual tension which pervades the ambience. Even though her house does not have a sanctuary-like situation, Tony's presence bears with it an aura of sanctuary. Tony's self-awareness, for example, that any characteristic of hers was part of her family tradition, part of the Buddenbrook heritage, and consequently should be respected, is a sustaining feature of a sense of sanctuary and strength in her inner being.

In the second paragraph that the windowpanes are described as being opaque could be viewed as symbolic of the mist which screens the truth about Grünlich's financial affairs. In Chapter VI there is an indication that Grünlich is in a very precarious financial condition. In the seventh chapter of Part Four, Consul Johann Buddenbrook, Tony's father, comes for a visit. He appears rather pale and worn, in part a response to the recent news that Thomas had a hemorrhage and will have to take a rest cure and to the news that Herr Grünlich is bankrupt. In the conversation with her father Tony admits that she never loved Grünlich. Except for the presence of her child, Erica, Tony has had a very unpleasant marriage with Grünlich. Consul Buddenbrook might have considered trying to save Grünlich from complete bankruptcy if Tony had genuine feelings of love and respect for him. However, as Tony makes it clear that she has always found her husband repulsive, the Consul is not willing to further undermine his own company's financial stability by extending a loan to Grünlich. At the end of the ninth chapter of Part Four Grünlich shows his true colors and reveals himself as the conniving businessman which he had previously appeared to be by proclaiming to Tony in a very harsh statement that he only married her for her money.

Both Tony and Thomas Buddenbrook have now returned home to revitalize themselves and to develop a new life. Tony lives a quiet life in the Buddenbrook house on Meng Strasse—she and her daughter live in second storey rooms in this rambling house. Maintaining her sense of dignity and respectability, Tony also shows a capacity for adaptability. Tony develops a stronger affection for her father, the Consul, who has shown her considerable patience and consideration during her personal crisis.

Consul Johann Buddenbrook and his wife become increasingly more religious as they become older. In the late summer of 1855 on a sultry and stormy day Johann Buddenbrook dies. The description of various aspects of nature reinforces or perhaps even initiates the aura of death in the family. Moreover, the atmosphere of a sanctuary which had existed in certain rooms by virtue of the furniture and tapestries is tainted and undermined to some extent—the oppressive ambience and somber gray sky of this tempestuous day is even depicted as diminishing the colors of significant objects in the rooms. The torrential rain which follows the sultriness appears to provide potential relief from the oppressive atmosphere; yet, the sadness of the day cannot be overcome for Consul Buddenbrook dies in his bedroom.

At the beginning of Part Five Tony is informed that the property of her grandparents outside the Castle Gate, which had represented a place of sanctuary for her, has been sold and will be split up into two dog-kennels. Tony is especially disappointed because she had always admired the spaciousness of the estate which will now be thoroughly undermined. On this day when Consul Buddenbrook's will is read Tony tries to create an aura of sanctuary in the room by closing the curtains and lighting the candles in the gilded candelabrum.

Thomas Buddenbrook becomes the head of the family business. Although Thomas does not have the religious faith which his parents had, he does display the same kind of intense work-ethic which his father showed. While Thomas does elevate the stature of the family business through his devotion, at least temporarily, Christian is not interested in the commercial world and much prefers a life of pleasure and dissipation. Yet, as Todd Kontje and other critics have discussed, there are striking similarities between Thomas and Christian underlying the public and outer differences and tensions between them. Kontje mentions the incident of Thomas' angry response to Christian's insulting "the integrity of the business world" (27): "As gradually becomes clear, however, Thomas' fury derives in large part from the fact that Christian has succumbed to the forces that also gnaw at his own soul" (27).

The description of Thomas Buddenbrook and his hands in this chapter is noteworthy. Thomas is depicted as pale and his hands are described as extremely sensitive and white, often by their movements implying an acute sensitivity and considerable reserve. That such qualities are unusual in the Buddenbrook family presence reminds of the assertion in *Tristan* and in other Mann narratives that at the end of a family's decline there is an artistic flowering. The presence of these characteristics in Thomas could be viewed as one harbinger of this inevitable condition. Yet, Thomas is professionally a conscientious businessman who is committed to preserving the vitality of the family heritage. After the death of his uncle Gotthold, Thomas assumes the title of Consul, that is, the office and title of the Royal Consulate of the Netherlands.

In Chapter V of this part of the novel the increasing spiritual devotions of Thomas's mother creates an aura of sanctuary in the house in Meng Strasse. She aspires to pay homage to the spirit of the deceased family members in various ways, from biblical readings and prayers to the visits of pastors and ministers. Tony has developed a critical awareness about pastors and ministers over the years and no longer believes that they are all models of piety and sanctity. The attempt of a Pastor Trieschke from Berlin to make advances to Tony reinforces her belief in the hypocrisy of such individuals and compels him to be removed from the house. While Tony has a semblance of security and comfort in the house in Meng Strasse, her cynical assertion that she has lost all faith in men implies that the aura of sanctuary here has been severely compromised and undermined.

The letter which Thomas Buddenbrook writes in chapter seven to his mother from Amsterdam on July 30, 1856 seems to suggest that the family fortunes are in the ascendancy. For not only does he approve of Clara's engagement to Pastor Tiburtius, but he also announces his own engagement to Gerda Arnoldsen, Tony's former schoolmate. Gerda, like her father, is a talented musician. Tom appears to love Gerda, but is also pleased that her father is a millionaire and a wealthy merchant, for her dowry will enhance the financial condition of his family's business. The aura of sanctuary at the house in Meng Strasse is revitalized in Chapter VIII as the Arnoldsens and Pastor Tiburtius come for a long visit. The mother of Thomas Buddenbrook is very pleased with Gerda and her demeanor. The prestige of the Buddenbrook family is also considerably enhanced by this personal and professional connection.

In Chapter IX when Thomas returns with Gerda from their honeymoon journey to Italy, they find that their house in Broad Street has been meticulously and splendidly prepared by Tony with the assistance of the upholsterer. The ground floor contains such architectural spaces as the vestibule, a small room next to the vestibule containing oak furniture, another room next to the vestibule which is more spacious, the kitchen, and the larder. The next floor of this impressive house is characterized by such features as a dining-room with red damask wall-paper, a prominent round table, a considerable sideboard, and various carved wooden chairs, a sitting-room, a salon, an expansive hall, and the bedroom with its mahogany furniture. The house also contains the servants' lodgings. Tony is pleased to see Tom and Gerda after their honeymoon but admits to her brother that she needs a change of scenery. In expressing her discontent with her personal situation Tony also articulates criticisms, which she has made or implied before, about the church, questioning the motivation of the various ministers who come to the house on Meng Strasse and take advantage of the family's generosity and even implying that there is no official need for such people as there is or should be a direct connection between the individual and God. Tony no longer feels content in this town, in part because of her status as a divorced woman and in part because she wants to travel and see more of the world. Tony also admits to Tom that she wants to try to make a match which will be worthy of the family. As the final chapter of Part Five ends one observes Gerda Buddenbrook standing before

Thomas and Tony talking in the twilight, a figure of vitality but also of pallor, an individual whose inner tensions create a dynamic character.

In Chapter I of Part Six the depiction of the house on Meng Strasse implies that it no longer appears to possess the aura of a sanctuary which it once did so prominently and exquisitely in its more prosperous times. For while the ground floor still possesses and preserves the vitality of a business, the upper floors are empty and isolated. The third paragraph of this chapter even proclaims that the social life of this house had ended with the death of Consul Johann Buddenbrook. A house that does not have a social life or an active social life may certainly still have a sense of sanctuary. In fact, the sense of sanctuary in such a house may even be more important than if the house were a focus of social activity. The first three paragraphs of Part Six of the novel suggest that the house in Meng Strasse was now a quiet place, in some sense a peaceful sanctuary for the Frau Consul who still received members of the family on Thursday afternoons and because of her religious piety occasional ministers. The focus of social activity for the Buddenbrook family has shifted to the house of Thomas and Gerda Buddenbrook on Broad Street, exemplified in the first important dinner they give after their honeymoon to which are invited various members of significant families in the town. The lavishness of the affair and the generosity of the new couple helps to ensure the personal and socioeconomic success of the evening.

In Chapter II of Part Six Tony, Frau Grünlich, returns from her pleasant visit to Munich to brighten the ambience of the house. This chapter also mentions further tensions between Thomas and Christian and the concerns which Thomas has about the weaknesses of the family. In Chapter III, Thomas arrives at the family business office on Meng Strasse in a disturbed state of mind. Thomas makes it clear to Christian that he is very upset with him for his remark made the previous evening that every businessman is a swindler, especially because he strives so hard to maintain the integrity of the family firm. The severe criticism which Thomas directs towards Christian shows that there can never be any genuine harmony between these two brothers. Thomas even concludes his argument by calling Christian a disgrace and suggesting that he should find another position. Soon thereafter, in June, 1857, Christian leaves to take a position at a company in Hamburg. Another point of interest which emerges from the conversation between the two brothers is the notion, espoused by Christian, that Thomas, unlike himself, has always been able to maintain a balance between his professional life and his private life, between his business interests and his artistic and emotional sensibilities. As long as Thomas is able to maintain such a balance, the stability of the family business is relatively secure.

In *Thomas Mann's World*, Joseph Brennan describes Thomas Buddenbrook as a quintessential bourgeois exemplifying the qualities which "are characteristic of the class—personal fastidiousness, love of good living, passionate devotion to respectable work, morbid dread of the irregular" (10–11). Brennan proceeds to say of Thomas Buddenbrook that "even his tendency to melancholy and pessimism follows the nine-

teenth century bourgeois pattern" (11). On one occasion Gerda reinforces this awareness of the bourgeois nature of Thomas when she proclaims, though perhaps too
critically, that he will never truly appreciate the artistic nature of musical expression
and will consider it only as an after dinner entertainment. In *Thomas Mann: Episches
Werk, Weltanschauung, Leben* Inge Diersen portrays Thomas Buddenbrook effectively in his position of social prominence: "An gesellschaftlichem Ansehen und
öffentlicher Position ist Thomas Buddenbrook allen ihm vorangegangenen
Buddenbrooks überlegen" (24). Even though Thomas Buddenbrook attains the position of Senator, the highest administrative accolade possible for him, this does not
lead to a secure socioeconomic situation for the family because of the various social,
economic, and personal problems which the Buddenbrooks must confront.

In Chapter IV Herr Permaneder arrives for a surprise visit to Tony Buddenbrook,
whose company he had enjoyed in Munich on several occasions. Although Tony and
Herr Permaneder appear to enjoy each other's company and seem to speak rather
freely to one another, Tony is evidently superior to her companion in background,
intellect, and spirit. The language which Herr Permaneder uses, his dialect notwith-
standing, is not on the same intellectual level as that of Tony. In the course of this
conversation, during which Herr Permaneder is also introduced to Thomas
Buddenbrook, Tony makes the poignant observation that everything good and beautiful in the world is fleeting. Such a statement applies not only to her own romantic
connections and to the sense of sanctuary which she has experienced in several phases
of her life but also to the solidity of the family's business establishment.

In defending Herr Permaneder's use of language, perhaps even more vitally than
she consciously wishes to do, Tony stresses the importance of the heart and soul of
the speaker. As a generous romantic Tony is willing to give Herr Permaneder the
benefit of the doubt in situations where his use of language is clearly incorrect and
where his linguistic idiosyncrasies are not understood and is eager to attribute to him
a kindness and a sensitivity which he, as one will later see, does not actually possess.
As in her previous connection to Herr Grünlich, Tony seems motivated here by a
strong desire to please the family and her brother Thomas in making a marital match.
At the end of Chapter V Tony speaks of the duty which she owes her family's name
and of her desire to compensate for the marital mistake which she made the first time.

In Chapter VI, as various Buddenbrook family members take an excursion, in
which they are joined by Herr Permaneder, Tony is delineated as having achieved a
spirit of revitalization, as having reenergized her sense of the importance of her existence in the world of her hometown and in the context of her family. This strong
sense of self culminates in Tony's marriage, despite certain valid concerns which are
not really developed, to Herr Permaneder at the end of the chapter.

Chapter VI is also significant because it offers a further insight into Gerda
Buddenbrook. It is evident that Gerda dislikes the kind of expeditions which the
family takes in this chapter. She is described as preferring the dusk ambience of her

curtained living-rooms and of disliking the dust, the crowds of people they would meet, and the heat. Such a statement could imply that Gerda, who, like her father, is a talented musician, has an instinctive desire for a sense of sanctuary. However, that Gerda is depicted as having a "morbid beauty" (282) might also suggest something more sinister, namely, that she, like Hedda Gabler in Henrik Ibsen's *Hedda Gabler*, is more intimately connected to the darkness than she might initially seem to be.

Chapter VII emphasizes the productive years of the Buddenbrook family business and the potential problems, financial and social, which could undermine their sense of solidity. The description of Thomas Buddenbrook in this chapter is very important because it emphasizes not only his exemplary work-ethic but also his sense of devotion to his firm and to the community. Thomas is also depicted as having one of the most cosmopolitan minds of his city and of his commercial community because of his intellectual curiosity, his interests, and his travels. It is also noteworthy that Thomas shows an interest in aspects of the business world which would not necessarily be of immediate concern to his colleagues who are focused primarily or exclusively on their particular work. Moreover, Thomas realized the importance of maintaining an active social existence and of entertaining various members of the socioeconomic elite of the city. Because of the dedication of Thomas to his work and to his socioeconomic presence in the community, his company appears to thrive. Yet, there is also the sense that problems such as Christian's activities, the poor health and suffering of Clara, the concern about having an heir, and the underlying worries about the life of Tony will have an impact on the halo of success which seems to encompass the Buddenbrook firm.

The next chapter describes the very sad misadventures of Tony in her second marriage. Tony soon becomes very unhappy with Herr Permaneder's boorishness, complacency, lack of ambition, and complete indifference to her family heritage. When Herr Permaneder receives Tony's dowry, he invests the money and retires from business to enjoy a comfortable life. Tony is appalled by this because she had hoped that her new husband would be commercially ambitious and would introduce her into the heights of Munich society. Moreover, she feels like a stranger emotionally, culturally, and linguistically in her new "home." Tony suffers quietly through this until she finds Herr Permaneder making sexual advances to their cook. Then Tony takes Erica, her daughter from her first marriage, and leaves Permaneder's house, with no intention of returning.

The issue of the complexity of Tony's character is effectively addressed by Judith Ryan in "*Buddenbrooks*: between realism and aestheticism," in which she writes that the "various aspects of Tony's personality find reflections in other figures in the novel" (123): "With Thomas and her father, Tony shares pride in family tradition; with Christian, high-spirited mockery; with old Johann Buddenbrook, distrust of conventional religion; with her mother, a concern for outward self-presentation" (123). Ryan also notes the interesting similarities between Tony Buddenbrook and the Goncourts' Renée Mauperin (122–23).

In Chapter X Tony and Thomas have a very significant and revealing private discussion about her situation. Tony makes it clear that she feels terribly insulted and demeaned by Permaneder and will never return to him. She says that as long as she has any self-respect, she can never even think of going back to such a household. Thomas's response is surprising in its lack of genuine concern for the emotional well-being of his sister. His argument is that since the insult to Tony is only known to herself, Permaneder, and the cook, her dignity and the dignity of the family would not suffer at all if she would return to her husband. It is interesting that the concern of Thomas is less for Tony than for the dignity and reputation of the family. Tony's strength of character shows dramatically in her response—for she asserts that what is really scandalous is allowing herself to stay in such a demeaning situation where she has to sublimate or forget her origins and family heritage and to pretend as if she were happy. In her conclusion Tony declares to Thomas that it is now his singular task to uphold the dignity of the family for she and Christian have failed in their attempts to do so. The sadness caused by Tony's manifold disappointments is reinforced by the fact of her relative isolation. Tony, who used to enjoy company, tries to be above the haughtiness and cold indifference of the daughters of the other prominent commercial families who used to be her friends. It is difficult to find a vital aura of sanctuary in such a town which used to value her presence and her congeniality.

Part Seven of *Buddenbrooks* begins with a christening at the Buddenbrook home in Broad Street. The birth of an heir, of the child of Thomas and Gerda Buddenbrook, is an apparent sign of rebirth in the family. Such is also Tony Buddenbrook's, Frau Permaneder's, suggestion at the end of Chapter I of Part Seven, for she believes that a new day is dawning for the family. And yet, even at this moment of celebration there are signs of potential decay and decline. For example, the physical description of little Johann notices shadows in the corners on the sides of the nose, making his face seem older than his four weeks. And, at the end of the ceremony, Grobleben says that everyone must return to mother earth at last. Such a sentiment is perhaps a foreshadowing of the inevitable decline of the family.

In Chapter IV of Part Seven Thomas Buddenbrook receives the distinctive honor of being elected a Senator. Yet, even at this moment of seemingly exuberant personal and public success, there is an indication of a problematic undercurrent in his life. For at the very beginning of the next chapter it is suggested that Thomas Buddenbrook, at age thirty-seven, is wearing himself out physically. He assumes too many private and public responsibilities and feels overwhelmed, although he does not openly admit this. To compensate for the stress and strain of his existence Thomas pays special attention to his physical appearance so that he always presents himself properly to the public. Walter E. Berendsohn describes this consistent focus on appearance effectively as follows: "His public appearance is a kind of theatrical performance for which he prepares himself daily by a tedious, careful toilet, and he has to strengthen himself with a selected wardrobe and frequent changes of linen" (25). The author himself defends the newly elected senator by proclaiming that what might appear to some people to be vanity, is essentially a strong desire to preserve a public persona of exemplary correctness. When the family doctor encourages Thomas to relax, his response is that he is not yet ready to allow himself such a luxury. However, that his mind is dynamically active, contemplating many ideas and situations, even at rest, implies that he is perhaps placing an excessive physical strain on his body. This is the early 1860s and the public reputation of Thomas Buddenbrook is at a high-point. He and his firm are considerably admired throughout the business community and the society of the city as well. Thomas, Senator Buddenbrook, feels so energized in the summer of 1863 that he even decides to build a new and grander house. While some people might have attributed this plan to the vanity of the senator, one might also say that he was motivated in this endeavor by a feeling of needing to rejuvenate and revitalize himself—the notion of creating a new architectural space invigorated him. Thomas Buddenbrook even selects the location of his new house, deciding on a property on Fishers' Lane in the ambience of good burgher-houses. Nevertheless, it is noteworthy that although Thomas seems determined to build a new and grander home, even he has concerns about this enterprise, admitting to himself that his present house in Broad Street has plenty of space for his family and the servants. Thomas finds reaffirmation of his plans to construct a larger house in his discussions with Tony, Gerda, and his mother, all of whom support the idea as a logical consequence of his socioeconomic success.

Of this decision on the part of Thomas Buddenbrook to build a new house Jochen Vogt writes that his plan is too grandiose, for the new residence is too big and "füllt sich nicht mit Leben" (33). Vogt distinguishes between the more communal and open atmosphere of the house in the Meng Strasse and the more secluded atmosphere of the individual rooms in the house of Thomas and Gerda in the Fischergrube (33). There is an abundance of architectural and architecturally interesting spaces in this mansion where the individual can isolate himself or herself or feel secluded.

The sense of transience is affirmed by the fact that the house in Broad Street, seemingly a solid feature of the Buddenbrook family existence, is relatively quickly sold to Stephan Kistenmaker, a prosperous wine merchant, removing the imprint of the Buddenbrooks forever. The transformation of the house in Meng Strasse is also evident in the fact that Thomas Buddenbrook planned to transfer the business offices of his firm from this older family house to his new house in Fischers' Lane. So the ground floor rooms of the house in Meng Strasse become empty and are soon rented by the City Fire Insurance Company. The public view of the construction of the new Buddenbrook dwelling on Fischers' Lane is interesting for it reveals that while the building appears to signify the finest house in the immediate community, some people admit privately that the old Consul Buddenbrook would never have spent money so exuberantly.

One evening after the new house with "its imposing brick façade with sandstone caryatides supporting the bow-window" (347) is finished and after the celebration has taken place Tony, Frau Permaneder, comes over to speak with Tom. Before Tony enters the office of Thomas she admires the lovely staircase of the new house "which as far as the first storey had a cast-iron balustrade, but at the distance of the second storey became a wide pillared balcony in white and gold, with a great gilt chandelier hanging down from the skylight's dizzy height" (349). She views this image of architectural elegance as a symbol of the power and of the success of the Buddenbrook family. The ensuing interesting conversation occurs, interestingly enough, outside for Thomas says to Tony that it is more pleasant in the garden, as if the pressing concerns relating to the business are too much for a discussion in an interior setting. The news which Tony brings to her brother is not pleasant, for Clara is very ill, presumably with tuberculosis of the brain, and seems to long for heaven instead of enduring more suffering on this earth. Tony, after also commenting that Christian is at the moment ill in Hamburg, encourages Thomas to be strong and to persevere despite these troubling events. As the conversation progresses Thomas admits that the new house sometimes seems to him to be "almost too beautiful" (351); he even admits that the anticipation of having the new house built was the best part of the experience. The pleasure of having this grand construction completed for himself and his family seems to have been diminished. After confessing that he feels older than he really is, Thomas offers some important insights about the human condition and about his own existence. For example, Thomas says that success is an inner force, "resourcefulness, power of vision" (352) and a belief that one's life influences the surrounding lives. Moreover, Thomas proclaims that fortune and success exist within himself. He believes that he must hold on to these tenaciously or he feels that the entire fabric and façade of his life and commercial enterprise will begin to slip away.

Thomas proceeds to reflect upon the recent apparent success of the family from the birth of his son to his election as senator and the increasing reputation of his business. Surprisingly, he concludes by saying that accomplishments such as the position of "senator" and the new house are superficial for "often, the outward and visible material signs and symbols of happiness and success only show themselves when the process of decline has already set in" (352). Such a statement implies that the new house, for all of its splendor, is not innately a sanctuary for him. Although Gerda does enjoy the music room, for Thomas the house becomes more of a financial burden. The burden is not only financial but also emotional, for despite the potent public persona which Thomas displays, the insightful awareness he shows of the nuances of the process of decline suggests that he might sense that such a decline is already beginning to effect his own family and firm.

Chapter VII of this part of the novel provides another example of the tension and underlying anxiety within the family. Thomas, Senator Buddenbrook, has a severe disagreement with his mother about the fact that she promised to Pastor Tiburtius, the apparently very self-serving spouse of the recently deceased Clara, her entire inheritance of more than one hundred and twenty-seven thousand marks. Thomas is angry with his mother for yielding to the request of the Pastor Tiburtius for this considerable amount of money. What makes Thomas especially upset is not only the fact that various family members do not show him the respect which he believes he, as the head of the household, deserves but also because he is aware that the firm has lost a lot of money recently. It is noteworthy that he proclaims that his business has declined since he built the new and extravagant house. It is as if this were an admonition to him that he should have been content with his previous existential condition instead of aspiring to possess such a lavish home.

Chapter I of Part Eight appears to offer a prospect of new beginnings and an opportunity for revitalization in the Buddenbrook family. As the birth and christening of Hanno Buddenbrook in the first chapter of Part Seven of the novel infused the family with a sense of energy and hope, so the marriage of Erica Grünlich, Tony's daughter, at the beginning of Part Eight, inspires a feeling of renewal. Tony feels especially revived by this event for she had been worried for years about the future of her daughter. As Tony shunned the society of the town because it treated her disrespectfully on account of her two divorces, her daughter did not have the usual opportunities for social exchange.

Tony, Frau Permaneder, feels especially revitalized by her daughter's engagement and marriage. In fact, it is even said that Tony feels very buoyant and hopeful, showing once again the ebullient spirits of her girlhood. Initially, Tony lives with Erica and her husband, Herr Weinschenk, to help with the housekeeping and ensure that everything runs smoothly. Even though Tony is very happy that her daughter is married and now has a little daughter, there are indications that this marital situation is less than perfect, for the husband is a rather boorish and coarse individual.

In Chapters II and III of Part Eight there are further indications of the emotional sensitivity and goodness of Tony, Frau Permaneder. In chapter two Tony tries to persuade Thomas to offer financial assistance to the husband of a friend of hers who is in serious financial difficulty. In chapter three Tony expresses her concern that Hanno is overly sensitive and that he feels everything too personally. He is particularly entranced by the stories and legends in *Des Knaben Wunderhorn*, the wonderful collection of folk songs by Brentano and Arnim. For Hanno represents a culmination and intensification of the sensitivity of his parents, Thomas and Gerda Buddenbrook.

The malaise and weariness of Senator Thomas Buddenbrook, which had been mentioned in previous sections of the novel, is discussed in more intensive detail in Chapter IV of Part Eight. Thomas is self-aware and realizes that he feels very tired and old. Of the decline of Thomas Buddenbrook Hugh Ridley writes: "The confident and elegant expression which Thomas puts on when dealing with the world... is shown to be a mask, and it slips off as his one recurring thought returns to haunt him: that at forty-two he is a broken and exhausted man" (42). Thomas acknowledges to himself that he is still rich and that he is valued by the mayor and various other civic leaders, although there are some people who believe that the firm of Buddenbrook is not as glorious as it once was. Yet, Thomas, as Gustav von Aschenbach in *Der Tod in Venedig,* has lost his inner vitality of spirit. And he has become more particular about expenditures, giving up the summer holidays and proceeding with other cost-cutting measures relating to meals and everyday life in the new and grand house.

This weariness is intimately connected to the notion of insight and knowledge about the world. In *The Ironic German,* Erich Heller describes knowledge "as the enemy of life, as the tempter to death, as the ally of disease" (13). Heller states insightfully that in *Buddenbrooks,* which "is the story of the fall of a family" (13) and Mann's "first allegory of the Fall of Man" (13), the "Buddenbrooks are doomed because they have come to know" (13). Heller describes Thomas Buddenbrook's inner conflict as leading to "a host of questions and doubts, paralysing his will, turning his actions awry, and making him into an actor who performs his burgher life as a kind of moral pretence—as though the real thing were something else, a thought, a play, an uncertain intimation of the spirit" (14).

The fourth chapter reveals various critical concerns which Thomas expresses about the commercial life, about the world of business. He reflects upon its ruthlessness, its brutality, its merciless sense of self-preservation and upon its lack of gentleness and compassion when someone is suffering and struggling financially. Unlike his father and grandfather who were more naturally businessmen, Thomas feels a conflict within himself, an instinctive conflict between the bourgeois and the artist, between the practical and the imaginative. Ignace Feuerlicht argues in *Thomas Mann* that Thomas Buddenbrook is elevated "above the crowd of lonely, frustrated, and aging business leaders" (18) by, "among other things, his cultural interests and, above all, his inner conflict" (18).To assuage his anxiety Thomas lights several burners of a chandelier and walks through various rooms of the house. As he gazes out into the moonlit garden, one is reminded of a similar constellation of images in *Tonio Kröger.* The patrician house of Tonio also has a garden with a fountain and a walnut tree. Whereas Tonio is usually revitalized by such a scene, Thomas, perhaps because of his inner emotional turmoil, is not comforted at all by this scenario. Thomas is troubled by the fact that he does not possess the absolute conviction in his profession which his competitors seem to have. Perhaps to compensate for and overcome such a feeling Thomas decides, after envisioning the harvests of Pöppenrade rustling vitally in the wind, to take a risk and offer financial assistance to the Herr von Maiboom, the husband of Tony's friend.

In Chapter V of this part of the novel there is further evidence of the weariness which Thomas, Senator Buddenbrook, feels regarding his professional life. Thomas seems to wish to pass over the imminent one hundredth anniversary of the founding of the Buddenbrook firm without any public announcement of the fact. It is Tony, Frau Permaneder, who encourages Thomas to celebrate the importance of this day, on the 7th of July, 1868. Yet, even during the family celebration Thomas cannot help feeling strongly that he wants to liberate himself from the routine and from the obligations of the everyday commercial world. As the celebration continues with the arrival of various visitors and telegrams to wish him and the family well, Thomas becomes increasingly depressed and dissatisfied. The business-related telegram which Thomas receives at the end of this chapter intensifies his inner despair, for it suggests that a commercial speculation which he had recently made has not been successful.

The inner conflict in Thomas Buddenbrook, the tension between the bourgeois and the artist, between the practical, realistic businessman and the romantic, the idealist, the dreamer, does not motivate a sense of productivity, as it does with some individuals such as Tonio Kröger. Instead, such a conflict has a deleterious effect on Thomas Buddenbrook, diminishing his capacities and producing a feeling of decreased self-worth. Ignace Feuerlicht asserts in *Thomas Mann* that Thomas Buddenbrook is not genuinely or instinctively at home in the world of everyday reality and practical affairs, "ages prematurely, does not see any purpose or real success in his life, 'hates life,' and dies at forty-nine" (17). Despite the talent for business endeavors and commercial activities which Thomas seemed to possess in his youth, as he gets older he feels increasingly estranged from an outlook on life which does not look beyond and is intellectually mired in the concern for economic profit and loss.

The inner emotional and spiritual despair and weariness which Thomas Buddenbrook feels reflects the philosophical outlook and inclinations of Arthur Schopenhauer. Erich Heller argues insightfully in *The Ironic German* that *Buddenbrooks*, "a work entirely in the manner of literary realism, is at the same time a philosophical novel in the sense that the imagination which has conceived it bears the imprint of Schopenhauer's thought" (27). Schopenhauer sees an inevitable and consistent conflict between the world, characterized by and permeated by the will, and the imagination or mind of the individual which can react against the will. In his essay "The Devil Secularized: Thomas Mann's *Faust*" Erich Kahler argues that "there is an exact correspondence between the consul Thomas Buddenbrook, who finds solace in Schopenhauer, and Tonio Kröger, with his nostalgia for the normal, blond, and respectable" (113).

In Chapters VI and VII of Part Eight Hanno's appreciation for and understanding of music are depicted in considerable detail. When playing the piano Hanno, like Gabriele Klöterjahn in Mann's *Tristan*, feels the music intensely and physically. As Gabriele, Hanno achieves an emotional union with the music and its vitality. As Thomas does not have the same appreciation for music which Gerda and Hanno have, the presence of music in the home widens the gap and increases the tension between Thomas on the one hand and Gerda and Hanno on the other. Moreover, Hanno is not interested in and rather indifferent to the everyday facts of the business world, for his soul is inspired and captivated by music. The tension between Thomas and his son is heightened at the end of chapter seven, for Hanno, in looking at the book which represents the Buddenbrook family tree, draws a double line under his name implying a sense of finality and foreshadowing the end of the Buddenbrook family.

In "The World Without Transcendence" Hans Egon Holthusen stresses the importance of music in *Buddenbrooks* and in other works by Mann, declaring that from "the beginning the theme of music occurs in Thomas Mann's work like a leitmotif" (124). Holthusen proceeds to say that music "is inherent in the 'Schopenhauerian' triad—'music, pessimism, humor'—that young Thomas Mann likes to strike in defining the mood of his own life" (124–25). With respect to *Buddenbrooks*, Holthusen says that in this novel "little Hanno's musicality moves into a sphere of decadence, alienation from the burgher's world, illness, dissolution, and death" (125). Hans Egon Holthusen's claim of Hanno's association with decadence is similar in spirit to Christoph Geiser's statements in *Naturalismus und Symbolismus im Frühwerk Thomas Manns* that the "Flucht in die Musikalität verhindert eine geistige Gestaltwerdung Hannos" (37) and that Hanno, despite his youth, is "kein Kind, keine kindliche Persönlichkeit" (37). Geiser proceeds to say of Hanno that his "Altklugheit bedeutet vollkommenes Desinteressement am eigentlichen Leben" (37). Hanno, by virtue of his extreme sensitivity, feels considerably separated and estranged from the mores of the world of everyday reality. Like his mother, Gerda, Hanno finds the greatest enjoyment in music, in a world of beautiful aesthetic expression which exists at a distance from the inclinations and motivations of the commercial realm.

In Chapter VIII of Part Eight the holiday celebrations seem to instill a sense of revitalization in the Buddenbrooks, despite the fact that criminal charges have been leveled at Director Weinschenk, Erica's husband. Thomas's response that what Weinschenk has done is no different from what many of his business colleagues have done except for the fact that they were not caught implies again a criticism of the world which Senator Buddenbrook has long inhabited professionally and the weaknesses of which he has gradually become more acutely aware of. The Christmas Eve party given by the Frau Consul at the old house on Meng Strasse is not only an exceptional present celebration—it is also in some sense a return to the glory of the past. For the novel begins with a house-warming to celebrate the house on Meng Strasse. The presence of so many of the family members at the Frau Consul's Christmas Eve party reinforces the atmosphere of family unity which the holiday festivity the previous day at the Senator's had initiated.

As Part Seven of the novel had concluded with Senator Buddenbrook's revelation of his weariness and malaise and with the images of war, so Part Eight of the novel ends on a negative note also. In Chapter IX the trial of Erica's husband, Director

Weinschenk, has upset Tony so considerably that her physical well-being has been affected. Moreover, Tony, once the romantic idealist, now appears to have shifted to a life-philosophy of melancholy realism. Tony says to Thomas that she has seen so much evil in the world and that she finds it difficult to believe in the innocence of people. Tony asserts that she has tried on various occasions to elevate the reputation of the family, but that she has sadly not been successful. The imprisonment of Director Weinschenk at the end of the chapter contributes further to the aura of decline in the Buddenbrook family. Tony's sense of sanctuary has been thoroughly undermined by events of the past couple of decades. At this point she feels particularly distressed for she and her daughter have now no home—she hopes to return to the house of her mother. The despair which Tony feels is epitomized by her concern about what will happen then. When the house of her mother will no longer be available to her, then she will feel completely abandoned and isolated. Ignace Feuerlicht stresses the child-like nature of Tony Buddenbrook, Frau Permaneder, throughout the novel while also suggesting that she is "deeply moved by her own and her family's failures" (19) and that she is always "concerned with the 'dignity' of her family" (19). Despite her apparent innocence and naivete or perhaps even because of it Tony Buddenbrook is the only individual who appears at the beginning and at the end of the novel. In the spirit of, and with the vitality of, a leitmotif, Tony maintains a consistent presence in the narrative, the history of her family, to which she has been so devoted and which she has enriched so immeasurably. One of the ways in which Mann uses the leitmotif, the repetition of certain words, phrases, clauses, or images, in *Buddenbrooks* is to provide a sense of coherence and continuity. The presence of Tony at the beginning and at the end of the novel reaffirms the aura of coherence and continuity in this narrative world.

The opening chapter of Part Nine is one of great sadness for Frau Consul Buddenbrook, the mother of Thomas and Tony, dies after suffering from pneumonia. At the end of her physical struggle with the painful disease the Frau Consul appears to be answering a summons from the world of the dead, from her dead husband and daughter, from her parents and other individuals who are calling her to join them.

At the end of Chapter II of Part Nine, after the angry and intense exchange between Thomas and Christian which reinforces their considerable dislike of one another, Thomas and Tony discuss the issue of selling the house on Meng Strasse. Thomas wants to sell the old family home while Tony is hesitant because of the many memories associated with it. After reflecting on the important occasion of the house-warming so many years ago, Tony starts to sob because she is so saddened at the idea of having to sell the home which has been for so long a sanctuary for her against the trials and tribulations of everyday mortality which she has been compelled to confront. Tony proclaims that this house has always been a "safe haven" (472) and a "refuge" (472) for her. While Tony seems ultimately to be persuaded by Thomas to realize the necessity of selling the house and of finding a smaller place, perhaps outside the Castle Gate, for her and her family to live, she is deeply saddened. For the house on Meng Strasse has been a very important place for her as for other family members. The strong emotional attachment to the house which Tony reveals here reminds us of the description of the house at the end of Part One. In the last several paragraphs of Part One, Johann Buddenbrook and his son, Consul Johann Buddenbrook, have just finished a conversation and proceed to their rooms. The last two sentences of the final paragraph depict the secure and stately atmosphere of the old house. As the house is dark and silent, so "hopes, fears, and ambitions all slumbered, while the rain fell and the autumn wind whistled around gables and street corners" (38). Not only was this house a sanctuary against stormy and tempestuous weather from the natural world; it was also a special place of serenity which had the capacity to diminish and sublimate fears and concerns and to generate hope and a spirit of optimism. These are the positive qualities which Tony remembers and cherishes about the old house and which make it so difficult to separate herself from it.

The moving funeral of Frau Elisabeth Buddenbrook in Chapter III of Part Nine is followed in chapter four by the problematic sale of the old family house on Meng Strasse to Consul Hermann Hagenström, one of the competitors of the Buddenbrook family. Both Thomas and Tony are displeased with the less than advantageous price which is decided upon for the sale of the house. The sale of this family house affects Tony Buddenbrook, Frau Permaneder, the most intensely for she does not believe that such deceitful competitors as the Hagenströms should be permitted to purchase such a lovely house and transform it with their coarse sense of taste. Thomas responds to Tony's concerns by saying that he envisions that the Hagenströms will attempt to preserve various aspects of the house, including the motto over the door, because they will view the purchase of such a house which belonged to another prominent family as a legitimization of their own effort to achieve socioeconomic ascendancy. Nevertheless, when Tony in the future passes the old house which has now been taken over and modified by the Hagenströms, she often cries, even in public. For Tony loved the old house dearly, a delightful abode which was always so meaningful for her— and it was difficult for her to have lost such a place of sanctuary. At the beginning of 1872 the Meng Strasse household is dispersed as family members assume possession of heirlooms and various important objects. The servants leave and the furniture wagons appear at the door to remove family possessions. The Senator takes the great carved chest, the gilt candelabra, among other things, to his house in Fischers' Lane. Tony takes various objects to her pretty apartment in Linden Place.

Helmut Koopmann argues effectively in *"Buddenbrooks:* Die Ambivalenz im Problem des Verfalls" that the biological decline of the Buddenbrook family is accompanied by the family's economic decline (48). Koopmann also says appropriately that the problematic letter from Gotthold which appears at the time of the housewarming party at the beginning of the novel represents an initial indication that the economic devaluation or demise of the family will develop from an outside source, and especially from "entfernter stehenden Familienmitgliedern" (48).

Chapter I of Part Ten paints a more detailed and vivid picture of the sense of malaise and weariness which Thomas Buddenbrook feels as his business appears to decline. Thomas has lost his energy and vitality—yet he still devotes a considerable time to his outward appearance. The vanity which others have noticed and of which he is himself aware has even increased recently. He spends hours in preparation for each public appearance, carefully selecting the appropriate clothes for each occasion. Christoph Geiser describes insightfully in *Naturalismus und Symbolismus im Frühwerk Thomas Manns* the apparent vanity and devoted attentiveness which Thomas Buddenbrook shows towards his physical appearance: "Die Eitelkeit Thomas Buddenbrooks gehört bereits nicht mehr zur Pflege des alten Namens, des Firmenschildes. Vielmehr gehört sie in dieser sublimen und aristokratischen Form eben auch schon zum neuen, ästhetischen Menschentyp" (35). Thomas does this out of a sense of personal inclination for aesthetic subtlety and elegance. What Geiser says about the awareness of a new, aesthetic type of individual is somewhat reminiscent of the emphasis on physical beauty in Oscar Wilde's *The Picture of Dorian Gray*. Although Thomas Buddenbrook does not share the hedonistic life-philosophy of Lord Henry, he does in some sense savor the devotion to beauty and to the attractiveness of a physical presence which Basil and Dorian believe in and cherish.

The description of the wardrobe of Thomas Buddenbrook could be described as that of an actor who must be prepared for different public roles. In this section Thomas Mann even depicts Thomas Buddenbrook as "an actor whose life has become one long production" (496). At this point in his life Thomas Buddenbrook is further delineated as someone who cherishes the public limelight and who lives for the moments when he can make a public statement which receives some praise. For Thomas Buddenbrook is very unhappy in his private life not only with himself but also in his relation to Gerda, his wife. There seems to be an underlying tension between Thomas and Gerda which has existed for a while. Moreover, Thomas finds it difficult to be alone for his inner emotional and spiritual malaise oppresses him. Even Hanno notices this. For example, in the next chapter when Thomas takes Hanno on social visits to various houses (as Gerda does not like to participate in these) Hanno sees how after each visit his father seems more pale and exhausted. Hanno observes not only the mask-like countenance of his father which would prevail before each visit and the artificial energy during the visit but also the mental and physical exhaustion after the visit when the public role has been completed.

A sense of sanctuary is delineated in chapter three of this part for Travemünde along the seashore is a beautiful place. Just as Tony appreciated the loveliness of this place in her youth, so Hanno appreciates it now. Hanno shows a profound admiration for the sea and for the subtleties of the ambience of the sea. He cherishes this environment and its natural beauty and tries to convince himself that the vacation there will last longer than it actually will. However, the flux of time and mortality is uncontrollable and inevitably brings the vacation to an end, compelling Hanno to return to the world of everyday mortality in which he does not feel truly at home.

The last paragraph of Chapter III is especially significant because it contains Tony Buddenbrook's reminiscences about her past pleasant times in Travemünde. Tony says that she will always remember the very congenial holidays which she spent in Travemünde and especially that she felt cared for by Morten Schwarzkopf and his family. In this passage Tony also expresses her realization that she would have been quite happy with and inspired by Morten. Even though Tony in her youth did not agree with Morten's critical statements about the nobility, when one considers the fact that Tony was for so long ostracized by such a socioeconomic class in her hometown, it is certainly possible that she would have been happier in her life if she had developed a longterm relationship with him. Tony's last two statements in this paragraph, which conclude the chapter, could be interpreted as metaphorical comments on her past marriages. Tony implies that she tried to transform essentially bad characters into good, but failed because such individuals (as her two ex-husbands) were not innately good and decent individuals. Despite the negative tone of the end of this paragraph Tony's very positive reflection on the beauty of Travemünde which she experienced in her youth is very important for it takes her and us back to Chapters VIII and IX of Part Three, if only momentarily. Tony's recollection of this delightful moment of her past is a personal sanctuary of emotional vitality which she carries in her heart and soul and which can revitalize her at difficult moments.

In Chapter IV of Part Ten, Tony acknowledges to herself that the only place in the world where she wants to live is her native city, although it is not nearly as pleasant and hospitable to her now as it was in her childhood. Tony also realizes how important it is for her to have a sense of repose and tranquility. The release of Weinschenk from prison does not dramatically alter the lifestyle of Tony and her daughter, Erica, for he leaves soon for a trip to London and never returns, after sending only one further note. Thus, Tony continues to live in relative contentment in Linden Place with her daughter and granddaughter.

Chapter V of this part of the novel begins with a discussion of the interest which the public still feels in the marriage of Thomas and Gerda and in their emotional lives. It is noticed that Gerda does not appear to show much emotional interest or warmth for anything except for music; moreover, her consistent contact with Herr Lieutenant von Throta is also observed with some curiosity and suspicion. Thomas becomes gradually tormented by the close contact between Gerda and the lieutenant and by their frequent musical interludes. On one occasion Thomas even shares his feeling of considerable concern and worry with Hanno—several days afterward Thomas feels a sense of decline. At age forty-eight, Thomas feels that he is approaching his own death in the near future. There are even moments when Thomas has the sensation that he is not sitting at the table with his family but actually "hovering above them somewhere and looking down upon them from a great distance" (522). Thomas Buddenbrook is very worried not only about the future of his firm, about his son's future, and about his wife's emotional situation and apparent interest in the company of the lieutenant—he is also oppressed by the thought that, as he faces his mortality, he is not prepared for death.

Thomas becomes more meditative and reflective—one day he even spends hours in the pavilion profoundly absorbed in a work by Schopenhauer, *Die Welt als Wille und Vorstellung*. Thomas is especially influenced by Schopenhauer's pessimistic life-philosophy and finds in this work a justification for his suffering. It is important that, as Hugh Ridley states in *Thomas Mann: Buddenbrooks*, "Schopenhauer gives a theoretical foundation" (63) to the suffering of Thomas, for in "Schopenhauer's system, to live in the world as will means to suffer" (63). Thomas finds this work comforting because it does represent an affirmation of what he has experienced in everyday life and what he has sensed about the emotional and spiritual essence of mortal existence.

For the rest of the day after reading in this work by Schopenhauer, Thomas feels exhausted. When he awakens after a short but deep sleep, Thomas experiences an epiphanic moment of inner illumination. It is noteworthy that the darkness is described as parting to reveal "an immeasurable, boundless prospect of light" (526). This sense of spatial expansiveness affirms the spatial expansiveness which has always been important in the Buddenbrooks houses. The revelation which Thomas Buddenbrook has encourages him to view death in a very positive light—he thinks now of death as a joyous occasion, somewhat similar in spirit to von Aschenbach's sense of death in *Der Tod in Venedig*. Thomas even imagines that death represents "the return from an unspeakably painful wandering, the correction of a grave mistake" (526) which would free him from limitation and give him a sense of freedom.

After asserting, as does Tonio in *Tonio Kröger*, that he contains within himself multiple existential possibilities, Thomas proclaims a sense of communion with those individuals who have expressed a strong individuality. Thomas realizes that the most important sense of communion and consanguinity which he feels or can feel with the world around him is not necessarily with persons in his family but rather with individuals who are similar in heart, soul, and emotional vitality. As he ponders with more intensity than ever before life and death, he feels as if he were already "free of all natural as well as artificial limitations" (527). In an epiphanic moment similar in scope and intensity to Joyce's notion of epiphany as a moment of timeless harmony, Thomas believes that the physical barriers of his world expanded and opened up to reveal a vision of the entire world. He feels liberated from the constraints of space, time, and history, and especially of family history. Thomas realizes his belief in an endless present of time and space through which he has access to eternity. The culmination of this epiphanic experience is Thomas's assertion that he will live, for he no longer fears death or sees death as an antagonist. Although he hopes to return frequently to the wonderful book which inspired such reflections, he also senses that his commercial obligations will prevent such study and meditations. In fact, numerous daily responsibilities interfere with any such plans in the future, so that Thomas not only does not return to the book, but reverts intellectually to the religious faith of his ancestors. He decides, consciously and outwardly at least, to leave everything up to God, and focuses instead on his earthly concerns, making his will.

In the latter part of this chapter Thomas tries to return to the accustomed images and faith of his earlier years but without considerable success. Unable to find an inner spiritual serenity, Thomas decides to make his will. In the autumn it is recommended by his doctor to take a short rest-cure by the sea—in fact, both Thomas and Christian go to Travemünde for a sense of relaxation. As the arrival of Aschenbach in Venice in *Der Tod in Venedig* is misty, so the arrival of Thomas in Travemünde is accompanied by a rainy atmosphere. Tony comes occasionally to visit Thomas during his sojourn along the sea and is reminded in certain locations of her congenial past experiences here with Morten, but tries to preserve a light heart and not let the past disturb her sense of calm. The vacation along the sea, and especially in Travemünde, has been a very important ambience for Tony and Thomas Buddenbrook. In one passage Thomas even emphasizes how soothing and comforting the sea is and can be with its spaciousness and its vastness, reinforcing his interest in a sense of endless space and time which he had expressed in the previous chapter. Thomas's praise of the consoling power of the sea culminates in the following statement: "But it is when one is worn out with turning one's eyes inward upon the bewildering complexity of the human heart, that one finds peace in resting them on the wideness of the sea" (538).

In Chapter VII Thomas leaves an assembly meeting early to see the dentist because of a terrible toothache. On his way home after this mid-winter visit to the dentist Thomas collapses in the street. In Chapter VIII Thomas, having been brought home in a condition which alarms Gerda, becomes increasingly weaker and then dies. Tony, in particular, is distraught, but distracts herself from her misery with the funeral arrangements. Chapter X of Part Ten ends with the public funeral of Thomas Buddenbrook, once an established and honored member of the town's society and its business community, now forever gone from the world of mortality. That Thomas is buried with a military honor guard in the Buddenbrook family plot in the cemetery does add a measure of dignity to this very melancholy and sad situation. Todd Kontje describes the destructive power of mortality against the Buddenbrooks as follows: "Death hangs heavy over the Buddenbrook family, gathering force with each successive generation until it crushes the life out of its final victim" (30). The death of Thomas Buddenbrook does show and reinforce the swift and merciless effect which mortality can and often does have on individuals in everyday life.

In Chapter 1 of Part Eleven the Buddenbrook house and firm are sold, reinforcing the sense of the family's precipitous decline. The aura of decline and death in this chapter is reinforced by the description of the demise of various individuals who used to be present in the society of this town. Tony, Frau Permaneder, is especially disappointed and upset not only by the fact that the family business was to end, but also by the proposed sale of the house which Thomas had created. Sadly, the firm, the granaries, and the warehouses are liquidated at a considerable loss. Gerda, for financial reasons, moves in the autumn of 1876 into a smaller villa just outside the Castle Gate. The depressing circumstances of this situation manifest themselves for Tony especially and presumably for Gerda as well not only in the fact that the house is sold at a notable financial loss but also because a number of the family's possessions will be taken over by the next owner of the house, who has no special affection for them, for Gerda can only take some of the household items with her. Two other signs of the family's decline as depicted in this chapter are the dismissal of Ida Jungmann who had served the Buddenbrooks for forty years and the placement of Christian in an institution by his current wife. When Tony visits Gerda she tries to counter the decline in the family fortunes by telling Hanno stories of the past greatness and glory of the Buddenbrook family encompassing in her narrative images not only of elegant architectural interiors but also of public prominence, such as the depiction of Hanno's great-grandfather as having driven through the country with his special carriage and four horses. Through the telling of such historically important narratives which affirm the past greatness of the Buddenbrook family Tony also certainly enhances her own state of mind and affirms her own existential vitality.

With respect to the issue of the decline of the Buddenbrooks Todd Kontje emphasizes in *The Cambridge Introduction to Thomas Mann* the role of philosophical pessimism: "Philosophical pessimism, not economic determinism, physiological degeneration, or moral depravity, is at the core of the Buddenbrooks' decline" (31). The economic, ethical, and physical problems and issues which the Buddenbrook family confronts also consistently challenge and drain its strength and vitality. Thomas Buddenbrook is the member of the Buddenbrook family who shows this pessimistic inclination most prominently in his reflections on Schopenhauer's *Die Welt als Wille und Vorstellung*, an inclination grounded at least to some extent in his sense that he is not instinctively suited to a career which is devoted ceaselessly to financial profit and gain.

In Chapter II of this part of the novel it is increasingly evident that Hanno was not destined to follow in the commercial, mercantile paths of his father and grandfather. He has no inclination for business but is thoroughly enraptured by the world of music and of aesthetic expression. Both Hanno and his best friend Kai exist in worlds beyond those of everyday mortality. Hanno and Kai are distinguished from their classmates in school not only by their artistic inclinations—Hanno concentrates on music as Kai on his writing—but also by their emotional sensitivity and gentleness. Hanno has read one of Kai's tales, written in a potently romantic spirit, and admires it greatly. Later in the chapter, after some of the teachers are presented in less than flattering terms as persons lost in their pedantic idiosyncrasies and without a genuine devotion to educating the students humanistically, Hanno admits to Kai his weariness and his despair. In proclaiming that he wants to sleep and to die, Hanno also reveals that his low self-esteem derives at least to some extent from the remark which someone had made that he is a member of a decayed family. After school Hanno plays the piano very capably and sensitively—he is able to improvise creatively. However, as Gabriele Klöterjahn in *Tristan*, when Hanno plays the piano intensely and passionately, his physical health is adversely affected. Hanno, although not interested in the world of business which is his father's domain, is definitely the heir to his mother's interest in and devotion to music. The importance of music has been manifest in the elegant life of Thomas and Gerda Buddenbrook from the beginning of their marriage, for Gerda was committed to preserving and nurturing her musical inclinations. Even in Chapter VI of Part Seven, for example, when Thomas takes Tony into the garden to discuss several problematic issues, they can hear the heavenly violin-playing of Gerda in the music-room. Such a moment metaphorizes the importance of music in the Buddenbrook home, for as the concerns about business seem to dominate and threaten the inner security of Thomas, Gerda enjoys her musical devotions—that the artistic triumphs symbolically over the bourgeois in this episode foreshadows the significance which the realm of art, music, and culture will have in the future of the Buddenbrooks.

The temporal setting of Chapter IV of Part Eleven, the final chapter of the novel, is appropriately the autumn. For the atmosphere of decay and decline which is so often an integral part of the autumn is abundantly present here. This chapter reveals that Hanno died of typhoid fever about six months before this autumnal evening. Unable to continue with the family business, Hanno nevertheless joins the family in death and participates in an aura of continuity as his grave exists in the family plot in the cemetery. Gerda, having lost both Thomas and Hanno, decides to return to Amsterdam. Tony, although saddened by this decision for it considerably diminishes the stature of the Buddenbrook family in town, says that she understands. That Tony even adds that she appreciates the fact that Gerda did not leave after the death of Thomas shows her generosity of heart, a characteristic which ennobles her person. It is noteworthy that Gerda, in returning home to Amsterdam, is taking nothing with her.

Helmut Koopmann states insightfully that *Buddenbrooks* describes not only the decline of a family but also the decline of an established way of life and of an entire century (51). In arguing thoughtfully that the housewarming party at the beginning as well as the final small family reunion at the end of the novel take place in the autumn, in an atmosphere of decay and decline (51), Koopmann also makes the observation that the initial family celebration has been dramatically transformed at the end to a "Totenfeier": "Das Einweihungsfest des Anfangs ist zu einer Totenfeier geworden" (51). For Tony remarks with profound melancholy and sadness that they will never see their deceased family members again.

And yet, one might say that the one individual whose attitude and presence mitigates at least to some extent the atmosphere of this "Totenfeier" is Tony Buddenbrook.

For she is not willing to accept the aura of decline and makes a valiant attempt to restore and preserve, if only symbolically, the inner vitality of the Buddenbrook family. Tony tells the several family members gathered on this occasion to wish Gerda farewell that they should have a weekly meeting to socialize and to read the family papers. Tony wants to preserve at least a semblance of the integrity and vitality of her family—she will now oversee the portfolio of important family papers and documents. In stressing the importance of the regular family meeting Tony also proclaims that she cannot live anywhere else, despite the fact that the home town no longer has the genuine appreciation of her which it should have and despite the fact that the stature of the Buddenbrook family has outwardly declined so considerably. As with other individuals who are so attached to their home towns, or to the domestic ambience in which they grew up, Tony reveals a generosity of heart and a nobility of spirit which is exemplary and inspirational.

Michael Zeller describes in "Seele und Saldo. Ein texttreuer Gang durch *Buddenbrooks*" the aura of Tony Buddenbrook's vitality: "Alles, was nicht Buddenbrook an ihr ist, hat sie als Ballast von sich abgeworfen. Sie ist das Ewige Kind ihrer Sippe, unberührbar von Leid und erinnerungslos. Und sie ist vital" (15). Zeller proceeds to say that Tony's "vitality" is diminished by her inability to make a decisive, momentously resolute decision (15). Yet, one might also claim that Tony's "vitality" is inextricably connected to her patient resilience, her humane kindness, and her capacity to stand above the vicissitudes of everyday mortality and signify the most salient characteristics of the Buddenbrook family.

Tony's lament about the various deaths of the members of her family during the course of her life follows her tearful and heartfelt declaration that she truly loved Hanno, perhaps even more than his mother. Her sense of unhappiness and despair that she will no longer see Thomas and Hanno and the other beloved people who have died receives a hopeful response from Friederike Buddenbrook, who exclaims that there will be a reunion, implying a spiritual reunion in heaven someday. When Tony begins to express a sense of doubt about such a reunion, although trying to maintain a spirit of hope that it nevertheless might occur, Sesemi Weichbrodt suddenly asserts with all her strength, the power of a "little prophetess, admonishing and inspired" (604), that it will definitely happen. Thus, the present and its overwhelming anguish and sadness for the members of the Buddenbrooks such as Tony who feel the decline and deterioration of the family so acutely and sensitively, is brightened a little by the prospect of having a family reunion in the future, a gathering in heaven, in a world beyond the exigencies and injustices of everyday mortality.

Perhaps Tony Buddenbrook is able to show resilience and survive despite her personal sufferings and despite the tragedies of her family because she has the capacity to see beyond the appearances of everyday reality and to understand the world as imagination in the spirit of Schopenhauer's emphasis on "Vorstellung." Although seemingly somewhat naïve, or perhaps just undervalued by people in society, as Helmer undervalues Nora in Ibsen's *A Doll's House*, who do not appreciate her innate intelligence, Tony is able to transcend the power and the influence of the Schopenhauerean will by her instinctively optimistic outlook and by her imaginative goodness.

Yet, it should be added that the outward decline of the Buddenbrook family does not reveal anything necessarily about the status of its inner heart and soul. For Tony, who symbolizes the family in this latter phase of its existence as she has always represented the dynamism and goodness inherent in it, is a noble character. Although Tony is not as outwardly successful, that is, not as wealthy or as socially prominent, or as socioeconomically powerful as the Hagenströms who were so competitive with the Buddenbrooks at one time and now have achieved a position of prestige in this society, in a sense Tony, by virtue of her character, her goodness, her kindheartedness, her sensitivity, her emotional wisdom, is very superior to the Hagenströms and others like them in society who dedicate their lives primarily, if not solely, to the pursuit of money and profit with little concern for humanitarian vitality. Tony Buddenbrook, as Cinderella with whom she shares various important characteristics and inclinations, possesses a great heart and a noble soul, which, one might say, is the most important accomplishment that any individual can strive for and attain in the world of everyday mortality. Having developed a profound appreciation for and devotion to her family's magnificent houses over the years, Tony preserves forever in her heart and soul a luminescent memory and a resplendent vision of these architectural domains which have been so important to the socioeconomic presence and prestige of the family and to her own emotional and spiritual integrity and well-being.

Tonio Kröger and *Tristan*—The House and Creative Vitality; the House and Transfiguration in Death

In *Tonio Kröger* the dynamic conversation between Tonio Kröger and Lisabeta Ivanovna in the middle section of the narrative in which they discuss such topics as the importance and vitality of literature, its healing power and its redemptive capacity, as well as the interconnections of art and life, is significant because it reveals Tonio's innermost thoughts and allows a means of self-expression while also emphasizing the supreme significance of literature and an aesthetic sensibility. In the autumn, presumably several months after this conversation Tonio tells Lisabeta that he needs a change of place and plans to travel to Denmark. Tonio reveals a longing to see the Baltic and to hear northern (implicitly north German and Scandinavian) names and words in their native context. Tonio feels that northern scenery and linguistic vitality will revitalize him emotionally and spiritually, for in the past his heart was alive here, even though he was treated as an outsider by those whom he admired and loved. It is also possible that some of the eloquent phrases which Lisabeta uses in their revealing conversation, such as declaring that the poet is not only the most highly developed of human beings and a saint but also a creator who has the capacity to produce the noblest intellectual reflections, remind Tonio of his artistic roots and of his "glorious" past, of the congenial vitality of his home area which had once been so inspirational for him.

It has been thirteen years since Tonio Kröger visited his home town, the place where his family used to be very prominent and represented one of the pillars of the commercial community. As a child Tonio was accustomed to feeling that his place in society was important, for his family's ancestral home was the most splendid residence in the entire town. Tonio was an exceptional child, very sensitive, thoughtful, and artistically gifted (for he not only wrote literary sketches but also played the violin capably). In his youth it is evident that Tonio, as Thomas Mann himself and as various characters in Mann's narratives such as Spinell and Hanno Buddenbrook, is not destined to pursue the family business, for practical commercial concerns are noticeably less important to him than the wisdom of the heart and the knowledge of the soul. In Tonio's childhood and youth his ancestral home represents a sanctuary against the degenerative presence and ravages of mortality. The natural ambience around the house enhances this sense of sanctuary. Tonio himself even contributes to the atmosphere of a sanctuary, for his violin playing creates an aura of harmony with the fountain and the walnut tree outside his window. In his childhood and youth the North Sea is also very important to Tonio—spending his summer holidays along the ocean creates a special bond between his sensitive soul and the beautiful natural environment.

The period of Tonio's youth is also characterized by a sense of isolation from contemporary society. As a sensitive, gifted, and intelligent youth, Tonio, despite his family heritage, was treated as an outsider by others. He did not typically share the inclinations and motivations of his schoolmates and was more interested in solitary literary and artistic pursuits. Inge Diersen describes this differentiation of Tonio from his peers, and especially from Hans Hansen and Ingeborg Holm, the symbols of the bourgeois world of everyday mortality, effectively in the following passage in *Untersuchungen zu Thomas Mann*: "Tonio Krögers Jugendgeschichte endete mit der Erkenntnis, daß es zwischen ihm und den anderen Menschen, den blond-blauäugigen Gewöhnlichen, keine Gemeinsamkeit gibt, er hat um sie geworben, sie haben ihn nicht verstanden und nicht verstehen wollen" (68). Tonio, unlike Hans and Inge, does not feel a sense of unity and consanguinity with his social and socioeconomic environment—he sees and feels more deeply and more sensitively than his peers the nuances, the idiosyncrasies, the subtleties, and the inconsistencies of the world of everyday mortality. The essence of Tonio's differentiation from his peers is not physical, as in the case of Hanno Buddenbrook, but emotional and intellectual, as Inge Diersen stresses so effectively in *Untersuchungen zu Thomas Mann*: "Er sieht Menschen und Dinge schärfer als seine Kameraden, er empfindet tiefer, differenzierter, und das sondert ihn ab" (66). Tonio appreciates and finds a spiritual soulmate in Don Carlos, the king in Schiller's drama, who is sad and emotionally expressive in his profound isolation.

Joseph Brennan describes the distinction and isolation of Tonio in *Thomas Mann's World* as "the theme of the artist who is sensitive to his aloneness in the world, conscious of his difference from other men" (13). Brennan thoughtfully states that "this consciousness of a gulf separating one from other men is doubly painful for an artist in whom the bourgeois element is inborn" (13). If we can assume that Lisabeta is correct in her characterization of Tonio as "ein verirrter Bürger," then Tonio is the kind of individual who feels this isolation especially acutely and poignantly. That the two idols of Tonio's childhood, Hans Hansen and Ingeborg Holm, do not share his interests, do not have his sensitivity for the world, and, especially in the case of Ingeborg, do not even pay any attention to him, causes him considerable emotional anguish and pain.

Since those difficult days of his childhood and youth when Tonio yearned for acceptance and appreciation, he has become successful as a writer. He has devoted himself to the art and craft of literary expression and has achieved works of significance. Tonio's return to his past, to his home town which he has not seen in years, is destined to kindle an emotionally dynamic response in him. When Tonio arrives in his home town in the early evening, he wishes that he could take an extended walk of dreamy solitude through the familiar streets. However, he also seems initially depressed by the fact that the gabled streets seem so close and restrictive. During the past thirteen years Tonio had occasionally dreamt of being back home—these reflections had been so vivid that he had even been unsure whether they were manifestations of dream or reality. The hotel room in which Tonio stays is reminiscent in atmosphere and spirit of his family's financial importance—the windows of the room look out upon a world of picturesque courts and gables with an aura of medieval vitality.

When Tonio awakes the next morning, he is greeted by an abundance of sunlight. Even though Tonio very much wanted to return to his home town for a visit, he is comforted by the fact that he would likely not be recognized by anyone. He is grateful that he can conceal his identity behind a dreamy mask of anonymity. After breakfast he wanders through the interesting array of gabled streets, visiting various familiar sights such as the Market Square and the Rathaus, which seem to be perpetual features of this urban landscape and which emphasize its continuity through the passage of time. Tonio also stands contemplatively in front of a house with a baroque gable on the Market Square—this is presumably the former house of Ingeborg Holm, with whom he had been in love as a child. However, as Tonio walks a little farther he comes upon a sign of decay and change.

In the Lindenplatz Tonio stops in front of one of the villas and looks into the garden. That his hand is stained with rust after touching the garden gate suggests that this villa, which had once been the pride of the Hansen family, is characterized by an aura of decay and is likely no longer in its possession. Then Tonio walks along the harbor and up a winding street to his family's former mansion. Here, too, of course, there is an indication of change and of the inevitable passage of time. For the mansion of the once prominent and wealthy Kröger family is now the public library. That Tonio experiences a momentary sense of fear as he enters his former house that he might encounter his father suggests that this northern journey is not only a present-day return to the ambience of his childhood and youth but also a dreamlike adventure into the atmosphere of the past.

Initially, Tonio is rather disconcerted that his former home has been transformed into the public library and a series of private apartments. It is interesting that although Tonio is a writer and devoted to literature he is skeptical of the presence of the public in this once privately revered place. After climbing up the splendid staircase Tonio enters the domain of the public library. As Tonio wanders through the different rooms he recalls various personal events which occurred in those once so vitally important architectural spaces. The breakfast room for intimate family meals, the large dining-room with its white statues of gods and goddesses suggesting a majestic aura, and the bedroom nearby where family members had died, are three notable spaces which he recalls with quiet melancholy. As Tonio even visits the room which had once been his own bedroom, he experiences a pang of poignant recollection. This was the room in which he had developed and preserved his first literary efforts and sketches. In his childhood and youth the walnut tree and the fountain in the garden outside had always been inspirational for him. Now, as Tonio gazes out the window he sees only a desolate garden, although the aging walnut tree is still a stalwart feature.

One of the primary comforts for Tonio in this scenario as he visits his former beloved home is finding one of his own literary works on the library shelves. One book which Tonio takes from the shelves is described as an excellent literary work which shows artistic talent. That this work is familiar to him and that he is able to follow the flow of the words so easily and effortlessly suggests that it is his own creation. This moment of experiencing the permanence of his own work, of finding his own work established in creative eternity in the library of his home town represents the conclusion and the culmination of this visit.

As the spacious upstairs rooms of his former house are now occupied by strangers, Tonio has no interest in further exploration and decides to leave this once vitally important place to return to his hotel. He subsequently prepares to depart by boat for Copenhagen. Unfortunately, as Tonio is on the verge of leaving the hotel he is questioned as a potential criminal, for he is actually mistaken for someone else. Tonio senses that the entire misunderstanding could be easily cleared up if he were to reveal that his name is Kröger and that his family were once very important members of the town society. Instead, Tonio clarifies his identity by showing the authorities a proof-sheet, a representative feature of his literary profession. This scenario underscores the inherent and even more overt conflict between the artistic and bourgeois worlds. It is noteworthy that Tonio could have defended himself and proved his innocence by asserting his connection as a member of the Kröger family to the bourgeois world. Instead, he chooses to remain elusive and unknown, showing the authorities a symbol of his connection to the artistic world.

Although he is somewhat distressed by the events surrounding his departure, Tonio shakes off his melancholy as the boat from Copenhagen enters the open sea and he observes the enchanting light of the moon. In the distance Tonio sees the beach where he had as a child listened to the ocean, its melodies, and its dreams. He also observes the lights of the Kurhaus where his family had spent a considerable time. Tonio's reflection on the power of the sea and this marine environment is similar in spirit to the passage in Fitzgerald's *The Great Gatsby* which emphasizes the importance of the transitory enchanted moment. Tonio's closeness to the Baltic and to its beautiful natural environment revitalizes him. The sound of the sea and of the wind connects Tonio to his past and revives him emotionally and spiritually, removing the anguish and pain of the present.

The passage on the evening sea is rather tempestuous. Even though Tonio is physically drained by the stormy swaying of the boat, he looks upon the vibrant and powerful waves with affection, with the appreciation which has lingered in him since youth. Tonio even finds some comfort in looking at the light of the stars. When the ship finally lands in Denmark, Tonio decides to spend several days in Copenhagen. The aura of Copenhagen, the architecture, the language, and the atmosphere of the city, reminds him vitally of his home town. Tonio is so emotionally moved by some of the familiar names and poignantly interesting faces that he decides to travel further.

The restlessness which "possesses" Tonio is an integral part of his sense of longing or Sehnsucht. In returning to his home environment Tonio hopes not only to revitalize himself but also to revive a sense of his congenial past, his materialistically pleasant and emotionally sensitive youth. This spiritual restlessness is also an important dimension of his aesthetic position as a Romantic writer. In describing Tonio's restlessness as "half memory, half hope" (119), Mann implies that his protagonist is motivated not only by his fond rememberance of the past, of some past events of his youth, but also perhaps by a hope of encountering notable symbols or representative individuals from that past.

Tonio's restlessness drives him further northward—he takes the boat along the coast of Seeland towards Helsingor. From there he travels by carriage to a small hotel in Aalsgaard. Thomas Mann's own short vacation at a resort in Aalsgard in the autumn of 1899 provided a foundation for the development of the narrative of *Tonio Kröger*. The bath-hotel here looks out onto the beach and the Swedish coast. Tonio revels in the sea air and in the beauty of the sea, the peaceful atmosphere of the locale, and the profound tranquility of the natural environment. He also enjoys listening to the local language, perhaps because it is symbolically reminiscent of the linguistic vitality of the northern dialect of his childhood years.

On one occasion Tonio is described as gazing out upon the sea enjoying the roar of the waves and then turning away to feel enveloped in an aura of silent warmth. Even though Tonio is not facing the ocean, he still feels its power and its allure. This passage is somewhat reminiscent of the ending of *Der Tod in Venedig*. For the sea in this paragraph of *Tonio Kröger*, as the sea in the last two paragraphs of *Der Tod in Venedig*, is depicted as luring and beckoning to the artistic individual. The notable difference between these two passages is that in *Der Tod in Venedig* Aschenbach is facing the sea and Tadzio, who appears to beckon him, smiles and motions "outward...into an immensity of richest expectation" (73). Aschenbach seems to wish to follow this gesture of hope and longing before collapsing. In *Tonio Kröger* Tonio turns away from the sea at the critical moment and smiles to himself as he feels the profound allure of the ocean, as if to say that as much as he loves the sea he is not yet ready to cease his literary productivity and to end his life. Tonio, as the persona in Frost's poem "Stopping by Woods on a Snowy Evening," still has "miles to go" before he is ready to sleep and much artistic work to create before he is willing to pass into another realm of existence.

From the hotel Tonio makes excursions into the surrounding natural environment. Tonio appreciates the isolation of the landscape and is content to lose himself in lonely paths and quiet refuges near the sea. One especially favored vantage-point is sitting next to a tree in the comfort of a grove and looking towards the sea. The splendid isolation of such moments inspires Tonio to feel a sense of sanctuary and a sense of "profound forgetfulness" (121) as if he were beyond space and time.

In such soothing endeavors and explorations which are characterized by a peaceful state of repose Tonio spends numerous days. The profound tranquility of the atmosphere of the natural environment near the sea is so potent that Tonio forgets all about the passage of time. Tonio even declares that he does not know specifically how many days passed as he enjoys the serenity of nature as well as an inner calm— nor does he express any interest in discovering how much time has actually passed by.

Then on one particular day when Tonio awakens early, something spectacular occurs. As he adjusts his eyes to the morning ambience he feels as if he is looking at "a magic illumination" (121). Various features of his room are "bathed in a serene and roseate light" (121) and suffused with an "unearthly brightness" (121). Tonio momentarily realizes that this beautiful radiance is the light of the sun in the sunrise.

The sunlight on this morning is especially inspiring because the previous several days had been cloudy and rainy. After breakfasting early, taking a swim, and then walking along the beach, Tonio returns to the hotel to find several omnibuses containing numerous guests having arrived for a family reunion. Even though Tonio realizes that the tranquility which he has been enjoying at the hotel will likely be diminished or interrupted by these new arrivals, his buoyant and joyful mood is unchanged. It is as if the appearance of the bright sunlight earlier in the morning assured him that the day would be pleasant, regardless of the vicissitudes which he might encounter.

A little while later as Tonio is having his second breakfast in the room as he gazes towards the ocean, two seemingly familiar individuals or types enter the room. To Tonio these appear to be Hans Hansen and Ingeborg Holm, looking just as they had in his childhood and youth. Not only are their features strongly reminiscent of Hans and Ingeborg, but they are wearing the same clothes which Tonio recalls them wearing in earlier days. Tonio seems exceedingly pleased to see these figures, these symbolic characters, from his childhood and from his congenial past. Their presence makes his heart glad. Tonio even admits as he reflects upon the fact that Hans and Ingeborg will return in the evening with the rest of their company for a dance that he feels a sense of happiness about this situation which he has not felt in years.

Inge Diersen describes this experience effectively in *Thomas Mann: Episches Werk, Weltanschauung, Leben*: "Es ist, als habe er gerade auf dieses Erlebnis gewartet, als habe er nur um seinetwillen die Reise unternommen.... Die Wiederbegegnung mit dem nördlichen Menschenschlag erleichtert es ihm, die Brücke zur Vergangenheit zu schlagen, zu seiner Jugend als der Zeit, da sein Herz noch lebte" (62). For it is the revitalization of his heart, his love for life, for the bourgeois realm of the happy, common, and pleasant, which is the primary goal of this return to the ambience of his childhood and youth.

It is very significant that Tonio observes the Hans- and Ingeborg-like figures so intently and carefully. For Tonio has returned to his home region to revitalize himself—he needs to connect or reconnect himself to the prominent characters and features of his youth. By recapturing the spirit of the past Tonio Kröger hopes and aims to revitalize and reenergize himself emotionally, artistically, and spiritually.

As the ball commences in the evening Tonio moves quietly and secretively to the veranda from where he can observe the entertainment seemingly unobtrusively. It is as if Tonio is traversing the hidden corridors of the past to return to the spirit of his youth. The entire scenario reminds Tonio of the dancing episode from his past. For not only are the Hans- and Inge-like individuals present, but there is the leader of the ball who is very reminiscent of the dancing master, Herr Knaak, from his youth. As Tonio watches the two individuals who seem to be Hans and Inge, he acknowledges that he views these two as symbolic of a particular race and type. In looking at these two characters Tonio reflects upon their similarity to the Hans and Inge of his childhood and is overwhelmed by a spirit of homesickness, by a sense of longing for the past.

As Tonio reflects upon Hans and Inge, their features, and the normal, everyday life which they appear to lead, he wonders whether his existence would have developed any differently if his approach to life had been comparable to or similar to theirs. Tonio considers whether, if he had lived a normal and more conforming and simple life as a child, he would have attained anything other than his current existential condition. The conclusion which Tonio reaches is that his life would have turned out just the same because of his instinctive interest in and capacity for creativity, for artistic achievement. Although Tonio longs for the apparent innocence and simplicity of the world of the bourgeois, of which Hans and Inge are conspicuous representatives, he senses or even knows that he would have never been truly happy in such a world. The artistic inclination and the creative urge in his soul would have felt stifled and repressed in such a milieu.

The dancing episode at the hotel contains not only individuals who are reminiscent of Hans, Ingeborg, and Herr Knaak, but also someone who reminds Tonio of Magdalena Vermehren, the young woman who in his youth was an awkward participant in the dance and who, unlike Hans and Inge, seemed to appreciate him. As in his youth, Tonio turns away from the young woman who is definitely an outsider in this society and yet who looks at him with appreciative and sensitive eyes, to the bourgeois world of Hans and Inge. Tonio even contemplates the possibility of approaching the figures who resemble Hans and Inge and addressing them briefly. And yet, even though Tonio says that such contact would make him happy, he feels at the same time that the Hans- and Inge-like figures in the current scenario would treat him as they did in his youth, namely, as a stranger and as someone outside their normal sphere of activity. In asserting that their language was not his language, Tonio reinforces the differentiation of the artist from the bourgeois realm of society.

In *Thomas Mann's World*, Joseph Brennan stresses the necessity of isolation in Tonio's existence, saying that the artist "must stand apart from life, self-conscious and alone, in order to obtain his perspective" (22). Tonio Kröger represents the consummate artist who "must live and move in two worlds" (21), for he exists not only in the world of everyday mortality but also apart from it, "standing off from it, over against it, transcribing it, seizing upon its most salient features and universalizing them" (21). It is noteworthy that Tonio Kröger has the resilience and the inner strength to develop and maintain such a challenging existence. Tonio does share various personal inclinations and qualities with Hanno Buddenbrook—for example, an aesthetic sensibility, a devotion to art, a belief in art (literature, music, and art in general) as the highest achievement of humankind, and a strong sense of the differentiation of the artistically inclined individual from society. Both characters also have a musical and lovely mother, grow up in a socioeconomically privileged environment, and are for a considerable time members of one of the most revered families in the town. Yet, as W. E. Berendsohn points out Tonio "bears the sufferings of his artistry with more power or resistance" (31). For Tonio has developed from childhood the vitality of his imagination and an inner life which is capable of transcending the frailties and limitations of the world of everyday mortality.

In reflecting upon Inge and her physical presence Tonio feels a sense of enchantment and longing for her aura and the world which she inhabits. In Tonio's further contemplations he wonders whether Inge laughed at him in his youth when he made the mistake in the dance and whether she would still laugh at him today after he had established himself as a writer. Inwardly Tonio realizes that even if his creativity had produced such great achievements as the nine symphonies of Beethoven and the Last Judgement of Michelangelo, Inge would still ignore him and treat him as an outsider. In gazing at Inge, Tonio thinks of a poetic line from Theodor Storm—"I would sleep, but thou must dance."

Tonio knows that he, as an instinctively sensitive and vital artist, will never be allowed and will never allow himself to be complacent and to live the life of simple, uncomplicated feeling. He recognizes that he is compelled and driven by his inner creative urge to consistently nurture his literary vitality and to produce artistic achievements. Like the pale young woman in the current dance, Tonio is inevitably an outsider in the world of Hans and Inge and from the perspective of the bourgeois society. It is noteworthy that this pale young woman, so reminiscent of Magdalena from his youth, also falls down in the dance. As Tonio helps her to her feet, she, as Magdalena years before, looks at him with dark and appreciative eyes. But Tonio is so focused on the existence of Hans and Inge, or their symbolic counterparts, that he ignores the Magadalena-like individual, though she is instinctively more suited to his heart and mind.

As Tonio goes to sleep that night and reflects on the evening's events and on his own past, he repeats over and over to himself the "few chaste northern syllables" (presumably words such as Hans Hansen and Ingeborg Holm) which symbolize love, happiness, and home for him. Tonio, the literary artist, also thinks about and is emotionally moved by various incidents from his own life, from intense intellectual adventures to passionate physical moments, from an acute awareness of the poignant and inevitable tension between the artistic and bourgeois worlds to a nostalgia for the domain of his childhood. Even though Tonio is melancholy and sad as he falls asleep on this memorable evening, he also acknowledges that his heart is alive. One might claim that such was actually the purpose of Tonio's return to the northern landscape—he wanted to revitalize himself, to reawaken his heart and spirit to the beauty and dynamism of the landscape of his childhood and youth.

The letter which Tonio writes to Lisabeta Ivanovna after this memorable experience is very important and represents a significant part of his developmental process as a writer. In this letter Tonio not only articulates thoughtfully the poignant tension in his soul between the artist and the bourgeois, between artistic inclination, aesthetic dynamism, and bourgeois stability, but also anticipates the future and a greater artistic activity. In the opening section of the letter (specifically, paragraph 2) Tonio reflects on the phrase which Lisabeta had used to describe him, namely, a "bourgeois manqué," that is, a bourgeois who has strayed into the artistic realm. In acknowledging that Lisabeta's intuition and characterization of him was rather accurate, Tonio equates his bourgeois dimension with his love of life.

Inge Diersen states in *Untersuchungen zu Thomas Mann* that Tonio Kröger "ist—wie Thomas Mann selbst—kein abtrünniger, sondern ein verirrter Bürger, einer, der sich von seiner Klasse distanziert hat, ohne recht zu wissen, warum er es tat, ja daß er es getan hat" (65). Tonio seems to be a bourgeois who has become lost in another realm and life-philosophy, in an artistic approach to life. He has distanced himself from his own social class and he feels this sense of distance acutely and poignantly. Even as a teenager Tonio realized that he was different, that he did not have the same bourgeois interests and inclinations as his peers. This sense of difference for Tonio is manifested in a heightened sensitivity for the world around him, for he observes more intuitively and thoughtfully and feels more intensively, and a greater aesthetic sensibility which is not dependent on and transcends the socioeconomic mores of his contemporary society.

Tonio proceeds to assert that he stands between the world of the artist and the world of the bourgeois without feeling at home in either. In this respect Tonio's existence is similar to that of Spinell in *Tristan*, of Tony Buddenbrook in *Buddenbrooks*, and of Castorp in *Der Zauberberg*. In fact, one could also claim that the threshold existence of Tonio in *Tonio Kröger* and Tony Buddenbrook in *Buddenbrooks* is similar to that of Sebastian and Cordelia in Waugh's *Brideshead Revisited* and to that of Conway in Hilton's *Lost Horizon*. All of these individuals exist at the threshold between two worlds without being completely at home in either. The vitality of their existence is generated by the tension of these two sometimes contiguous and sometimes distant worlds, a tension which can make life difficult but which can also engender very meaningful and pleasant moments and memories.

Although Tonio proclaims, understandably, that he has suffered because of this tension and because of this feeling of not being at home in either realm, there is also the implication that his literary activity has benefited from this tension. As for other writers and artists, this existential conflict between the artistic and bourgeois domains has generated, motivated, and stimulated his creative vitality. Tonio also states that it is "the bourgeois love of the human, the living and usual" (131) which makes a writer or any individual with literary inclinations a true poet.

The experience in his home area, in the beautiful northern landscape, has been so important and inspirational for Tonio that he declares to Lisabeta that from now on his work will be superior to what it has been. In the second-to-last paragraph of the letter to Lisabeta, Tonio affirms the significance of the sea and of nature in his life. He says that as he writes he hears the sea whispering to him and he closes his eyes. As Michelangelo in the presence of his marble blocks and stone formations from which he would liberate beings, so Tonio states, as he closes his eyes, that he is gazing into an unborn world which "needs to be ordered and shaped" (131). This is a sanctuary of creative energy, the manifestations and possibilities of which Tonio will fulfill in his artistic work—Tonio will exhibit in his work the redemptive power of the word and of letters which Lisabeta had attributed to the literary artist earlier in the narrative.

In emphasizing that his most profound love belongs to the happy, lovely, and everyday beings, Tonio also implies that such a love is an integral part of his artistic existence, of his creative expression, and of his creative vitality. Tonio's letter to Lisabeta and his northern trip to his childhood home, which revitalizes him emotionally, intellectually, and spiritually, represent sanctuaries of light and hope. These are places of harmonious and peaceful refuge in Tonio's heart and soul which will perpetually guide and inspire him in the future. These are places of sanctuary which embody and signify the spirit of the architectural splendor of Tonio's childhood home, its sense of security and stability, its beauty, and its congenial comfort and which represent his sensitive emotional and spiritual connection to the natural environment.

Another narrative by Mann in which the motif of an architecturally vital sanctuary, a sanctuary of light, plays a significant role is *Tristan*. The very first paragraph of the story describes Einfried, the sanatorium, as a place of seclusion and natural beauty surrounded by mountainous heights. The setting is permeated by a picturesque quality for the main building is depicted as being in a garden with bowers and pavilions. That this ambience is distanced from the world of everyday mortality is reinforced in the declaration that even an author is in residence here "stealing time from God Almighty" (318). Such a statement implies that the sense of time in this sanatorium environment, the awareness of time which this environment creates, is distinctive and extraordinary. That any individual has the capacity here to "steal time" from the divine being suggests that is a place with an unusual temporal sensibility and with a potential to transcend mortality.

The sense of distance from everyday mortality is further reinforced by the fact that the porters have to carry the trunks of the guests from the carriage which stops in front of the gate because there is no direct drive up to the house. The old mansion, which represents the central architectural feature of the sanatorium, exemplifies this aura of distance by its representation of the Empire style. Gabriele Klöterjahn, as ethereal and unworldly as she seems with her beautiful hands and her delicate head, appears in her diseased state to be a manifestation of the Empire style. Gabriele's physical vitality was undermined in the birth of her child. One might say that the art versus life theme is especially manifest here in the contrast of the ethereal beauty of Gabriele with the physical robustness of her son.

Gabriele's husband, Herr Klöterjahn, is depicted as the quintessential bourgeois. By contrast, Spinell, the resident author at the sanatorium with a sensitive appreciation of the Empire style, is strikingly similar to Gabriele in heart and spirit. The pure and ethereal nature of Gabriele is complemented by the youthfulness and gentleness of Spinell's presence. Spinell is an aesthete who values manifestations and images of beauty in the world around him. As an intuitive disciple of the aesthetic movement nurtured by Wilde among others, Spinell admires various man-made and natural objects for their beauty and grace. The literary work which he created shows, not surprisingly, a considerable devotion to this approach to life, to the attempt to find and cherish the beautiful. The scenes of his work take place in elegant boudoirs filled with rich art objects and treasures from delicate porcelain to antique furniture and tapestries.

Although Spinell seems typically antisocial and does not actively seek companionship in the sanatorium world, he is very attracted by the presence of Gabriele Klöterjahn. Spinell appears to be captivated by Gabriele and her physical beauty at first sight and shows her great reverence and admiration. Inge Diersen states in *Thomas Mann: Episches Werk, Weltanschauung, Leben* that Spinell does not truly love Gabriele and is not really interested in the real person Gabriele Klöterjahn. Instead, Spinell is using Gabriele's presence to create a sense of aesthetic harmony or unity between her inner being and her lovely appearance (Diersen 50). It is noteworthy that Gabriele does not repulse Spinell and even asks him various questions about his life and the sanatorium. Spinell even admits to Gabriele that he is really in Einfried because of his feeling for style, suggesting that there is no dangerous illness with which he is dealing. He appreciates the fact that Einfried has an interesting architectural history and used to be a castle. Spinell proclaims that he admires the Empire style, of which the sanatorium is a perfect example, considerably and that its "brightness and hardness, this cold, austere simplicity and reserved strength" (327) gives him a sense of purification and rebirth. Gabriele's response that she is able to appreciate what he means by this statement suggests that there is an emotional and spiritual consanguinity and connectedness between them which she does not seem to have with her husband.

In a subsequent conversation which occurs after several days of lovely weather which reinforces the sanctuary-like atmosphere of the sanatorium world, Spinell asserts that he prefers to view beautiful women with a fleeting glance because then he does not have to take into account the reality of their blemishes and imperfections. Gabriele seems to understand the essence of Spinell's claim. There is an aura of independence and freedom which such a stance of distance from the exigencies of everyday reality offers and which Gabriele appreciates and admires. At the end of this particular conversation Spinell appears to imply that he admires Gabriele greatly and believes that she has a countenance of "lofty nobility" (330). Gabriele's conversations with Spinell and her reflections on him and his unusual ideas revitalize her emotionally and lead to a more personal and introspective understanding of herself and her inclinations.

The increasing conversational intimacy between Spinell and Gabriele is revealed in the verbal exchange in which he says that he detests the name "Klöterjahn" as a vile designation and asks about her maiden name. In approving of her maiden name, Eckhof, Spinell asks Gabriele to tell him more about herself if this would not exhaust her. Gabriele begins her personal narrative by saying that she was born in one of the old gabled merchant houses of Bremen and that her father was an artist and a businessman. She praises exuberantly the violin playing of her father, saying that his exquisite musical artistry would bring her to tears. Spinell says to Gabriele that he believes her contention that her father's violin playing could bring her to tears. He proceeds to inquire whether her family has been living in the same old revered house for generations. Gabriele's answer in the affirmative leads Spinell to make an especially subtle observation about the interrelation of the artistic and bourgeois worlds.

Spinell declares insightfully that "a race with sober, practical bourgeois traditions will towards the end of its days flare up in some form of art" (332). This is a vital theme in Mann's work, manifesting itself in such other narratives as *Tonio Kröger*, *Der Tod in Venedig*, and *Buddenbrooks*. What Gabriele says about her own personal and musical background and her father's violin-playing is reminiscent of the musical ability of Gerda Buddenbrook and her father. Not only Gabriele and Gerda, but also their fathers are capable and sensitive musicians. While Spinell, in making the above statement about the artistic culmination of a seemingly solid bourgeois tradition, is presumably thinking primarily of the Eckhof family and dynasty, one might suggest that such an observation could apply to his own situation as well. The appreciation which Spinell shows for Gabriele's socioeconomic background and heritage implies that this milieu is not unknown to him and that his own past life was at least to some extent rooted in such an environment. In fact, one might claim that this is an essential personal characteristic which Spinell and Gabriele share—each is an "artist who is at the same time a bourgeois" (Brennan 24) and thus "must cope with inner tension as well as external isolation" (Brennan 24). Gabriele and Spinell are kindred spirits who have strong artistic inclinations and sentiments as well as bourgeois interests and values.

Gabriele's further statements are especially revealing about her past and about her world-view. Her statement that her father is more of an artist than some who promote themselves as such and receive public acclaim suggests a capacity for critical awareness which one might not have expected from the initial description of her character. Gabriele's subsequent delineation of the special moments when she and her father performed musically together (she on the piano and he on the violin) leads her to describe as well the lovely garden in the back of her house where she spent many hours. This garden is presented as a hermetic, "timeless" place of decay. It is described as very overgrown and "shut in by crumbling, mossy walls" (333). There was a fountain surrounded by lilies in the center of the garden. Such a garden is a sanctuary, an enclosed place of personal beauty secluded from the world of everyday mortality. Like the garden in the back of the Kröger house in *Tonio Kröger* which Tonio admires so much, this special garden in the back of the Eckhof mansion possesses a timeless atmosphere and an extraordinary charm for the individuals such as Gabriele who have the sensitivity to appreciate it.

This conversation displays and reinforces what the other exchanges and discussions between Spinell and Gabriele have suggested both implicitly and explicitly:

namely, that Spinell seems to see a special beauty in Gabriele which no one else, not even her husband, Herr Klöterjahn, does. For example, Spinell, in reflecting upon the image of Gabriele and her friends in the garden, says that she was a queen among all of them and that she wore a little gold crown in her hair. Even though Gabriele outwardly denies this, although inwardly she is undoubtedly flattered by such a contention, Spinell states further that if he had been present in this garden scenario, he would have seen the crown on her head. The beautiful image and aura which Spinell has tried to create, which illustrates his admiration of Gabriele, is diminished and sublimated when she speaks about Herr Klöterjahn's arrival and proposal.

Gabriele reflects often upon the comments and ideas of Spinell which had encouraged her to think more about her own life. When Spinell talks with her he does so in a quiet demeanor of reverence and admiration "as though he would lift her higher and higher on the tide of his devotion until she rested on billowy cushions of cloud where no shrill sound nor any earthly touch might reach her" (335). Such an emotionally vital statement is reminiscent in spirit of the comment which Daisy makes to Gatsby in Fitzgerald's *The Great Gatsby* that she would like to push him around in a pink cloud. Gabriele experiences inwardly a sense of elevation of spirit through this feeling of being soothed so immeasurably. That Spinell's comforting words and descriptions have a positive resonating effect on Gabriele is seen especially by the fact that on one occasion she asks him whether he really would have seen the little gold crown on her which he had mentioned in a previous conversation. Spinell responds with strong feeling that he knows he would have seen her wearing the little gold crown as she sat among her friends in the garden of her youth, for he views her in the present, and envisions her in the past as an extraordinary individual, as an individual whose exceptional artistic capacities have been undermined and undervalued by her existential circumstances. It is also noteworthy that the gleam of this crown is described as fleeting, suggesting perhaps a glory which is transient or even that the atmosphere of a sanctuary which permeated this garden would not last.

The cold and clear day at the end of February when many of the residents participated in a sleighing party provides a further opportunity for Gabriele and Spinell to meet and converse, for they are not joining the excursion. In the afternoon Spinell and Gabriele happen to meet in the salon of the sanatorium. In one remark Spinell considers the issue of the sunlight. He says that after several weeks of exuberant sunshine a little cloudiness would be welcome. Spinell's comment that the absence of the direct sunlight may inspire profundity of thought is somewhat reminiscent of Ruskin's statements, in speaking enthusiastically about Turner's paintings, that cloudiness is one of the hallmarks of modern art and that cloudiness reveals the possibility of multiple meanings.

Spinell then asks Gabriele to play the piano, if only briefly. She is very hesitant, declaring that both her doctor at home and Dr. Leander of the sanatorium have forbidden her to play because it might endanger her health. It is noteworthy that Spinell, who has seemed previously to be so concerned about her health and about speaking quietly in her presence so as not to disturb her, now pleads with her several times to play, even though she responds that such activity would probably be injurious to her health. Spinell's aim is to re-create her past, or the glorious past which he has conjured up for her, in a living present. His final appeal to her is generated in his suggestion that if she plays as she used to in her youth then perhaps the little gold crown will once again glisten and shine in her hair. It is also possible that Spinell views Gabriele not as an individual but as a symbol of an existential domain of aesthetic vitality which he had enjoyed in the past or as a type of character whom he had admired in the past. As Spinell is able to afford living in the sanatorium and as he has no conspicuous source of income, it is likely that his socioeconomic background was at least middle-class or upper middle-class or that his family was relatively well-to-do. Perhaps Gabriele might remind Spinell of a musically inclined family member, even a sister, who is deceased or has moved far away and with whom he no longer has contact—his encouragement of her playing the piano might be an implicit attempt to conjure up a vision of part of his own congenial past.

Gabriele's yearning for the pristine past, for the delightful past of her childhood, coincides with Spinell's quest for beauty, for a rich aesthetic experience, and she decides to play. The first composition which Gabriele plays is Chopin's nocturne in E-Flat major. Her beautiful playing inspires her to play two more nocturnes, which she does with grace and sensitivity. Even her dress with its velvet arabesques contributes to the aesthetic vitality of the moment, for it reinforces her unearthly appearance. Spinell is enraptured by her playing and finds a special piece in one of the black-bound volumes which he gives to her. This is Wagner's important operatic version of *Tristan and Isolde*.

Gabriele plays with brilliance and reverence. The culmination of her playing is described as follows: "Here two forces, two beings, strove towards each other, in transports of joy and pain; here they embraced and became one in delirious yearning after eternity and the absolute"(341). Such a moment could be seen as symbolic of the relation of Gabriele and Spinell. For in this musical scenario their spirits achieve a dynamic unity in their mutual longing for beauty and eternity. In the Second Act the emotional, physical, and spiritual union of the lovers Tristan and Isolde is reinforced. The dynamic intensity of this poignantly powerful music represents the emotional and spiritual connectedness and unity of Gabriele and Spinell. As the music soars in profound longing the spirits of Gabriele and Spinell are united in a precious moment of ecstasy. Or one might interpret this episode as signifying two individuals each of whom enjoy this aesthetic experience in his or her own emotional and intellectual realm.

There is also an implication here that through this exquisite musical performance Gabriele is also connecting her past and present selves in a vital spirit of continuity. Her marriage to Herr Klöterjahn had distanced her and separated her spirit from her beautiful past, her very congenial childhood and youth. Spinell's presence and encouragement have enabled her to reestablish the emotional and spiritual connection with this beautiful past, as fleeting as it might be. The transient dimension of this moment is implied by the presence of Frau Pastor Höhlenrauch, the patient who had born fourteen children and had lost her mental vitality—she is an indication of death and a sign that love does not last forever. As the Frau Pastor leaves the room Gabriele plays the finale, Isolde's song of love and death. As Gabriele plays the little blue vein in her brow becomes especially prominent. Her extraordinarily sensitive playing captures the passion, redemption, and fulfillment of the artistic work. She plays with such sensitivity that this moment could be described as an artistic fulfillment of her life. The negative dimension of this experience is that Gabriele has by such excessive physical activity ensured her imminent physical demise. Todd Kontje says in *The Cambridge Introduction to Thomas Mann* that on "one level, *Tristan* is a burlesque of Wagner's opera, with Klöterjahn in the role of King Mark, Gabriele as Isolde, and Spinell as Tristan, although in this case the infidelity never goes beyond the shared passion for Wagner's music" (39).

When Gabriele finishes playing, there is a profound silence, for both she and Spinell are entranced by the performance. W. E. Berendsohn describes this shared musical experience of Gabriele and Spinell, nurtured by both the sensitivity of the pianist and the enraptured attentiveness of the listener, as a "noble converse of souls" (34). Through "the mighty elevation of the music" (Berendsohn 34) Gabriele and Spinell have attained a dynamic sense of emotional and spiritual union and a sense of transcendence. The silence is disturbed by the sound of bells—the return of the sleighing party reintroduces the time of everyday mortality which had been seemingly suspended during the rapture of the musical performance. Spinell does not verbally thank Gabriele for her delightful playing; however, as he is on the verge of leaving the room he falls upon his knees holding his hands clasped in a gesture of emotional vitality. One might describe this as Spinell's prayer of thanks or expression of gratitude to Gabriele, for she has given him an exquisite aesthetic experience. In fact, one could argue that she has more than fulfilled his longing for a beautiful and moving aesthetic experience. In kneeling down perhaps Spinell is also praying for Gabriele and her well-being. For, despite his apparent disregard of her physical condition by asking her to play the piano in the first place since he knew this might be dangerous, he does feel emotionally attached to her and does not want her life to be diminished or shortened. And he senses that she signifies a soul-mate. Spinell might even be praying to the aura of the Empire style which had allowed him to have such a rich aesthetic and sensual adventure. Perhaps Spinell is even praying to a divine realm to preserve the well-being of Gabriele and to allow him to sustain the memory of this entrancing experience for many years to come.

There is no direct verbal exchange between Gabriele and Spinell after this momentous occasion, for there does not need to be. Their souls have achieved an eternal communion in the world of the spirit which does not require conversational expression. The musical performance, as impressive as it was, has certainly placed a considerable strain on Gabriele's physical well-being. And yet, there is a simultaneous sense that despite this physical weakening, Gabriele's spirit has been healed: "Fancy and thought alike are lost, merged in the mystic shade that spread its wings of healing above their madness and despair" (342). Gabriele knew intuitively that playing the piano would harm her physical well-being, but she is willing to proceed because she also is aware that her musical performance will heal her heart and soul. Such a devotion to music coupled with an awareness that musical performance will have a negative impact on one's physical condition is seen in various works of romantic literature. There is in Gabriele something of the demeanor and life-philosophy of Antonia in E. T. A. Hoffmann's *Rat Krespel* who is willing to sing although she knows that such physical exertion will cause her demise.

The letter which Spinell subsequently writes to Herr Klöterjahn emphasizes the necessity of writing and of creative expression, tries to elevate Gabriele's personal story to the level of myth, and reinforces the distinction between the life-philosophies of the artist and of the bourgeois. Spinell effectively captures the scene from Gabriele's past when she enjoyed a blissful and emotionally pure existence in the sanctuary of the garden behind her patrician house. In accusing Klöterjahn of having spoiled the purity and integrity of this scene, Spinell also suggests that this businessman never understood the qualities which made the garden sanctuary so special such as the "presence" of the golden crown on Gabriele. Spinell's depiction of Gabriele's family, the Eckhofs, as having become too exhausted and refined for the action of everyday life and as having reached a culmination in vital aesthetic expression is strongly reminiscent of the description of protagonists in other narratives by Thomas Mann. Tonio Kröger, in *Tonio Kröger*, is not interested in pursuing a business career as so many of his forbears and devotes himself to writing and aesthetic expression—he signifies the last of the Krögers and the artistic culmination of the family and its commercial enterprise. Hanno Buddenbrook in *Buddenbrooks* is similarly not interested in the family business and is instead attracted by more aesthetic pursuits—as Tonio Kröger in his narrative, Hanno appears to represent in *Buddenbrooks* the conclusion of the family line.

In his emotionally intense letter Spinell criticizes Klöterjahn as being a "plebeian gourmand" (349) who lured Gabriele out of the pleasant refuge of her overgrown garden into the misery and ugliness of everyday mortality. Spinell's disdain for Klöterjahn is manifest throughout the letter, from his implication of the businessman's infidelity and flirtatious activity with chambermaids to his direct avowal of his hatred for him. In Schopenhauerean terms Klöterjahn represents the will to live while Spinell signifies the capacity of the imagination to create a vision of a better, more beautiful, and more humane world. Even though Spinell effectively makes his critical argument against Klöterjahn, who is clearly not worthy of the beautiful

Gabriele, he does not seem to be aware of the fact that his treatment of Gabriele is less than reverential in its own right. For example, one might wonder whether Spinell views Gabriele as an individual worthy of admiration in her own right or as a symbol of artistic vitality who may inspire others to greater aesthetic feeling and expression. This issue is reminiscent of a similar theme in Nathaniel Hawthorne's "The Birthmark." In this narrative Aylmer, a scientist, treats his noble and self-sacrificial wife, Georgiana, as an object and as a symbol of potential earthly "perfection" in persuading her to undergo an experiment to remove her birthmark. Aylmer selfishly does not think about the consequences which the dangerous experiment might have for Georgiana—instead, he desires to prove his ability as a scientist and uses Georgiana as a pawn in this endeavor which ultimately kills her.

As Klöterjahn has used Gabriele to achieve some of his desires and goals in the world of everyday mortality, Spinell has in a sense used her to attain a heightened experience of aesthetic vitality. He knew that playing the piano could jeopardize her health, but he implored her to play nonetheless. Spinell accuses Klöterjahn of having coveted the deathly beauty of Gabriele—yet, one might also say that he is to some extent guilty of having done this by imploring her, despite her fragile physical condition, to play the nocturnes and *Tristan*.

Spinell even admits that he has to some extent contributed to Gabriele's physical weakening when he asserts that "if at the very last she has lifted herself out of the depths of degradation, and passes in an ecstasy, with the deathly kiss of beauty on her brow" (350), he has been responsible for that. Spinell views himself as the one who has liberated Gabriele from the degeneration of everyday mortality and has enabled her to achieve a heightened spiritual and aesthetic awareness. The ecstasy of which Spinell speaks is reminiscent of the emotional intensity and ecstatic energy which Walter Pater mentions in *The Renaissance* as being essential to a vital existence. Spinell's aesthetic philosophy is also infused with the spirit of the l'art pour l'art movement and he certainly shares the motivation of such writers as T. Gautier who believed in the supreme importance of art and in the power of art over the exigencies and idiosyncrasies of everyday mortality.

The animosity which Spinell feels towards Klöterjahn and the bourgeois world which he represents is very evident in the last paragraph of the letter. In reaffirming his strong dislike of Klöterjahn, especially because of what he has done to Gabriele, her aesthetic capacities, and the spirit of beauty which she represents, Spinell declares that his letter is an act of revenge. Yet, he acknowledges that his only weapon is the word and that his only defense against the bourgeois world of Klöterjahn is his linguistic vitality. The last three paragraphs of the letter demonstrate that Spinell, although not overtly conscious of his own possible negative impact on Gabriele's well-being, vigorously defends her and her potential to create artistic beauty in a world, the bourgeois world of everyday mortality, which does not instinctively or truly appreciate such beauty and such aesthetic refinement. That Gabriele played the piano so melodiously and dynamically supports Spinell's claim, made both implicitly and explicitly, that she is a very sensitive and talented artist and a symbol of the world of beauty.

Herr Klöterjahn's response to Spinell's caustic letter is to address him directly, not only angrily criticizing the author and various phrases which he uses but also suggesting that he would be contacting his lawyer at home regarding the issue of defamation of character. In the midst of his verbal attack on Spinell someone comes to inform Klöterjahn that his wife has brought up a considerable amount of blood and that her demise seems inevitable. Spinell is certainly to some extent responsible for the physical demise of Gabriele for he encouraged her to play the piano although he sensed or knew that such musical activity could or would harm her physical health. Inge Diersen discusses this situation effectively in *Thomas Mann: Episches Werk, Weltanschauung, Leben*, stressing the blame which should be attributed to Spinell: "Die Verführung zur 'Todesschönheit' hat wirkliches Sterben zur Folge" (52). After Klöterjahn leaves to see his wife, Spinell admits to himself that he cannot endure too many of life's crude and harsh experiences. He decides to take a walk in the garden to restore his inner tranquillity. As Spinell walks outside he looks up at one of the sanatorium windows, presumably that of Gabriele, in profound reverie. The spacious garden is bathed in golden afternoon sunlight. He is enjoying the luminescent tranquility and even hums the motif of longing from the musical composition which he had recently heard. Farther down the path Spinell suddenly sees the figure of a robust child, Gabriele's son, joyfully screaming in the presence of his nurse. Shocked and dismayed to view this figure who had been the cause of a considerable amount of Gabriele's physical suffering and who reminds him so unerringly of Herr Klöterjahn, Spinell walks away from the noise to recover a sense of serenity in another destination.

In *Tristan*, unlike in *Tonio Kröger* and *Der Tod in Venedig*, life, in the literal and symbolic figures of the bourgeois world, appears to triumph over art, over the artistic life-philosophy. In *Tonio Kröger* Tonio is emotionally rejuvenated and spiritually revitalized at the end of the narrative. He declares to Lisabeta that when he returns from his northern visit he will devote himself with renewed energy to his creative endeavor. In *Der Tod in Venedig* Aschenbach experiences mortality and dies. However, one might say that he has also achieved artistic and literary fulfillment in his life. For his works are appreciated and valued. And in Venice, although he endures his physical demise, he also experiences an aesthetic awakening in the sense that one of his characters or character-types, namely Tadzio, comes to life. That is, Aschenbach in a sense gives him life by naming him and by depicting him as displaying certain similarities with some of his literary characters. The artistic life-philosophy and the artistic approach to existence is ultimately very potent in both *Tonio Kröger* and *Der Tod in Venedig*.

In *Tristan*, on the other hand, Spinell, the figure of the artist, seems to be running away from the clamor and noise of everyday mortality. Yet, one might also claim that Spinell is merely distancing himself from the disturbing and discordant auditory impressions which confront him. Perhaps Spinell escapes or compels himself to escape outwardly from the coarseness and uncongenial sounds of everyday mortality so that he can return to an inward tranquility. Even if the outdoor environment of the sanatorium has lost its sanctuary-like atmosphere by the presence of the young Klöterjahn, Spinell can always find a sense of spiritual sanctuary within himself, within his memory of the beautiful music which Gabriele played on that special, if at the same time physically debilitating, occasion, within his memory of their intimate conversations which revealed a definite consanguinity of souls, and in his aesthetic experience of the Empire style which, as he claimed earlier in the story, has the effect of a purification and rebirth on him. If one interprets the last paragraph of *Tristan* as suggesting that Spinell will seek within himself the sense of sanctuary, of a special place of self-revitalization and purification, which is so important to him, then perhaps one could argue that the artistic life-philosophy is, as in *Tonio Kröger* and in *Der Tod in Venedig*, strong and vibrant. The noisy presence of the young Klöterjahn causes merely a temporary diminishing of the artistic voice which will be reenergized in the congenial atmosphere of a private sanctuary of aesthetic appreciation and a devotion to beauty infused with the blissful memory of lovely experiences. The title of the story also suggests that the most important event is the musical interlude of Gabriele's playing the lovely music which is motivated thematically by the union of the souls of the two lovers. Ultimately, Spinell's experience of sanctuary is not only an aesthetic one in his room and in the aura of the exquisite musicality but also an emotional one in the communion of two souls who understand and value each other deeply. After the tragic demise of Gabriele, this sense of sanctuary will be perpetually preserved in Spinell's memory of such a profound moment of spiritual awakening and self-revitalization.

Der Zauberberg—Polarity and Spiritual Enhancement

In the essay "Not an Inn, but an Hospital," C. E. Williams emphasizes the connection between the emotional and intellectual adventure which the protagonist of *Der Zauberberg*, Hans Castorp, undergoes and the tradition of the *Bildungsroman*, the novel of personal development and spiritual education (37). The education of Castorp, Williams argues, is achieved by the "process of *Steigerung*, an alchemistic term implying purification, concentration, and intensification" (39). Williams proceeds to say of Castorp that "the hero, relatively callow and conventional to begin with, matures and gains a depth of insight which would have been out of the question in any other context" (39). Castorp is receptive to numerous intellectual and spiritual influences and dimensions of the magic mountain environment, not the least of which are the features of spatial and temporal expansiveness.

Hans Castorp's quest for the magic mountain, characterized by the dynamic process of "Steigerung" (which is based on Goethe's perception of "Polarität" and "Steigerung"), derives its vitality from the following qualities, tendencies, or events: Castorp's familiarity with and intuitive affinity for death; his adoption of the sanatorium world's value-system; his emotional, intellectual, and spiritual attraction to images of timeless, or seemingly timeless, continuity; his hermetically intense discussions with Settembrini, among others, which lead to a greater historical awareness; his own mythological vitality; his burgeoning knowledge of and understanding of time; and his participation in the timeless harmony of nature.

Castorp develops early in his life an intuitive understanding of death, an instinctive appreciation of images of death. The most conspicuous memories of Castorp's parental home are associated with illness and death. The deaths of Castorp's mother, father, and grandfather within the space of only a few years is a tragic experience, although Mann describes this period in his protagonist's life as not seeming to be overwhelmingly or unbearably painful. In his grandfather's house, where Castorp stays after the death of his parents, Castorp develops and strengthens a sense of tradition and continuity which is most effectively expressed through the symbol of the christening basin which exudes a sense of antiquity and timelessness. The house of Castorp's grandfather has interesting architectural features. This house is depicted as "a mansion...built in the early years of the last century, in the northern-classic style of architecture" (19). The parterre contains "chiefly reception-rooms, and a very light and cheerful dining-room, with walls decorated in stucco" (20). The three windows of this room, "draped with wine-coloured curtains, looked out on the back garden" (20). The aura of seclusion and conservative devotion to the past in the mansion is especially exemplified by the portrait of the grandfather, Hans Lorenz Castorp. The spirit of the house seems to emanate from and be affirmed by this impressive painting.

The intuitive understanding of death in the "flatland" becomes an affinity for death on the magic mountain in the spirit of the sympathetic attitude towards death expressed by several German Romantic writers. Novalis, for example, asserts the necessity of physical illness to inspire creative vitality. Friedrich Schlegel views illness as a spiritual force. E. T. A. Hoffmann writes in *Rat Krespel (Councillor Krespel)* of an artist whose physical weakness is the source of her creative genius, her stunningly beautiful voice, as well as of her ultimate demise. The awareness of illness as the spiritual means to an intellectual and emotional awakening and not as something problematic, disturbing, or disgraceful is found in several of Mann's early narratives, especially in *Der kleine Herr Friedemann, Little Herr Friedemann,* 1898 and later in *Der Tod in Venedig, Death in Venice* (1912).

The eight-year-old Hans Castorp is described as having a sensation of time as both flowing and persisting, of recurrence in continuity. The experience of a sense of timeless continuity is associated with Castorp's intuitive appreciation of death. As he listens to his grandfather mention the family names on the christening basin,

Castorp appreciates the profound connectedness between the present and the past and seems to have a sensory experience of the solemn and tranquil atmosphere of church vaults and of other such secluded places. Castorp's appreciation of and reverence for death are intimately connected to his feeling of religious awe.

The christening basin is one of various objects in the mansion of Castorp's grandfather which have an aura of tradition. Another important image is that of the grandfather's life-size portrait which had previously hung in his parent's house and now had been returned to the grandfather's mansion. This painting, which shows Senator Hans Lorenz Castorp in his official role as Councillor, is permeated by the spirit of a past world of administrative and commercial vitality. This painting is very important to Hans Castorp for he feels that it signifies the true image and essence of his grandfather. Such an image is also very similar to the final posture of his grandfather as he lies dead in his coffin. The young Castorp, although emotionally saddened by this individual's death, feels that even in death this figure represents the authentic and official image and spirit of his grandfather. The figure of his grandfather is vitally important for Castorp, as Michael Beddow asserts in his essay, *"The Magic Mountain"*: "With hardly any recollection of his parents, his most influential memory from early childhood is the figure of his grandfather, who had to the last used his considerable political influence to fight the 'spirit of the new age'" (141).

Mann speaks of Castorp's familiarity with death at an early age and his mature, responsible, and thoughtful response to such familiarity. Castorp sees death as a two-dimensional condition: on the one hand, it represents a holy and spiritual state, characterized by mournful beauty. On the other hand, it is a material and physical condition which does not have anything spiritual about it.

After the death of his grandfather, Castorp is taken in by the family of his guardian, Consul Tienappel, an uncle of his deceased mother. The sale of the firm of Castorp and Son provides Hans with a substantial inheritance. Castorp, while growing up in this luxurious environment, develops a sensitive awareness of the world around him as well as an appreciation of fine living. For example, he does not at all like to have a rough spot or blemish on his shirt cuffs. And he considerably enjoys fine dining, although his teeth have developed a number of cavities. While Castorp believes in the importance of work, he also finds that he can become overly tired with excessive and prolonged stress. The Tienappel house possesses the ambience of a solid bourgeois existence, reinforced by the surrounding garden in which all of the weeds were removed.

As a child and as a young man Castorp reveals certain qualities which will later distinguish him as an appropriate member of the Berghof world. Of paramount importance are Castorp's personal sensitivity and his intuitive familiarity with death. Castorp's difference from the "flatland" world to which he seems to belong so perfectly is suggested by his artistic talent, as undeveloped as it still is. For example, at age fifteen Castorp produces a watercolor of a graceful ship which shows artistic talent. Castorp, being peaceful and interested in a solid career, chooses, with encouragement from a family friend, to study ship-building. Perhaps he also senses that he may fulfill at least some of his artistic inclinations in such a career. When Castorp appears very fatigued after completing his examinations, the family doctor, Dr. Heidekind, recommends a short rest-cure of several weeks in the mountains after which he would join the ship-building firm of Tunder and Wilms.

Another quality of Castorp which suggests that he may adapt well to the sanatorium world where he plans to take his three-week rest-cure, is his penchant for mild pleasures and material comfort—his strong respect for work is balanced by his disinclination to become overwhelmed by it and to devote himself to it too strenuously. Such an attitude is reminiscent of the strategy of Hugh Conway in James Hilton's *Lost Horizon*: "He was enjoying that pleasant mingling of physical ease and mental alertness which seemed to him, of all sensations, the most truly civilized" (85).

Castorp's journey to the Berghof Sanatorium in Switzerland foreshadows the tumultuousness and the timeless vitality of his sanatorium experience. As the journey from Hamburg to the mountainous region of Davos culminates in a steep and steady climb that seems endless, Castorp's Berghof experience will be a dynamic and intense emotional and intellectual adventure. The description of Castorp's journey foregrounds the predominant importance of space—"Space...possessed and wielded the powers we generally ascribe to time" (4).

The experience of novel and seemingly endless space leads Castorp to a sense of inner freedom and forgetfulness, which will manifest itself as an increasing lack of concern for the responsibilities of the world of the flatland as he spends more time at the Berghof. Through his experience of an expansive space Castorp gains a profound sense of timelessness. There is also the implication in this passage that an experience of a vibrant sense of space can produce a self-transformation in an individual. As the train proceeds away from the flatland into the mountainous domain Castorp neglects the book, *Ocean Steamships*, a symbol of his future profession, which he had brought along. This is significant because it suggests the possibility that as Castorp ventures farther into the mountains he will be less dependent on previous conceptions and more open to new influences.

The ambience of timeless space is at the heart of the Berghof experience. The sanatorium world, like the world of Shangri-La in Hilton's *Lost Horizon*, possesses and affirms a sense of timelessness through its physical isolation from the everyday world. In the initial conversation between Castorp and his cousin, Joachim implies not only that Hans will experience things which he has never dreamed of but also that he will encounter a new sense of time. Castorp is initially skeptical about Joachim's notion of spending so much time at the Berghof and is not overly impressed by the alpine landscape. However, Castorp gradually does develop an appreciation of the sense of time, that is, the aura of timelessness, which the Berghof offers. And he assumes in time, and without much difficulty, the carefree, even Bohemian, approach to life and mortality at the sanatorium.

The Berghof Sanatorium with its luminescent halls, reception rooms, elegant restaurant, individual rooms for the patients and residents, the dining hall with its seven tables, arched bays, pillars, and electric chandeliers, general rest-hall, domestic offices, and other essential chambers signifies a magnificent architectural creation with a distinctive aura of timelessness. The lovely natural landscape surrounding the Berghof helps to affirm and sustain the atmosphere of timelessness and decay which pervades it. On the one hand, the Berghof represents a medical establishment which is focused on the reality of trying to cure or ameliorate the pain and suffering of the ill or seriously ill patients. On the other hand, for those patients who are only slightly ill and who are not in a life-threatening situation and for those individuals who are visiting or who work at the sanatorium, this environment offers an extraordinary ambience for reflection, solitude, aesthetic appreciation, and admiration of the beauty of nature as well as for companionship and interesting conversation.

The room, Number 34, which Castorp is given at the International Sanatorium Berghof, appears to possess the aura of a sanctuary of light. When the ceiling light is turned on, the room is flooded with light and reveals an ambience of cleanliness and purity. Yet, despite the peaceful luminescence which pervades the room, reinforced by the gesture of Joachim's placing a bouquet of flowers on the chest of drawers, the fact is that a woman had died in that room shortly before Castorp's arrival. Castorp's sensation of feeling cold and his hearing the horrific cough of the Austrian aristocrat as they proceed to the restaurant, however, dampen somewhat the positive impressions. That the Berghof may be interpreted as a "sanctuary" not only of light but also of decay and death is suggested in this episode, for example, by the presence of the isolated woman in the restaurant, who, it is said, has lived from her early youth in various tuberculosis sanatoriums and has never been a part of the everyday world.

Castorp's room number 34 is one of various instances in the novel which suggest, implicitly or explicitly, the importance of the number seven. Castorp will spend seven years on the "magic mountain." Ignace Feuerlicht argues effectively in *Thomas Mann* that the number seven has an essential significance in this novel:

> Castorp is orphaned at seven and he makes the fateful decision to leave for Davos 'in the last days of July' (the seventh month) of 1907.... Castorp stays there for seven years.... There are seven tables in the dining room;... Toward the end of his stay in the *Berghof*, Castorp sits at a table with six others.... The novel has seven chapters; the first volume ends after seven months; and the crucial section "Snow" is the seventh section of chapter VI. (29–30)

Feuerlicht suggests that one reason for such a consistent use of the number seven in the novel is that Mann believed in the special significance of certain numbers (30).

At the beginning of Chapter III it is evident that the aura of sanctuary which his room at the sanatorium had initially seemed to be is further undermined, not only by the raucous noises from the couple next door but also by his observation of the pallid elderly lady walking the garden below. While his room is not always the most tranquil place because of the discourteous neighbors, Castorp does occasionally experience a sense of timelessness or atemporality in this location. For example, in "Mental Gymnastic" in Chapter III, Castorp sits on the comfortable chair in his loggia looking out upon the sunny landscape. From this vantage-point the natural landscape "looked like a framed painting as viewed through the arch of the loggia" (67). It is as if the flux of mortality has ceased. This experience of an aura of timelessness is reinforced in the section "Changes" in Chapter VI when Castorp gazes at the silent winter landscape from the chair in his room. The mountain peaks and forests are depicted as being silent as "mortal time flowed over and about them" (346). For at least six months every year these features of the natural landscape are covered with snow. It is as if the mountains and forests, whether illuminated by the sun or shrouded in mist, express a permanence, an existential solidity, which cannot be affected or influenced by the flux of mortality. Such magnificent spaces are beyond the reach of mortality. Their existential vitality may change moderately with the flow of the seasons, but the significant features of the landscape are always revitalized through their eternal cyclicality. The timelessness is further enhanced by the transformational capacity of the natural landscape. For example, in "Changes" Castorp and Joachim observe from the distance an apparent cover of snow on the pasture which upon closer examination turns out to be an extensive display of crocuses.

When Castorp meets Hofrat Behrens the latter says immediately that there is something comfortable about Hans and that he would make a better patient than his cousin Joachim. Soon thereafter Castorp is introduced by Joachim to Settembrini. Castorp's initial impression is that Settembrini reminds him of foreign street musicians in Hamburg. Even though there is some awkwardness in the initial conversation between Castorp and Settembrini, it is noteworthy that the conversation flows.

When Settembrini tells Castorp that he is audacious to have come to the sanatorium as a guest, to have descended into this realm permeated by "the vacant and idle dead" (57), he seems to ascribe a mythological vitality to Castorp or perhaps merely the potential to achieve such a mythological vitality. Settembrini also asserts that the shortest unit of time in the sanatorium world is the month, implying that Castorp's intended three-week stay is not even worth mentioning. In response to Settembrini's praise of Castorp's chosen profession as representing the world of work, Castorp admits later in the conversation that he is actually not a physically robust individual and feels most comfortable when he is not doing anything. Castorp is impressed and entertained by Settembrini's eloquence and his manner of speaking. At the end of the section "Satana" Castorp even admits to Joachim that he especially liked Settembrini's emphasis on human dignity and on the importance of the humanist to express beauty and dignity.

Victor Lange in "Thomas Mann the Novelist" describes the Berghof experience of Castorp thoughtfully as follows:

> Inescapably drawn into the rhythm of life and death, day and night, health and disease, waking and dreaming, musical transcendence and medical diagnosis, all of these soon felt and understood as inescapable polarities, Hans Castorp gradually gains an intense sense of self as well as a heightened perception of the intellectual and political convictions of Europe before 1914. (3)

One might say that Castorp is not merely drawn into such a perpetual rhythm. For he shows instinctively, if not intuitively, a proclivity to participate in and to understand such a rhythm of seemingly irreconcilable oppositions.

Horst S. and Ingrid G. Daemmrich in *Spirals and Circles* interpret the "magic mountain" experience of Castorp in the following insightful manner:

> Hans Castorp moves during his exposure to learning experiences on the Magic Mountain within an infinite spiral of perception—understanding, objectified perception—enhanced understanding toward increasing self-insight and an understanding of the historical forces that shaped the modern world. (2:4)

They proceed to emphasize effectively not only the versatility and devotion but also the sense of liberation which characterize and motivate his learning process:

> Seen in its entirety, his education reveals the story of the human spirit's search for self-explication through the forms of Eros, reflection on nature, historical thinking, metaphysics, science, art, and magic. A series of encounters with representative groups and figures initiates a dialogue between Castorp and human existence.... The incessant dialogue that transforms every observed phenomenon into a living substance propels Castorp from an embryonic stage upward on a spiral that liberates him spiritually. (2:6–7)

Hans Castorp's conversations and discussions with Settembrini signify not only his intellectual awakening; they also offer him a sense of timelessness, a distraction from the momentum of mortality. One reason why Castorp can develop himself intellectually in the magic mountain environment is that he arrives at the Berghof sanatorium with "a mind which is open and impressionable" (69), as W. H. Bruford suggests in his essay "'Bildung in *The Magic Mountain*." Of the importance of Settembrini for Castorp, W. H. Bruford writes: "It is Settembrini who first makes him aware of 'Geist,' of all that the exercise of his inner freedom can mean for him, while confined by illness to the Berghof. It becomes his university, and his spirit blossoms here, as his intellectual interests are gradually aroused" (70). Later in the novel Castorp's appreciation and understanding of the intense intellectual exchanges and oppositions of Settembrini and Naphta are also seemingly timeless moments, moments when he seems doubly removed from the flux of mortality (removed from the physical and intellectual ambience and demands of everyday reality), though the two antagonists often discuss and debate the past or present state of the world.

Fritz Kaufmann argues in *Thomas Mann: The World as Will and Representation* that Mann, by placing Castorp on the magic mountain "lets him thus transcend the world of the plain...and, in a way, transcend himself as well" (97). Although Castorp does not reveal the silent heroism of Joachim "he becomes worthy of being chosen the hero of *The Magic Mountain* because he is venturesome enough to create himself" (98). Such an individual who attempts to create himself anew in a conspicuously different existential context from that to which he is thoroughly accustomed and to rejuvenate and enhance his aesthetic and intellectual awareness shows a distinctive nobility of character. Perhaps Castorp is in a sense even trying to implicitly fulfill the claim of dignity which Settembrini makes in the section "Satana" for the humanist.

In his conversation with Joachim after the initial encounter with Settembrini, Castorp appears to be intellectually enlivened. It is as if the potential within him for intellectual vitality and philosophical speculation has been inspired by the contact with Settembrini's wide-ranging mind and by the Berghof climate. In an ensuing section, "Satana Makes Proposals That Touch Our Honor," Castorp admits to Settembrini that even though he has only been at the Berghof for a day, he feels to some extent as if he has been here for much longer and has gained wisdom during the sojourn.

Despite Settembrini's admonition to leave the Berghof because the environment does not seem to be conducive to him physically or mentally, Castorp intends to stay, not only because he feels he could develop and strengthen his intellectual vitality through Settembrini's guidance, but also because of his attraction for Claudia Chauchat. Moreover, Castorp feels an instinctive attraction to Albin's condition of carefree indifference to society and to the pressures of social responsibility. Castorp appreciates Albin's life-philosophy, especially when he is overwhelmed by the physical, atmospheric effects of the Berghof environment. For example, at one point Castorp describes himself as extremely fatigued and also feeling as if he were dreaming and trying to awake from such a state but is unable to do so.

In one of his dreams in "Satana Makes Proposals" at the end of Chapter III Castorp encounters Hofrat Behrens walking along the garden path. Not only does he imply that Castorp seems suitable as a patient, but he also expresses disappointment that the new arrival will not even give the Berghof one year of service. Ultimately, however, one might claim that instead of taking his apprenticeship at the Hamburg shipbuilding firm, Castorp, perhaps more unconsciously than consciously, fulfills it at the Berghof, giving Behrens considerably more than just one year of dedicated service.

After experiencing intriguing dreams involving Claudia Chauchat and the borrowing of a lead pencil and Dr. Krokowski and the attempted flight from a psychoanalytic evaluation, Castorp has an interesting dream about Settembrini. While Castorp is trying to compel Settembrini, whom he describes as a hand-organ man, to remove himself from the scene, he experiences a sudden epiphanic moment, a moment of personally vital revelation. Castorp gains an insight into the genuine nature of time, realizing that it is "nothing more or less than a 'silent sister,' a mercury column without degrees" (92). This passage is important not only because it suggests that Castorp, despite his own burgeoning mental vitality, feels threatened occasionally by Settembrini's intellectual prowess, but also because it emphasizes the relativity of time, the notion that time is dependent on an individual's perception and conception of its flux.

Such an understanding of time reinforces Castorp's previous philosophizing about time in the section "Mental Gymnastic" when he stresses that the existential condition of time depends on an individual's perception of and perspective on time. With respect to the measurement of time Castorp raises the question how we can possibly measure something about which we know so little and whose characteristics we cannot really adequately describe. After asserting that one assumes that time flows evenly, without knowing absolutely whether this is true, Castorp concludes this reflection on time by saying that the units by which we measure time are merely "arbitrary...conventions" (66). Michael Beddow makes the important point in "*The Magic Mountain*" that Castorp's living "in a perpetual present" (146) and his "loss of a sense of time leads him to start questioning other categories he has previously taken for granted" (146). The aura of timelessness which Castorp feels intuitively and in which he participates so readily also signifies a potent source of his intellectual awakening, a stimulus for his intellectual explorations and investigations.

One other dream which Castorp has on that mentally eventful night when various images and figures cross his fervent imagination is that of Claudia Chauchat coming into the dining room with the seven tables and letting the door crash as usual. However, instead of going to her usual table, she comes quietly to him and gives him the palm of her hand to kiss. As Castorp kisses her hand, which he notices is not well taken care of, he experiences a potent sensation of "reckless sweetness" (92) and carefree abandon.

At the beginning of Chapter IV on the third full day of Castorp's visit, after a pleasantly warm and sunny early August day, there is a snowstorm. Castorp is perturbed by the sudden change in the weather and remains in his room. Joachim's explanation the next day that it may snow during any month of the year and that there are no real seasons in the Berghof ambience reinforces the sense of temporal confusion or continuity which Castorp occasionally feels in this context. One might say that Castorp achieves a sense of timelessness in the Berghof world because it possesses its own sense of time. The sanatorium world reveals an aura of timelessness through the consistent presence of significant features of nature as well as through the existence of a regular schedule of activities at the Berghof.

When Castorp and Joachim return from making certain purchases in the village, they meet Settembrini who is also returning to the sanatorium. The temporal confusion caused by the inclement and uncertain weather seems to be dissipated or sublimated by the conversation of Settembrini, who speaks, for example, of the power of reason, of rationality, and of enlightenment to liberate humanity from its fears and misconceptions and guide it towards a more congenial and humane existence. While Castorp is impressed by the linguistic vitality of Settembrini, Joachim admits that he senses that Settembrini has a considerable respect for humankind. The rich vocabulary of Settembrini and his humanistic precepts will influence Castorp considerably as he refines his own intellectual powers.

In *Thomas Mann: Episches Werk, Weltanschauung, Leben,* Inge Diersen suggests insightfully that through Settembrini's significant influence, Hans Castorp is given the opportunity to experience manifold ideas and intellectual adventures which he never would have encountered in his previous lifestyle (142). Diersen proceeds to argue that the most important influence which Settembrini has on Castorp is to encourage him to develop a sense of humanitarian responsibility: "Er erfährt von einer veränderungsbedürftigen Welt und von der Lebenseinstellung und –haltung eines Menschen, der bereit ist—wenn auch durch Krankheit gehindert—, etwas für die Veränderung zu tun" (142).

In the subsequent excursus on time in Chapter IV, Thomas Mann offers further important reflections on the nature of time and on the relation of habitual activity and the flux of time. Mann suggests that when one performs the same action or does the same thing for an extended period of time the individual experiences an awareness of the slowing-down of time and develops the sense that the flux of time is considerably diminished. Monotony and repetition may contract and dissipate the larger units of time to a sense of being nothing at all. At the end of these reflections about time Castorp, although he has been on the magic mountain only for a short while, says to Joachim that it seems as if he has been here for an eternity.

Hans Castorp, perhaps because he is, like Hugh Conway in Hilton's *Lost Horizon,* not instinctively aggressive or ambitious, enjoys the idea of a rest-cure—Castorp is described as having the capacity to sit for hours without having a distinct occupation. Another reason for this capacity is that Castorp loves to see time spaciously before him—he enjoys the conception or sensation, or perhaps even the illusion, of an ocean of time stretching endlessly before him.

Castorp develops a diastolic sense of time (a sense of the fluidity and openendedness of time) on the magic mountain in the world of the Berghof Sanatorium which becomes a hermetic sense of time upon his departure at the end of the novel to participate in the world war. He also develops a diastolic sense of space, especially in the section in Chapter VI entitled "Snow" where he experiences the aura of an endless landscape. In contrast to Wordsworth's persona in *The Prelude* who achieves a diastolic sense of time through a diastolic sense of space (that is, space precedes time), Mann's protagonist attains a diastolic sense of space after developing an expansive sense of time (that is, time precedes space).

Castorp achieves an expansiveness of self in the spirit of the sublime of Longinus. In his *Analytical Inquiry into the Principles of Taste*, Richard Payne Knight describes the theory of the sublime of Longinus as follows:

> All sublime feelings are, according to Longinus, feelings of exultation and expansion of the mind, tending to rapture and enthusiasm; and whether they be excited by sympathy with external objects, or arise from the internal speculations of the mind, they are still of the same nature. In grasping at infinity the mind exercises these powers...of multiplying without end; and, in so doing, it expands and exalts itself, by which means its feelings and sentiments become sublime. (36)

Such a grasping at infinity is precisely what Mann's protagonist and Wordsworth's "majestic intellect" do in expanding and enriching the self.

Walter E. Berendsohn in *Thomas Mann: Künstler und Kämpfer in bewegter Zeit* describes Hans Castorp as having a capacity "to reflect on everything that crosses his path" (73) and as being "a passive yet very attentive observer and listener in life's theatre with its changing repertoire" (73). Although he is not a grail seeker in the medieval tradition, Castorp does seem to possess a semblance of the modern seeker of the grail of "timelessness." Castorp's intellectual curiosity is essential to any individual seeking to achieve a sense of "Aion." Castorp's "grail-seeking" quest is enhanced not only by his profound simplicity and clarity of thought, which are somewhat reminiscent of the character of Sir Galahad, but also by the fact that he may remain at the Berghof Sanatorium for as long as he wishes to.

Castorp also seems to experience a sense of timelessness through music. Settembrini's discussion of music offers an insight into the capacity of music to express or reinforce a sense of timelessness. Settembrini, though preferring the word to music, says that music through its "life-enhancing method of measuring time" (114) provides a sense of "spiritual awareness and value" (114) to the passage of time. As part of this positive dimension, music accelerates the flow of time so that the individual gains a sense of constructive and meaningful enjoyment in the flux of mortality. To be truly effective, Settembrini suggests, music should be associated with or connected to literature, for otherwise it might only stimulate the emotions without necessarily engaging the reason.

In this discussion about music in "Politically Suspect" Settembrini also expresses his concern that music may also have the effect of an opiate, producing lethargy or inaction. Settembrini claims that music is politically suspect for it is ambiguous—it may lead either to a heightened spiritual awareness or to an intellectual lethargy. One might argue that either aspect of music may encourage the development of a sense of timelessness, but especially the latter. For in its narcotic effect, in its encouragement to inaction, music causes time to slow down or be suspended. A piece of music has its own inner time which replaces the normal flux of time—when one is absorbed in or captivated by a musical composition, external time ceases to exist. The individual establishes his own sense of time from the inner time of the music.

Castorp also experiences a strong sense of timelessness in the Berghof ambience when he gets a cold and a slight fever. The fact that he has become ill affirms Castorp's instinctive association with the sanatorium world. That Castorp "belongs" to the Berghof existential context is reinforced by Behrens who declares that he senses initially that Hans was one of them. Castorp tries to persuade his fellow sanatorium residents that his fever does not mean anything, but they also sense that he instinctively belongs to the Berghof. The sense of timelessness which Castorp experiences when he is sick is emphasized in the section "Soup-Everlasting" which opens Chapter V. The statement is made that when a sick person spends time in bed, time appears to be an everlasting present. Soup-everlasting, the midday broth which is brought everyday, symbolizes the endless temporal continuity of this experience.

Castorp's sense of timelessness when he is sick is reinforced by the fact that he is isolated not only from the Berghof society but also from the community in the world of everyday mortality down below, from the north German community. The protagonist of *Der Zauberberg* responds both positively and negatively to this sense and semblance of timelessness. The splendidly serene isolation pleases him because he may indulge in various reflections and meditations and be free from any arduous responsibility. Yet, he does occasionally miss the contact with some of his fellow Berghof residents. Castorp is grateful to Joachim for his multiple daily visits to bring him companionship and news and to Settembrini who, through his discussions and discourses has provided an endless source of intellectual stimulation and entertainment. It is also noteworthy that Settembrini, when he appears at Castorp's sickchamber, turns on the light, thus literally and symbolically illuminating the patient's existence. Castorp even declares that he almost wishes to keep his fever so that he may continue to listen to Settembrini's thought-provoking ideas for an extended period of time.

In "Soup-Everlasting" after Castorp sends the letter to his uncle saying that he is required to stay longer at the Berghof to achieve a more complete recovery, he follows as carefully as possible the regimen established for him which is motivated by a consistent uniformity of regular activities. On the one hand, this is very convenient because it takes away from the patient the burden or responsibility of making decisions—every part of the day is planned. On the other hand, because of the pervasiveness of the regularity of Berghof time, Castorp feels occasionally that he does not have enough time to focus on and contemplate his own reflections. Despite the negative undertone which such uniformity of daily activities may suggest, this condition also contributes to and leads into the implication of the mythological vitality of the protagonist.

One evening during his sickness Castorp, having just finished the meal which was brought to his room, looks out into the dusk and reflects on the fact that each day appears to fuse indistinguishably with the next. He also senses that time is passing too quickly, for even though it is now evening, he feels that it was just morning.

The day has ended too abruptly. Castorp's reflections culminate in the declaration that "from the beginning of time he had been lying and looking thus" (192). The concern about the inevitable passage of time which is expressed in one of Castorp's statements is balanced by the proclamation in the above-mentioned quotation which evokes the image of the protagonist as a quasi-divine figure, a Promethean personality, in control of time. This is an individual who by the continuity of his physical condition and stance complements the regularity of the Berghof ambience. In assuming an emotional, intellectual, and psychological posture of timeless vitality, Castorp presents himself as a mythological force of hermetic wisdom.

In the section "Sudden Enlightenment" Castorp not only observes Joachim in the X-ray machine in an eye-opening, mind-expanding experience, but he also becomes poignantly aware of his own mortality. As Castorp looks at the skeleton of his own hand and the dissolution of his flesh, he envisions that he is looking into his own grave. The power of this light-ray may be said to be comparable to the vitality of Settembrini's intellect which sheds light on and inspires Castorp's intellectual life challenging and confronting any decline or weakening of the patient's mind. As Castorp experiences a poignant awareness of his own mortality, a penetrating realization that he would someday die, his face wears the same "sleepy, and pious" (219) expression that it does when he listens to music.

Perhaps partially as a self-fortifying and self-revitalizing response to the sudden awareness of his own mortality Castorp writes a declaration of independence from the "flatland" mentality in the next section of the novel. In stressing that the conceptions of time in the Berghof are different from those down below, the patient-engineer suggests his familiarity with various temporal conceptions and strategies and even with time itself. By writing this letter to James Tienappel, an eminent representative of the world of everyday mortality, and saying that he must for health reasons prolong his sojourn at the sanatorium, Castorp reaffirms his sense of timelessness. Even though Castorp supports his experience of timelessness by articulating his situation so effectively, he nevertheless feels the physical strain of such activity. For Castorp, as for Mann himself, who asserted that writing was an arduous and a challenging endeavor, the completion of such a literary composition is not achieved without paying a price for "plucking a leaf off the laurel-tree of art."

One interesting point which Mann makes at the beginning of "Whims of Mercurius" in Chapter V is that there is never a major natural event or loud celebration to designate the beginning of a new month or year. There are no outward signs or indications to mark such an event for time moves quietly onward. In the Berghof world various individuals do not feel a need to loudly proclaim the beginning of a new month or year. Castorp reveals a similar approach to the flux of time. In "Whims of Mercurius," for example, he is described as not concerning himself with the flow of units of time. He had not noticed the beginning of October of this particular year, for example, instead telling time by the physical sensations which the season was arousing. The elaboration of the importance of sensation continues and leads into the description of the intensification of Castorp's infatuation with Claudia Chauchat. The anguish which he feels after the careless look which she gives him is transformed into a sense of rapture when she smiles at him and says good-morning on another occasion.

In the next section of Chapter V, "Encyclopedic," Settembrini admonishes Castorp to be wary of the Eastern carelessness and recklessness with respect to time. Settembrini seems to be concerned not only about the excessive influence of Eastern ideas on his young protégé, but also about the potentially dangerous presence of that symbol of intellectual lethargy and sensuality, Claudia Chauchat. Settembrini presents a generalized argument that the individuals from the East are so reckless with time because they are a people of seemingly endless space and expansive spaces. In contrast, Settembrini asserts that the Europeans, because of a less exuberant and in some cases limited space, must be more economical with time. He concludes this line of argument by reasserting part of the rationalist's credo: "Time is a gift of God, given to man that he might use it...to serve the advancement of humanity" (243). As a member of the International League for the Organization of Progress, Settembrini maintains a fervent belief in the possibility of humankind to achieve a more humane and more noble existence in the future. As a corollary to this point Fritz Kaufmann asserts that Castorp liberates himself from the connections and privileges of the bourgeois world, of the nineteenth-century Buddenbrooks society, in the quest for a higher realm of existence and social awareness "which is ultimately not Hans Castorp's mystical trance but the true world-citizenship, the loyalty to earth and man, for which he is secretly fitted by his education on the magic mountain" (101).

At the beginning of the section, "Humaniora," the description of the serene and radiant alpine environment around the Berghof appears to displace any lingering thoughts about the violent potential of nature exemplified in the catastrophic earthquake previously mentioned. The sky possesses a deep blue color, the pastures are a pleasant green, and the sound of cowbells creates an ambience of peacefulness in the natural environment as a complement to the aura of solemnity in this mountainous region. One of the most important aspects of the aura of timelessness which Castorp tries, consciously as well as unconsciously, to sustain at the Berghof is such a mood of solemnity. In its own right solemnity is not only conducive to affirming a sense of timelessness and atemporality; it is also intimately related to the intuitive familiarity with death and with the atmosphere of death which Castorp experienced in his childhood and youth.

The seclusion which Hans and Joachim feel as they sit at the end of the garden on this bright October day appreciating the natural landscape is a prelude to their experience of Behrens' secluded private apartments and painting gallery as this section develops. As in other narratives by Mann, for example, *Buddenbrooks,* there is a room or a special space in a sizeable house or great house which contains artworks of supreme significance. The middle-class atmosphere of the furnishings of the rooms of Hofrat Behrens is transformed by his art and artistic explorations into an aesthetic wonderland. The paintings which Behrens shows the two cousins signify various interesting landscapes and several portraits. There are paintings and photographs of his deceased wife, as well as a portrait of Claudia Chauchat in the living-room. There are also mountain landscapes, pastoral sketches, still-lifes, and flower-pieces. Such a gallery is at the heart of the Berghof sanatorium. Or, one might say, such rooms with Behrens' artistic expressions, represent part of the heart and soul of the International Sanatorium Berghof. Castorp is most struck and intrigued by the portrait of Claudia Chauchat, which Behrens says was the result of numerous sittings. As Castorp moves the portrait of Claudia Chauchat to a spot where it will receive more light, he is inspired to offer several interesting reflections, especially the notion that an interest in form, a desire for the attainment of a beautiful form or beautiful forms, is at the heart of the humanistic endeavor. The quest for the beautiful is a noble endeavor. The congenial discussion between Hofrat Behrens and Castorp ends with the Hofrat saying that he feels rather melancholy, although he also declares that he enjoyed the presence of Castorp and Joachim considerably.

In "Research" Castorp preserves his increasingly more resilient Berghof sense of timelessness, which may even be described as atemporality, by not celebrating the Christmas season with his family in the world below. Christmas represents a temporal landmark, a particular moment which one may use to transcend intervening spaces. Castorp seems not to cherish the notion of the Christmas holiday because it undermines the fluidity of Berghof time and challenges the continuity of timelessness which has become so important to him. One particular depiction of the natural environment on a November evening captures the essence of the Berghof atmosphere which at least some of the patients seem so unwilling to leave. The surrounding natural environment is permeated by an enchanted splendor, by the aura of a spellbound trance, sublimating the frailties of the mortal world. The qualities of purity and enchantment are essential to the experience of timelessness in the Berghof environment.

The description of life later in this section as "the existence of the actually impossible-to-exist, of a half-sweet, half-painful balancing...in this restricted and feverish process of decay and renewal" (275–76) applies also to the depiction of the experience of timelessness. For Castorp's condition of timelessness is also an inner warmth created by a moment of ambiguity, an inevitable tension between eternity and mortality, between form and matter. Timelessness, the experience of the timeless moment and a concatenation of timeless moments, is neither life nor death, but a threshold phenomenon. Castorp's experience of timelessness depends at least in part on the presence of an inner tension between life and death and on the provisional unity of such apparently opposing forces.

As a corollary theme to the importance of intellectual awareness and development it is interesting that most of the reading at the Berghof is done by the new-comers and the "short-timers," for the long-term patients of the sanatorium had learned to diminish the significance of time and to overcome the flux of mortality. Castorp, however, reads extensively. After finishing *Ocean Steamships*, his immediate intellectual connection with the "flatland," Castorp orders books from the village on anatomy, physiology, and biology. One culmination of this reading effort, which reflects Castorp's fascination with life and its sacred and impure mysteries, is the sensual daydream which he experiences at the end of "Research" in which a female image of life blossoms over and envelops him in its softness. Inge Diersen discusses thoughtfully in *Thomas Mann* the importance which the atmosphere of the sanatorium and the sense of love have on Castorp and his developing studies: "Angeregt durch die Sanatoriumsatmosphäre, in der sich alles um die Krankheit und somit um den Körper dreht, angeregt aber ebenso durch seine Verliebtheit, beginnt Hans Castorp Studien zu treiben" (144). Castorp is especially interested in books about anatomy and physiology which he studies regularly during the rest-cure.

Castorp's awareness of and reverence for solemnity, intimately linked to his concern for timelessness, is revitalized in the next section of Chapter V, "The Dance of Death." Castorp evokes here the image of a caretaker which places him above the daily anguish and misery of many of his fellow Berghof residents and gives him a semblance of timelessness. In asserting his disagreement with the attempt of the Berghof authority to spare the resident-patients who are not near death from the wretchedness and dying of the difficult cases, Castorp says that he decided to concern himself with the individuals who are seriously ill. In visiting occasionally the "children of death," Castorp satisfies a spiritual need within himself while also fulfilling his inclination as a "caretaker" of other souls. One might think that such visiting of terminally ill patients could endanger the life of Castorp, "life's delicate child" (308), as Settembrini calls him. Yet, perhaps such an inclination is also a sign of Castorp's own heroic, self-sacrificial approach which will ultimately lead him back down into the world to participate in the military cataclysm at the end of the novel.

In the process of visiting the dying patients, Castorp, who has an innate desire to treat suffering and death with reverence, becomes increasingly more serious and reflective. Or perhaps one might claim that the Berghof environment has inspired Castorp's potential for contemplation and reflective thought and has encouraged his instinctively charitable nature and humanistically motivated capacity to blossom and to thrive. As Henry Hatfield astutely points out, the visits which Hans makes to the dying show not only his fascination with death but also suggest "that truly felt knowledge of death makes a person more humane" (43).

One afternoon Castorp and Joachim even take one of the dying patients, Karen, to the theater in the Platz to view a pageant of vibrant mortal existence. They also escort Karen to the cemetery on the slope of the Dorfberg which contains mostly graves of people who died when they were young, who were usually not more than twenty years old. That the genius of this place seems to be a stone angel or cupid which embodies the profound silence could be viewed as a parallel to the rooms of Behrens which contain his paintings and which, in some sense, could signify the artistic heart of the Berghof. The cemetery visit constitutes a sobering experience; yet, it is also a symbolic reinforcement of the aura and tone of the sanatorium world, an existential context pervaded by decay and death but also by a sense of everlasting peace, a sense of timelessness, of timeless serenity, of a deep and profound stillness. That Castorp is not concerned about his contact with terminally ill patients is also perhaps a sign of his instinctive and subconscious awareness of his own mythological vitality.

The beginning of Chapter VI, entitled "Changes," does describe significant alterations in the life of the Berghof Sanatorium. There is the gradual, difficult birth of the spring from the pervasive presence of the long winter. Such determination to overcome the omnipresence of snow reflects and reinforces the courageous persistence of the Berghof residents in confronting and combating death. Finally, spring emerges radiantly, infusing the solemnity of the sanatorium environment with a vital glimmer of hope. However, the arrival of spring also suggests the flow of mortality, the inevitable flux of time which is or seems to be less prominent when there is "eternal" snow on the magic mountain.

The departure of Claudia Chauchat, for whom Castorp has developed a strong infatuation, upsets the aura of enchantment, of painfully sweet enchantment, which Castorp feels in her presence, whether direct or indirect. Even though Castorp is emotionally distraught by her apparently temporary departure for Daghestan, that he remains in the Berghof world might solidify his sense of timelessness because it demonstrates his capacity to survive and his persistent existence at the sanatorium despite the aura of decay and despite the manifold vicissitudes of life and death which encroach upon its solemn silences.

The move of Settembrini from the sanatorium to a lodging of a chandler in the village nearby is also unsettling to Castorp. In this conversational exchange when he announces his departure Settembrini also emphasizes to Castorp the importance of the positive implications of the motto "Placet experiri." In the spirit of his enlightenment humanism Settembrini argues for the approach to life which engages reason in confronting the powers of darkness. Henry Hatfield in *From The Magic Mountain: Mann's Later Masterpieces* claims that Castorp, in appreciating the importance of Settembrini's motto, "possesses Nietzsche's double perspective. Conservative yet daring, he accepts the traditional "Respice finem' (Think of the end) but corrects it with the Goethean 'Remember to live'" (41). In experiencing such a metaphysical tension Castorp heightens his capacity for intellectual development, for the intellectual awareness which he is eager to strive for and achieve and the guide for which Settembrini is more than willing to be.

Castorp's reflections on time and mortality in "Changes" show not only that his intellectual awareness is being sharpened and strengthened but also that he possesses the inner dedication to the conception of time which an individual who aspires to achieve a sense of timelessness should have and cherish. In the next section, "A New-Comer," Castorp's interest in comprehending the breadth of knowledge is further evidence of his burgeoning intellectual development and vitality. Not only does he make progress in his botanical endeavors and studies, but he shows that he has gained knowledge of the zodiac and of ancient civilizations. Castorp, like his mentor, is strongly interested in the cultural and intellectual progress of humanity. This section reveals Castorp's humanistically ecumenical acceptance of the complexity of the human condition.

In this same passage Castorp asserts his strong awareness of the flux of time and his critical response to the normative perception of time especially wondering about the problematic transitional shifts from one season to another. Castorp also meets Naphta, another tenant of the tailor's house where Settembrini lives. Helmut Koopmann argues effectively in *Thomas Mann* that Hans Castorp represents a mediating figure between Settembrini and Naphta, a figure sustaining the vitality of "die Mitte," the bourgeois realm raised to new heights of feeling and thought and signifying the position of the middle-class and moderation (105).

In the spirit of his role as an intellectually aware spectator of the world around him and of the intellectual development of humankind, Castorp functions effectively as a mediator between Settembrini and Naphta. Feeling that these two antagonists appear to be sometimes confused in presenting their views on the world order, Castorp aims for clarity and shows his willingness to reconcile the intellectual and emotional tensions in the otherwise relatively serene mountain air. Castorp not only mediates but he also disregards the admonitions of Settembrini to avoid contact with Naphta because of the potentially dangerous nature of some of his ideas. Such a strategy suggests that Castorp, as much as he respects Settembrini, is determined to develop and enrich his intellectual awareness at all costs, perhaps in the tradition of Gustav von Aschenbach in *Der Tod in Venedig* who consecrates himself completely to the challenge and the privilege of refining his aesthetic awareness.

Castorp's potential as a mediating spirit is linked to his capacity to represent the universal human condition, to universalize the human spirit. Of this capacity Kaufmann writes: "Although Hans Castorp is not a poet, he nonetheless evinces a trait belonging to a poet's very essence, namely, pure receptivity. In this substratum of the artistic a certain satisfaction is already given to man's yearning to unite his individual life with the life of the universe" (105). Kaufmann proceeds to assert that "just as art is capable of representing the particular in its universal significance, so Hans Castorp's openness to ideas and impressions of every kind helps him to acquire a universality within his own being" (105).

Inge Diersen emphasizes effectively in *Thomas Mann: Episches Werk, Weltanschauung, Leben* not only Castorp's capacity for listening sensitively to the discussions and conflicts of Settembrini and Naphta but also the notion that Castorp is at the center of a mythical struggle between symbolic representations of god and the devil for his soul (151). Castorp listens attentively, sometimes asking questions and sometimes challenging Settembrini and Naphta, eventually refining and strengthening his own intellectual capacities and preserving a sense of independence in the discussions and tensions between these two resolute and vital individuals.

In "Choler. And Worse" Castorp does not look forward to his first anniversary at the Berghof sanatorium. As other established patients, Castorp is indifferent to such an event and to the concern for or interest in private time. Most of the Berghof residents approach the notion of their anniversary with a deep silence. They do not typically show a genuine interest in it: some residents may let the anniversary slip past and others may even forget it. Perhaps they react in such a way because they wish to preserve at least a semblance of continuity with their pre-Berghof lives; or perhaps they feel a more profound sense of timelessness if they view their lives as a smoothly flowing temporal continuum uninterrupted by various events. The aura of timelessness which is experienced by Castorp and other residents of the Berghof is described in the following manner: "The settled citizens preferred the unmeasured, the eternal, the day that was for ever the same" (413). It is possible that the established residents do not wish to celebrate and remember the anniversary of their arrival at the Berghof because the recollection of such an event would remind them of a time and of a world which they would like to forget.

The relatively vital sense of timelessness which Castorp has achieved and nurtured prior to his discussion with Joachim about nature and prior to Joachim's departure is somewhat challenged and undermined when in the section "An Attack, and a Repulse" Castorp is given a place at a new table in the dining room, and even assumes Settembrini's former seat. Moreover, Castorp receives a visit from the "flatland"— his uncle, James Tienappel, comes to see how he is progressing. Tienappel is astonished to learn that Castorp is not intending to return soon but instead plans on remaining at the Berghof for at least another six months. Tienappel leaves abruptly after a short visit, perhaps because he has gained all of the information he needed to about Castorp's situation, or perhaps because he senses that a longer stay might require a significant readjustment to life at home, or perhaps because he feels endangered by the aura of decay and death in the Berghof world.

Tienappel's sudden departure from the Berghof world signifies the final affirmation of Castorp's liberation from the north German "flatland" which had once been his home. Castorp realizes that such an event represents a crisis moment in the connection between himself and the world of everyday mortality. Castorp, the increasingly wise and emotionally and intellectually aware protagonist, is so much at home in the Berghof ambience that he no longer feels any inclination or compulsion to leave and to assume the job and the responsibility which awaits him in the world below. Castorp's situation has become similar to that of Naphta as it is described in "Operationes Spirituales." Having been in the Berghof world for six years, Naphta's presence becomes a fixed existential situation, having the aura of a permanent residence in this atmosphere of seclusion.

In the section "Snow" of Chapter VI Castorp achieves an epiphanic moment, a profound moment of awareness about life and time. The Berghof environment has a tremendous snowfall—the snow covers everything, reinforcing the isolation of the Berghof from the world below. The sunlight is minimal as the snow continues to fall in considerable amounts. Most of the Berghof residents wish that they would be allotted more light and less snow. Yet, as a compensation for this sometimes problematic climate of the Berghof environment and as a compensation for the fact that they cannot enjoy the same kind of active life which people in the world down below may do, the Berghof residents are given an existence which is permeated by a spirit of carefree forgetfulness in the sense that one may forget the flux of mortality. Despite the excessive amount of snow in the mountains in this particular winter, Castorp seems enchanted by this ambience, especially when he thinks about its similarity to life at the seashore. For the snow on the mountain and the sand on the seashore are similar in spirit, each signifying an aura of existential uniformity and deep serenity.

In his essay "'Bildung' in *The Magic Mountain*" W. H. Bruford affirms the connection for Thomas Mann between the expansiveness of the sea and the endlessness of the snow in the mountains. Mann said that the sea was one element of nature which always fascinated him: "The sea is not a landscape, it is something that brings us face to face with eternity, with nothingness and death, a metaphysical dream, and to stand in the thin air of the regions of eternal snow is a very similar experience" (78).

Castorp goes skiing to admire the natural beauty of these wintry heights which are permeated by a profound stillness and seemingly endless silences which arouse feelings of awe similar to those one might feel along the seashore. Castorp also embarks on this adventure to search, perhaps more unconsciously than consciously, for the mysterious and intangible and to challenge himself beyond his accustomed limits of existence. Here Castorp fulfills the potential for mythological vitality which he had displayed earlier in the novel. On his skis Castorp explores increasingly more isolated regions. While he finds the deep solitude which he desires, he is also aware of the potential danger of his situation. Although Castorp feels a sense of communion and connectedness with the forces of nature, he is also sensible of the destructive power of elemental and primeval nature.

The figure of Castorp in the "Snow" episode is analogous to the lonely, isolated individuals in several of Caspar David Friedrich's paintings—for example, in *Monk By the Sea* (1809), *The Abbey* (1810), and *Cross in the Woods* (1812). In these paintings, the figure, invariably and inevitably dwarfed by the landscape, confronts a seemingly elemental and primordial natural environment. As the personae in Friedrich's paintings, Castorp achieves a sense of emotional and spiritual unity with nature which is so vital to them as well.

In feeling a religious awe for nature, Castorp senses the fascination of venturing so far into the unknown wilderness and eternal silences that the experience appears to be perilous. His exploration of the profound wintry solitude and vastness of the mountain ambience is comparable to his intellectual adventures with Settembrini and Naphta. One might also declare, as do Inge Diersen and other critics, that Castorp is accompanied in spirit by Settembrini and Naphta in his adventure in the snow because he considers and reflects upon their ideas and arguments as he confronts and explores the mountainous heights. Diersen describes effectively in *Thomas Mann: Episches Werk, Weltanschauung, Leben* the intellectual presence of these two adversaries in Castorp's potentially perilous adventure: "Hans Castorp wird bei seinem Schneeabenteuer geistig von Naphta und Settembrini begleitet, er wägt ihre Positionen, ihre Ratschläge gegeneinander ab, während er sich in immer bedrohlicherer Lage praktisch zurechtfinden muss" (153). In this intellectually and physically challenging and demanding process Castorp feels a sense of association with his "antagonists," but also establishes a respectful critical distance from them. As in his mediating role in the frequently intense exchanges between Settembrini and Naphta, so in his exploration of nature Castorp assumes a Faustian perceptiveness. Castorp climbs up high into the mountains, into the snowy haze, without a definite destination guiding him, ever higher into the upper regions seemingly blended with the sky. Even though he is inwardly somewhat disturbed by the absolute stillness, Castorp is proud that he is able to venture so far into the mountain wilderness.

Castorp's experience of the "magic mountain" and his dream-vision in the "Snow" episode are prefigured by Friedrich Schiller's visionary experience on the "magic mountain" in "Der Spaziergang." Schiller's persona finds aesthetic, emotional, and intellectual rejuvenation in the presence of the "magic mountain" in "Der Spaziergang." Schiller's "Ich" in this poem, as Castorp in the "Snow" adventure, exists at the threshold of two emotional and physical antitheses or extremes, between "Schwindeln" and "Schaudern" as between "Höh" and "Tiefe," and symbolically between life and death. Yet, this is an existential tension which resolves itself in the poet's conception of the "Äther" as a dynamic, fluid unity and in his anticipation of following the continuity of the trellised path.

The ascension by Schiller's persona of the mountain is an occasion to comprehend in his field of artistic vision the expansiveness of the world of humankind and of nature. His contemplation of the growth of human civilization is generated by a sense of dynamic space, by the spatial metaphor of "ein schimmernder Streif, die länderverknüpfende Straße." After a consideration of the constructive, positive evolution of the human spirit in conjunction with divine assistance, Schiller's "Ich" proceeds to reflect also upon the dark, destructive aspects of humankind. As Castorp in his dream-vision in the snowy mountain wilderness, so Schiller's "Ich" on the "magic mountain" experiences an intellectual and aesthetic adventure and epiphany that encompasses polarities of human existence and resolves them ultimately in the unified conception of the innately harmonious, eternal cyclicality of the natural environment.

The sense of youthfulness and vernal vitality culminating the poem, which reinforces the rejuvenation of the "Ich" in this "magic mountain" experience embracing and fusing life and death as well as dream and reality, signifies not only the emotional and intellectual condition of the "Ich" but also the spiritual aura of Nature. For the "Ich" is not only reenergized in the purifying presence of Nature; he is also aware of participating in the eternal cyclicality of the natural world. The poem concludes with an image of the expansiveness of time, not only in the sense of the eternal vitality of nature and of humankind, but also in the realization that the congenial past may infuse the present with an inspirational energy, represented by the sun of Homer smiling upon the present.

In contrast to Castorp who internalizes a sense of time before an awareness of space, Schiller's "Ich," like Wordsworth's poetic voice in *The Prelude*, achieves a sense of the expansiveness of space before he attains a realization of the expansiveness of time. Despite this difference, I would claim that Schiller's "Ich" and Castorp ultimately achieve similar "magic mountain" experiences. What they share are an instinctive awareness of the threshold nature of the "magic mountain" ambience, a profound sense of personal revitalization after confronting heroically the primeval solitudes of the mountain wilderness, a renewed commitment to the potential dignity and vitality of life and humanity, and a visionary capacity that not only apprehends the inextricable interrelation of life and death, but also intuits the connections and tensions between the conceptions of spatial and temporal expansiveness.

The inspirational power of the sublime landscape, expressed by Thomas Gray in his letters describing his visit to the Grande Chartreuse in 1739, is felt as well by Castorp in his magic mountain context. Gray writes: "I do not remember to have gone ten paces without an exclamation, that there was no restraining: not a precipice, not a torrent, not a cliff, but is pregnant with religion and poetry" (Wilton 70). While Gray perceives the power of the intellectual and spiritual breadth of the majestic intellect primarily in nature, Mann, as Wordsworth's persona in *The Prelude*, conceives of it in the mind and in nature.

Thomas Gray, in describing his experience in the mountainous landscape, also speaks of seeing spirits at noon and sensing the presence of death perpetually before his eyes. The following passage exemplifies Gray's sense of the mountain adventure as a threshold experience between the realms of life and death: "It is six miles to the top; the road runs winding up to it, commonly not six feet broad; on the one hand is the rock, with woods of pine-trees hanging overhead; on the other, a monstrous precipice…at the bottom of which rolls a torrent" (Wilton 62). Gray's depiction of the mountain exploration as signifying the fragile edge of life and death anticipates the mountain experiences of Wordsworth and Mann, both of whom portray the sublime ascent and subsequent descent as an interaction and fusion of gloom and glory.

This awareness of the threshold nature of the magic mountain experience is rein-forced by Gray's sense (affirmed in their own way by the protagonists in Mann's *Der Zauberberg* and Wordsworth's *The Prelude*) of being caught between the beautiful and the sublime. Immanuel Kant says that whereas the sublime is signified by bound-lessness, the beautiful is characterized by form and limits. Kant goes on to say that the sublime represents a dynamic state of mind while the beautiful is observed by a mind at rest. Kant, in locating the sublime within the creative mind, says that the observation of objects such as mountain peaks, chasms, or high waterfalls elevate the energies of the soul above their customary height and allow us to consider ourselves in the context of the seemingly almighty power of nature.

For Mann's protagonist the magic mountain is a dynamically and effulgently vital threshold space at the fragile edge of time and eternity, life and death, the beau-tiful and the sublime. As for Hilton in *Lost Horizon*, so for Mann in *Der Zauberberg* the mountain environment is a place of intellectual vitality and rejuvenation, although with a somewhat different motivation. Hilton's Shangri-La aims to preserve the cul-tural heritage of human civilization in anticipation of a future international cata-clysm. Mann's Berghof Sanatorium offers intellectual stimulation and the prospect of creative development not only as a distraction, a diversion from the pervasive aura of decay and death but also as a foundation for the emotional, intellectual, and spiri-tual expansion of the self in its attempt to cultivate a more insightful understanding of humanity.

In *Thomas Mann: Profile and Perspectives* André von Gronicka writes of Castorp's quest for timelessness: "In the snowswept wilderness of his *Munsalväsche*, his 'wild mountain,' in the grip of death, at a moment of heightened perception, Castorp finds the strength to break death's fatal fascination and to dedicate himself to life, kindli-ness, and love" (139). Gronicka emphasizes effectively the significance of this protag-onist's striving to confront and transcend death by commiting himself to the ideal of a new humanism which would emphasize "the dignity of life" (139) and "which would profess a steadfast faith in man's nobility, while being deeply cognizant of the dark, mysterious depths of human nature" (139).

In "Mann and History" T. J. Reed describes the images of Castorp's vision dur-ing the snowstorm experience as representing "transformations of what Hans Castorp has been hearing debated: Settembrini's life-affirming Enlightenment activism and Naphta's ruthlessness that embraces darkness and death" (11). Reed proceeds to emphasize the balance which the people in the vision are striving to maintain: "The 'sun people' in Castorp's vision are living out a balance: neither sunny optimism nor defeatist pessimism, but a humane solidarity informed by their knowledge of the worst, the darkness that always presses us round" (11). In mediating, sometimes con-sciously and sometimes unconsciously, between the contrasting philosophies of Settembrini and Naphta, Castorp aspires to achieve such a balance in his own life.

Castorp experiences a vital sense of freedom as he moves among the snowy heights and mountainous solitudes, feeling as if "his feet were like wings" (480). Even though Castorp also feels a sense of fear as he confronts the snowladen silences in the increasing darkness of the afternoon, he appears to relish this freedom and asserts that he wants to make full use of the time which this wandering adventure provides him. The image of the seven-league slippers is important not only because of its inherently enchanted, romantic vitality but also because it suggests the capacity of the protagonist to cover considerable spaces, great expanses of space, relatively easily, a feat beyond the capability of most mortals. The experience of spatial expansiveness, of diastolic spatiality, contributes to and reinforces Castorp's sense of timelessness in this environment. As in the Berghof ambience there is a dream-like quality to the experience of timelessness in this natural space which makes it all the more ethereal and vital.

The challenge of this epiphanic moment intensifies in the immense snowstorm which permeates the landscape. Castorp feels emotional and physical excitement and stress in confronting the elemental forces of nature, just as he does after a discussion with Settembrini and Naphta. Castorp's resistance of the storm represents not only his extraordinary effort to persevere in this perilously frigid environment but also symbolizes his attempt to remain intellectually alive in the Berghof context. Castorp finds a semblance of shelter at the isolated hut. At the climax of "Snow" Castorp senses a presence in nature as powerful as the presence that uplifts Wordsworth's persona in "Tintern Abbey" with the joy of elevated thoughts who feels

> a sense sublime
> Of something far more deeply interfused,
> Whose dwelling is the light of setting suns,...
> A motion and a spirit, that impels
> All thinking things, all objects of all thought,
> And rolls through all things. (95–102)

Such a "sense sublime" is analogous to the spirit of transcendent awareness which culminates Castorp's experience in the "Snow" episode. Castorp's outward-directed awareness of participating in the "motion" and the "spirit" of the universe is described insightfully by Horst S. and Ingrid G. Daemmrich in *Spirals and Circles* as follows: "He reaches the decision to establish a productive relation with the world by reconciling spiritual existence with a reverence for the dynamic forces of nature" (2:7).

Castorp, as Wordsworth's persona in "Tintern Abbey," experiences a dynamic, universal motion and spirit that pervades all dimensions of his "Snow" adventure. For example, one of the most intriguing dimensions of the "Snow" section is Castorp's dream of a southern climate filled with images of life, of loveliness, and of vitality. Yet, there is also a temple-like structure where two old women are dismembering a child. This intense perceptual moment signifies the heightened intellectual and spiritual awareness of Castorp. In reflecting on the inner tension of this lovely and horrible dream Castorp realizes that life and death are part of each other's domain and are inextricably linked. In asserting ultimately that he has made a "dream poem of humanity" (496), Castorp emphasizes the importance of love and that love has the capacity to be stronger than death. The epiphanic moment of the "Snow" episode culminates in the following assertion: *"For the sake of goodness and love, man shall let death have no sovereignty over his thoughts"* (496–97). With this realization Castorp awakes from his dream—he has attained his goal of supreme awareness and of an awareness of a transcendent power.

In his discussion with Settembrini and Naphta in the next section in which they expound on the Jesuits, the Freemasons, and alchemistic endeavors, Castorp says that the use of the word "hermetics" reminds him of the conserve jars which the housekeeper in Hamburg used to keep in the larder. The food items which are preserved in these jars are protected from and hermetically sealed from the influence of time and mortality. Such a notion of being hermetically secure and separated from the effects of time applies directly and effectively to Castorp's own experience in the world of the Berghof Sanatorium. For Castorp has attempted, in his own quest for timelessness, to attain a sense of being hermetically sealed and concealed from the influence of the world down below, from the responsibilities, pressures, and flux of mortality. He has even tried, explicitly and implicitly, to achieve a transformation of the self in the alchemistically vital aura of the Berghof.

Settembrini attempts to dissuade Castorp from his pious reverence for death. For Settembrini believes that death is the end of a process of organic growth and decline and argues that the only appropriate way to think of death is as part of life. Naphta counters by asserting that without death there would not have been the rich cultural heritage of architecture, painting, music, poetry, or any other art. Settembrini especially emphasizes the importance of literature and literary endeavors, proclaiming in the same language which is used in *Tonio Kröger* to praise the poet, the "purifying, healing influence of literature" (525) and asserting that the spirit of literary creativity represents "the noblest manifestation of the spirit of man" (525).

It is significant and simultaneously exceedingly sad that chapter six, which has spoken eloquently of death imagery and of an ambience of alchemistic endeavor and transformation, ends with the death and burial of Castorp's cousin, Joachim Ziemssen. According to Hofrat Behrens, Joachim, who had recently left the Berghof to engage in his military service in the world down below, had done so too precipitously. Behrens says that Joachim took a considerable risk in doing this when he was still feverish and should have remained convalescing in the sanatorium. In the final paragraph of Chapter VI Mann stresses the lonely vantage-point on which his protagonist stands as he looks towards the world below. Castorp seems now to exist forever at a distance, emotionally, physically, intellectually, and spiritually, from the world of everyday mortality down below. Yet, it is not necessarily as negative an isolation as some might suggest—for this is an existential seclusion of intellectual and emotional potential, of transformational possibilities, and of transcendent vitality permeated by an aura of Berghof timelessness. However, one could also say that Castorp's position as a figure at the threshold of life and death, time and eternity, has only been underscored and intensified by the passing of his cousin. For Joachim's death does allow the presence of mortality to encroach to some extent upon the vital aura of timelessness which consistently pervades the realm of the Berghof Sanatorium.

At the beginning of Chapter VII in "By the Ocean of Time" Mann describes Castorp's conspicuous indifference to the passage of time. He states that if Castorp had been asked to answer questions regarding specific dates and durations with respect to his experiences in the Berghof world, he would not have been able to do so. As this section continues, the question is raised whether the conserve jar which is hermetically preserved exists outside of time. Castorp even appears to counter his inclination towards an experience of timeless eternity by watching time flow, by observing the second-hand of his watch intensely so that he could attain a sense of holding on to time and of prolonging the passing moments.

In the section "By the Ocean of Time," as previously in the novel, the image of the ocean is evoked to suggest eternity. The snowy expanse of the mountain landscape reminds the protagonist of the ocean dunes of his familiar flatland environment. In such an environment one may achieve a sense of timelessness. As one walks and keeps walking along the ocean's shore, one may attain a sense of unity with the surrounding landscape with which one feels so much at home that time has vanished or appears to have vanished. Participating emotionally and spiritually in the aura of expansiveness along the shore or in the snowy landscape is an essential dimension of the experience of timelessness. The roar of the waves protects and shelters the individual from the clamor of the world of mortality. An aura of forgetfulness, of indifference to the rapacious flux of time, is engendered which leads to an awareness of participating in an ambience of eternity, of eternal peacefulness.

The section "By the Ocean of Time" ends with an ambivalent undertone. On the one hand, Mann asserts, in the spirit of Settembrini and in honor of Joachim, the fundamental importance of a sense of duty. The final sentence of the section, however, raises the question whether Castorp's quest for metaphysical solace and timelessness is not strengthened by his realization that Joachim's zeal for conformity, for the "flatland" approach to life, and for a philosophy of life dependent on the "flatland" conceptions of time, had brought him to his fatal demise.

In "Fullness of Harmony" later in Chapter VII the appearance of the gramophone at the Berghof causes considerable excitement and fascination. Castorp feels instinctively that he should be in charge of it. Castorp is energized and inspired by the presence of this object, feeling a new enchantment and inclination in his life. By himself Castorp plays several recordings all of which have a romantic undertone. When listening to one song in particular, Schubert's "Linden-Tree," Castorp feels an intimate emotional participation. Castorp's profound feeling is described as a conception of the spirit aware of its own significance and reaching beyond itself to express a more expansive world of feeling. Such a feeling is analogous in intensity and scope to the transformation of Beethoven's personal experience of despair in the Funeral March of the "Eroica" into a representation of a broader and more ecumenical human experience. Castorp's awareness of his own significance is effectively discussed by Erich Heller in *The Ironic German*: "Down in the plain his responsibilities were within the world. Up here he is responsible for the world. Day after day he sits on a grassy slope and 'governs.' For he knows, and knowledge is power; yet, ironically, it is also loneliness, feebleness, and sickness to death" (15).

The questionable séance and the passionately primitive duel between Settembrini and Naphta challenge and perhaps even undermine the aura of timelessness and time-less serenity which Castorp feels in and has come to consider as an essential aspect of the Berghof Sanatorium world. At the painful and problematic duel Settembrini proclaims that he will not kill and fires into the air. Naphta is disturbed by this response and shoots himself in the head. This cataclysmic event certainly undermines the aura of timeless tranquility which has been a fundamental part of the Berghof world. The sudden removal of Naphta as an intellectual presence on the magic moun-tain and from the dynamic exchanges between Settembrini and Castorp negatively effects the seemingly timeless ambience. For an aura of timelessness or atemporality can only be properly and effectively preserved without such dramatic changes. The duel also foreshadows the ending of the novel by introducing the theme of mortality, of violent death, in conjunction with the theme of personal and social responsibility.

In the final section of the novel, "The Thunderbolt," Castorp, having spent seven years on the magic mountain, is treated with relative and polite indifference by the world around him, which is perhaps the goal to which he, as a mythical figure, was intuitively striving. His existential condition has become that of the individual who is no longer given considerable responsibilities or even less onerous tasks, who is allowed to revel in his own inclinations and interests. Mann suggests that Castorp himself has become relatively indifferent to his outward appearance, as if such a con-cern implies a concern about the passage of time and an interest in participating in the flux of mortality. Not only does Castorp feel relatively established in this magic mountain environment, but the authorities of the sanatorium appear to view him in this light as well, for they do not feel the need to examine his situation very carefully and they have no concern about the possibility of abruptly wild or unusual behavior on his part.

When Castorp is informed of the death of old Consul Tienappel, Hans' great-uncle and foster-father, he is reclining in his chair, as if he is in a position of mythical vitality unable to be dramatically effected by various events from the world down below or even from the Berghof realm. The death of Consul Tienappel is, moreover, noteworthy in the life of Hans Castorp because it reinforces his complete separation from the flatland world, for he ceases from now on to desire to have any contact with the everyday world of mortality as represented by the world beyond the Berghof Sanatorium. For example, Castorp, after producing the letter of condolence to his uncle-cousins, no longer sends letters to individuals in the flatland world of reality, from which he no longer receives any epistolary communications. Castorp's rather complete indifference to time and to the passage of time is emphasized in the fact that he no longer carries a watch because it had fallen and he had never desired to have it repaired. Such indifference to mortality coupled with a sense of his mythical vitality is captured effectively in the following passage: "Thus he did honor to his abiding-everlasting, his walk by the ocean of time, the hermetic enchantment to which he had proved so extraordinarily susceptible that it had become the fundamental adventure of his life" (708). No ordinary mortal has the capacity to stroll along the ocean of time and to survive as effectively as Castorp does. The above statement reinforces the mythical prowess of the novel's protagonist and also suggests that he seems to have been fated to come to the Berghof Sanatorium to participate in the quest for timelessness, an existential condition to which he seemed to be so well suited. One might even say that Castorp's childhood and youth, characterized to a considerable extent by an aura of solemnity, decay, and death, prepared him to be an appropriate resident of the Berghof Sanatorium. For the "hermetic enchantment" with timelessness, the sense "of time as both flowing and persisting, of recurrence in continuity" (23) was, as Feuerlicht and other critics have effectively asserted, already present in Castorp's childhood, for example, in his experience of the baptismal bowl which his grandfather shows him.

Then, suddenly, the thunder-peal occurs, as primitive and abrupt and as potentially destructive as the duel between Settembrini and Naphta, and effects even the distant heights of the sanatorium world. Castorp is affected not only by the newspaper reports of the aggression and the hostilities of the military conflict but also by Settembrini's observations about the state of Europe. For the first time in many months Castorp feels himself compelled to reconsider his seemingly permanent position in this ambience of enchantment as he contemplates a return to the flatland to participate in the war. Mann captures the metaphysical tension evoked by the thunder-peal in a letter to Paul Amann in which he suggests that the novel entails a Rip van Winkle-like experience which will end in the outbreak of war. Mann reinforces this tension in describing the spirit of the work as humorous-nihilistic with an inclination to show sympathy with death.

Castorp does leave the Berghof world out of a vague and slowly evolving sense of social responsibility and duty to his country. One might also argue, as do Horst S. and Ingrid G. Daemmrich effectively in *Spirals and Circles*, that "the narrator is compelled to abandon Castorp once the hermetic spell of the atmosphere is broken by the clash of societies which collectively failed to gain historical awareness" (2:8). Castorp's departure from the Berghof could also result from the fact that his sense of timelessness has been disrupted and undermined, for the Berghof no longer seems to represent a serene sanctuary from the world, or at least Castorp is persuaded, by external factors, to believe that it does not.

One might wonder whether the intense awareness of this disruption of a sense of atemporality and timelessness is as strong for Castorp as it is for Robert Faehmel in Heinrich Böll's *Billard um halbzehn, Billiards at Half-Past Nine* (1959). Whereas Faehmel's sense of timelessness, articulated as an enchanted moment in the realistically ethereal aura of the Prinz Heinrich billiard room, is agitated and undermined permanently by a figure from the past—by the return of Schrella—Castorp's sense of timeless enchantment, nurtured so assiduously for several years, is disturbed, though not thoroughly displaced, by the rememberance of the past, of Joachim's dream, and by a renewed awareness of the exigencies of the present. Moreover, Castorp has had for a long time a silent, unconscious appreciation and yearning for solemnity and death—and perhaps he feels that he might even function as a substitute for Joachim on the flatland battlefield. In attempting to fulfill Joachim's dream Castorp feels that he is a part of an experience larger than himself—in serving his country and his cousin's memory Castorp will strive to realize and sustain a sense of social and personal responsibility.

Perhaps one might even claim that Castorp reveals himself as an existential humanist, fulfilling the intellectual and social challenge of Jean-Paul Sartre in *Existentialism and Humanism*. Sartre writes in *Existentialism and Humanism* of the importance of transcendent aims: "Man is all the time outside of himself: it is in projecting and losing himself beyond himself that he makes man to exist; and, on the other hand, it is by pursuing transcendent aims that he himself is able to exist" (432). While Castorp certainly shows a strong capacity for self-surpassing—a capacity which he has consciously as well as unconsciously nurtured on the magic mountain—he has perhaps not completely realized, as Sartre would say of the existential humanist, that he is himself the heart and center of his transcendence.

Sartre describes existential humanism as the relation of transcendence as constitutive of man with subjectivity:

> This is humanism; because we remind man that there is no legislator but himself; that he himself, thus abandoned, must decide for himself; also because we show that it is not by turning back upon himself, but always by seeking, beyond himself, an aim which is one of liberation or of some particular realization, that man can realize himself as truly human. (432)

Castorp, once the timeless enchantment of the magic mountain is challenged and diminished, appears to act upon his gradually developed conviction that there is no legislator but himself and affirms his intuitive existential humanism by seeking beyond himself in a potentially self-destructive gesture of dynamic social responsibility.

The transcendent aim of timelessness and of timeless enchantment which Castorp aspired to achieve and which motivated his existence for at least seven years— one might say, at least, because it appears as if the prelude of this inclination was developed in his youth—is sublimated and transformed into his participation in the horrific military upheaval which undermines the world of everyday life, feeling, and thought, namely, the First World War. *Der Zauberberg,* despite the fact that its final scenario involves destruction and war, ends with a question which wonders in a seemingly hopeful and optimistic undertone whether love may one day arise from the ambience of decay and death which permeates the world of mortality. Perhaps Castorp's self-sacrificial, heroic gesture at the end is an expression of his love for humanity and his faith that his individual effort will ultimately create a more humane, thoughtful, and humanistically vital world. As Conway at the end of Hilton's *Lost Horizon,* Castorp returns to the world of everyday mortality because he believes in the timeless vitality of the human spirit and because he hopes to inspire that world to greater enlightenment and to a more rational outlook and perspective. Such a heroic gesture could also be construed as a manifestation of his quest to affirm the timeless vitality of the human spirit. As Conway tries to return to Shangri-La after his self-sacrificial effort in support of Mallinson's inclination to reconnect with the world of everyday mortality, so Castorp perhaps hopes intuitively to return after his participation in the military conflict in a spirit of heightened humanitarian awareness to the timeless enchantment and intellectual expansiveness of the magic mountain, to the serene timelessness of the Berghof Sanatorium, where he may contribute to a profoundly humane and deeply sensitive caring and attentiveness for those individuals who exist at the threshold of life and death, time and eternity. For "his walk by the ocean of time" (708) had given Castorp not only a prolonged feeling of "hermetic enchantment" (708) and a sense of his capacity to achieve a consistent and thoughtful transcendence of the flux of mortality which was the essential experience of his life, but also an awareness of his own mythical vitality and of his potential to shape constructively, to contribute in his own personal way to, a new world of humanistic vitality and humanitarian dignity.

CHAPTER 2

Evelyn Waugh

In *Brideshead Revisited* (the excerpts from the novel in this chapter are from the Little, Brown edition of 1946) when Sebastian Flyte takes Charles Ryder for the first time to Brideshead on a morning in June, the first view of the house and surrounding estate is notable. After passing through a series of gates and a spacious parkland there was a turn in the drive and "suddenly a new and secret landscape opened" (34) before them. In the distance "shone the dome and columns of an old house" (34). The seclusion of the house and the domestic interior is emphasized from the beginning of the description of the estate not only through the series of gates which represent the initial contact with the outside world but also through the presence of the parkland, the lakes, and the hills which envelop and protect the house. The aura of seclusion is further reinforced by Sebastian's initial statement that he wants to show Charles the garden front and the fountain, that is, features external to the house and not an integral part of the interior. The sense of isolation from the world of everyday reality is also emphasized in Sebastian's own personal distance from the house in his statement that this is where his family lives, thus not directly stating that this is "his house."

The vital seclusion is further emphasized in Sebastian's claim that the house is closed because the members of his family are away in London. Instead of entering the house at the front, Sebastian takes Charles to a side court and to the servants' quarters, for he wishes to introduce him to Nanny Hawkins. One indication of the magnificence of the interior is the presence of the dome. The labyrinthine interior of the domestic ambience is suggested in the ascension to the room of Nanny Hawkins, for Sebastian and Charles climb up and through various passages and past a number of minor staircases before reaching the nurseries at the top. The initial description of Nanny Hawkins as being serenely asleep and seated at the window which looks out over the landscape vistas including in its scope the fountain, the lakes, and the temple is important because it captures the essence of the tranquility which is embodied by this splendid home.

The room of Nanny Hawkins is a delightful sanctuary of secular and religious proportions. The secular aspect, the collection of presents from her children and other individuals on her chest of drawers, of this sanctuary is balanced by the religious dimension, the rosary in Nanny's hands and the oleograph of the Sacred Heart over the mantelpiece. The aura of sanctuary is enhanced by its aesthetic vitality, for it is described as an exceedingly congenial room with the wallpaper of ribbon and roses. The serenity of Nanny Hawkins' elderly face, having served for so many years in the Marchmain family, reinforces the essential serenity of this domestic environment. In saying in "Places of the Mind: Locating *Brideshead Revisited*" that Brideshead is "an enchanted place in the way that the places of childhood and first love are enchanted places" (141–42) Ruth Breeze also states insightfully that "the central room in the house, one of the rooms which survives to the end unchanged, is the nursery under the dome" (142). Sebastian feels especially comfortable in the ambience of this important room not only because it reminds him of his pleasant childhood but also because it contains an aura of faith which is instinctively, and sometimes more subconsciously than consciously, important to him as well. Sebastian's childhood represents for him a period of carefree innocence and youthful vitality. In his life at Oxford Sebastian is trying at least to some extent to recapture and preserve a semblance of this innocence and carefree attitude in a romantic vision of the past.

After Sebastian and Charles leave the room of Nanny Hawkins, Sebastian asserts that he wants to depart before his sister Julia returns. His explanation is that he does not want any of his charming family to connect with Charles and undermine their friendship. When Charles asks to see more of the house, Sebastian reluctantly assents and leads his friend into a dark corridor where he opens a mahogany door into a dark hall which becomes flooded with light when one of the window shutters is opened. A luminescent sanctuary is revealed containing "vast, twin fireplaces of sculptured marble, the coved ceiling frescoed with classic deities and heroes, the gilt mirrors... and the islands of sheeted furniture" (38). Even though this is only a momentary glance into this splendid interior, for Sebastian soon closes the shutter, one can see the magnificence of this room as well as its aura of seclusion. The vastness of the fireplaces and the frescoed ceiling suggests an inner spatial expansiveness which is to some extent tempered by the covered furniture, an image of beautiful objects sheltered from the encroachment of the world of everyday mortality and temporality.

Although Sebastian's sense of serenity which he seemed to have before entering Brideshead and during his visit to the sanctuary of Nanny Hawkins changes noticeably when he thinks of meeting Julia or having his family charm Charles away from a congenial friendship, he does want to show Charles the family chapel before they leave the estate. The chapel, the wedding present of Lord Marchmain to Lady Marchmain, represents one of the most recent architectural modifications at Brideshead. This chapel, a prominent example of the art nouveau style, signifies a special place of aesthetically and spiritually vital refuge with the brightly colored images of angels, lambs, and saints on the walls, the triptych of pale oak, and the sanctuary lamp.

The conflicted emotional connection which Sebastian has towards his lovely mansion, Brideshead, is seen throughout this particular visit. The lighthearted mood which Sebastian displays on the way to Brideshead and which appears in flickering moments of contentment and serenity during the visit, such as when they visit Nanny Hawkins or when he shows Charles the splendid room or the chapel, is clearly disturbed and undermined when Sebastian thinks of encountering members of his family or of his presence and position in the family. This episode could suggest that Sebastian wants to achieve a sense of sanctuary and seclusion not only from the world of everyday mortality but also from his family and from the personal encroachment of his family in his life.

The initial presentation of Sebastian in the first several pages of Chapter One of Book I of *Brideshead Revisited* reveals indications of his desire for a sense of sanctuary. In his first statement of the novel Sebastian implores Charles to escape from Oxford for the day, for the city has become too noisy and rambunctious and has temporarily lost its aura of tranquility. The aesthetic sensibility of Sebastian is also manifest in this initial statement for he speaks of the combination of strawberries and the special wine he is bringing as heavenly. That Sebastian is not especially enamored of everyday reality and mortality and that he consciously tries to maintain a sense of distance from the exigencies and the vicissitudes of the world around him is implied in his self-awareness that he does not drive well and in his search for an openness of space beyond the urban environment. The knoll under the elms where Sebastian finally stops to enjoy the strawberries and the wine has an aura of atemporality and timelessness about it for Charles states that the fusion of the scents of summer and the scent of the tobacco and the fumes of the wine "seemed to lift us a finger's breadth above the turf and hold us suspended" (24).

Sebastian's sense of enchantment here culminates in his statement that this is the kind of special place where one could deposit a pot of gold. Sebastian says that he would like to bury something significant in various places where he has been happy—then later in his life when he feels old and miserable, he can come back, unearth the notable object, and conjure up congenial past memories. The idealistic motivation of such a sentiment has a fairy-tale quality to it. Moreover, the notion of revealing or illuminating a precious object, thought, or memory after a period of disuse or darkness, whether literal or symbolic, appears more than once in the first chapter in the discussion of Sebastian's interests and capacities. For example, when

Sebastian opens the shutters to illuminate the magnificent room at Brideshead, he is doing precisely the same thing—he is revealing a collection of precious objects which have been shrouded, although just temporarily, in darkness. A similar instance of such revelation is when Charles returns from a lecture to find his college room full of golden daffodils the day after Sebastian had been sick through the window. That the flowers are accompanied by a note from Sebastian in which he declares his contrition and hopes that Charles will come to lunch because Aloysius, his teddy bear, will not speak to him until he thinks that he is forgiven, suggests not only the playful nature of Sebastian's imagination but also the capacity of Sebastian for emotional expression and attachment. One might even claim that Sebastian, as Gatsby in Fitzgerald's *The Great Gatsby*, represents a patron of light, a special individual with an Apollonian aura about him who has the ability to illuminate the world and its moments and phases of darkness. Yet, such individuals are often undervalued and devalued by the world of everyday mortality which they are trying to enlighten— Sebastian and Gatsby both exemplify such characters of Apollonian motivation who are undervalued and mistreated by the world of everyday mortality.

One could say that Sebastian's statement about the significance of burying a crock of gold in various places of personal importance is influenced at least to some extent by his wealthy family background. For the light and the luminescent motivation which Sebastian represents is golden. The daffodils which Sebastian contritely gives Charles are golden; the light which streams into the splendid room at Brideshead and which fuses with the aura of the precious objects there is richly golden and disperses the darkness; and the object which Sebastian wants to bury in preparation for a congenial future is golden. Although Sebastian's statement implies the inevitability of mortality and the passage of time, for he speaks of growing old and of the necessity of deleterious physical change, there is the sense that the discovery or rediscovery of a beautiful object such as the crock of gold would revitalize the heart and soul of the individual. In conjunction with the statement at the end of the previous paragraph about feeling suspended above the turf, this passage emphasizes the capacity of a special place to create an ambience of spatial expansiveness, an expansiveness which can, even if only modestly or in a transient fashion, postpone or transform the flux of mortality. It is also noteworthy that such an endeavor to bury a crock of gold or a precious object in various special places suggests a desire to find locations which are primarily distinctive for their personal significance and for the fact that they cannot be easily accessed by others.

One might describe Sebastian's interest in burying a beautiful object in a place where he can later unearth it and remember pleasant memories, as well as his interest in living alone at Brideshead Castle, as signifying a philosophy of enclosed space, a strategy of aspiring to achieve a sense of sheltered and protected space. Robert M. Davis in "Imagined Space in *Brideshead Revisited*" emphasizes the desire of Charles to attain such an enclosed space as well: "In the body of the novel...Charles characteristically seeks not liberation but enclosure as an escape from the complexity of the outside world through what Ryder images as 'that low door in the wall…which opened on an enclosed and enchanted garden'" (24). Davis proceeds to argue effectively that Lord Marchmain aspires in his palazzo in Venice to "sustain the illusion that he can maintain a private, sensual-aesthetic world isolated from social, political, and domestic demands" (26).

As Charles reflects on his initial encounters with Sebastian at Oxford University, he states that he dates his Oxford life not from the time of his matriculation but from the day when he first met Sebastian. It is noteworthy that such a meeting was accidental and only happened because Sebastian, after a night of revelry, became ill as he was at the threshold of Charles's ground-floor college rooms. Charles had been advised by his cousin Jasper to change these rooms because he suspected that they would eventually become a place where other people would inevitably congregate and consistently meet. In stating that he never consciously followed any of the abundant advice which Jasper gave him with respect to college life and study at Oxford, Charles suggests that one of the reasons why he never wanted to change his rooms was because of the lovely, fragrant gillyflowers growing below his windows. Such is the kind of reason which Sebastian might also have given for not wanting to change his rooms, if he had been in a similar situation. For both Charles and Sebastian have a vital and subtle aesthetic sensibility, a sensibility which they share and nurture during their friendship.

In this section of Chapter One Charles even addresses the issue of aesthetic vitality. While admitting that he wished that he had possessed more exquisite things to display in his college rooms, Charles does describe several objects which are rather revealing. For example, that he would place a reproduction of Van Gogh's *Sunflowers* prominently in his room is significant in light of the importance of light and illumination in his life and in light of the Apollonian presence of Sebastian which such an image anticipates. One might even say that Charles's selection of such an image to grace his rooms implies that he has an Apollonian interest and motivation as well. Although Charles describes his books as commonplace, at least one of the selections could be considered as especially revealing. For A. E. Housman's *A Shropshire Lad* contains diverse poems about mortality, beauty, and the transience of the beautiful, all of which are themes of special importance for Charles and Sebastian.

In describing the objects and the books in his college room Charles also reflects on the types of friends which he had initially made at Oxford and their essential difference from Sebastian. Charles distinguishes between the intellectual approach of his early friends, exemplified by Collins, and the emotional approach of Sebastian to his studies and the world around him. The capacity of Sebastian in his seemingly innocent manner to illuminate various aspects of the world for Charles and for others is affirmed in this section of the narrative. When Sebastian says, in the spirit of his pristine or simple approach to life and to beauty, that he has the same kind of emotional feeling for a butterfly or a flower that he has for a cathedral or a picture, Charles is very positively impressed. While Charles appreciates the intellectual vitality of such individuals as Collins, he is more influenced by and seems personally to favor the emotional approach of Sebastian.

The presence of Sebastian, the second son of the Marquis of Marchmain, at Oxford is well-known to Charles even before he actually meets and gets to know him. Sebastian is a conspicuous character at college because of his physical appearance and beauty and because of his seemingly eccentric behavior. It is interesting that such eccentricity of behavior is described as knowing no bounds, which parallels the expansiveness of soul and spirit which generally informs Sebastian's approach to and philosophy of life. One of the most prominent examples of this apparent eccentricity is that Sebastian carries a teddy bear around with him. It is noteworthy that Sebastian gives the bear a name, Aloysius, and speaks of him as if he were an individual, suggesting that a seemingly inanimate object deserves such personal attention and consideration. One might even view Aloysius as a kind of alter-ego for Sebastian or of Sebastian—he is not just a sign of Sebastian's connectedness to his childhood and youth, but he is also a dimension of Sebastian's self. One might consider Aloysius as a congenial symbol of Sebastian's "golden" childhood which he likes or needs to keep with him as a reminder of goodness and innocence in his confrontation of the coarseness, the meanness, and the mundanity of everyday reality. Sebastian's personal differentiation from others is further emphasized by the fact that he is portrayed as being so different from his elder brother, the Earl of Brideshead, and also from Collins, who, it is implied, analyzes Sebastian in less than glowing terms.

The name of Sebastian Flyte, as Annette Wirth and other critics have thoughtfully pointed out, is of special significance. Wirth states in *The Loss of Traditional Values and Continuance of Faith in Evelyn Waugh's Novels: A Handful of Dust, Brideshead Revisited and Sword of Honour* that Flyte could suggest "the urge to flee" (62) and that Sebastian's "moods are changeable" (63). One may, of course, view Sebastian in the tradition of the suffering and martyrdom of St. Sebastian, an experience which is alluded to in the presence of Anthony Blanche at the luncheon party in Sebastian's Oxford rooms. Annette Wirth also appropriately points out that the Latin origin of Sebastian's name is significant: "The name 'Sebastian' means 'august' or 'venerable' which is defined as 'worthy of reverence'" (90). There is a holiness and a sanctity in Sebastian's character and in his heart and soul which is only gradually displayed to the world. Cordelia has the warm-heartedness to sense and to appreciate this dimension of Sebastian's character.

Charles Ryder candidly admits that the luncheon party to which Sebastian invites him after the unfortunate incident of the previous night marked the beginning of a new era in his life. In choosing to lunch with Sebastian in his college rooms in Christ Church instead of with his more intellectual friends, Charles is influenced by the generous contriteness which had filled his room with the golden daffodils, by his

search for love, for a sense of friendship and appreciation which he instinctively felt
he would not find with his current friends, by a sense of curiosity to meet Sebastian,
and by a feeling that he would find that special entrance "which opened on an enclosed
and enchanted garden, which was somewhere, not overlooked by any window, in the
heart of that grey city" (31). That Charles feels instinctively that his contact with
Sebastian would offer a sense of enchantment and a sense of sanctuary is noteworthy. For Sebastian fulfills both of these possibilities abundantly in the course of their
developing friendship.

The first several paragraphs describing the arrival of Charles at Sebastian's rooms
in Christ Church are very revealing about the character of Sebastian. In his college
rooms Sebastian is initially presented as a singular individual who is alone and who
has a sensitivity for nature. The generosity of heart and spirit which is an essential
dimension of Sebastian's nature is also evident for he aims to give the other students
attending his luncheon party more of the plover's eggs than he intends for himself.
In saying that he has taken various medications to help soften the anguish of the previous night's experience and in stating that he does not want to be awakened Sebastian
implies his interest in achieving a sense of differentiation and isolation from the world
of everyday mortality. Such an interest is further affirmed by the physical location
of Sebastian's rooms, which are high in Meadow Buildings in Christ Church College.

The entrancing nature of Sebastian, which is also enchanting, is enhanced not
only by the awareness that his epicene beauty could possibly be as transient as it is
vital, but also by the cosmopolitan array and by the eclectic series of objects which
are present in his rooms, such as the harmonium in a gothic case, the large Sevres
vases, and the drawings by Daumier. The large luncheon table suggests not personal
gluttony but a capacity for generosity and for sharing with others. That the chimney-
piece contains numerous invitations from presumably socioeconomically wealthy
women in London implies that his presence is socially desired without his having any
particular personal interest in or attachment towards such individuals. Perhaps one
reason for this is that Sebastian might sense that people are interested in him less for
the kind of person he is than because of his socioeconomic prominence. Even his presumed "friends" from the college who attend the luncheon party observe Sebastian
only after they have reached for the plover's eggs, suggesting that he might be more
appreciated for the material objects and the material ambience which he can provide
than for the integrity or inner beauty of his person. In contrast, it is noteworthy that
Anthony Blanche, when he arrives, does speak to Sebastian directly. Both Sebastian
and Anthony have an aesthetic sensibility which is of comparable vitality, though it
is more publicly and ostentatiously displayed by the latter.

Robert Murray Davis makes important observations in *Brideshead Revisited:
The Past Redeemed* about Sebastian and his college room: "The narrator says that
Sebastian is beautiful; he gives details about the incongruous furnishings of the room,
works of art mingling with mere souvenirs, which reflects the furnishings of

Sebastian's mind; Sebastian's dialogue reveals directly...that his conversation is easy" (68). As Gatsby's mansion in Fitzgerald's *The Great Gatsby* represents a cosmopolitan mixture of various interesting objects from different historical periods which reflect his own inner inclinations, so Sebastian's Oxford room signifies an amalgam of aesthetically intriguing objects which mirror the richness of his aesthetic sensibility. Davis also emphasizes Sebastian's superiority to London society: "Sebastian is so superior that he does not bother to frequent it" (68). Sebastian and Gatsby also share the characteristic of an instinctive generosity—both individuals give parties without being actively engaged in the entertainment, instead maintaining an aloofness and emotional distance from most of their guests.

As Anthony departs later in the afternoon his parting comment makes reference to the mythological nature and heritage of Sebastian's name. For Saint Sebastian, according to one narrative of his life, suffered martyrdom by being attacked with spears and shafts. In art history Saint Sebastian, a Christian saint and martyr, is typically portrayed as a handsome youth pierced by arrows. Notable paintings of Saint Sebastian by Andrea Mantegna, Sandro Botticelli, Titian, Hans Memling, Guido Reni, Carlo Saraceni, and El Greco sensitively display the nobility and the suffering of this important religious figure. One of the most moving paintings of Saint Sebastian tended by Saint Irene is by Georges de La Tour. That Anthony would say that he would like to stick Sebastian full of arrows like a pin-cushion is significant for it suggests that Anthony might be more violently and not as kindly disposed towards Sebastian as one might have initially thought. While the use of the pin-cushion, instead of a barbed arrow, in his statement softens its intensity and violence somewhat, this remark does foreshadow some of Anthony's later comments about Sebastian as the novel develops. That the narrative does not describe Sebastian's farewell response to Anthony or to any of the other attendees at the luncheon party might imply a sense of distance between them. It is as if Sebastian senses that his connection with Anthony and with the other undergraduates who are at lunch will be fleeting.

The first day of Charles's personal association with and friendship with Sebastian concludes with their visit to the Botanical Gardens, which Sebastian exclaims he must see. That Sebastian is very interested not only in beauty but also in nature is affirmed in his mention of the beautiful arch and the various kinds of ivy. It is moreover interesting that Sebastian suggests that he needs to visit the Botanical Gardens occasionally, that he cannot imagine his life without the presence of the Botanical Gardens. Perhaps Sebastian feels such a close connection to the Botanical Gardens because their natural beauty reminds him of the lovely landscape around Brideshead. Or perhaps he feels a sense of emotional and spiritual communion with nature which he does not instinctively feel in the human domain. When Charles returns to his college rooms at the end of his first day with Sebastian, the entire atmosphere seems to have changed. That he feels that only the golden daffodils appeared real suggests not only his profound appreciation of Sebastian's gift but also his awareness, as yet perhaps as unconscious as it is conscious, that he has found that special door, or an indication or a trace of that special door leading to an enchanted and secluded garden.

At the beginning of Chapter Two of Book I Jasper visits Charles near the end of the summer term to give him further advice regarding life and studies at Oxford. Jasper feels a sense of responsibility for Charles as his cousin because he believes that Charles's father lives isolated from the world and does not really provide his son with good counsel. Jasper even provides interesting information about Sebastian Flyte and his family, especially about the great wealth of the family and the fact that Lord and Lady Marchmain are living separate lives. Jasper not only criticizes the attitude of the very wealthy students who think that they can do anything they wish but also raises a concern about Charles's financial situation and the apparent frivolity and excessive drinking to which he has recently devoted himself. As Charles reflects after the farewell of Jasper on the emotional exuberance and festive dynamism of his recent life with Sebastian and others, he says that he feels as if he were being given a trace of the "happy childhood" which he had never known, for his childhood and boyhood had been rather lonely and influenced by war and sadness over the death of his mother.

The human skull in a bowl of roses bearing the motto 'Et in Arcadia Ego' on its forehead, which Charles has in his room at Oxford in 1923, while disturbing Jasper does suggest Charles's aesthetic vitality and his awareness of the connectedness of beauty and transience. According to Vergil, Arcadia was the home of pastoral simplicity and happiness. Philip Sidney's famous pastoral romance (written in 1580 and published in 1590) entitled "Arcadia," established the genre in England. Two paintings by Nicholas Poussin (one in 1627, the second in 1637–38) focus on the theme of 'Et in Arcadia Ego'—these are pastoral paintings showing shepherds, idealized figures from classical antiquity, around a tomb containing the inscription 'Et in Arcadia ego.' The title of Book I of *Brideshead Revisited*, 'Et in Arcadia Ego,' could be interpreted in different ways. In his book, *Visible Words—A Study of Inscriptions in and as Books and Works of Art*, John Sparrow discusses various interpretations of this statement. One possible interpretation of 'Et in Arcadia Ego' is that Death is saying that even in Arcadia he is present. Another possible interpretation, which involves a transposition of the words to "Et ego in Arcadia" would be that the speaker is saying that he once lived in Arcadia and that he now, having been separated from such a congenial place, thinks about it and longs nostalgically for it (Sparrow 80, 82).

Jean Louis Chevalier in "Arcadian Minutiae: Notes on *Brideshead Revisited*" also describes this image effectively: "For Charles, to rest a skull in a bowl of roses is to evince an exquisite sense of the ephemerality of human existence and to display poetic intelligence of mystical imagery, since roses are not merely emblems of youth and beauty, they are also procession and altar flowers" (41). Chevalier proceeds to state that the "bowl in which the skull is set to rest amounts to an altar of repose, which lends the skull a quasi-sacramental value" (41). Such an "altar of repose" contains at least a semblance of the flame of faith, which at this point of the narrative is more aesthetic than religious in its motivation.

The day after Jasper's attempt to give Charles sound advice for his life at Oxford Charles receives a dinner invitation from Anthony Blanche. Charles hears about Anthony's recent unpleasant experience with Lord Mulcaster and some of his friends. Anthony, in keeping with the spirit of his earlier statement at the luncheon party, shows his jealousy of and animosity towards Sebastian when he is alone with Charles. While saying that Sebastian has such charm, Anthony says it in such a way as to imply a negative undertone. There is certainly an undertone of jealousy in Anthony's statement when he declares that Sebastian was the only boy at school who was not beaten and mistreated. Despite the negative, critical attitude which Anthony reveals in his comments about Sebastian, he can be astute in his observations. For example, Anthony asserts that Charles is an artist, for he has seen some of his drawings. Yet, at the same time Anthony, who cannot seem to control his critical inclinations, says that Charles as an individual is rather ordinary and not exquisite, that is, not exquisite as his drawings are.

Once he allows his critical tendencies to surface and develop Anthony is not readily capable of stemming the tide. He proceeds to offer various critical assessments of and negative remarks about the members of the Marchmain family. After describing Brideshead, Julia, and the other sister in very unflattering terms, he offers an intensive depiction of Sebastian's parents, stressing the fact that Lord Marchmain, although a potent and Byronic character in his own right, has been destroyed and undermined by Lady Marchmain. For of the four children only Sebastian will see his father. According to Anthony, Lord Marchmain, who seems to live contentedly in Venice, has been forced out of society by Lady Marchmain. Of course, later in the narrative when Sebastian and Charles travel to visit Lord Marchmain in Italy, we are given a different perspective on the family history.

For Charles perhaps the most disturbing and disconcerting part of the evening is Anthony's final point that Sebastian, while charming, is not really intelligent. The next day, after a poor sleep caused by reflections on some of Anthony's terribly negative remarks about the members of the Marchmain family, Charles tells Sebastian about the attempt which Anthony had made to undermine their friendship. Sebastian's response, as Anthony interestingly enough had predicted, is to talk about Aloysius, his teddy bear, and that he would not have approved of Anthony's treacherous endeavor. And yet, it is important to note that Anthony merely says that Sebastian will start talking about his bear and does not say or predict what he might say. Sebastian's statement to Aloysius is characterized by an innocent charm and a simple kindness, qualities which Anthony seems neither to admire nor to praise. Perhaps not insignificantly Charles even describes Anthony's verbal assault on the Marchmain family as devilish. Even though Sebastian brushes off Anthony's searing and perhaps even sometimes bitterly jealous statements (that is, the statements which

Charles told Sebastian that Anthony had made) as silly, there is the sense that both Sebastian and Anthony are vying for the soul of Charles. Sebastian sees Charles as a kindred spirit and though he might seem casual and relaxed in his concern about what Anthony has tried to do certainly does not want his friendship with Charles to be undermined.

Chapter Three of Book I describes Charles's return home at the beginning of the Long Vacation without any special plans. The lonely atmosphere of his youth is affirmed in the description of him wandering alone throughout the house when he comes home from college, as his father remains ensconced in the refuge of his library until just before dinner. The atmosphere of the dinner is one of considerable loneliness, for Charles's father shows no genuine interest in him or in his presence and even props a book next to himself, pretending or seeming to read. When the two of them proceed to the garden-room after dinner, Charles expresses an awareness of his father's capacity to put himself mentally in distant epochs where he felt very comfortable. The desire of Charles's father for isolation and seclusion is further manifest in his claim that he forced Aunt Philippa, who had tried to be a comforting presence in the house after the death of Charles's mother, out in the end. Mr. Ryder, as Prince Bolkonsky in Tolstoy's *War and Peace*, aspires to achieve a sense of distance from contemporary society—his library is a special place of sanctuary.

The dinner which Mr. Ryder has for Sir Cuthbert and Lady Orme-Herrick, their daughter Gloria, her fiancé, a publisher, and Mr. Jorkins, is a painful affair which no one particularly seems to enjoy. This event reinforces the inner tensions between Charles and his father, who appears not to wish to have his congenial isolation disturbed by anyone. The unhappiness and loneliness which Charles feels at home is heightened considerably when he receives the short missive from Sebastian which says that he will soon be travelling to Venice to visit his father and that he is not truly alone for various members of his family keep appearing and then departing for various destinations. Even though Sebastian even states in the letter that he wishes Charles were coming on the trip and that he were there, Charles is unfavorably impressed and discontented by the tone, and seems to be influenced by and to hear in his mind the admonishing voice of Anthony from their earlier dinner expounding on the "charm" of Sebastian.

However, one Sunday afternoon Charles receives a telegram from Sebastian which says that he has been injured and asking if his friend would come immediately to Brideshead Castle. This telegram revives the profound emotional feeling which Charles has for his friend, a feeling which had been disturbed by the initial laconic note which he had received from Sebastian earlier in the vacation. The decision of Charles to leave right away does not appear to trouble his father, for he even says that his son should not hurry back. When Charles arrives at Melstead Carbury after taking the train from Paddington Station, he is met by Lady Julia who is grateful that someone is available to care for Sebastian. Even though Julia shares certain characteristics and qualities with Sebastian, it is clear that she does not wish to have the responsibility of caring for him. When they arrive at Brideshead, Charles sees Sebastian in a wheelchair with one foot bandaged.

The room where they dine that evening is 'the Painted Parlour,' an aesthetically interesting refuge in this beautiful house. The octagonal space of this room contains wreathed medallions on the walls, pastoral groups of Pompeian figures across the dome, satin-wood and ormolu furniture, a bronze candelabrum, mirrors, and sconces, reflecting the work of one individual. From this room Sebastian and Charles adjourn to the library where they spend almost every night of the following month. Not only is the library a space of sanctuary in and of itself; but its location is also very comforting and picturesque for it "lay on the side of the house that overlooked the lakes" (78) and its windows "were open to the stars and the scented air, to the indigo and silver, moonlit landscape of the valley and the sound of water falling in the fountain" (78). What makes this mansion so extraordinary is not only the splendid sense of sanctuary which it contains and affirms but also the mythical vitality which is an integral dimension of its atmosphere. The history of Brideshead, the narrative of its architectural creation and development, helps to create a mythical vitality about the house. One might even say that the myth or mythical narrative of the house generates and sustains the aura of sanctuary, for such a myth is at least to some extent the "foundation stone" of the great house.

It is noteworthy that Sebastian in both rooms, 'the Painted Parlour' and the library, emphasizes the beauty of being alone. The 'Painted Parlour' possesses not only octagonal spaciousness and an Arcadian aura, affirmed in the various pastoral figures on the dome, but also an ambience of coziness and privacy embellished by the presence of the satin-wood and ormolu furniture and the bronze candelabrum which reflect the work "of one illustrious hand" (77). Inspired by the lovely atmosphere of the library where they will spend considerable time during this summer holiday, Sebastian says to Charles that they will have "a heavenly time alone" (78). At the beginning of the next chapter, Chapter Four, Charles agrees with Sebastian's comment, saying that during those summer days at Brideshead he felt himself to be "very near heaven" (79). Sebastian is so happy about having the house to himself without the presence of his family members that he expresses his ardent wish that this special place would always possess such an aura of splendid isolation—"always summer, always alone, the fruit always ripe and Aloysius in a good temper"(79). This is Sebastian's vision of Arcadia, a vision of aesthetic beauty and pastoral serenity, which will sustain him at least to some extent even when he is distant from his beloved Brideshead. Years later as he reflects on his past life, Charles says that the way Sebastian was that summer as they enjoyed the quiet, the beauty, and the vitality of the "enchanted palace" (80) is the way that he always likes to think of him.

Sebastian has an exceptional aesthetic sensibility and appreciates various distinctive and spacious interiors at Brideshead Castle—one such important architectural interior is the library which possesses an aura of great vitality. Such an inner sanctum is similar in spirit and aesthetic splendor to the extraordinary libraries in England at Blenheim Palace (where the picture gallery was converted into a library by the 9th Duke of Marlborough), at Chatsworth (where the long gallery was transformed into a library in the early nineteenth century), at Castle Howard (with its spacious luminescence), at Blickling Hall (where the long gallery was converted into a library in the eighteenth century), and at Syon House (where the long gallery was converted by Robert Adam into a library and a withdrawing room in the mid-eighteenth century). Such an inner sanctum also contains the spirit of beauty and cultural vitality exemplified by the exquisite libraries of the Schönbrunn palace in Austria, the libraries at Sans Souci, at the Charlottenburg Palace, and at Wörlitz in Germany, and the libraries of Versailles, the Alhambra, Buckingham Palace and of other delightfully spacious palaces or country estates. Sebastian has the kind of profound aesthetic sensibility which would appreciate any such lovely and magnificent interior in a great house.

Charles states that he enjoyed an aesthetic education at Brideshead as he roamed "from the Soanesque library to the Chinese drawing-room, adazzle with gilt pagodas and nodding mandarins,...from the Pompeian parlour to the great tapestry-hung hall which stood unchanged, as it had been designed two hundred and fifty years before" (80). Although Charles does not admire and love Brideshead Castle as deeply as Sebastian, he does have a very sensitive appreciation for the mansion, saying that if such a residence belonged to him he would not live anywhere else. That Charles agrees implicitly with Sebastian when he says that he is glad that his family in the past had decided to pull down the original structure and build a new castle about a mile away in a more propitious location affirms his appreciation for this great house and its ambience.

Charles and Sebastian not only roam through various parts of the castle but also sit for hours looking out onto the terrace. The terrace, which represented "the final consummation of the house's plan" (80) overlooked the lakes and was encompassed by "the two arms of the colonnade" (80). Beyond the edge of this were groves of lime leading to "the wooded hillsides" (81), creating a vision of ultimate pastoral tranquility. At the center of the terrace, part of which was paved and part of which was planted with flower-beds and box, was the splendid fountain, bought and imported by one of Sebastian's ancestors from a piazza in southern Italy a century before, now embellishing the artistic dynamism of this paradise. Encouraged by Sebastian, Charles draws the fountain and even admits that he manages to create an image reminiscent of Piranesi. In admitting that he had developed an appreciation of architecture since his childhood, Charles also declares that while his inclinations were initially medieval, his experience at Brideshead represented a conversion to the Baroque. Entranced by the high dome and the coffered ceilings, by the arches and broken pediments, and by the fountain, Charles feels emotionally and intellectually energized and revitalized. Frederick L. Beaty writes in *The Ironic World of Evelyn Waugh* that "even while sensing the architect's desire to embody the vitality, variety, and grandeur of divinity" (153) in the dome, the arches, and the pediments of Brideshead, "Charles is totally unaware that his 'conversion to the baroque' is a prelude to his religious conversion" (153). Beaty proceeds to say that Charles cannot at this point "consciously realize that man may reach the sacred through the profane or that God may work His will through man's aesthetic sense" (153).

Charles appreciates the architectural history of the house and the fact that it was built in the time of Inigo Jones using the stones from an earlier structure which was a castle. He also admires the aesthetically interesting fountain. Katharyn W. Crabbe states in *Evelyn Waugh* that as "Charles's role in the world changes, the fountain changes to express the change" (99). Crabbe proceeds to assert that in the course of the novel the fountain serves as "a central part of the idyllic long vacation in which Charles and Sebastian are perfectly happy" (99), and later as a mirror of "the passionate intensity of Charles's love for Julia" (99), and still later a place without color and light after Julia's remarks on the topic of sin (99). Ultimately, the fountain is empty of water and appears to be a place without comfort. As Katharyn W. Crabbe thoughtfully suggests, the "modern age, which Charles calls 'the age of Hooper,' has thoroughly overrun the last vestiges of gentleness, honor, and beauty" (100), negatively impacting both the house and the fountain.

One day Sebastian and Charles find a box of oil-paints in a cupboard; Charles subsequently paints a romantic landscape in one of the small oval frames in the office. Such a landscape which encompasses a summer scene of natural beauty and spaciousness as well as an ivy-covered architectural ruin might even be said to foreshadow literally and symbolically later experiences in the novel—for the image of nature in the painting bears a certain resemblance to the natural beauty of the Brideshead landscape and the house itself becomes an object of decline and undervaluation during the war. After this successful venture of Charles's painting in the office, the two friends are inspired to explore the wine cellar and to take a serious interest in the appreciation of the various vintages stored there. Alone and encroached upon by few visitors, Sebastian and Charles decide to get drunk every night as they enjoy the fruits of the abundant wine cellar.

Brideshead Castle contains in the house and grounds a notable semblance of the spirit of several great country houses of England, and especially of Castle Howard. Lord Carlisle, who commissioned John Vanbrugh in 1699 to build a castle and garden, wanted a sublime creation. The revolutionary estate which they developed is described by Torsten O. Enge and Carl F. Schröer in *Garden Architecture in Europe*: "there was no secular building in the whole kingdom with a larger dome, no other house with such a forest of vases, statues, busts and chimneys on its roofs, and no garden with such delightful miniature architecture as Castle Howard in North Yorkshire" (192). From the terrace walk to the artificial lake to the Temple of the

Four Winds, Vanbrugh's last work, to Nicholas Hawksmoor's impressive mausoleum, the spacious estate around the magnificent house contains various splendid views in keeping with the strong sense of expansiveness which Lord Carlisle desired. Castle Howard was built by Charles, 3rd Earl of Carlisle, an important and powerful member of the royal court who became Earl Marshal of England. It was highly appropriate for Castle Howard to be selected as the great house of the Marchmain family in the 1981 movie version of *Brideshead Revisited*—each of these mansions is a sublime architectural masterpiece which was in the same family for generations. In Castle Howard the Great Hall, the elaborate dome, the State Rooms with various splendid objects, and the bedroom in which Queen Victoria slept in 1850 are notable interior features which possess a spirit similar to the architectural magnificence of several interior spaces at Brideshead Castle. And the natural landscape around each of the great houses was modified or altered to suit the aesthetic sensibility of the owner of the great house and of the architect.

One might also say that Brideshead Castle represents the spirit of Blenheim Palace, another of John Vanbrugh's great architectural creations, which celebrates the Duke of Marlborough's military prowess, and especially his defeat of the French at the Battle of Blenheim in 1704. Queen Anne gave the Duke of Marlborough, John Churchill, the royal estate of Woodstock and a huge amount of money to build a grand house in gratitude for his military victories over France and Bavaria. The original garden design by Henry Wise, court gardener to Queen Anne, was modified by Lancelot "Capability" Brown who in 1764 was put in charge of the gardens. He created two entertwining lakes under Vanbrugh's considerable bridge and developed a sweeping landscape for he believed "that park and countryside should merge into one another with no visible transition" (Enge and Schröer 199). The beauty and splendor of Brideshead Castle, which is so similar in spirit to the magnificence of such great houses as Castle Howard, Blenheim Palace, Stowe, and Chatsworth, and the lovely natural environment of the estate are intimately and profoundly appreciated by Sebastian and Charles.

In *Three Modern Satirists: Waugh, Orwell, and Huxley*, Stephen Greenblatt describes Brideshead Castle effectively as representing "order, stability, goodness, civilization, and above all continuity with the past" (4). The individual who is in charge of and responsible for such a noble heritage must be exceptional and devoted to the aristocratic heritage. Annette Wirth suggests in *The Loss of Traditional Values and Continuance of Faith in Evelyn Waugh's Novels* that Sebastian withdraws "subconsciously and consciously from this noble heritage" (63). This is especially sad because Sebastian has, it seems to me, greater potential than any of his siblings to carry on the tradition of a noble aristocrat as the owner of a splendid house. He has the appropriate character for it, seen in his aristocratic emotional and physical presence, in his generosity of heart and spirit, in his profound appreciation of, love for, and commitment to Brideshead Castle and its architectural ambience and natural environment, in his capacity to be appropriately social (for example, in the party which he gives in his Oxford rooms) and associate with his peers, in his religious potential which would eventually have desired, as Cordelia did, to preserve the chapel as an integral part of the Brideshead aura, and in his admiration for the past and the tradition of the house, evident in his dedication to Nanny Hawkins and her place in the family. Instead, however, Sebastian is undervalued and misunderstood by various people around him, including tragically by most of his family members. As Annette Wirth correctly suggests, Sebastian's "conscious effort to escape from the reality of the world is also expressed in his seeking solace in alcohol" (63). If the world of everyday reality which Sebastian inhabited in his youth and young adulthood were characterized by and shaped by a predominance of characters of noble spirit and generous heart or even just by people who truly cared about him and his problems and worries, it is possible that he could have been saved and prevented from his flight into distant silences and unfamiliar places and from his abdication of personal responsibility.

Ruth Breeze argues in "Places of the Mind: Locating *Brideshead Revisited*" that Brideshead Castle offers not only a sense "of wholeness and harmony" (140) in aesthetic terms but also signifies a microcosm of the world: "...Waugh's great house is a microcosm, not only artistically, in that it embraces different styles and periods in harmony, but also in its vegetation, with gardens that contain a world of different climates" (141). Breeze also makes the interesting observation that in the conflict between Brideshead and the world of everyday mortality "there is a suggestion that the real embodiment of civilisation, the true heir to Greece, Rome and Renaissance Italy, is the country house" (142). In the consideration of such a proclamation and its implications one might think not only of the aesthetic and cultural tradition of which the English country house is an integral part but also of other similarly vital and aesthetically interesting houses in European literature such as the Buddenbrooks House in Thomas Mann's novel which offer a similar ambience of cultural dynamism. And one might also observe an inherent similarity between such a magnificent house and the "great house" of Rivendell in J. R. R. Tolkien's *The Lord of the* Rings and the "great house" of Shangri-La in James Hilton's *Lost Horizon* both of which attempt in an aura of timelessness to preserve the cultural legacy of civilization.

The tranquility of the castle is interrupted by the Agricultural Show when Sebastian's older brother, Brideshead, and his younger sister, Cordelia, arrive. It is interesting that Sebastian and Charles are sunbathing on the roof of the house and watching the Agricultural Show in the park below through a telescope. They want to maintain their distance from the world of everyday mortality, but it is not consistently possible to achieve this. As he is talking about his brother and the inner conflicts between religious piety and secular expectations which seem to be tormenting him, Sebastian also states that he was the only one of the children who did not hate his father for leaving the family so abruptly and moving to Italy. In this passage Sebastian also invites Charles to travel with him to Venice to meet his father.

When Sebastian and Charles dine with Brideshead and Cordelia in the evening one of the seemingly inescapable topics is religion. Sebastian had discussed religion and religious issues to some extent before with Charles, saying, for example, that whereas Brideshead and Cordelia are ardent Catholics, he and Julia are less religious and religiously vital. One of the pressing concerns of Brideshead and Cordelia is the possibility that the chapel on the estate will be closed for there are not enough Catholics living in the area to make it viable, at least according to the Bishop in London with whom Brideshead had recently met. The family chapel is a quintessential sanctuary which signifies a self-contained religious ambience. Three of the Marchmain family members, Lady Marchmain, Brideshead, and Cordelia, as fervent Catholics, would very much like to retain the Blessed Sacrament at the castle. Cordelia's effusive statement that the chapel is beautiful, whether or not it fulfills the expectations of good art as Bridey wonders, is reminiscent of Sebastian's comment earlier in Chapter Four that the dome is pretty, so it really does not matter to him when it was built. Both Sebastian and Cordelia have an essential appreciation of art and artistic objects which is not naïve, but rather profoundly direct and pleasantly subtle.

The declaration of Sebastian that Catholics have a different perspective on life reflects not only the state of Lady Marchmain's family which, as J. V. Long asserts in "The Consolations of Exile: Evelyn Waugh and Catholicism," "has kept its religion since the time of the Elizabethan persecution" (13) and the sense that English Catholics lived in a relatively isolated and circumscribed circle but also the essence of Evelyn Waugh's conversion to Catholicism. J.V. Long proceeds to say that Waugh admired and felt a consanguinity with the sense of exile and alienation which the English Catholics experienced and with their capacity to survive: "Catholics in England were, in Waugh's mind, a community who had suffered and survived persecution and exile. The key component of survival was a willingness to develop strategies of resistance, of non-conformity, of recusance. Waugh appropriated this attitude, and it permeated his sensibility" (19–20).

At the end of the day as Brideshead takes Sebastian away to show him various documents which he needs to take to his father in Venice to sign, Cordelia stays to talk with Charles. In their conversation once again the topic of religion surfaces, which seems perfectly natural for Cordelia, but certainly not for Charles. Cordelia, sensing intuitively that Charles is truly the agnostic which he claims to be, exclaims that she will pray for him. As the evening party ends, Charles thinks to himself that although he has spent considerable time with Sebastian, he does not really know the inner being of his friend. Once again the issue of seclusion emerges, as Charles reflects on his observation that Sebastian had tried to separate him from the rest of his life in the sense of protecting him from being involved with or encroached upon by other aspects of and by other individuals in his life.

As the Agricultural Show ends and as Brideshead and Cordelia leave, the blissfully relaxing month which Sebastian and Charles have enjoyed and savored at the castle also concludes. The sense of enchantment nurtured at Brideshead during the past month is not completely ended but rather transferred to a different geographical ambience; one might even say that the sense of enchantment is transformed to one of congenial rapture as Sebastian and Charles travel to Venice to visit Lord Marchmain. The façade of the palace where Lord Marchmain lives does not seem so imposing. Yet, when the doors are opened and Sebastian and Charles are taken up the stairs into the light "the *piano nobile* was in full sunshine, ablaze with frescoes of the school of Tintoretto" (96). This is a luminescent sanctuary sheltered from and against the outer darkness. The sense of sanctuary is also present in the description of the rooms where Sebastian and Charles will be staying during their sojourn in Venice. When they arrive, these rooms are shuttered to keep out the afternoon sun; yet, when they are opened, the vista is one of colorful brilliance, for they look out onto the Grand Canal. It is as if this set of rooms, a special space within the luminescent sanctuary of the interior of the palazzo, opens up onto a further imaginative world, even though such a world is actually a vision or version of the world of everyday mortality. Yet, such a space does have an aura of splendor, of opening up onto and into a world of dreamy and lovely imaginings.

Charles first observes Lord Marchmain on the balcony of the saloon. The description of the face of Lord Marchmain as noble and simultaneously as having an aura of being somewhat sardonic, somewhat weary, and somewhat voluptuous seems appropriate for the socioeconomic and cultural context in which he has chosen to reside. For such qualities are an embodiment in miniature of the aesthetic vitality, the cultural dynamism, the commercial success and decline, and the emotional and spiritual languor of Venice, its recent historical development, and its existential presence. The interior ambience of Lord Marchmain's palazzo is characterized by and permeated by splendid objects and an atmosphere of marble, velvet, and gilt *gesso*.

The experience which Charles has in Venice is in its own right as much of an aesthetic education as was his sojourn at Brideshead. Yet, such a vital experience is also different in the cast of characters which informs it and in the reflective observations which are inspired in him. For example, Charles has an interesting conversation with Cara, the middle-aged, well-mannered mistress of Lord Marchmain who is received cordially in Venetian society. First, she tells Charles that Lord Marchmain stays with her not because he truly loves her, but because she protects him from Lady Marchmain whom he hates passionately. Cara also clarifies a point which was raised earlier in the novel when it was suggested that Lord Marchmain was a social pariah. Here Cara asserts that quite the opposite is true, for it is Lord Marchmain who has driven people away whom he thinks have had contact or might have contact with Lady Marchmain.

Cara also reveals to Charles two poignant observations about Sebastian. She declares that Sebastian is in love with his own childhood, symbolized especially by his attachment to his teddy-bear and to his nanny, and that he drinks too much and will become a drunkard if no one intervenes to dissuade him from such excess. This conversation ends the visit to Venice for Sebastian and Charles, which the latter describes as having passed swiftly and sweetly so that he feels as if he were "drowning in honey, stingless" (101).

When Sebastian and Charles return after their glorious Italian trip to London one day before the new term at Oxford begins, they part in the forecourt of Sebastian's mother's house. When Sebastian states that he will not invite Charles to come in because the house is probably full of his family members and that they will see each other again at Oxford, there is the sense that the golden aura of the carefree and blissful summer which they have shared together has been undermined. The unhappy sense of unpleasant expectation which Sebastian reveals at the threshold of his mother's house is matched by the emotionally cold response which Charles receives from his father when he returns home. The lack of genuine communication between the two is reaffirmed in the verbal and psychological tension which informs their terse and laconic conversational exchanges and the space which remains unfulfilled by words and feelings left unsaid and unexpressed.

The beginning of Chapter Five of Book I also signals a change in the aura of happiness which made the summer so consistently pleasant. Oxford, at the beginning of the academic year, is permeated by an autumnal atmosphere, symbolized by the falling leaves and the twilight decay. On this first Sunday evening of the term Sebastian, having lost the exuberance of the previous summer, declares that he feels very old. One reason for the change in Sebastian's demeanor is the fact that he has been gently admonished by Monsignor Bell to be more studious and academically focused. Charles believes that he and Sebastian have lost the spirit of discovery and the sense of curiosity which had made their previous collegiate year so interesting and so exciting.

Whereas Charles writes his weekly essays, attends occasional lectures, and also joins the Ruskin School of Art, Sebastian feels increasingly constricted and melancholy about the loss of the blissful freedom which he had enjoyed during the previous academic year. As the term progresses they become increasingly isolated and separate themselves further from others, making no new friends. After admitting that he missed the presence of Anthony Blanche, who had left the university, Charles also reveals that he and Sebastian seemed to try to avoid their Oxford companions and sought pleasant company in less exalted taverns.

At this point in the dismal term Lady Marchmain arrives for a weeklong visit to Oxford. She wants to create a memorial book for her brothers who were killed in the war and finds Mr. Samgrass of All Souls to help her with this endeavor. Although a history don and genealogist who has various social connections, he does not have a genuine religious faith and is described intuitively by Charles as someone who is rather artificial and emotionally cold beneath his genial appearance.

Soon after Lady Marchmain's visit to Oxford, during which she invites Charles to spend an extended vacation at Brideshead, Julia and her companion, Rex Mottram, arrive to have lunch with Sebastian. During the lunch, which Charles hosts at his rooms, one observes that Rex is as superficial and artificial in his way as Mr. Samgrass is in his. Sebastian's perceptive remark about Rex that all of his friends are manipulative, scheming, and superficial politicians effectively summarizes the essence of Rex's character as an extremely aggressive and ambitious person of questionable integrity.

The dinner party which Rex soon thereafter gives for the charity ball with which Julia is involved affirms some of the negative qualities already perceptible regarding Rex and also has disturbing consequences for Sebastian and Charles. After first going to Marchmain House in London with Boy Mulcaster to get dressed, they proceed to the dinner party, already somewhat drunk. Mulcaster's suggestion to leave the party and go to Ma Mayfield's, to the Old Hundredth, is disastrous. When Sebastian, who is driving in a drunken frame of mind when they leave, abruptly stops the car in the middle of the road, he is approached by two policemen, who might have let the passengers go if Mulcaster had not selfishly and with bravado made a statement suggesting that he could bribe them to look the other way. The policemen respond by taking the young gentlemen to the nearby jail. This is certainly one of the low points of Sebastian's youth. From the beginning of this affair Sebastian, who was not overly enthused about following Mulcaster, was simply trying to be generous and helpful to others. Instead, Sebastian is the one who bears the brunt of the deleterious consequences.

With the assistance of Rex Mottram, who was really more interested in being or seeming to be impressive than in providing genuinely supportive help, Charles and Mulcaster are let off with a minor fine. When Sebastian appears for trial a week later he is fined ten pounds and suffers the public representation of the unfortunate event in the newspapers. It is said that the magistrate would have been much harsher with Sebastian if it had not been for the testimony of Mr. Samgrass who proclaimed that Sebastian had an exemplary character and a promising future at the university. The narrative makes clear that the helpfulness of Rex Mottram and Mr. Samgrass in this incident derives considerably more from their own sense of selfishness and self-oriented ambition to be considered useful by the Marchmain family than from any genuine concern about the situation of and well-being of Sebastian.

The paragraph in *Brideshead Revisited* which mentions the two newspaper headlines declaring that the marquis's son was unused to wine and that a model student's career was at stake contains a double irony. It is ironic that the first headline suggests that the marquis's son was unused to wine for Sebastian is, of course, a rather heavy drinker at this point in his life. It is even more ironic that the second headline in content and in tone, in the spirit of Mr. Samgrass's testimony, implies something negative about Sebastian and his character. For, when one reflects upon the initial depictions of Sebastian and his aesthetic motivations and emotional inclinations at Oxford, one could easily make the argument that he actually does have an exemplary character and a generosity of heart and spirit which is noteworthy anywhere, whether at a prominent university or in any other public setting. It is also very ironic that Sebastian, whose character and intentions are so superior to those of Mr. Samgrass, is subject to his parasitic and controlling whims and fancies at the university.

As Ruth Breeze insightfully notes in "Places of the Mind: Locating *Brideshead Revisited*" the London of the charity ball which Sebastian and Charles attend and which has such dire consequences is depicted as signifying a dismal and blighted landscape (132). Breeze also points out that the London which Ryder visits again in the General Strike has an aura of nightmarish excess (133). When Ryder returns to London later from his tour of Latin America and encounters Anthony Blanche, the city is also permeated by an atmosphere of emotional and spiritual degeneration. Marchmain House, "a doomed relic of a former age of glory" (Breeze 138), is one site in the city which is of special aesthetic interest to Sebastian and Charles, but sadly, this lovely architectural creation seems destined to vanish. Marchmain House signifies a vision of elegant harmony, a symbol of a world of aesthetic refinement and vitality no longer appreciated by the urban society now increasingly permeated by a sense of aggressiveness, chaos, disorder, and haste.

Charles is not especially surprised to find Mr. Samgrass at Brideshead Castle when he visits there for the vacation. Mr. Samgrass is ingratiating to the prominent members of the Marchmain family in public, but in private can imply a critical attitude towards them. For example, when Charles arrives at Brideshead after Christmas, Samgrass is sitting in the Tapestry Hall in a possessive attitude as if he owned the mansion; moreover, he suggests a criticism of the family's activity by calling the meet of the hounds an archaic spectacle. One of his statements which might seem outwardly positive, but which is actually characterized by a very negative undertone, is that he would like to see Brideshead and Sir Walter Strickland-Venables, the two masters of the hunt, included in the tapestries in the room because this would add a colorful note to their rather mundane appearance.

The sense which some of the members of the Marchmain family have that Samgrass is a charlatan who is adept at pretending to pursue interests which others want him to while really only interested in his own self-aggrandizement is expressed by Sebastian who, after the hunt and at the beginning of this vacation, proclaims that he wishes Samgrass would leave, for he is weary of being grateful to him.

In this part of the narrative Charles already senses that Sebastian feels threatened by various aspects of the outside world, that is, by dimensions of his private and public life which confined and restricted him and his spirit and did not allow him to be comfortably or congenially alone. One of Sebastian's concerns has consistently been that some of his family members would annex Charles as their friend. Sebastian is especially disturbed about the "little talks" which his mother desires to have with Charles, for he senses that these will cause a rift or distance between the two of them. The setting of some of these talks during colder weather is typically Lady Marchmain's sitting-room on the first floor. Brideshead Castle, while naturally signifying a splendid sanctuary in its own right as a magnificent house, has within its domain multiple rooms and halls which represent sanctuaries as well. One of these inner sanctuaries, one of these smaller sanctuaries within the larger spatial expansiveness and refuge of the mansion, is the sitting-room of Lady Marchmain. The room, which she modified to fit her own tastes, is so distinctive that when one enters it one seems "to be in another house" (126). This room, permeated by the pleasant scent of fresh flowers as well as of diverse musty objects, contains not only various water-colors and a small library of works of poetry and piety but also an inner sanctum of personal treasures relating to her faith and to her family. During the course of his conversation with Lady Marchmain, Charles, although feeling somewhat influenced by her charm and faith, asserts that at that time he was primarily focused on and concerned about Sebastian and his personal crisis.

It is noteworthy that Charles seems to be the only one in the Marchmain family circle who is attuned enough to Sebastian and his feelings to be aware of the fact that Sebastian is experiencing a very serious personal crisis. In astutely observing that Sebastian considered not only members of his family but also his conscience and affection as intruders into his peaceful inner world, Charles is poignantly aware that his friend's days in Arcadia were coming to an end. Charles also perceptively realizes that as his connection with the Marchmain family developed, his friendship with Sebastian became strained. For by enhancing his intimacy with the Marchmain family members Charles seemed to be becoming a part of the world from which Sebastian wanted to separate himself.

The sense of sanctuary which Sebastian had recently felt at Brideshead during that glorious summer has been considerably, if not completely, undermined by the presence of so many family members and guests at the castle, and especially by the continuing contact with Mr. Samgrass. To escape the implicitly menacing influence of Samgrass, Sebastian leaves Brideshead to spend time in London at the house of Charles. When they return to Oxford, Charles observes more clearly than ever before that Sebastian is suffering from a sickness of heart and an unhappiness of spirit. Now when Sebastian is merry it is because he is drunk. As E. A. Robinson's Miniver Cheevy, Sebastian drinks to escape the world of everyday mortality and its inadequacies.

During the following Easter vacation at home Sebastian's personal troubles and the tension with his family are amplified. On one particular day Sebastian gets very drunk. The responses of several family members are noteworthy because they show a lack of genuine concern and affection for Sebastian and his predicament. When Charles tells Julia that Sebastian is drunk, she responds by saying that this is a boring situation and no business of hers. Brideshead's reaction is merely to say in a rather impersonal manner that one cannot stop an individual who desires to get intoxicated. Lady Marchmain definitely seems to show more concern, but is willing to postpone a personal discussion with Sebastian until the morning. Cordelia, while seeming to care more than her brother and sister about Sebastian and his condition, does not really try to do anything to help him or perhaps one should say is not sure what can be done to assist him in this crisis. The evening ends on a note of painful tension for Sebastian, pale and haggard, comes to the room where the family members are gathered to make a point of apologizing not to them but to Charles, whom he describes as his only friend.

The next morning Sebastian comes early to the room where Charles is staying to say that he is leaving right away. Although Charles is unwilling to depart so suddenly without saying a formal farewell to Lady Marchmain, Sebastian still aims to leave soon and meet up with Charles again at his house in London. When Charles says goodbye to Lady Marchmain they talk about Sebastian and his plight. In saying that she does not want Sebastian to be ashamed of his problem with alcoholism, Lady Marchmain states that she has seen this before in the family, namely, in the figure of Lord Marchmain, who used to get drunk in the same manner. She even compares Lord Marchmain and Sebastian, claiming that they were both not happy, ashamed, and trying to run away. As kind as Lady Marchmain can be, there is also the sense that she, as Julia, does not want to have the responsibility of trying to help and improve Sebastian with his alcoholism, as she did not try to help and improve Lord Marchmain. She seems to abdicate her responsibility in part by contrasting the behavior of Lord Marchmain and Sebastian in their drunkenness with the behavior of her brothers when drunk, seeming to suggest that the latter were in some way superior to the former. At the end of the conversation when Lady Marchmain gives Charles a copy of the newly published book about her dead and heroic brothers and he leaves her inner sanctum, he feels as if he had been freed from her influence. When Charles returns to his home in London later in the day, he finds Sebastian there and is reassuring, in response to Sebastian's query, that he is supportive of his friend and remains devotedly on his side.

When Charles and Sebastian return to Oxford where the gillyflowers were abundantly present under the windows of Charles's room, Charles senses that his friend is suffering inwardly and is despondent. Sebastian admits to Charles that he would be all right if his family members and presumably other people like Mr. Samgrass would just leave him alone and not encroach upon his privacy and his solitude. In the course of Lady Marchmain's visit to Oxford she comes to Charles to tell him that it has been arranged that Sebastian will live with Monsignor Bell in the Old Palace, thus ruining the plans which Sebastian and Charles had to share rooms together in Merton Street.

Charles, severely disappointed, responds to Lady Marchmain by stressing that if she wants to make Sebastian a drunkard the way to do it is to confine and watch him, as placing him with Monsignor Bell, and not to allow him to feel free in his inclinations and motivations. That night Sebastian and Charles get drunk in a spirit of unrestricted freedom of expression as they had in the past. For Sebastian senses that the aura of congenial sanctuary and of splendid personal freedom which he had enjoyed in the past at Oxford and which he had enjoyed richly during that special summer at Brideshead is being completely undermined and destroyed.

The ending of this chapter is pervaded by considerable melancholy and by an atmosphere of personal loss and tragedy. After Sebastian leaves Oxford with Lady Marchmain, Charles helps Brideshead look through the objects in Sebastian's rooms to decide what should be sent on; Brideshead shows little, if any, genuine feeling for Charles or for Sebastian in their conversation. The sadness of this conversation is intensified when Charles then proceeds to visit his former friend Collins. Even though Collins has one room available, it is not offered to Charles and when he leaves, they never see each other again. When Charles soon returns home to his father's house in London, he raises the issue of not taking a university degree and instead preparing for his future career, which is to be an artist, a painter. The father's impersonal and relatively uncaring response, even suggesting that Charles might consider an art school abroad, reemphasizes the lack of kindness and thoughtfulness to which Charles has been recently subjected. The profound melancholy and emotional despair permeating the end of Book One culminates in the letter which Charles receives from Lady Marchmain. The letter makes evident that she has taken control of their friendship, for she is the one who writes and not Sebastian. In saying that Mr. Samgrass will be taking charge of Sebastian she counters the suggestion which Charles had made earlier to allow his friend a sense of freedom. It is almost as if she is implying that the role of Charles will be replaced by Samgrass who will be travelling with Sebastian to the Levant. Even though Lady Marchmain says that she hopes that Charles's domestic arrangements for next term have not been too drastically changed by the plan for Sebastian to live with Monsignor Bell, there is the implication in this statement that she has gotten what she wanted. Her final sentence in the letter has a biting undertone. As one reads the last sentences of the letter, one might be reminded of the criticism which Anthony Blanche had earlier expressed regarding Lady Marchmain. Although outwardly the letter, and especially its last several sentences seem relatively innocuous, when one reflects on the tone and on what might have been said and done by Lady Marchmain to ameliorate the tension and rectify the situation, the negative undertone of the epistle is conspicuously apparent. The approach implied in the letter is reminiscent of the attitude which Lady Marchmain revealed in her response to Lord Marchmain's and Sebastian's proclivity for drunkenness, a kind of drunkenness which was incomprehensible to her. Saying that she is "so very sorry" appears to be a reasonable and compassionate response. Yet, if she really cared about the friendship of Sebastian and Charles and if she were really grateful for the devotion which Charles had for so long shown to his friend and if she really wanted to help Sebastian, would she have said what she did and would she have allowed Samgrass to exert such an influence over Sebastian. It is somewhat ironic that Lady Marchmain, an ardent Catholic, would allow or even think of allowing Samgrass, who was earlier in the novel described as someone who is definitely lacking a genuine religious faith, to superintend the potential revitalization of Sebastian. The ending of Chapter Five of Book I is particularly melancholy and sad when one reflects upon the profound happiness which Sebastian and Charles had enjoyed during that exuberant summer at Brideshead and the great appreciation which they had showed for the sanctuary-like atmosphere of the castle, an appreciation more sensitively expressed by them than by anyone else. For it is evident by this point in the narrative that such former happiness will never again be achieved, that it is as transient as the autumnal leaves which fall and swirl over and around the stones of Oxford.

At the beginning of Chapter Six of Book I (which is Chapter I of Book Two in the later revised edition) of *Brideshead Revisited*, Mr. Samgrass is showing the Marchmain family slides of his tour of the Levant with Sebastian. From the very beginning of the slide show one can tell that something is amiss, for while Samgrass tries to offer considerable detail about the images, Sebastian is typically not present. Sebastian explains his absence from the photos by stating that he was ill, while Samgrass states that Sebastian sometimes held the camera. This slide show occurs on the first evening of Charles's holiday visit, two days after Christmas. It is noteworthy that Charles receives a note of invitation from Lady Marchmain three weeks prior to the holiday—the tone of the note is softer than her previous epistle and seems to express a genuine interest on behalf of Sebastian to see his friend. That Sebastian visits Nanny Hawkins with Charles and Cordelia represents perhaps an attempt to revitalize the spirit of childhood and early youth which had pervaded the first occasion on which he had brought Charles to Brideshead.

Of the members of the Marchmain family, Lady Marchmain, Cordelia, and Bridey especially exemplify the aura of the Catholic aristocracy. All three have a strong faith which is very important to them. Julia is rather indifferent to her Catholic upbringing at this point of the novel; Sebastian seems to be outwardly not overly concerned about his religion, yet inwardly he, perhaps more than any other member of the Marchmain family, signifies a pious individual. The presence of Nanny Hawkins is important not only as a symbol of the innocence and happiness of the childhood of some of the Marchmain children but also as an affirmation of the religious devotion which various family members feel. Nanny's presence in a sanctuary-like atmosphere in the upper story of the house reinforces the notion that there is a very devout religious aura in one integral part of Brideshead Castle. John H. Wilson writes in *Evelyn Waugh—A Literary Biography, 1924–1966* that Waugh "felt kinship with Catholic aristocrats" (82) not only because the "Catholic aristocrat defends old, unfashionable values" (82) but also because he sympathized with the suffering which they had experienced because of their beliefs. Wilson proceeds to say that in "1944, after he had experienced disillusion and humiliation in the war, Waugh wrote *Brideshead Revisited* and conveyed the grace of an aristocratic Catholic family from the perspective of a convert like himself" (83).

John H. Wilson also makes the important point in *Evelyn Waugh—A Literary Biography, 1924–1966* that the portrayal of aristocrats in *Brideshead Revisited* differs from the representation of such individuals in his earlier novels in its declaration that some aristocrats have a vital aesthetic sensibility (104). Both Sebastian and Charles admire the beauty of the estate, the "exquisite man-made landscape," an appreciation certainly shared by Lady Marchmain, Bridey, Julia, and Cordelia to different degrees. Wilson also argues effectively that Waugh "had long been conscious of the connection between aristocracy and beauty" (104), quoting various statements from Waugh to reinforce this. Waugh believed that genuinely supportive aristocratic patronage could not only help artists greatly in various ways but could also contribute to the preservation of a humanitarian culture by creating a spirit of courteousness in discourse and in maintaining the integrity and vitality of the English language. Of the suffering of the Flytes, Wilson says: "The Flytes suffer not only because they appreciate beauty in an ugly world, but also because they retain their faith when they could conveniently abandon it" (106). Lady Marchmain's family background is typical of the Catholic aristocracy, for during the past several centuries the Catholic squires had led isolated lives among themselves, wealthy but without notable opportunities for political and public advancement.

Several critics, including John H. Wilson, have emphasized that although Brideshead Castle "becomes the object of love when Charles sees it" (108), it "is only a vehicle for the real hero, none other than God himself" (108). Wilson emphasizes the interpretation of Waugh himself with respect to the importance of religion in the novel: "As Waugh explained...*Brideshead* is an 'attempt to trace the workings of the divine purpose in a pagan world, in the lives of an English Catholic family, half-paganised themselves,' in the world of 1923–39'" (108). Although the Marchmain family is over time considerably, and even severely, encroached upon and influenced by the outside world, for example, by such individuals as Charles, Mr. Samgrass, Rex Mottram, and Beryl Muspratt, most of them survive as individuals, diminished and saddened by the suffering which they have experienced and observed, but nevertheless at least somewhat hopeful about the future.

Sebastian, as Charles, appreciates and admires the architecture of Brideshead, although in a more sentimental and intellectually innocent manner. Whereas Charles is curious about the architectural history of Brideshead Castle, Sebastian is content to enjoy its beautiful presence. One might say that Sebastian has a very refined aesthetic sensibility, seen especially in his desire to live in certain lovely architectural and natural environments, and a quiet appreciation for the picturesque and the sublime. Horace Walpole wrote of Castle Howard in the eighteenth century: "Nobody had informed me at one view I should see a palace, a town, a fortified city, temples on high places, woods worthy of being each a metropolis of the Druids, the noblest lawn in the world fenced by half the horizon,...; in short, I have seen gigantic palaces before, but never a sublime one" (*Great Houses of England and Wales* 299). More intuitively and more devotedly than any of his family members Sebastian has a genuinely profound admiration for Brideshead Castle, for its picturesque and sublime interiors, architecture, and natural views and vistas. In *Evelyn Waugh* Katharyn W. Crabbe argues that in "making Brideshead Castle the central image of the novel, Waugh for the first time employs the symbol of a building without being ironic" (101–2). Crabbe proceeds to contrast the positive nature of the construction and development of Brideshead with the architectural activity in *Decline and Fall*, for example: "In *Decline and Fall* he had presented the creation of Llanabba Castle as economic exploitation and a failure to recognize the spirit of existing architecture" (102). Both Sebastian and Charles appreciate (Sebastian more emotionally and Charles more intellectually) the spirit of architectural genesis, development, and growth leading to the creation of Brideshead Castle.

In Chapter Six of Book I, Charles observes that Sebastian looks physically pale and haggard, a worn-out version of his former self. Moreover, Charles also notices that the wariness in Sebastian which he had previously seen has intensified. When Charles is going to dress for dinner, he is addressed by Brideshead who tells him that his mother has ordered that no drinks are to remain in any of the rooms—the tacit reason is to prevent Sebastian from being tempted to indulge in his inclinations. Brideshead reinforces this arrangement by telling Charles that Sebastian was actually lost over Christmas and was only discovered by Samgrass on the previous evening. Even though the dinner that evening is described as very gloomy, especially because of the anxiety about Sebastian and his possible behavior and also because of the underlying sense that there is something fundamentally shady about the self-promoting slide show of Samgrass, the evening ends with a sense of hope, as Lady Marchmain reads to everyone and as Sebastian expresses an interest in participating in the hunt which is planned for the next day at Flyte St. Mary. Yet, later that evening Sebastian admits to Charles that he is merely going to pretend to partake of the hunt and instead endeavor to reach the nearest pub so that he can spend the day there drinking with carefree ease.

As this conversation continues we learn how problematic the life of Sebastian has become and how deeply unhappy he truly is. Sebastian tells Charles that his family has stopped his bank account. He also offers perceptive observations about Samgrass's real intentions in taking the trip to the Levant—namely, that he had always wanted to visit various interesting sites in Turkey and the Middle East and as

Lady Marchmain was generously paying for everything and as he was travelling in a first-class style, he could not resist taking advantage of the opportunity. Sebastian tells Charles the intriguing story of how he managed to escape from Samgrass in Constantinople and again in Athens and how he met Anthony Blanche in Constantinople.

The next morning Charles relents and despite his misgivings, and knowing that the Marchmain family would not approve, gives Sebastian some money (two pounds) so that he can enjoy himself during the day. Charles spends the day painting in the garden room, where he continues the tradition of completing one of the medallions on each of his visits to Brideshead. Sebastian returns from his day's adventures in a rather drunken condition and the hope, which the previous evening had implied, of achieving a pleasant atmosphere after the hunt is postponed, if not undermined. The next morning marks the beginning of the end for the friendship of Sebastian and Charles; for, in response to a question from Charles, Sebastian states that he does not really want Charles to stay longer at Brideshead, for he is no help in his profoundly tragic personal dilemma. When Charles goes to Lady Marchmain to say his farewell, she is very harsh towards him, accusing him of being wicked and cruel because he gave Sebastian money, knowing that he would likely use it to go to the local pub.

As Charles drives away and takes his last look back at the house, he expresses the melancholy sentiment that he is leaving part of himself behind, while also implying that it will be difficult to revitalize in the near future the aura of happiness which he experienced there. It is noteworthy that the language which he uses in this context is reminiscent of the image which Sebastian had used the first time he took Charles to Brideshead. On that occasion Sebastian had said that he wanted to bury a crock of gold in places where he had been happy so that when he was old and unhappy he could return and retrieve the precious object and remember the pleasant past. On this occasion Charles uses the image of burying treasure not in a positive sense, as an anticipation of future bliss, but as a means to pay for the trip to the world of the dead. The low door in the wall leading to an enchanted garden which Charles had eagerly sought and discovered, or thought he had discovered, in Oxford seems to have closed irrevocably.

Charles returns to Paris and his aesthetically dynamic life there in a melancholy state of mind. He is not terribly surprised to receive a cordial letter from Cordelia several weeks later, for he realizes that life typically does not have absolutely clear separations. It is interesting that Cordelia in the letter says that she, as Charles before, was sympathetic towards Sebastian's plight and got whisky for him. And now she is in disgrace. Approximately a week later Rex comes to his apartment—he was supposed to be taking Sebastian to see a specialist in Zürich, but Sebastian managed to escape.

The dinner which Rex and Charles have at Paillard's, the small and exclusive restaurant which Charles suggests, is very revealing. Rex tells Charles that the Marchioness thought she might have been too harsh on Charles at their last meeting. She felt this way especially after the downfall of Samgrass, whom Julia described as a fraud. Rex also mentions what Cordelia herself had said in the letter to Charles, namely, that she had for a while helped Sebastian to whisky; and he also states that the Marchioness is seriously ill and that the financial condition of the family is not as robust as it appears to be. As Charles listens to Rex talk about mortal illness, debt, money, and power he tries to focus on the delicious meal and block out the self-aggrandizing, self-directed world which Rex represents. Rex admits that he was not only aiming in his continental trip to take Sebastian to a doctor but also to visit Lord Marchmain because he sensed that he would agree to anything regarding his engagement to Julia which would disturb Lady Marchmain. At the end of this chapter Charles mentions that he later heard about the marriage of Julia and Rex in a small, nondescript chapel with no royalty present and not even any members of Julia's family. Such an outcome is especially dismal because it is the antithesis of what both Julia and Rex, and especially Rex, in his lust for power, had desired.

In Chapter Seven of Book I (which is Chapter II of Book Two in the later edition of the novel) we learn about the developing relationship of Julia and Rex, the conflicts and struggles involved in this relationship and finally their engagement. The chapter begins with the description of Julia's first London season in which she shone like a star. Julia is portrayed as inhabiting a sanctuary-like world, a very exclusive socioeconomic ambience of several prominent families. The power of Julia to charm is encapsulated in the depiction of her as a very special individual in possession of a magic ring. Yet, this apparent fairy-tale capacity to enchant the world around her is diminished and undermined by her connection with Rex, an arch-realist whose intrigues and resolute self-aggrandizement inevitably clashes with such a charming capacity and obliterates the aura of a sanctuary-like atmosphere in Julia's life.

One example of this potential of reality to encroach upon any sanctuary-like atmosphere is Bridey's explosive announcement which occurs in the library of Marchmain House which is where the family had gathered one day among the abundance of presents. Brideshead had made various inquiries about Rex's past and had discovered that he had once been married but had neglected to tell Julia about this fact. As Julia is a Catholic, this fact is a serious impediment to her impending marriage with Rex. It is evident that Lady Marchmain and Brideshead want to stop the marriage from taking place. Rex does not give up so easily and asserts that if he will not be allowed to marry Julia in the cathedral then he will marry her in a Protestant church. The other family members are appalled by this suggestion. Nevertheless, Rex telegraphs Lord Marchmain to ask his approval for this and his response is, not surprisingly, that he is delighted. Julia later confesses that the wedding was a squalid affair, for while some of her friends and some of Rex's friends attended, all of the members of the prominent families originally invited did not. At the end of this chapter as Julia is reflecting upon her past and especially upon her relationship and life with Rex in conversations with Charles on board a ship in the Atlantic, she says that such an inauspicious beginning necessarily doomed the marriage. Rex, consistently interested in appearances, had wanted a much more exuberant and publicly popular event. The glowing debutante whom he thought he had married, however, was really a kind of outcast. The sadness of Julia is heightened in her admission that after being married to Rex for about a year she realized that he was not a complete human being but rather a "tiny bit of a man pretending he was the whole" (200). It is interesting that Julia elaborates on this point saying that only the modern age could produce such an artificial and superficial individual, who, because of his ability in one particular area, can appear to be more intelligent, more compassionate, more effective, and more talented than he really is. Even to Cordelia earlier in the novel Rex had seemed to be a self-directed, self-oriented person driven by money and power to succeed in a material sense but with little, if any, humanitarian instinct and motivation.

In Chapter Eight of Book I (which is Chapter III of Book Two in the later edition of the novel) Charles Ryder returns to England from Paris in 1926 for the General Strike. Julia calls Charles and asks him to come to Marchmain House for her mother, who is dying, wants to see him and apologize for her critical attitude on the occasion of their last meeting. The aura of death seems to permeate the house which has a diminished splendor—that the library with its bookcases of Victorian oak is not appreciated as a private chamber for reflection and thought and even possesses more of a public atmosphere as if prepared for a formal committee meeting reinforces the ambience of imminent change and decay which is so prevalent here. Julia also asks if Charles would try to find Sebastian to tell him that his mother is ill. So Charles, who has not been in contact with Sebastian for a long time, travels to Morocco and visits the British Consul near Fez. The consular porter takes Charles to the house in the old town where Sebastian is presumed to live. As Charles observes the dusty silences, the quietly robed figures and the air scented with incense and cloves, he thinks he realizes what especially attracts Sebastian to this place.

As Sebastian is at the hospital kept by the Franciscans, Charles goes there the next morning to see him. Sebastian is an alcoholic and because of his physical frailty is in no condition to travel back to England. Despite the outwardly wretched condition of Sebastian's life, it is noteworthy that he, as the doctor in the hospital affirms, does not complain and is very kind and patient. On the last day of Charles's visit the news reaches them that Lady Marchmain has died. When asked by Charles if he considers returning to England, Sebastian replies that he would find it pleasant in some ways. Yet, he wonders whether his new companion, Kurt, would like it. Charles, who has been helpful to Sebastian by visiting the hospital daily during his visit and by contacting the branch manager of the bank to ensure that his friend will receive a regular amount of pocket money drawn from his quarterly allowance, is appalled at the prospect of his friend from those delightful Oxford days spending his life with the seemingly vagabondish Kurt. Sebastian makes an interesting statement about his friendship with Kurt which resonates more with Charles as he reflects upon its implications later—Sebastian says that in contrast to his previous life in which he was always looked after, it is congenial to have the opportunity to look after someone else, even if it is someone as hopeless as Kurt seems to be. The last image which Charles has of Sebastian is that of him and Kurt in the "little enclosed house at the end of the alley" (216). Although it appears publicly and outwardly as if Sebastian has failed in his life, when one thinks of the splendid existence he enjoyed at Brideshead and the wonderful possibilities of his life, in a symbolic sense he has achieved the sense of sanctuary which was always very important to him. If one reflects upon the ambition which he stated at Brideshead during that special summer which is notably informed by a sense of being happily alone and of being in a congenial place of refuge, this has been fulfilled, although not in the socioeconomic context or with the material abundance that one would have expected of someone of Sebastian's upbringing.

Even though Sebastian lives away from Brideshead and from England I would say that he has a deeper appreciation of his family castle and estate than his brother and sisters who will have more direct contact with Brideshead in the future. Sebastian seemed to have a profound appreciation of and close attachment to Brideshead when he was at Oxford. For he wanted to be at the family mansion in the summer when it was relatively quiet and was quite happy to wander among its glorious halls alone while Bridey and Julia seem more inclined to come to Brideshead when they are compelled to for a social event. More than any of his siblings Sebastian carries the spirit of Brideshead Castle with him wherever he goes, either in England or abroad. Perhaps this is one reason why he enjoys the ambience of his house in Morocco. For it has a semblance of the quiet seclusion and the relative isolation which was so important to him at home. And the ambience directly outside his house in Morocco has qualities of religious and secular significance which Sebastian would appreciate and admire—the quietly robed figures, the passages opening onto the stars, the air scented with incense and cloves. Such a context could symbolically remind Sebastian of some of the magnificent rooms and halls within Brideshead or even of the ambience in a church.

In contrasting the very congenial childhood and youth of Sebastian with its anticipation of abundant happiness with the Sebastian who is living marginally in Morocco, I am reminded of two poems by Edwin Arlington Robinson, "Richard Cory" and "Miniver Cheevy." The persona in "Richard Cory" is strikingly similar to Sebastian Flyte in character, in temperament, and in motivation. In stanza one of the poem the physical description of Richard Cory is very similar to that of Sebastian Flyte in his Oxford days, "a gentleman" (3), "Clean favored" (4), and "imperially slim" (4). As Richard Cory is a focus of the observation and admiration of the public, so is Sebastian. In the second stanza Richard Cory is described as being naturally elegant and capable of a warmth of expression. He is so elegant and regal that he "fluttered pulses" (7) when he speaks to people. The extraordinary nature of this individual is affirmed in his capacity to glitter when he walks. Very few mortal individuals possess or even have the potential to demonstrate such a rare ability. Sebastian, too, "glitters" when he walks and is very capable of speaking sensitively with other people. One difference between Richard Cory and Sebastian, which is evident in the first two stanzas of the poem, is that Richard is more subdued and less "flamboyant" than Sebastian. For Sebastian at Oxford is content to walk around with his teddy bear and to be noticed by others. Yet, Sebastian is not aggressively or actively flamboyant or ostentatious. Rather, one might characterize Sebastian's motivation in this context as innocent and playful, for he appears to wish to be observed so that he may be appreciated.

The portrayal of Richard Cory in stanza three of the poem is also very reminiscent of Sebastian Flyte. Both individuals are extremely wealthy and are "admirably schooled in every grace" (10). The perception of these two individuals by the public is also somewhat similar. Both Richard and Sebastian certainly have various admirers who wish they would have a semblance of his wealth, family heritage, or physical attractiveness. Yet, there is a difference in the nature of the public which admires these two individuals. In the Robinson poem there is a potent contrast between the socioeconomic class and material wealth of Richard Cory and that of the society around him. In Sebastian's case, such a contrast is less prominent, for there are many undergraduates at Oxford and various individuals in the world which the Marchmain family inhabits who are also relatively wealthy. And yet, one comment which Charles makes when observing Brideshead Castle is relevant here. When Charles says that if Brideshead Castle were his house, he would not live anywhere else, he could be said to be speaking not only for himself but also for anyone who has an appreciation of such a beautiful place and who would be very content to live in such a place for many years.

The impoverished public in stanzas three and four of the poem which is struggling to survive financially keeps working and striving for a better life. The suicide of Richard Cory at the end of the poem ends the dream and removes the image of a regal life which can be inspirational. Unfortunately and tragically, Richard Cory was too unhappy in his personal life to continue living. The situation of Sebastian Flyte is very similar. Sebastian, while not literally commiting suicide, does in a sense commit a symbolic suicide. For the promise of his younger life seems to have been vanquished when one sees his painful struggles with alcoholism and the details of his life in Morocco. From a public perspective Sebastian seems to have lost the glory of his former life in England, a life of carefree exuberance and socioeconomic abundance. He seems to have abandoned his youthful strivings and the responsibility of his position as a prominent member of society.

And yet, from a private perspective, that is, when one examines Sebastian's inner life, one might notice that his life in Morocco is very similar in spirit and motivation to his life at Oxford and at Brideshead. For Sebastian's ambition was to live in an aesthetically interesting ambience and to be happy in a relatively carefree way which would allow him an appreciation of the natural beauty in the world around him. His life at Brideshead, at Oxford, and in Morocco all fulfill these goals. Robert Murray Davis affirms this notion as well in *Brideshead Revisited: The Past Redeemed* saying that "Sebastian has attempted to re-create, in Fez and with Kurt, the Arcadia he inhabited at Oxford with Charles and from which he has been exiled" (102). The spirit of the earlier Arcadia has been to some extent, if not to a considerable extent, preserved with respect to its architectural and natural atmosphere and its serenity. However, from the perspective of the participating individuals one might say that the earlier aura of Arcadia has been dramatically transformed because now Sebastian has adopted the role of taking care of another individual, namely Kurt, whose condition is rather problematic. Whereas Sebastian is clearly the superior individual in this relation, in the Arcadia at Oxford and at Brideshead Sebastian and Charles complemented each other and were equals in developing and nurturing their aesthetic and emotional sensibilities and their intellectual inclinations.

The religious aura of Brideshead (exemplified in the chapel and the domed ceilings of some of the rooms and halls) is manifested, though in a much simpler manner in Sebastian's experience in Morocco. Charles himself notices and acknowledges the importance of the sense of the passageways outside Sebastian's small house in Morocco as opening to the stars, the quietly robed figures, and the scented air— Charles knows instinctively that this sense of serenity, of spatial expansiveness which can symbolize an expansiveness of soul, and of a religious atmosphere is significant to Sebastian and his emotional well-being. With respect to the issue of whether Sebastian is representing responsibly his position in society as a young English lord, one could say in his defense, as his outward behavior might be construed by some as irresponsible, that he is trying to be kind and thoughtful towards the world around him, even taking in a stray and lost individual—in that sense Sebastian exemplifies a humanitarian philosophy of life, which various other people and especially some of his family members do not seem to readily appreciate. One might also claim that Sebastian is following the model of his father, Lord Marchmain, who left England and seemed to abandon his public responsibility as a prominent English lord. As Sebastian, Lord Marchmain lives in an environment, namely Venice, which he finds aesthetically appealing and interesting.

Sebastian's existential situation is also reminiscent of the plight of the persona in Edwin Arlington Robinson's "Miniver Cheevy." Miniver admires the heroic past, the glorious myths and legends of the classical and medieval periods and of the Renaissance. His ideal would have been to be a member of the Medici family. Miniver is also perceptive enough to realize, as is implied by the first two lines of stanza four, that many individuals in contemporary society who are considered "heroic" and important are really not so at all—such superficial people are merely adept at appearing to be capable and impressive. The social criticism of this fourth stanza culminates in its last two lines: "He mourned Romance, now on the town, / And Art, a vagrant" (15–16). In other words, love and art, two of the most important ideals of the heroic periods about which Miniver dreams, have been cheapened and sullied by contemporary society. Miniver's only viable response to such a world is to think about the past and to affirm the contrast between its mythical vitality and the sordidness of the present. He finds a congenial escape from this painful fate in drinking consistently.

Sebastian is similar to Miniver in that they both yearn for a more lovely and noble world, for a world permeated by beauty. While both long for the past, Miniver is interested in the distant past, whereas Sebastian is more focused on his pleasant personal past. Both Sebastian and Miniver live relatively isolated and secluded lives away from the exigencies of everyday mortality. Miniver is happiest when he can enjoy his solitary dreams of the heroic days of old, an interest which other people do not appear to share. Sebastian is happiest when he is alone at Brideshead Castle, in a sanctuary-like atmosphere of carefree serenity, natural beauty, and architectural magnificence. Sebastian, as Miniver, finds solace in escaping the anguish of everyday mortality by drinking excessively.

In leaving Sebastian in his less than splendid state of isolation Charles seems disappointed that not more could be done for his friend. Even though Charles says that there was nothing more that he could do for Sebastian, he does show much more sensitivity for his friend and is much more helpful to him than either Bridey or Julia. Perhaps Charles does not want to intrude further into Sebastian's personal life or perhaps Charles is so repelled by the presence of Kurt that he does not feel comfortable in remaining. That Charles does not return again later to visit Sebastian might even suggest that he has given up on his friend, that he has given up believing in his friend and in his potential for improvement, as various members of the Flyte family have already done. What Charles misses consciously, although he might sense this subconsciously, is that Sebastian is essentially a pious and holy individual. As Jacqueline McDonnell says in *Evelyn Waugh*, "Sebastian is a major romantic creation, drawn from the heart of the Christian tradition: the hopeless sinner saved" (95). And yet, there is an innocence and kindliness at the heart of Sebastian's character which suggests that his inner life has been from childhood more or much more than hopeless. It is primarily or exclusively from the perspective of the aggressively ambitious realm of everyday mortality, represented by some of his peers, that Sebastian's life might or does seem "hopeless." Yet, by his generosity of heart and spirit Sebastian preserves an inner faith in his goodness and in his capacity to fulfill a quiet Christian existence which the criticism and harshness of the outside world cannot eradicate.

When Charles travels to England after his short visit with Sebastian so that he can discuss Sebastian's financial situation with Brideshead, he is asked if he would like to paint Marchmain House so that a record of the house can be preserved when it is pulled down to be replaced by a block of apartments. Charles begins work on this commission immediately because the contractors will soon be starting their destructive work. This commission of four paintings was especially important for

Charles because it represented the beginning of his career as an architectural painter. It is noteworthy that while Charles considers Marchmain House to be one of the most beautiful houses he has ever seen, Bridey says that he never considered it to be aesthetically interesting. As with Brideshead Castle, it seems as if Charles has a more profound appreciation of the architectural beauty of the place than most of the members of the Flyte family except for Sebastian, who loves the mansion more dearly than anyone. The house possesses an aura of glorious continuity and past splendor, exemplified by such an exquisite interior as the lovely drawing-room, an "elaborate, symmetrical Adam" (218) creation and by the fact that the furniture has been in the long drawing-room since the beginning. Moreover, this drawing-room contains bays of windows which open onto a vernal, green park of young trees, suggesting an instinctive and intimate consanguinity between the house and nature.

When he is finished working one evening he and Cordelia have dinner together during which she reveals that she loves Sebastian more than anyone and that it was necessary to sell Marchmain House to revive the financial stability of the family, for Lord Marchmain has been in debt for a while. Cordelia also tells about other notable changes in the Marchmain family circumstances. She is especially saddened by the fact that the chapel at Brideshead was closed—the requiem for her mother was the last ever said there. When this was finished the priest came in and took out the altar stone, emptied the holy-water stoop and extinguished the lamp in the sanctuary. Cordelia also talks about her mother, suggesting that she was closer to her than any of her siblings. She also makes an interesting statement about her deceased mother, saying that she was saintly, although she was not a saint. One might make the same comment about Sebastian for he has a saintly aura and saintly qualities as well, qualities which are perhaps too subtly presented for the world of everyday mortality to easily appreciate and value them. The sense of finality and decline is also apparent in Cordelia's recounting of what Julia said when she heard that Marchmain House would be sold—she said that Cordelia would not have her coming-out ball. Cordelia elaborates on this sad point by saying that her dream of being a bridesmaid at Julia's wedding did not materialize either, for the event was really a rather squalid affair.

The architectural painting which Charles does so adeptly at Marchmain House was to become his life's work. Even though his connection with the Marchmain family is ultimately severed, his career owes everything to those early days at Brideshead when he created landscapes in the garden room and when he painted Marchmain House before it was torn down to build various apartments. In Chapter One of Book II (which is Chapter I of Book Three in the later edition of the novel) we see that the success which Charles has achieved in his public career is not matched in his private life. Book II of *Brideshead Revisited* is appropriately titled "A Twitch Upon the Thread." In his public life Charles attains some prominence as an architectural painter, creating artistic renderings of numerous country houses which would, primarily for financial reasons, be soon abandoned or torn down. One of the hallmarks of his success is the publication of three folios of his work, *Ryder's Country Seats*, *Ryder's English Homes*, and *Ryder's Village and Provincial Architecture*. One of the important statements which Charles makes about his appreciation of architecture is that he "loved buildings that grew silently with the centuries, catching and keeping the best of each generation" (226). One might say that such an approach to architecture is a main reason why he admires Brideshead Castle so much, for Brideshead exemplifies such a gradual and delightful developmental process.

In his private life Charles is less fortunate. A primary reason why Charles travelled extensively abroad was to escape the presence of his wife, Celia, Mulcaster's sister, whom he has ceased to love. Charles and Celia are returning by boat from New York to England. In organizing a cocktail party, Celia and Charles discover that Julia is on board. Charles, reflecting upon the fact that he has not seen Julia and that he has not had any contact with the members of the Flyte family in a long while, also mentions that he knows that Sebastian is still abroad. When Charles and Julia meet again on the ship they have an interesting conversation in which Charles thinks that the reward for all of Julia's sufferings over the years is a "haunting, magical sadness" (239) which represents the "completion of her beauty" (239). Perhaps one of the reasons why Charles is so intrigued by Julia is that she reminds him in various ways of Sebastian. One might claim of Sebastian, as of Julia, that his sufferings engendered in him a "haunting, magical sadness" which represented the completion of his beauty, physical and spiritual. One might even describe this as an inner sanctuary of sadness or as a sanctuary of the inner self which is permeated with and motivated by sadness, and even by melancholy.

Charles and Julia spend a lot of time together, sharing various thoughts and feelings of the past and present. When Julia tells of her childhood at Brideshead, Charles feels as if he were reliving some of those golden days which he had experienced there years ago with Sebastian. Both Julia and Charles have been very unhappy in their respective marriages and both admit that they dislike their respective spouses. Julia says that she and Rex now live in their discontented state at Brideshead, while Bridey occupies a couple of the upstairs rooms near Nanny Hawkins. She and Bridey now occasionally visit their father; Sebastian, sadly, has disappeared. Julia also says that her daughter was born dead and that she has been punished for her mistakes. Yet, she believes, in the spirit of her earlier religious upbringing, that everything is part of a plan.

When the ship arrives in England after a rough crossing for Celia and after giving Julia and Charles an opportunity to become verbally and physically intimate, Charles tells his wife that he cannot come home right away because of the exhibition of his paintings. One of the noteworthy aspects of the public viewing is the arrival of Anthony Blanche, whom Charles has not seen in years. Anthony is the same emotionally direct, uninhibited, and volatile self which he had displayed in earlier years. In contrast to many of the other viewers who like the paintings, Anthony is caustically critical of the works of Charles. Shortly thereafter as Charles, in a spirit of reminiscing, is listening to Anthony in a little bar talk so glibly, he feels as if he were back "in Oxford looking out over Christ Church meadow through a window of Ruskin Gothic" (271). However, the momentary sense of refuge which Charles feels is obliterated when Anthony launches his very harsh verbal attack of Charles's work as an artist. There is no potential here for even a tentatively misty glimpse of the "enchanted garden" which Charles had so longed for at Oxford. Anthony's essential criticism of Charles's art is that it is merely "charming" and not substantial or provocative—he proclaims that "charm" has destroyed Charles and his art. Anthony even reminds Charles of the dinner which they had together years ago at Oxford when he had warned Charles about the potentially deleterious effects of "charm."

The exceedingly critical tone of such a statement, of such an assessment of his artistic work, from someone whom Charles had admired is certainly devastating. Yet, it is somewhat softened by the fact that he soon thereafter travels with Julia to Brideshead Castle, which has been taken over by Rex and his aggressive political friends. The verbal violence and acquisitive, pushy demeanor of the other people at Brideshead ensure that Julia and Charles will be left alone together. Even though Julia and Rex are still officially co-residents of the castle, Julia admits to Charles that for her Rex no longer exists. The presence of Rex and his cronies at Brideshead offers a dramatic and melancholy contrast to the glorious summer at Brideshead when Sebastian and Charles spent a blissful time alone. The quiet and subtle appreciation of the house, of its radiant beauty and of the lovely surrounding natural environment which Sebastian and Charles showed in the past and which have been and still are, whether directly in person or implicitly through memory, so vital to their emotional and spiritual existence has been undermined and diminished by the brutal, harsh, and coarse presence of Rex and his associates. The house, it seems, also yearns for a more serene and golden past when its beauty and magnificence were truly and profoundly appreciated and loved.

At the end of this chapter, Chapter Two of Book II, Charles makes an interesting statement which is reminiscent of an image and a remark from earlier in the novel. In Chapter Five of Book I, Sebastian, who is waiting for Charles at his house in London, asks him when he arrives whether he has gone over to his mother's side. Charles responds that he is with Sebastian against the world. Now in Chapter Two of Book II Charles says that he feels as if love is making him hate and distance himself from the world. He even states that he feels as if there were a conspiracy by mankind and God against him and Julia. After Julia affirms such a perception, both seem to sense that their mutual love, as vital as it appears to be, will not last forever. Whereas the first love and admiration of Charles was for Sebastian, his second love is for Julia, his sister. James F. Carens argues in the Introduction to *Critical Essays on Evelyn Waugh* that "These profane loves, we eventually understand, are but earthly manifestations of Ryder's longing for God" (11).

Such a perception of love and its capacity is reminiscent to some extent of the philosophy of love in Emily Dickinson's "The soul selects her own society" and in Matthew Arnold's "Dover Beach." The notion which Charles expresses (and Julia affirms) at the end of Chapter Two of Book II is that the love which he shares with Julia inspires him to separate himself from the world of everyday mortality. This is also the motivation of the persona in Dickinson's "The soul selects her own society," who, once she has found a companion, a lover, distances herself from the world. In Arnold's "Dover Beach" the persona says to his lover that they should be true to one another and encourages her to realize the importance of this idea in a world which has so much conflict, tension, and aggression. The only solace in such an uncertain and violent world, the persona suggests, is that which is provided by a true and abiding love. The assertion by Charles in Book I in support of Sebastian against the vicissitudes of the world and the similarly vital declaration by Charles in Book II regarding his love for Julia possess the motivation and the underlying emotional intensity which is manifest in the last stanza of Arnold's "Dover Beach." Lines 2–6 of the final stanza of this poem signify an especially poignant parallel to the experience of Charles at Brideshead. For Charles at the Marchmain family castle in his Oxford days the world does seem momentarily to lie before him "like a land of dreams"—when he visits Brideshead at the later stage of his life he is inevitably and pleasantly reminded of those earlier glorious summer days with Sebastian. And yet, Charles senses, what the development of the narrative will ultimately show, that such happiness cannot endure and is not destined to endure in a society and in a world which is not genuinely or consistently characterized and permeated by joy, devotion, or tranquility.

However, at the beginning of Chapter Three of Book II Julia and Charles do experience a temporary sense of genuine tranquility at Brideshead, reminiscent of the aura of splendor which Charles had enjoyed there with Sebastian so many years ago. Charles has just finished painting Julia as he has done so often before; he and Julia had dressed for dinner, and when they had come down, the world seemed transformed. It was as if nature was affirming the beauty of the moment which they were experiencing, for the lovely summer sun had appeared from behind the clouds, a soft wind was blowing and the fragrances of various features of the natural environment merged to create a harmonious sensation. As Charles and Julia sit by the fountain and reflect on their recent lives together characterized by "not a day's coldness or mistrust or disappointment" (278) Julia says that she wants to marry Charles soon and that she wants to experience at least a short period of peace before the war comes. However, as Julia speaks of making more concrete plans for the future, such as the fact that each of them would need to get a divorce from the respective spouses, the chill of mortality seems to encroach upon the congenial sanctuary of summer light and serenity which they have been enjoying. Julia's comment at the end of this passage that she feels as if the past and the future were so threatening that the present can barely exist and survive foreshadows an imminent doom.

In the next section of this chapter Bridey's presence at Brideshead seems to usher in an atmosphere of gloom, for he does not really approve of the relationship of Julia and Charles and persistently asks questions about Rex. After Bridey makes the surprise announcement of his engagement to Mrs. Muspratt, he offends Julia deeply by saying that he could not bring her and her children to Brideshead because of Julia's living with Charles while she is still officially married to Rex. The other problematic aspect of Bridey's marriage plans, at least for Julia, Charles, and also for Rex, is that Bridey will now be in possession of Brideshead and will want to live there with his new wife and step-children. Julia is clearly upset by Bridey's statement and its implications. Later that evening as she and Charles are again by the fountain, he makes a statement which angers her and she hits him in the face with a switch made from one of the lime shoots. This moment destroys utterly the sanctuary-like atmosphere of the fountain and of the external environment of the house, and anticipates the ultimate degeneration of the sanctuary-like atmosphere of the interior of the house which has been initiated by Bridey's callous remark.

In Chapter Four of Book II (which is Chapter IV of Book Three in the later edition of the novel) on one November afternoon later that year Julia and Charles are standing at a window in the drawing-room at Brideshead looking out at the leaves swirling over the landscape. Although both Julia and Charles have been working to finalize their divorces, their statements as they watch the yellow leaves outside sweeping over the lawn seem to portend an ending and not a bright shared future for them. Julia says with quiet melancholy that they will not see them in the spring and perhaps never again. For Bridey and his new family will then be living at Brideshead. Charles responds by saying that once before he had left Brideshead, that is, on the day when Lady Marchmain had accused him of such cruelty because he had given Sebastian money to go to the local pub, thinking that he would never see it again. Julia's next remark also is pervaded with a sense of profound melancholy and gloom as she raises the possibility of returning years later to a dramatically changed natural landscape and personal situation. One might simply consider such phrases as reflective of Julia's current sadness, and yet, they do clearly anticipate and foreshadow an ultimate cessation of the "us" and an eventual conclusion of her relationship with Charles.

Cordelia soon arrives at Brideshead after a long period of absence. First, she became a nun and entered a convent; when this did not work out, she went to Spain and helped out with the war effort. When Cordelia, Julia, and Charles are in the nursery visiting with Nanny Hawkins, Cordelia says that she even visited Sebastian, who is not doing well, in Tunis recently where the monks are taking care of him. As at other moments of the novel, it is noteworthy that when various of the Flyte children return to Brideshead, they always want to visit Nanny in the old nursery. It is as if Nanny Hawkins represents a sense of sanctuary, as if the nursery which she so resolutely inhabits, signifies a golden place to which they desire to return periodically not only because it reminds them of their pleasant childhood and youth at Brideshead but also because this contact inspires and revitalizes them for the future. During this conversation with Cordelia, Julia, and Charles, Nanny makes an interesting observation which is similar to what she has said before—she says that she could never understand why various members of the Marchmain family always seem to need to go abroad. One might interpret this statement as suggesting that Nanny Hawkins loves England and the English landscape and does not see the need to travel away from their country so frequently. However, when one reflects on a similar remark which she made earlier in the novel when she observed that Julia spends a lot of time away from Brideshead in the summer, perhaps what really surprises Nanny is that any of the children of this family would wish to be away from such a beautiful creation as Brideshead Castle.

The story about Sebastian which Cordelia tells Charles the next day is very moving and reinforces observations which had previously been made about Sebastian's character, interests, and motivations. Cordelia had first visited the consul and was told various details about Sebastian's life. He had wanted to be accepted as a missionary lay brother by a monastery in Tunis but the Fathers did not want the responsibility of looking after him. Then Sebastian started drinking intensively again. Yet, people do in some sense watch over him, for when he wandered away from the rather unimposing little hotel where he lived, they sometimes followed him to make sure that he did not come to any harm. Cordelia is clearly pleased when she says of Sebastian that they loved him in Tunis: "He's still loved, you see, wherever he goes, whatever condition he's in. It's a thing about him he'll never lose" (304). Cordelia says that even though the people there stole his money, they thought of him as a good person and cared about his well-being. There is even a measure of self-criticism and criticism of her family in Cordelia's commentary, for she says that the people there said that they thought Sebastian's family was very uncaring and improper for leaving him in such a state with no concern for his condition—and she agrees with them.

The way Sebastian is viewed by the people in Tunis and the affection which some of them develop for him is reminiscent of the manner in which Sebastian was treated during his early, happier days at Oxford. When one thinks of the first lunch at Sebastian's college rooms which Charles attended, the other undergraduates who come to this appreciate first the luncheon offerings and the material atmosphere which Sebastian offers and secondarily the presence of Sebastian himself. One might even reflect on statements which Anthony Blanche made to Charles about Sebastian's being the only youth during their earlier school days together who was not beaten by the older boys. This could have been due to Sebastian's socioeconomic position as the younger son of Lord and Lady Marchmain; and yet, one could also make the argument that the reason for the positive treatment which Sebastian received even in those early days at school when other students were being bullied and punished goes much deeper. Sebastian has an aura of innocence and of goodness, a quietly extraordinary presence, which is either consciously observed or unconsciously felt by those around him. This aura of innocence and goodness manifests itself in various ways in his life and actions, from appreciating the beauty of the Botanical Gardens with a seemingly simple reverence to having a devotion to the sublime serenity of Brideshead to enjoying visiting with Nanny Hawkins as a reminder of his happy childhood to wanting to become a missionary lay brother, while always never intentionally harming or hurting others. It is noteworthy that Cordelia stresses in her account of Sebastian that the people whom she met in North Africa, in Tunis, in Morocco, all thought of Sebastian as a good man, and that it disturbed them to see him in a condition of apparent misery engendered particularly by his alcoholic excesses. Sebastian is the kind of person who through the aura of innocence and goodness which is at the heart of his character and being perpetually signifies a sanctuary of light. He is an individual of Apollonian motivation and vitality who tries, whether consciously or subconsciously, to illuminate and to shed light on the world around him, to disperse and to scatter the shadows and the darkness, symbolic and literal, permeating and encroaching upon contemporary society.

Another way to view this capacity of Sebastian to illuminate the world around him with his innocent charm and kindness is to reflect on the notion of being called to a special service in life or having a vocation. Donat Gallagher addresses the issue of vocation thoughtfully in the essay "The Humanizing Factor: Evelyn Waugh's 'Very Personal View of Providence'," saying that "Waugh certainly shared the Puritan/ Victorian belief that everyone is 'called by God to—a specific worldly vocation'" (22). Gallagher states that Waugh believed that "acts of service will give life new meaning and fulfill the actor's 'function in the divine plan'" (29). By his very presence in the small community in North Africa where he lives his modest existence Sebastian gives not only his life but also the lives around him new meaning—for the people here sense to various degrees that Sebastian represents an essential goodness in a world too often fraught with and affected by evil and negative influences. The quote which Donat Gallagher mentions from Cardinal Newman's *A Meditation* is of special relevance for the life of Sebastian and for his position in society: "God has created me to do him some definite service; he has committed some work to me which he has not committed to another. I have my mission—I may never know it in this life but I shall be told it in the next" (29). Such a statement, it seems to me, represents perfectly the spiritual and emotional state of mind of Sebastian in this latter phase of his life. Exiled from his home and estranged physically from his family and from the English Catholic community, Sebastian nevertheless feels intuitively, and perhaps even subconsciously, a sense of vocation. One might even argue that Sebastian only truly realizes that he has a special capacity to positively influence and to illuminate the world around him and that he has a special vocation when he is distanced from the aristocratic world of elegance, pleasure, and material wealth in which he grew up.

Cordelia also tells about her discussion with the Superior of the monastery, an elderly, pious individual from Holland, who had spent fifty years in Central Africa.

He relates the story of Sebastian's first visit, when he wanted to be accepted as a lay brother and asked if he could be sent into the bush to the simplest people, far away from society. As the conversation with the Superior continues, Sebastian ultimately admits that he would like to be at a small church by a river, perhaps reminiscent of the sanctuary of Brideshead with the nearby lakes. Astonishingly, when the Superior then asks Sebastian to tell him about himself, his response is that he is nothing, suggesting not only a great lack of self-esteem but also a sense that the world of everyday mortality would not really appreciate or understand his personal story. How profoundly sad such a statement is or seems to be when one thinks of Sebastian at Oxford or at Brideshead during that summer of his glorious isolation. And yet, in a sense, his experience in northern Africa is comparable to and similar in spirit to his past life in England. The innocence, the simplicity, the generosity, and the kindness which he exhibits in different variations at Oxford, at Brideshead, and in London manifests itself also in his presence in Morocco. Cordelia even applies the word "holiness" to Sebastian—she seems to be the only member of her family who truly appreciates this quality in Sebastian.

Cordelia said that she spent about two weeks with Sebastian to help him get over the worst of his illness, for he was very ill and apparently looked terrible, although he preserved his sweetness of manner. Because of his illness, caused by his excessive drinking, Sebastian is kept in the infirmary of the monastery and will be looked after by the Superior. Cordelia proceeds to make the interesting observation that Sebastian is one of those people who live a threshold existence as they do not belong either to the world or to the monastic rule. She even admits that she is such a character herself, although she adds that she can function more effectively in society because she does not drink. Cordelia's prediction of Sebastian's future is especially important. For she suggests, and there is every reason to believe that her prediction will be correct, that Sebastian will work as a kind of under-porter in the monastery for as long as he can, someone who is appreciated by the older members of the religious community and somewhat laughed at by the novices. Every once in a while Sebastian will disappear on a drinking binge and then return to spend an abundance of time in the chapel. Cordelia even says that he will "probably have little hiding places about the garden where he keeps a bottle and takes a swig now and then on the sly" (308). On the first occasion during their Oxford days when Sebastian had taken Charles to Brideshead he had made a statement about the importance of such hiding places. Sebastian had said at that time that he would like to bury something meaningful in every place where he had been happy so that when he grew old he could return to such distinctive sites, dig up the important objects, and enjoy pleasant memories. Perhaps in the future when he drinks from the bottle which he has hidden in the garden of the monastery Sebastian will not only appreciate the quiet serenity of the environment, isolated or seemingly isolated from the conflicts and cataclysms of contemporary society, where he now lives but he will also remember the happy days of his existence at Oxford when he could look out buoyantly over the world from his rooms in Christ Church as well as the glorious days of his childhood and youth at Brideshead when he lived in a paradise of architectural splendor surrounded by exceptional natural beauty.

Sebastian has always wanted a sense of sanctuary, whether in a religious or in a secular sense or as an harmonious fusion of the two. Even though he is not physically well enough ever to return to Brideshead to enjoy the loveliness of the place and to revive a sense of his happy childhood, he is described by Cordelia as living in a "very beautiful place...by the sea—white cloisters, a bell tower, rows of green vegetables, and a monk watering them when the sun is low" (309). When one reflects on the consistent and sensitive appreciation of beauty which Sebastian showed from his youth and which was especially manifest at various times during his undergraduate days at Oxford and during his life at Brideshead, his final resting-place in the world of everyday mortality could be said to be rather similar in spirit to his favorite places of aesthetic vitality in England. For what Sebastian most appreciated in an aesthetically interesting environment was a sense of natural beauty, of quiet isolation, of architectural purity and simple elegance. Even though Sebastian is in an environment which is aesthetically pleasing, he still experiences considerable suffering, as Cordelia believes and as one might imagine. As Cordelia concludes her reflections on Sebastian she makes the important observation that "No one is ever holy without suffering" (309). She believes that Sebastian displays such holiness and possesses such holiness in his inner being.

Chapter Five of Book II (which is Chapter V of Book Three in the later edition) begins with a noteworthy disruption of the plans of various individuals, for Lord Marchmain has decided to return to Brideshead to spend the remaining months or years of his life in his former home. Thus, Bridey and Mrs. Muspratt are compelled to move out and readjust their plans; Julia and Charles are able to return to Brideshead, which they thought they might never see again. When Lord Marchmain arrives, he looks much older and much less vital than he did just months ago in Monte Carlo. As he does not feel able to climb stairs, Lord Marchmain decides to reside in the Chinese drawing-room on the ground floor. One of the first comments Lord Marchmain makes after he settles in is to criticize Bridey's choice of Mrs. Muspratt as his wife for he believes she is very common and ordinary. In continuing to express his critical concern a little later in the narrative Lord Marchmain says that he is very disturbed and appalled at the idea of Mrs. Muspratt, Beryl, assuming the place which his mother had formerly held in this majestic house. It is a very troubling image for him to think of Bridey, Mrs. Muspratt, and her children taking over while the house appears to decline and deteriorate. That Lord Marchmain would make the latter statement suggests that he is aware that the house is on the verge of decline, despite its past greatness. Lord Marchmain asserts that he is going to modify his will and make Julia the heir, for she appears to him to be a more suitable resident.

When Bridey and his wife return from their honeymoon they spend several days at Brideshead, but Lord Marchmain, who is now suffering regularly, will not see them. During the Easter holidays Lord Marchmain's condition worsens—Bridey returns and says that they should call a priest. As on a couple of previous occasions in the narrative, Bridey introduces a statement or a problem into the family circle which has serious consequences or repercussions for other individuals. Both Julia and Charles sense that this issue of calling in a priest will infuse the scenario with a problematic tension. While Charles criticizes this plan as hypocritical because Lord Marchmain has been estranged from religion for so many years, Julia sees nothing wrong with the notion of her father seeing the parish priest regarding the last sacraments.

One of the ways in which Lord Marchmain strives to keep alive, or perhaps one should say to hold off the grip of death, is to talk to himself, to say that he is feeling better, to describe what he sees in the room around him, for example, the figures in the wallpaper, the little gold men who are able to live so long. Lord Marchmain also thinks about his family's past in the house, reflecting not only about particular individuals of exemplary longevity such as Aunt Julia, his father's aunt, but also about the creation and the development of the house and the fountain. In mentioning the fact that one can still see the original location of the old house near the village church before it was moved to the new site and in pondering the historical progress of the family from knights to barons to positions of higher prominence in the Hanoverian period of royalty, Lord Marchmain affirms not only his appreciation of the continuity of the family from its origins and of the house from its physical roots but also strives implicitly to see himself as an integral part of this mythological vitality. It is noteworthy that Lord Marchmain considers the future as well, making a prognostication about a potential child of Julia's. The image of his father's aunt, Aunt Julia, is especially important to Lord Marchmain for she presumably lived at Brideshead, where she was born and died, for most of her long life—while Lord Marchmain aspires, against seemingly insurmountable odds, to experience a comparable longevity, that he thinks so intensively about the development of the house and of the family might suggest an undertone of regret that he distanced himself for so long from this lovely mansion and its regenerative powers.

Just before he dies Lord Marchmain receives absolution from the priest and makes the sign of the cross. Later that evening Julia and Charles have their final conversation. Julia proclaims suddenly that she cannot marry Charles and that she can never be with him again. For although Julia has hardly been religious over the years and although she has even criticized the Catholic faith of her youth, she now wants to return to it. And she sees no opportunity of doing that in a life with Charles who is an agnostic and skeptical about religion. Julia needs to have a life which believes in the possibility of God's mercy, for she has come to believe that her life is part of a divine plan, motivated by a sense of faith. James F. Carens stresses the importance of this return to the church in his introduction to *Critical Essays on Evelyn Waugh*: "Thus the ultimate returns to the Church of Lord Marchmain, Sebastian, and Julia—who sacrifices the possibility of marriage to Ryder in order to return—and the conversion of Ryder himself, all reveal God's providence and his sanctifying grace" (12–13). Annette Wirth emphasizes that the spiritual awakening of Charles Ryder occurs "in the moment of Lord Marchmain's death-bed repentance" (80). Through this experience Charles is given "a glimpse of the mercy of God" (81).

Stephen Spender discusses effectively the role of religion in the lives of several of the major characters in *Brideshead Revisited*: "Despite their folly, failure, and disorder, their religion is capable of saving them and it gives their lives significance" (68). Spender proceeds to say that the "presence of their faith in the lives of this family, sometimes clear, sometimes obscured, is vividly felt" (68). Spender states that a primary goal of the novel is to clarify and emphasize the distinction "between the love of God and the love of man" (68).

Various critics such as Donald Greene have argued that although there is a wide range of aristocratic characters in the novels of Evelyn Waugh, only several of them are truly admirable ("A Partiality for Lords" 454–56). John H. Wilson emphasizes a similar point in *Evelyn Waugh, A Literary Biography 1924–1966*, saying that while Waugh "did not admire the aristocracy" (162) generally, he did admire "aristocratic qualities, including leisure, freedom, patronage, and privilege" (162). Waugh attributed such qualities to some of his aristocratic characters and also achieved them to a considerable extent in his own life. Wilson summarizes the importance of faith for the two families of Catholic aristocrats, the Flytes and the Crouchbacks, which appear in four of Waugh's novels, *Brideshead Revisited* and the war trilogy: "Faith guided everyday conduct, but it also provided integrity and perspective: it explained the purpose of human life, and it affirmed that suffering was only transitory" (162–63). For the ultimate spiritual reward was great. Lady Marchmain, Sebastian, and Cordelia feel this instinctively and signify a natural sense of faith and holiness in their lives. Bridey has an orthodox Catholic view, but this is somewhat artificially presented because he is not as naturally pious as Cordelia or Sebastian. Julia seems to sense near the end of the narrative that the absence of faith in her life will undermine her future and wants to return to a semblance of the faith of her childhood. Wilson discusses the interest of the Flytes and the Crouchbacks in art and in collecting aesthetically interesting objects, and addresses the issue of art in relation to faith, saying that "art was a means to understand history and faith" (163) and that art "should edify the patron, the family, and ultimately the public" (163). Wilson states further that the artist, fulfilling such a responsibility, necessarily "had to create on the basis of faith, since one's life affected one's art" (163)—in the spirit of such a statement one might think not only of Waugh but also of some of his characters as having the capacity, the desire, and the motivation to integrate art and faith. Perhaps Charles eventually achieves, or develops the potential to achieve, such an integration through his conversion. Sebastian, in aspiring to live his quiet, unassuming life in an environment which preserves the aesthetically vital aura of Brideshead and even of Oxford, might be said to achieve an integration of art and faith as well. The outward appearance of Sebastian's life might challenge such a claim, but inwardly Sebastian exemplifies the quiet piety, the gentle humanity, the serene dignity, and the noble generosity which he has always shown and which has been consistently undervalued and devalued by his peers and by contemporary society.

Alvin B. Kernan makes an interesting analogy between Charles Ryder and Evelyn Waugh in his essay "The Wall and the Jungle: The Early Novels of Evelyn Waugh." Kernan argues that "Waugh is ultimately, like the chief character of *Brideshead Revisited*, a painter of old houses" (85) and, "like Charles Ryder, Waugh finds his ultimate values in building, holding it to be not only the highest achievement of man but one in which, at the moment of consummation, things were most clearly taken out of his hands and perfected, without his intention, by other means" (85). Kernan also makes the important observation that Waugh "defends tradition, not the status quo; social order, not the establishment" (85). Of the Flyte family members, Lord Marchmain, Lady Marchmain, Sebastian, and Cordelia, especially exemplify such an interest in tradition and an orderly existence. While expressing such an interest in tradition in different ways, these individuals derive at least some of the vitality of their lives from a sense of tradition, of family tradition and history, and from an inner sense of faith and order, which is occasionally misinterpreted or undervalued by various individuals in contemporary society.

In the Epilogue of *Brideshead Revisited*, Charles, stationed with the army at Brideshead, hears that the house now belongs to Lady Julia Flyte, as she calls herself. She is abroad on a service mission; a caretaker and a couple of servants are still living on the top floor of the once majestic house, now suffering in an atmosphere of neglect. Charles wanders around some parts of the house, walking down familiar corridors and looking into rooms piled high with furniture as they were the first time he visited with Sebastian. A housemaid carrying a cup of tea happens to recognize Charles and he takes the tea to Nanny Hawkins instead. After recovering her composure, Nanny tells him about the fortunes and misfortunes of various family members, that Julia and Cordelia left for service in the war and that Bridey joined the yeomanry just as Lord Marchmain had done in his time. She also speaks about the difficult time which Bridey's wife and children are having finding a safe location in which to reside. Mr. Mottram seems to have become a public success, finding an outlet for his considerable aggressiveness as a minister in the war effort. Nanny says that Julia and Cordelia appear to be in Palestine, which is where Bridey's regiment is stationed. They are all planning to come home after the war.

In the last several paragraphs of the novel Charles, having described himself to Hooper as "homeless...middle-aged, loveless" (350), revisits the chapel and says a prayer. As Charles walks back to the camp he has an array of conflicting emotions and reflections. On the one hand he thinks about the fact that the builders did not and could not know the "uses to which their work would descend" (350–51). Each generation added something to the house and the estate; yet, now in the war everything seems bleak and dismal, as if affirming the point that all is vanity. However, despite the apparent omnipresence of transience in this place, Charles thinks that a special sign emerged out of the work which had not been part of the original design. He states that he found a small flame that morning "burning anew among the old stones" (351). One might describe this as the "flame" of faith and love which once burnt for and inspired the old knights and now burns for the soldiers who are far from home. It is a flame to which he, as one of the tragedians of which he speaks at the end, contributed. For Charles always admired Brideshead, this magnificent house, as much as most of the members of the Marchmain family. Even though Charles is very self-critical at the end of the narrative, he also implies that his future life will be at least somewhat influenced and inspired by this newly discovered, or rediscovered, flame of faith and love and by the rememberance of those past very congenial and glorious days at Brideshead when his heart, mind, and spirit were emotionally enraptured, aesthetically enchanted, and profoundly blissful. For this flame of faith, which has an essentially religious dimension, is important not only for Charles, who had converted to Roman Catholicism, but also for any individual who strives for a sense of existential unity and wholeness.

Katharyn W. Crabbe stresses in *Evelyn Waugh* the religious nature of the notion of faith at the end of the novel. Crabbe writes of the chapel: "What is significant is not the décor but the flame…which comes to symbolize faith. It is faith, not art, that assumes different forms through the years and still continues unchanged" (101). Crabbe writes that Charles ultimately finds a sense of continuity and happiness not in the vestiges of the material world but in "the flame from the lamp of deplorable design and its reminder of God's love" (103). This seems to give him the feeling of transcendence which he had so consistently desired. Annette Wirth argues similarly that this flame "symbolizes the Catholic faith and transcends the mutability of wartime England" (81) and gives Charles the sense of "permanence, inspiration, and stability" (82) which he has been looking for since those blissful days at Oxford. After his conversion to Catholicism Charles does eventually appreciate the significance of the chapel at Brideshead. The chapel is important, as Wirth appropriately says, because of "its preservation of the eternal flame" (96), the flame which gives Charles and other individuals "the strength to hope" (96) and which symbolizes the spirit of faith despite the ravages of war and the dramatic physical changes which have occurred at Brideshead Castle.

Ruth Breeze affirms the importance of faith and of the chapel in "Places of the Mind: Locating *Brideshead Revisited*" saying that Charles Ryder ultimately viewed the chapel at Brideshead as "the heart of the great edifice" (143), for this is where his soul feels at home. I would agree that the chapel is supremely important as a vital source of the flame of faith and very important in its own right as an architectural phenomenon. However, I view the house, the aesthetic spirit of the house, as very important and vital as well. Although a house such as Brideshead may have been weakened and despoiled materially and physically and although it may seem to have degenerated from its former state of glory, it still possesses an inner spirit, an inner emotional, aesthetic, and spiritual being, which cannot be eradicated by the deleterious effects of the flux of time. Such an aesthetic and emotional spirit exists in a great house from the moment of its creation, from the moment of the initial placement of the "foundation stone," and develops organically over time. In the case of Brideshead Castle such an aesthetic and emotional spirit is inextricably interwoven with the spiritual source of the house. One might say that the heart and spirit of Charles, as the heart and soul of Sebastian, can envision and rest in the lovely ambience of Brideshead and its chapel eternally. The spirit of faith which individuals such as Lady Marchmain, Cordelia, Sebastian, and Charles develop is infused with an aesthetic sensibility enriched by its appreciation and admiration of the extraordinary beauty of Brideshead Castle.

Ian Littlewood also emphasizes the contrast at the end of the narrative between the material desolation of Brideshead Castle and its ambience and the flame of faith which burns with quiet intensity in the lamp: "...the decline of Brideshead is of slight importance; to exaggerate its loss is to range human values against divine. What matters is that the lamp—even a lamp of deplorable design—still burns in the chapel" (*Critical Essays* 173). Of the sanctuary lamp Gene Phillips writes in *Evelyn Waugh's Officers, Gentlemen, and Rogues* that its "rekindled flame heartens Charles, who feels it indicates that the flame of faith will continue to burn in him, and in those who were part of his life at Brideshead" (74). This flame restores the life-giving aura which Charles had earlier experienced at Brideshead and signifies the faith through which Charles gives meaning to his suffering.

On the one hand such a flame, the flame of faith, which the old knights could see from their tombs and which now burns for other distant British soldiers in the war, appears to have a purely religious motivation. Yet, given the past richness of experience of Charles in Brideshead Castle, perhaps one could also say that the flame or aura of faith which is engendered here derives not only from religious vitality but also from the memory of halcyon and blissful days in this architecturally beautiful space. Charles Ryder has become a convert to Catholicism, but he is also essentially an architectural painter and has a profound appreciation of architectural loveliness— such an aesthetic sensibility is gently fused with and vitally supplements his newly found and newly developing religious faith.

George McCartney in the essay "Helena in Room 101: The Sum of Truth in Waugh and Orwell" argues effectively that *Brideshead Revisited* "is concerned with something far more important than a wealthy family's losses" (62). McCartney emphasizes the candle burning before the tabernacle in the chapel, "testimony that God's

Presence continues to work in history" (62). McCartney also makes the important point that Brideshead Castle, although originally built for an aristocratic family and for its development, ultimately "provides shelter, physical and spiritual, to all classes" (62–3). Despite the physical degeneration and degradation which Brideshead Castle has endured, it still preserves a glimmer of hope and faith in the chaotic world of everyday mortality which does not appear to appreciate its effulgent beauty. The flame of faith burns anew at the end of the narrative not only for Charles in England, for Bridey, Julia, and Cordelia who are abroad in service associated with the war, for numerous other individuals serving the war effort and its associated commitments, but also for various individuals signifying goodness and kindheartedness in their daily lives such as Sebastian in his seemingly melancholy state of exile which actually reaffirms his sense of vocation.

Robert M. Davis in "Imagined Space in *Brideshead Revisited*" emphasizes the fact that at the end of the novel Charles, despite the material changes and alterations which are conspicuously evident in the house, including the drastic modifications of his paintings on the garden room panels, "is undismayed...because the climax of Lord Marchmain's submission has enabled him to move...to a conception of process in which, under the aspect of eternity, value is preserved even though things and places are destroyed" (33). The glimmer of hope which Charles feels at the end of the narrative is generated to a considerable extent by the spirit of faith which has been gradually developing as an important part of the inner self and by the rememberance of the lovely past sojourn which he had enjoyed at Brideshead.

Frederick L. Beaty argues effectively in *The Ironic World of Evelyn Waugh* that the Flyte family, despite their negative influences on Charles, ultimately is "instrumental in bringing him to wholeness, though Charles could never have imagined the nature of that wholeness or anticipated the way in which it would come about" (154). Beaty stresses the painfully poignant process of personal connectedness and loss which Charles experiences leading to his spiritual awakening and conversion: "Only after the relationships fall apart, only after Julia and Lord Marchmain return to their religious faith, does Charles's acquaintance with Brideshead enable him to progress beyond mortal passions to a love of God" (154). Beaty declares that Charles has ultimately "acquired a positive frame of reference and a definite set of values on which to rely" (154) and that his cheerful attitude at the end of the Epilogue "indicates the renewal of an inner strength capable of influencing all aspects of his life" (154). If it were not for his contact, whether blissful, pleasant, melancholy, or painful, with the Flyte family and with Brideshead Castle, Charles might never have developed and nurtured the faith and the hope which he has internalized at the end of the novel, which have become such a vital dimension of his life, and which now illuminate and sustain his inner being.

The glorious, perhaps one should say gloriously brief and transient, past experience at Brideshead, especially during that delightful summer, was very much due to the generosity, romanticism, and emotional sensitivity of Sebastian Flyte who truly loves the magnificent house which is the heritage of his family. Sebastian, an eminent representative of the individual in literary history who has a profound appreciation for a great house in and of itself, as a beautiful architectural phenomenon in its own right, is in the tradition of such characters as Darcy in Austen's *Pride and Prejudice*, and Emma and Mr. Knightley in Austen's *Emma*. As Darcy loves and appreciates Pemberley, so Emma loves and admires Hartfield and Mr. Knightley his Donwell Abbey. And one can assume that in time Elizabeth in *Pride and Prejudice* will come to develop as profound an admiration for and devotion to Pemberley as Mr. Knightley will develop with respect to Hartfield. Such a devotion to and love for a house is also seen in Hoffmann's *Der goldne Topf* in the feelings of Lindhorst, Serpentina, and Anselmus towards the fascinating home of Lindhorst in Dresden, and by extension, Atlantis, and in Chekhov's "The Cherry Orchard" in the love of Lyubov for her beloved childhood home and cherry orchard. Sebastian's appreciation for and admiration of Brideshead Castle is also intimately and profoundly connected to his love of nature, of the lovely natural environment surrounding and encompassing the house.

Of these literary precursors one might say that Sebastian is most similar in temperament and in personal qualities to Anselmus in *Der goldne Topf* and to Mr. Knightley in *Emma*. For Sebastian, Anselmus, and Mr. Knightley are all deeply romantic characters and instinctively forces for goodness and light in a world often shrouded by darkness or by the mists of twilight and in need of their Apollonian wisdom. The essential difference between the life of Sebastian and the lives of Anselmus and Mr. Knightley is that while Sebastian is compelled by the exigencies of the world of mortality to live apart from his beloved Brideshead Castle, the spirit of which he will nevertheless always carry in his heart, Anselmus and Mr. Knightley are fortunate in that they are able to live in the existential contexts which they admire and desire with the individuals they love. In narrative endings which have the aura of a fairy-tale Anselmus in *Der goldne Topf* will live happily ever after with Serpentina in Atlantis, which appears to be an extension, partially literal and partially symbolic, of Lindhorst's magnificent house in Dresden, and Mr. Knightley in *Emma* will enjoy a blissful future with Emma in Hartfield while still being able to feel connected to Donwell Abbey in its joyous proximity. The nobility of heart, generosity of spirit, and goodness of character which Sebastian, Anselmus, and Mr. Knightley show in their respective narrative worlds reaffirm the exemplary nature of their lives.

In some respects Sebastian is also similar to Mr. Rochester in Charlotte Brontë's *Jane Eyre*. Both individuals are from a wealthy family background, have a very congenial mansion where they can live, but choose or are compelled to leave this lovely house for personal reasons. One essential difference in the approach of these characters to their respective houses is that while Rochester only appears to gain an enhanced appreciation of Thornfield after the arrival of Jane, Sebastian instinctively loves Brideshead from his childhood on. Although the reasons for the departure from the family mansion are different, the outcomes for Rochester and Sebastian are to some extent similar. After Thornfield burns down and Rochester is severely injured in the conflagration, he lives in complete isolation at Ferndean, attended by only a couple of trustworthy family servants. Sebastian, after the bouts of drunkenness, unhappiness, and mistrust at Brideshead, also leaves his beloved house never to return. Rochester is fortunate that his kindred spirit, Jane Eyre, returns to revitalize him. Sebastian, on the other hand, feels an instinctive desire and need to escape further attempts by his family to encroach upon his life by fleeing to North Africa where he tolerates a marginal existence in his splendid and melancholy isolation. Sebastian, as Rochester, has an instinctive faith which has burgeoned over the course of time; for Rochester, this faith is motivated considerably by the presence of Jane, while for Sebastian this faith is generated to a considerable extent by his rememberance of things past, by his recollection of the beauty and innocence of his childhood in a lovely environment.

Sebastian's desire to live quietly and peacefully by a river in the latter phase of his life is extraordinarily similar in motivation and in spirit to the fundamental life-philosophy of Siddhartha in Hesse's *Siddhartha*. Although not publicly or overtly as holy or pious as Siddhartha, Sebastian, as Cordelia properly points out in her conversation with Charles, has a dimension of holiness and piety which is an important part of his character and his existence. It is perhaps ironic that Bridey was the Marchmain child who had initially wanted to be a priest, yet Sebastian, initially seemingly and outwardly more social and less religious, is the member of the Marchmain family who ultimately represents an individual of profound, if mortally imperfect, holiness and serenity. One of the essential features of this "holiness" is a generosity of spirit which is manifest from the beginning of the novel, exemplified in Sebastian's luncheon party in Christ Church. Sebastian is magnanimous to those individuals around him at the party as he is generally to other people, whether in his family or in society, even if he knows that they merely or primarily value his socioeconomic prominence and do not really appreciate his inner being and even if he senses that they considerably undervalue or devalue him.

Brideshead Castle signifies the spirit of Arcadia, especially during the blissful summer which Sebastian and Charles enjoy there. The notion of Arcadia initiated by Virgil in his *Eclogues* is presented in a mythical age and celebrates pleasant and virtuous country life. In his essay "Gardens—Models of a Better World" in *Garden Architecture in Europe*, Carl F. Schröer describes Arcadia, the allegorical ideal of Arcadia, as "a secularized paradise which represents—in a similar fashion to the Garden of Eden—an idyllic *locus amoenus*, in which a timeless existence of peace, leisure, and love is possible, free from the demands of everyday life" (12). As an allegorical ideal Arcadia offers "a Utopian vision of happiness" (12); however, as "an artistic product" (12) Carl F. Schröer says that Arcadia represents "an intermediate realm which lies somewhere between paradise and reality and which contains aspects of both" (12–13). During the Renaissance and in more recent periods of literary and artistic vitality the theme of Arcadia signifies a longing for a glorious or congenial past, especially in a pastoral ambience. In this Arcadian existence love "is experienced not sensuously but rather longingly" (13), for the "desire for love, rather than its fulfillment, is the true Arcadian sentiment" (13). The aura of Brideshead which Sebastian especially appreciates and admires is that of an Arcadian idyll, motivated at least to some extent by a serene faith, personal and religious, in a harmonious ambience. Sebastian's happiest times at Brideshead, and perhaps the most enjoyable months of his entire life, were spent in the peacefulness and solitude which the mansion and estate offered, when he had a sense of the harmonious communion of his soul with itself and with his serene faith as well as with the spirit of beauty in the house and with the architectural elegance and splendor of the house, and with the loveliness of the natural environment encompassing and reaffirming such grandeur and wholeness in its expansive and luminescent spaciousness. By internalizing the aesthetically most congenial aspects and the emotionally most pleasant moments of this past Arcadian idyll which was generated and nurtured by the beauty and the magnificence of his childhood home, by preserving his religious faith, and by allowing the innate kindness, generosity, and quiet holiness of his heart and soul to develop and to present itself naturally in the public domain in his life in England and abroad, Sebastian is able to create and to nurture a philosophy of life and a survival mechanism which enables him to endure the hardship and the suffering of his present existence in the world of everyday mortality and the anguish of living at a perpetual physical distance from his ever admired and beloved Brideshead Castle.

CHAPTER 3

J. R. R. Tolkien

There are various aesthetically interesting and lovely houses in J. R. R. Tolkien's *The Lord of the Rings*, comprised of *The Fellowship of the Ring*, *The Two Towers*, and *The Return of the King*. In the Prologue to *The Fellowship of the Ring*, the first part of the trilogy, Tolkien writes that the craft of building among the Hobbits, as other crafts, probably was learned from the Dúnedain. Yet, there is also the suggestion that this creative capacity was learned directly from the Elves. For at the time that the Hobbits began to expand their building of homes beyond burrows and holes in the ground the Elves of the High Kindred were still in Middle-earth, living at the Grey Havens and in other locations accessible from the Shire. It was even possible at that time to see three Elf-towers beyond the western marches. With respect to the architectural inclinations of the Hobbits, they typically preferred houses which were solid, comfortable, on or close to the ground, and long or extended. There existed a distinct preference for round windows and round doors in the architecture of the Hobbits as it developed. The dwellings of the Hobbits of the Shire were often large, as sizeable families generally lived together in one extended house. For example, Brandy Hall, the ancestral mansion of the Brandybucks, contained numerous tunnels where many family members lived in relative harmony.

The house of Bilbo Baggins, Bag End, is described at the beginning of *The Fellowship of the Ring* as a place of security and stability containing hidden wealth. After Bilbo returned in 1342 (at the age of fifty-two) from his adventures with Gandalf the Grey and the dwarves he was believed to have concealed a considerable treasure, or so it was popularly thought, in the Hill at Bag End. In Chapter 1 of *The Fellowship of the Ring* Bilbo is planning for his eleventy-first birthday celebration. People were astonished that Bilbo seemed to be relatively unchanged with the passage of time, for even at the age of ninety he looked very well-preserved. As he was generous towards numerous individuals, this physical idiosyncrasy was typically overlooked. At the age of ninety-nine Bilbo, who did not have close friends or family, adopted his younger cousin, Frodo, as his heir and invited him to live at Bag End. Not only do Bilbo and Frodo share the same birthday, September 22, but they also have similar characters, personalities, and interests.

In the second paragraph of J. R. R. Tolkien's *The Hobbit* the interior of the house of Bilbo Baggins is described. The round door opened onto a hall which resembled a tunnel "with paneled walls, and floors tiled and carpeted, provided with polished chairs" (3). The tunnel was rather extensive and contained numerous round doors opening on both of its sides, leading to a multitude of rooms on the same floor including "bedrooms, bathrooms, cellars, pantries, wardrobes, kitchens, dining-rooms" (3). The best rooms in the hobbit-hole or hobbit-house, as depicted in the second paragraph of *The Hobbit* are those which have a pleasant view of the natural environment: "The best rooms were all on the left-hand side (going in), for these were the only ones to have windows, deepset round windows looking over his garden, and meadows beyond, sloping down to the river" (3). Matthew Dickerson and Jonathan Evans elaborate on this point insightfully in *Ents, Elves, and Eriador: The Environmental Vision of J. R. R. Tolkien,* saying that "the best rooms look out not only on gardens—that is, nature in cultivated form—but also on meadows and the river, natural features that, though by no means truly wild, are less domesticated or cultivated" (12). Dickerson and Evans proceed to emphasize the closeness of the Hobbits to the earth, asserting that "their dwelling in the ground is fundamental to the nature of Hobbits" (12). Dickerson and Evans also emphasize the importance of simplicity and simple comforts for the Hobbits (14). Tolkien explains the origin of the word "hobbit" in an appendix of 1955, suggesting that it derives from the combination of two Old English words, *hol* ("hole" or "hollow") and *bytla* ("built structure, building, or dwelling").

It is also important to consider briefly the family history of Bilbo Baggins, which is discussed in *The Hobbit,* for this influences and shapes his life considerably. His mother was Belladonna Took, one of the daughters of Old Took, a prominent figure in a neighboring region. A legend was in existence that one of the Took ancestors had taken a fairy wife—this was given as the explanation for the occasional inclination among the Tooks to leave the area and have an adventure. Belladonna Took married Bungo Baggins, a rich and respectable hobbit who built a magnificent hobbit dwelling for his wife, a hobbit-hole which was widely considered as one of the most splendid anywhere. When Bilbo was about fifty years old and seemingly perfectly comfortable in his existential situation with no desire to leave the Shire and have an adventure, he is visited by Gandalf and a number of dwarves. The song of the dwarves about having a heroic adventure exploring mountains, pine-forests, and caves and searching for gold and lovely objects awakens a desire in Bilbo, seemingly inherited from his Took ancestors, to join them. Gandalf's strong and unwavering encouragement to Bilbo to join the dwarves on their expedition leaves the seemingly complacent and well-situated hobbit no choice—he is compelled to join the treasure-hunters.

To return to *The Fellowship of the Ring*, a couple of days before Bilbo's extraordinary birthday party Gandalf arrives, ostensibly to help with the fireworks displays but really for much more important reasons. As he and Bilbo are sitting in a small room of the house which looked westward into the garden, there is the feeling of a considerable sense of sanctuary. Not only is the ambience of the house at Bag End peaceful, but the flowers in the garden, the snapdragons, the sunflowers, and the nasturtiums, are resplendent in red and gold. Such an aura of serenity will not last, for the imminent birthday party will transform the ambience of Bag End, the neighborhood of The Hill, and the Shire. The birthday party is especially noteworthy not only because of the exceedingly generous array of food and drink which is provided along with the numerous presents and the colorful fireworks but also because of Bilbo's distinctive speech, after which he completely disappears. Bilbo's purpose was, of course, to celebrate the birthday which he and Frodo shared and also to highlight his departure from the Shire. At the end of his speech to the one hundred and forty-four guests at the dinner, specifically chosen to combine the ages of himself and his heir, Bilbo slips on the magic ring which he had found so many years before and becomes invisible.

As Bilbo, having quietly returned to his house after this magical disappearance from the party, prepares to leave the Shire forever, he takes a special book and bundle from his study and puts these in his travelling bag. He also has an envelope into which he puts the golden ring and its chain, seals it, and addresses it to Frodo. Yet, instead of placing this on the mantelpiece, Bilbo, seemingly inadvertently, places this in his pocket. Soon thereafter Gandalf comes in to talk with Bilbo about several important things before his departure. As Bilbo had slipped on the ring to disappear from the party and from the presence of his guests Gandalf had created a flash of light to distract from Bilbo's sudden vanishing. Bilbo admits to Gandalf, who is not completely pleased about the use of the ring which will cause unnecessary gossip, that he feels old and weary and desires to see the mountains again before ultimately finding a place where he can enjoy great serenity, a special spot where he can finish writing his book. As Gandalf and Bilbo finish their conversation, the envelope with the ring and important documents is placed on the mantelpiece for Frodo, whom Gandalf says he will protect and watch over. Bilbo, who previously had shown a capacity for Wanderlust, then walks off into the night with several dwarves as his companions, never to return again to his once beloved home. Yet, he will always preserve in his mind images of this beautiful sanctuary of peacefulness and tranquility. The aura of continuity and tranquility at Bag End is to some extent reinforced by the fact that Sam Gamgee's father has been Bilbo's gardener for forty years.

The Shire which Bilbo has admired for so many years is characterized by a picturesque natural beauty. This is a domain of quaint gardens and soft hills, not of mountains, of extensive forests, and of sublime chasms. In *Tolkien's World* Randel Helms writes of the Shire: "The hobbits' homeland, the tradition-bound, backward-looking Shire, is an idealized version of preindustrial England that clearly grows out of Tolkien's own conservative, nostalgic view of the land of his youth" (73). It is not surprising that one of the most important individuals in Bilbo's life is his gardener; nor is it surprising that Sam, the gardener's son and an avid and very capable gardener in his own right, is the intimate friend of Frodo. The appreciation for and the devotion to the natural environment and to the preservation of its beauty is a supremely important theme from the beginning of *The Lord of the Rings*. While Bilbo asserts that he wants to travel and to experience more sublime aspects of nature than the Shire offers, he still loves the Shire when he departs after his distinctive birthday-party. His professed destination, Rivendell, is, like the Shire, a sanctuary of natural loveliness and peacefulness.

That evening Frodo, in the company of Gandalf, takes the vital envelope from the mantelpiece—Gandalf exhorts him to keep the ring safe and secret. The next day various individuals come to the house to collect presents, which are piled up throughout the hall. Even though numerous objects are given away, Frodo, as Bilbo's heir, still retains the most precious objects, from the ring to the furniture, books, and pictures. As Chapter 1 of *The Fellowship of the Ring* concludes Gandalf leaves for a long while, assuming that Frodo will remain safe within the confines of the Shire.

The Shire which Bilbo loved and lived in for so many years and which Frodo similarly cherishes is a place of natural beauty, serenity, and peacefulness. When J. R. R. Tolkien, born in Bloemfontein, South Africa in 1892, returned with his mother to England and spent several years in Sarehole, then a village outside Birmingham, he thought of this as "a kind of lost paradise." Tolkien spoke later of the deep love which he developed for his own countryside, for a place which he knew and admired so profoundly. Patrick Curry in *Defending Middle-Earth: Tolkien, Myth, and Modernity* makes the excellent point that the "sense of place comes through powerfully in Tolkien's fiction, and it is reinforced by his naming of places, which also reflects his love and knowledge of language" (60). Curry proceeds to say that "the various races of people in Middle-earth are rooted to and unimaginable—both to themselves and to us—without their natural contexts" (61). Such a statement is especially true of the Hobbits, whether they are physically living in or wandering away from the Shire. Bilbo will always be emotionally and spiritually rooted to his beloved Shire, as will Frodo. Regardless of where they are in the world of Middle-earth and regardless of the circumstances in which they find themselves, Bilbo and Frodo will always have congenial memories and visions of the Shire, sometimes perhaps even more pleasant than they are consciously willing to admit to themselves. And they will be consistently sustained and strengthened by a vision of the blissful and peaceful life, by a remembrance of the sense of paradise, which they enjoyed in the Shire. Yet, there is a sense, manifest from the opening chapters of *The Fellowship of the Ring*, of the inevitability of change and of the intervention of mortality and history in the peacefulness of the Shire. For Bilbo's departure from the Shire initiates a new phase in its historical development. And in Chapter 2, "The Shadow of the Past," Sam even mentions that he has heard tales about the movement of the Elves toward the west, toward the Grey Havens, from where their ships would sail into the beyond, into an ethereal world, and would never return. The narrative itself reinforces this important point saying that many of the Elves are leaving Middle-earth for a more secure and more congenial environment.

The beginning of Chapter 2 of *The Fellowship of the Ring* affirms Bilbo's importance as a figure of legend because of his exploits and strange activities and depicts Frodo as exemplifying a lifestyle similar to that of his benefactor. Although Frodo has friends, he lives alone and has an interest, as did Bilbo, in exploring the forests and the hills and shows a curiosity in learning more about the areas beyond the Shire. It is even believed by some, especially by Frodo's close friends, that he visits the Elves. As Frodo approaches his fiftieth year, he seems to show an interest in further exploration—this inclination coincides with significant events in the world, especially the fact that many Elves appear to be heading westward and leaving Middle-earth while numerous Dwarves are also seeking refuge in the west from various dangers. There are hints that the power of evil, once driven out of Mirkwood, had reemerged in Mordor.

After a relatively long absence Gandalf once again visits Frodo and explains the significance of the great ring, the ring of special power. It is noteworthy that the house at Bag End signifies a sanctuary of security and stability at this point in the narrative—for it is a special place where Gandalf feels comfortable enough to narrate the story of the ring. If this house did not have such an aura of pleasant solidity one would presume that the wizard would not have used it as a location to tell such a vitally important narrative. In this narrative Gandalf proclaims that any one of the great rings gives the wearer a sense of prolonged life, although this is really illusory because the ring eventually makes life very wearisome. Moreover, if an individual persists in using the magic ring frequently to make himself invisible, then ultimately his physical presence will fade and he will become invisible, a phantom subject to the caprice of the dark power which governs such rings. Gandalf discovers that the ring which Bilbo had taken from Gollum and had given to Frodo is the most powerful ring of them all. It is, as the lines from a verse in Elven-lore declare, the "One Ring to rule them all, One Ring to find them / One Ring to bring them all and in the darkness bind them" (I, 81).[1]

---

1 This and all further quotations from *The Fellowship of the Ring*, the First Part of *The Lord of the Rings*, in this chapter are designated as I in addition to the page number of the quotation. Quotations from *The Two Towers*, the Second Part of *The Lord of the Rings*, are designated as II in addition to the page number of the quotation. And quotations from *The Return of the King*, the Third Part of *The Lord of the Rings*, are noted as III in addition to the page number of the quoted passage.

Gandalf, convinced that the ring which Bilbo had found years ago and which is now in the possession of Frodo is the master-ring, then proceeds to tell Frodo the narrative of the nine rings—Gandalf emphasizes in a tone of considerable concern that if Sauron, the dark lord, regains control of this potent ring which he had formerly made, then evil will have an opportunity to triumph over good and the world as he knows it will be problematically and perilously transformed.

As Gandalf tells the fascinating tale of the history of this potent ring he speaks of the victory of Gil-galad, King of the Elves, and Elendil of Westernesse over Sauron, although they both died in the battle, and of Isildur, Elendil's son, who slashed the ring from Sauron's hand and took it himself, before being killed by orcs. Gandalf also senses that Gollum, formerly Smeagol in the earlier part of his life, strangled a friend to take the ring for himself. Gandalf makes the interesting point that the ring is an active participant in its own destiny and history—he believes that the ring left Gollum and that Bilbo was destined to find the ring. Moreover, Frodo, as Bilbo's heir, was fated to bear the ring as well.

As Frodo listens to Gandalf's discussion about the ring, he realizes that he must leave the Shire, for his presence as the bearer of the ring is perilous for it. As Matthew Dickerson and Jonathan Evans state effectively in *Ents, Elves, and Eriador: The Environmental Vision of J. R. R. Tolkien*: "Frodo is a steward not so much of the Ring as of the *responsibility* that his possession of the ring places on him" (46). Frodo makes the important statement that as long as he knows that the Shire is safe and congenial, he shall be able to leave and to wander towards his destiny more effectively. Simon Malpas in his essay "Home" describes this sense of home insightfully as follows: "The Shire is presented here as a foundational space, an ontological ground for the Hobbit's identity, that lies securely outside of the conflict he is about to enter" (96). Malpas proceeds to say that "Frodo's journey will be bearable given that there is always the possibility of imaginative recourse to the stability of a home that retains its life-sustaining virtues irrespective of the threats and difficulties of the protagonist's unhomeliness" (96). Yet, this sense of a secure home environment which can revitalize the protagonist emotionally and spiritually will be dramatically transformed in the course of the narrative. Gildor's comment to Frodo even before he leaves the Shire suggests that this area will be subject to the vicissitudes of history and change. And yet, might one not argue that it is the "imaginative recourse" (to use the effective phrase of Simon Malpas) to his memory or vision of the Shire which is of enduring value for Frodo and which will inspire and revitalize him during the horrific and painful days in the future? This is relatively analogous to the declaration which is made in Siegfried Lenz's *The German Lesson* that those individuals who are firmly rooted are able to weather and withstand the treacherous storms and vicissitudes of the world of everyday mortality. Such a statement may be interpreted as suggesting having a firm foundation either in a "real" remembrance or in an imaginative vision of a cherished location. And sometimes the apparently "real" recollection of a beloved place may be or may seem to be as creative as the seemingly more imaginative memory.

The passage in Chapter 2 of *The Fellowship of the Ring* in which Frodo stresses his desire to save the Shire as well as his personal connectedness to the Shire and its picturesque beauty shows his capacity for self-sacrifice for the cause of goodness, a capacity which will be increasingly heightened and strengthened in the course of the narrative. In *Ents, Elves, and Eriador: The Environmental Vision of J. R. R. Tolkien* Matthew Dickerson and Jonathan Evans say insightfully that Frodo's words in this situation show a strength of character which develops and matures during the course of his quest (88). Frodo decides, as the beginning of Chapter 3 makes clear, to leave on his fiftieth birthday and he will take Sam Gamgee, his faithful friend and gardener, with him as a dependable travelling companion. Gandalf advises Frodo to leave his home very quietly and to aim first for Rivendell. Frodo feels inwardly that this is a sage decision for he would very much like to visit the house of Elrond and to enjoy the profound serenity of that beautiful place. In addition to presenting a concise history of the ring and of various individuals involved with it, Gandalf makes it clear to Frodo that he must leave the Shire for his own sake and for the safety of others. That Gandalf suggests that Frodo change his name from Baggins to Underhill affirms the dangerous nature of this enterprise.

Gandalf is a supremely important character in *The Lord of the Rings*, a very insightful and wise wizard who assumes different forms and represents an "Odinic wanderer," as Tolkien once said of him. Gandalf is devoted to the preservation of the good and worthy individuals and animate beings in general as well as of the good and worthy aspects of society and of the world. Gandalf is a steward, and one of the most significant stewards of Middle-earth, who is deeply committed to its caring management. Of the expansive concerns of Gandalf, Matthew Dickerson and Jonathan Evans write in *Ents, Elves, and Eriador: The Environmental Vision of J. R. R. Tolkien* that while Gandalf aims to organize and support various forces of good against Sauron and his malevolence, "the ultimate purpose of his work is the protection and preservation of all life in Middle-earth" (44). Gandalf represents a supremely attentive and vital force not only for what is good and noble, in support of goodness and its inclinations and manifestations, in the world of Middle-earth, but also against evil and the evil and malicious individuals and proclivities that are conspicuously evident. Gandalf also has the resilience and the strength to transform himself from Gandalf the Grey to Gandalf the White when circumstances require a personal transformation. Gandalf has a close and caring connection to all of the major good characters in the narrative, especially Bilbo, Frodo, Aragorn, Legolas, Elrond, Galadriel, Treebeard, just to name a few. Gandalf is very adept at using magic and is very sensitive to the use of language. In *Hobbits, Elves, and Wizards*, Michael N. Stanton argues that "magic, as practiced by Gandalf, seems to consist of using language as a tool to gather and concentrate and focus the ambient energies of nature" (47). Stanton suggests that what appears to be magic or magical "may be only a powerful sympathy with nature" (47). Patrick Curry suggests in *Defending Middle-earth: Tolkien, Myth, and Modernity* two interesting parallels with Gandalf, "the Celtic Merlin and the classical Hermes Trismegistus" (113). Gandalf has a profound knowledge of numerous individuals and many peoples of Middle-earth which he uses constantly and sensitively to create and sustain a wholesome, vitally humanitarian, and environmentally sensitive existence.

One of the necessary preparations for Frodo is sadly the sale of Bag End, which is purchased by one of his least favorite relations, Lobelia Sackville-Baggins. The public believed that Frodo's wealth had diminished and that he was compelled to sell and move to Buckland to live among his Brandybuck relatives. Gandalf leaves again but promises to return for Frodo's farewell celebration. However, as the late summer fades into early autumn and as Frodo's birthday approaches there is no sign of Gandalf. Gandalf does not arrive for the party—Frodo is definitely very concerned about the fact that the wizard is not present for this event. On the evening of the next day as Frodo makes ready to depart, a profound sense of melancholy pervades the scene. The house is described as being "sad and gloomy" (I, 104), qualities which apply to Frodo as well for he is melancholy about leaving his cherished home and about the absence of Gandalf from the festivities. One indication that Frodo is leaving at a most appropriate time is that just before he makes his final good-bye to the house, a stranger is heard asking Mr. Gamgee about Mr. Baggins—there is the sense that the aura of sanctuary which had prevailed at Bag End is on the verge of being undermined. As Frodo finally departs with Sam and Pippin on the first part of the journey there is no complete security, for at one point they are perilously close to being accosted by a black rider at night. Fortunately, this shadow is forestalled and dispersed by the sudden sound of Elves wandering and singing. It is moreover important that the Elves are singing of the beautiful Elbereth, her luminescence which gives them hope and faith, and their beautiful homeland beyond the sea. The sense of flux in the world of Middle-earth is suggested by the fact that Gildor, the leader of these several High-Elves, describes himself as an exile and declares that most of his kindred have long ago returned to their Elven-home across the sea, although some still reside in the serenity of Rivendell. In saying farewell Gildor gives Frodo special encouragement by naming him an Elf-friend and wishing that the stars will illuminate his path.

As their journey continues they encounter Farmer Maggot and his family, then cross the Brandywine River into Buckland where Frodo's new house is located. One of the most conspicuous architectural creations in Buckland is Brandy Hall, the ancestral home of the Brandybucks. This location is also sadly memorable for Frodo because it is the site of a family tragedy. Years ago Frodo's parents, Drogo Baggins and Primula Brandybuck, were staying with Master Gorbadoc, the head of the Brandybuck family, at Brandy Hall when they were drowned as their boat capsized on the Brandywine River. After living for a while at Brandy Hall, Frodo was eventually brought to live at Bag End as Bilbo's heir.

With respect to the Brandybuck (originally Oldbuck) family, it is noteworthy that as their population increased, their ancient house expanded as well, eventually encompassing the entirety of a low hill, and being characterized by several front doors, numerous side-doors, and many windows. The continuing growth of the Brandybuck family, the members of which built consistently all around the main house, established Buckland. In this area the authority of the Master of the Hall, the owner of Brandy Hall, was unquestioned. The sense of security of Brandy Hall is reinforced by the fact that an imposing hedge, the High Hay, is built on the eastern portion of the land. As the forest closes in on the hedge in various places, the Bucklanders do keep their doors locked at night.

Frodo's new house at Crickhollow was chosen for its seclusion and for its distance from other dwellings—originally, this house had been built by the Brandybucks as a guest house or for those family members who wanted temporarily to live in a more quiet location than Brandy Hall. The structure is very similar to a typical hobbit-hole for it is long and low. Some of its other distinguishing features are the round windows and a round door. As Frodo and the other hobbits are welcomed in by Fatty Bolger, he notices how welcoming everything looks, for his personal belongings had been carefully arranged by his friends to approximate the ambience of Bag End. Sadly, Frodo's sojourn here will be very brief, for he and his companions depart the next day, hoping to avoid any contact with a black rider and deciding first to venture through the Old Forest.

As one reflects on Tolkien's creation of various extraordinary individuals and places I think it might be helpful to keep in mind one of his major points in his essay "On Fairy-Stories." In this essay Tolkien writes: "What really happens is that the story-maker proves a successful 'sub-creator.' He makes a Secondary World which your mind can enter. Inside it, what he relates is 'true': it accords with the laws of that world. You therefore believe it, while you are, as it were, inside." One might describe not only the author of the novel but also Gandalf, Bilbo, Tom Bombadil, Elrond, and the other story-tellers within the narrative context of *The Lord of the Rings* as very effective sub-creators. The world of mythical vitality which they create is extraordinary and epically real.

In the Old Forest the hobbits encounter the large and grasping willow tree along the River Withywindle. After being rescued by the fortuitous, or seemingly fortuitous, appearance of Tom Bombadil from their potentially life-threatening encounter with "old man willow," the hobbits follow Tom to his house for a comforting and rejuvenating rest. Of the importance of Tom Bombadil for Frodo, Randel Helms writes in *Tolkien's World*: "Tom's arrival is purely providential, necessary because the hobbits have yet to grow sufficiently to help themselves and because his instructions are vital to the continuation of the quest" (86). Helms proceeds to say that Frodo learns through Tom Bombadil about the "malice implicit in the cosmos, malice entirely independent of Sauron and of which he is only the personified though immensely powerful spirit" (87).

The house of Tom and Goldberry is on a slope above a grassy knoll. The four hobbits are welcomed into this lovely abode with golden light and with mellifluous song. The intimate connectedness of Tom and Goldberry to the natural environment is manifest at the threshold of the house, for Goldberry says that they should sing of the sun, the stars, the moon, the mist, the clouds, the light, the wind, the lilies, and other aspects of nature. The description of the voice of Goldberry as "young and as ancient as Spring, like the song of a glad water flowing down into the night from a bright morning in the hills" (I, 171) reaffirms her close and congenial connection to the natural ambience.

As the hobbits cross the stone threshold they enter a long low room with various lamps and a solid wooden table with candles. Goldberry, seated on a chair in the room, appears as an elf-queen surrounded by vessels of white water-lilies. Frodo is enchanted by the lovely and soothing presence of Goldberry. In response to Frodo's query about Tom, Goldberry says that he is the master of wood, water, and hill. One might view Tom Bombadil as a nature-spirit who guards and nurtures the natural environment, making sure that each aspect of the environment is allowed to maintain its identity and its integrity. In *Hobbits, Elves, and Wizards* Michael N. Stanton says that Tom, "since he was in Middle-earth before the forms of nature itself…can be thought of as a kind of ground for nature's being" (29–30). In *Ents, Elves, and Eriador: The Environmental Vision of J. R. R. Tolkien* Matthew Dickerson and Jonathan Evans describe Tom Bombadil similarly as "the representation or personification of nature" (19) which can be seen in "his unpretentious naturalness, even his earthiness" (19). The marriage of Tom Bombadil and Goldberry is very appropriate in its fusion of the embodiment of an earth spirit and a water spirit. In one of his letters Tolkien even says that "Goldberry represents the actual seasonal changes in such lands (*Letters*, 272). One of the most noteworthy characteristics of Tom Bombadil is that his use of language, often in song, can influence and shape reality. When he demands that the old willow tree release Merry and Pippin, it does. And when Tom exhorts the barrow-wight to depart, it does, and the hobbits are liberated from their peril. Tom Bombadil has a profound interest in the natural world and in the natural environment which encompasses and permeates his existence. Of such a devotion M. Dickerson and J. Evans write insightfully in *Ents, Elves, and Eriador: The Environmental Vision of J. R. R. Tolkien* that Tom Bombadil shows a great interest in gaining knowledge about numerous aspects of the created world and its history in a spirit of selfless inquiry with no concern about the acquisition of any sense of power which such knowledge might afford (21).

The rooms of the dwelling of Tom Bombadil and Goldberry are so delightfully and aesthetically decorated that the house itself could be seen as an inward extension or manifestation of nature—likewise, one might claim that the immediate natural environment around their residence affirms the natural vitality and the love of nature which Tom Bombadil and Goldberry express and represent in their daily lives. The room with the sloping roof at the north end of the house where the hobbits sleep exemplifies this situation for its stone walls are draped with green hangings and yellow curtains while the floor is strewn with green rushes. The mattresses with white blankets on one side of the room, the earthenware basins on a bench on the other side of the room, and the green slippers next to each bed create a very hospitable atmosphere. The ordinary is fused with the extraordinary in the house of Tom and Goldberry. While various features of the house may seem ordinary, the spiritual essence and the aesthetic aura of the house are mythical. It is not surprising that Frodo feels a sense of enchantment after entering the house. That Tom and Goldberry live in intimate and sacred connectedness with the natural environment enhances the mythical presence of this effulgent house. After a refreshing dinner the hobbits sit in the room with the large hearth, where Goldberry says goodnight to them, encouraging them to sleep peacefully for the only presences around the house at night are the moonlight, the starlight, and the wind. In their ensuing conversation with Tom he reveals that it was rather fortuitous that he found them in the clutches of the old willow, for that was the final time this year when he was planning to wander in that region looking for water-lilies and lilies for Goldberry. Yet Tom also admits that he was on the lookout for the hobbits for he had heard news of them.

When asked by Frodo who Tom Bombadil really is, Goldberry responds that he is the "Master of wood, water, and hill" (I, 174). She proceeds to emphasize the integrity of each living thing in nature, saying that each animate feature of the natural environment has its own sense of being and independence. Tom Bombadil signifies a nature-spirit who watches over the many features of the natural environment to create an aura of natural harmony and unity. In *Defending Middle-earth: Tolkien, Myth and Modernity* Patrick Curry makes the important point that "in Lórien, Frodo experiences the truth" (93) of Goldberry's statement "in a tree" (93) when he touches the tree and experiences "the delight of the living tree itself" (I, 455).

In the morning after a relatively serene sleep for most of the hobbits, although at least two of them have somewhat disturbing dreams, Frodo looks out of the eastern window of the room and observes a kitchen garden. Out of the western window one can see the forest and the valley of the Withywindle in a mist. As it is a rainy day the hobbits can remain at this special house and listen to the interesting stories of Tom and the mellifluous singing of Goldberry. The narrative of Tom encompasses the mythical breadth and diversity of creation and of nature for he speaks of the trees, of the flowers, of the bees, of good things, of evil things, of streams, and of the Great Barrows and the development of the barrow-downs. Tom also sings of past ages when the world was younger and of the Elves in the earlier days. As the story, or as the series of interwoven stories, continues Frodo loses all sense of the passage of time, for in the silence of the starlight he is unsure whether one day or whether many days have passed. It is noteworthy that Tom feels comfortable enough with the hobbits who are present to tell them, in response to Frodo's question, something of his personal history. Tom is an old and venerable nature-spirit for he was present there before the river and before the trees, before the kings and before the barrow-wights. Tom asserts that he remembers the first raindrop and the first acorn and that he was present when the Elves began to travel westward. When Goldberry appears as a figure framed in the light streaming through the door the tale comes to an end and they enjoy a sumptuous supper. The songs which Goldberry sings after the supper are of hills, of pools, of the sky, and of soothing silences. Before they go to sleep that night Tom talks with the hobbits and asks them more questions, even inquiring about the ring. Tom's handling of the ring suggests that he is not at all interested in such a material object. Michael N. Stanton effectively describes in *Hobbits, Elves, and Wizards* Tom's lack of interest in the ring, saying that he is beyond the power struggle which encompasses those who are concerned with the history and the destiny of the ring (30).

On the next day the four hobbits depart in a somewhat melancholy frame of mind, for the stay with Tom Bombadil and Goldberry was exceedingly refreshing and soothing, mentally and physically. It is as if they have experienced not only a beautiful natural refuge and a lovely house but also two noble spirits of the world of nature whom they might never see again. After the breathtaking view of the surrounding countryside from the upper slope where they say farewell to Goldberry, the travellers proceed on their journey which becomes suddenly perilous again when they experience the mist on the barrow-downs. As in the confrontation with the old willow, the hobbits are almost fatally trapped and lost in the barrow-downs. However, Frodo, though weakened is able to sing the short rhyme which Tom Bombadil had taught them to use if in danger, and once again Tom emerges to rescue them. From the horde of glittering objects, jewels, and swords Tom chooses a brooch set with blue stones for Goldberry and well-crafted daggers, which were made many years ago by the Men of Westernesse and which seem untouched by time, for each of the hobbits. Tom is extremely helpful to the hobbits, even guiding them to the road and directing them to go to an inn, The Prancing Pony, in Bree, which is four miles away.

At The Prancing Pony Frodo and his companions are extremely fortunate to encounter Strider, Aragorn, who is referred to in the letter which Gandalf left in haste a while ago with the innkeeper. While the first four of the eight lines are seemingly designed to portray Aragorn, they may also implicitly characterize Frodo and some of his companions on the quest:

> All that is gold does not glitter
>> Not all those who wander are lost;
> The old that is strong does not wither,
>> Deep roots are not reached by the frost. (I, 231)

One could apply the fundamental points of this stanza to Frodo as well, for he is an individual of extraordinary capacities and great determination whose appearance might not suggest such hidden depths. Frodo's sense of connectedness or rootedness to his home, to his beloved Shire, and to other beautiful places such as Rivendell and Lothlórien which he comes to cherish on his journey is also important because it represents a continual source of comfort and revitalization during the bleak and miserable times which he experiences and which threaten his existential vitality and his life.

The next aesthetically interesting house in *The Fellowship of the Ring* is Rivendell, where Frodo is recovering after his wound from the attack of the black riders. Frodo was in a very perilous situation after being attacked on Weathertop—he survives through his own resilience and with the invaluable assistance of Glorfindel and his white elf-horse, of Aragorn, and of Elrond who, in commanding the river at the ford to flood, overwhelmed the horses of the black riders pursuing Frodo. And ultimately the healing powers of Elrond removed a splinter from the dangerous blade of the enemy and saved Frodo. One of the important points which Gandalf makes in his conversation with the convalescing Frodo is that the power of the Elves in Rivendell as a capacity for good and as a capacity to resist and challenge the evil of the dark lord is great. The Elven-wise, the lords of the Eldar from beyond the sea, have no fear of the ringwraiths, for they have resided in the Blessed Realm and thus have the capacity to live in the realms of immortality and mortality. Gandalf also reaffirms the considerable significance and majesty of Elrond and Glorfindel. Bilbo had long ago described Rivendell as "a perfect house" (I, 296) whether one likes eating, sleeping, thinking, storytelling, or singing. This is an extraordinary place which can diminish or remove physical malaise, unhappiness, and weariness. In *Master of Middle-Earth: The Fiction of J. R. R. Tolkien* Paul Kocher speaks of the welcoming nature of Rivendell: "Rivendell stands for the horizontal capacities of elf society to reach out, touch, and influence the other intelligent peoples of Middle-earth" (94). In *J. R. R. Tolkien's Sanctifying Myth: Understanding Middle-earth* Bradley Birzer writes that in "Tolkien's mythology, Rivendell best represents living with nature, the Shire represents the agrarian use of nature, and Orthanc and Mordor represent the exploitation, domination, and, consequently, the destruction of nature" (128).

When Sam takes Frodo to see the other companions he leads him to a garden overlooking a river. Rivendell is very pleasantly situated for from the eastern side of the house one can see the valley below and the mountains above. Such a physical location is reminiscent of the sanctuary of Shangri-La in James Hilton's *Lost Horizon*. The magnificence of Rivendell is affirmed and enhanced in the presence of such figures as Elrond, its Lord, and his daughter, Arwen, who is portrayed as a queenly woman and the Evenstar of her people. The beauty of Arwen is especially reinforced in the statement that Frodo had never before seen "Such loveliness in living thing" (I, 300). The splendor of Rivendell is also strengthened by the presence of Gandalf, Glorfindel, Aragorn, and the other important characters who are attending the

Council of Elrond. After the feast celebrating Frodo's recovery, Elrond, Arwen, and the other dignitaries and significant individuals proceed to another hall which contains a great hearth between carved pillars. This hall is typically a place for quiet and reflection, but on this occasion it is used for the presentation of music by minstrels and for storytelling. Frodo is also very happy to find Bilbo in a corner of the hall writing a song and enjoying the serenity. While suggesting that Rivendell is an ideal place for thinking and quiet reflection Bilbo also makes the interesting remark that "Time doesn't seem to pass here: it just is" (I,305). Such a statement does imply that Rivendell creates its own sense of time and that it has an implicit potential to affect and transform the flux of mortality.

The congenial seclusion and sense of sanctuary which Rivendell represents and offers derives not only from its physical and geographical location and from the intellectual and the spiritual power of the Elf-Lords and of the Elves which permeate it but also from the magical quality of the Elven-tongue. The language of the Elves typically has the capacity to enchant and inspire those individuals with an inherent goodness and to thwart the intentions of those who are less good or evil. When Frodo listens attentively to the Elven words and melodies his mind is transported and he has visions of distant lands and of luminescent things which he had never before imagined. As the enchantment which the words and music of the Elves produces is heightened, Frodo feels as if he were having a profound dream in which a river of serene gold and silver is flowing over him which ultimately becomes a melodious dream of the chanting of verses. As Frodo leaves the great hall with Bilbo, he hears a lovely song to Elbereth and as Arwen looks at him, the light of her eyes enraptures him. One might say that the sanctuary of Rivendell is in part created and sustained by the beautiful resonances of the Elven words and music. Michael N. Stanton describes the importance of the Elves effectively in *Hobbits, Elves, and Wizards*: "The Elves are the height of what human beings might be, and their relation to the world of nature and of society is one of harmony and wisdom.... Their languages are lovely, their music ethereal, and their architecture at once gracefully proportioned and made for Elven and human use" (35).

In Chapter 2 of Book II of *The Fellowship of the Ring* before the Council of Elrond takes place Frodo is described as walking on the terraces above the loud-flowing Bruinen and watching the sun rise above the mountains and shine down through the mist. The aura of exceptional natural beauty here is represented not only by the image of the sunrise but also by the fact that the dew is glimmering on the yellow leaves. The autumn morning is pervaded by a peaceful and rejuvenating luminescence. After Elrond introduces various members of the company he emphasizes that the enterprise against the dark lord is a communal one, that the individuals and different groups who are fighting on the side of goodness do not stand alone. One of the highlights of the Council of Elrond is the history of the Ring narrated by Elrond himself. Other individuals, Glóin, Aragorn, Boromir, Bilbo, Frodo, and Gandalf also speak and Aragorn is revealed to all as the heir of Isildur. Michael N. Stanton says effectively in *Hobbits, Elves, and Wizards* that each "participant brings a particular perspective from his own corner of Middle-earth" (36) to this vitally important council. Elrond's conclusion and advice to the company is to take the ring on the very dangerous road to Mordor and try to destroy it in Mount Doom in the fire in which it was made. Frodo senses that it is his responsibility to try to take the ring to this terrible place and a voice within him, which in a sense does not seem to represent his entire will, proclaims to the Council of Elrond that he will do this. Elrond answers respectfully that if Frodo assumes this responsibility freely, then he concurs.

The awareness of time, of an extensiveness of time, is at the heart of Elrond's narrative. He proclaims, for example, that his memory can reach back to the Elder Days, that he has experienced three ages in the West, has seen many defeats and many victories, and that he was the herald of Gil-galad at the terrible battle before the gate of Mordor. That Elrond uses the word 'fruitless' as an attribute for 'victories' in this context might not only reflect his personal experience, for example, at the Battle of Dagorlad, but also suggest his uncertainty and his subconscious doubt about the quest which he knows intuitively will have to persevere to liberate the world from the evil which threatens it so severely. In his essay "Time" Barry Langford states that Elrond's revelation of his age "opens up an unusual, but characteristically Tolkienesque, perspective: a vast reach of time to which the present is not only inheritor or successor, but to which it is bound in active and conscious relation" (37). Langford describes this sense of time as "ethically compelling" (37), a notion which Gandalf reinforces when he proclaims that they must find a way to permanently resolve the problem of the one perilous ring.

As Frodo discusses his situation with Bilbo, Sam, Merry, Pippin, and Gandalf, there is a glimmer of hope that the future is not as dark and gloomy as it might currently seem. For Gandalf says to Frodo that he will accompany him on this treacherous journey—and Bilbo makes the seemingly naïve remark that books should have good endings. He projects an ending for his book which will declare that they all lived happily ever after. The presence of such a statement in the context of planning for a very dangerous journey, the making of such a statement in a place, Rivendell, where words are precious and valued, is important because it does suggest that although the mission to take the ring into the depths of Mordor may seem impossible, there is yet a glimmer of hope that it may be accomplished. There is also a fragile sense of hope in Gandalf's statement that the path which they have chosen does not signify despair—for he appears to believe instinctively that the quest, although seemingly impossible and overwhelmingly treacherous to many, may succeed. Gandalf also makes the important observation that Sauron's belief that everyone is motivated by a lust for power might help them in their mission. For Sauron, as Milton's Satan, is so self-directed, that he will not conceive of the possibility that someone might wish to reject the power of the ring and destroy it. Elrond decrees that the Company of the Ring will be comprised of nine individuals, to counter the nine black riders. Elrond chooses Aragorn, Legolas, Gimli, Boromir, Merry, and Pippin to accompany Frodo, Gandalf, and Sam.

One of the most important aspects of Rivendell in addition to its natural beauty and the luminescent and noble spirit of existence which permeates it and which is exemplified in various individuals such as Elrond and Arwen who live here is its intellectual devotion to culture, lore, and history. In preparation for the journey Aragorn and Gandalf examine and discuss the books of lore and maps which are contained in the house of Elrond. The rejuvenating capacity of Rivendell is also manifest in the new weapons which are prepared for Aragorn and for Frodo. The Sword of Elendil has been forged anew by the smiths of the Elves and infused with mythically potent images of the sun, moon, and stars as well as various runes. The brightness and the apparent power of the remade sword encourages Aragorn to rename it Andúril, Flame of the West. Bilbo gives Frodo the sword Sting and a shirt of silver mail which he had been given by Thorin.

Despite the spirit of revitalization which the individuals of the Company feel while staying at Rivendell, there is, understandably, a profound sense of sadness which pervades their farewell from this lovely place. Elrond wishes them well while also making a short speech exhorting the ring-bearer not to cast away the ring or to give it to the enemy or to give it to anyone who is not a member of the Company or the Council, and then only in an emergency. Elrond also stresses the fact that the others travel with Frodo as free companions and may choose to end their participation in the quest at any time. Yet, it is clear, as Gimli effectively says, that only a faithless individual would give up on the quest when everything seems bleak and desolate. When the Company finally leaves at dusk on a grey day near the end of December, they are not cheered by song or music. The only hint of hope at this somber departure scenario is Bilbo's optimistic remark that he expects a complete account of the quest from Frodo when he returns and that he should not take too long in this adventure. Many people who are present at the departure of this Company would not share, either consciously or unconsciously, such an optimistic vision of the quest and of the capacity of Frodo to return very easily or quickly. Yet, the fact that Bilbo makes the statement does illuminate this somber moment with a faint ray of hope. After the members of the Company climb the steep paths leading out of the vale of Rivendell and reach the windswept moor they look back and observe the light of the Last Homely House before they vanish into the darkness.

The emotional and intellectual aura and physical ambience of Rivendell is very reminiscent of the sanctuary of Shangri-La in James Hilton's *Lost Horizon*. I would like now to discuss several parallels between Rivendell in *The Lord of the Rings* and Shangri-La in *Lost Horizon*. There are also several interesting parallels between the characters of Frodo in *The Lord of the Rings* and Conway in *Lost Horizon*. In chapter three of *Lost Horizon* the first sight of the lamasery of Shangri-La is a lovely and serene vision of a seemingly timeless world, of a timeless universe of dynamically subtle thought and refined feeling. For Conway the initial perception of the lamasery might have been a vision deriving from his profound sense of physical tranquility and harmony which he feels during the climb. The depiction of the initial view of Shangri-La is memorable not only for its ethereal quality, but also because it initiates Conway into this seemingly timeless world. A group of pavilions "clung to the mountainside with none of the grim deliberation of a Rhineland castle, but rather with the chance delicacy of flower-petals impaled upon a crag. It was superb and exquisite" (67). Hilton suggests that the aura of this mountainous ambience is comparable to and as "tremendous as the Wetterhorn above Grindelwald" (68). Beyond this lofty image and affirming its majesty through its own vitality are "the snow slopes of Karakal" (68). Rivendell, permeated by an ethereal timelessness and a vital inner harmony, is also effulgent and extraordinary in its lovely natural seclusion with the mountains nearby.

One might argue that Rivendell and Shangri-La represent aesthetic embodiments of E. M. Forster's internally harmonious work of art. Forster declares in *Two Cheers for Democracy* that a work of art is unique "not because it is clever or noble or beautiful or enlightened or original or sincere or idealistic or useful or educational— it may embody any of those qualities—but because it is the only material object in the universe which may possess internal harmony" (90). Rivendell, Lothlórien, and Shangri-La all reveal the internal stability and harmonious order which are essential to the eternally significant and humanistically vital work of art.

The otherworldliness of the Tibetan mountain ambience of Shangri-La is reinforced by the sense that the air, "clean as from another planet, was more precious with every intake" (62). The conscious and deliberate breathing which resulted inevitably in such an atmosphere produced ultimately "an almost ecstatic tranquility of mind" (62) and "a single rhythm of breathing, walking, and thinking" (62). Conway's serene personality achieves an emotional and a spiritual unity with the profoundly tranquil aura of Shangri-La.

Rivendell also offers such a sumptuous peacefulness and serenity as a complement to its aura of timelessness. Rivendell is an exceptional realm of emotional and spiritual vitality and cultural refinement, not only for the Elves but also for other special individuals such as Bilbo and Frodo. Both Bilbo and Frodo, who feel instinctively at home in and suited to Rivendell, have a profound appreciation of the beauty, the tranquility, and the mythically vital aura of this gorgeous place which rejuvenates their emotional, aesthetic, and spiritual sensibilities.

Hilton's *Lost Horizon* suggests on several occasions that Conway is destined to participate in a quest for a timeless space, for the world of Shangri-La, because he has the appropriate character and life-philosophy to appreciate the extraordinary beauty and the profound serenity of this sanctuary. Conway's personality reveals a resilient balance of inner energy and dynamic spectatorship. Hilton elaborates on this quality in Conway to participate with an intuitive perceptiveness in life by saying that his seeming indecisiveness at the approach of the strangers after the relatively tempestuous journey by plane was not courage or self-confidence but "a form of indolence, an unwillingness to interrupt his mere spectator's interest in what was happening" (57). This passivity might be linked for Conway, as it is for Castorp in Mann's *Der Zauberberg*, to the fact that neither protagonist creates the aura of timelessness in which he participates. Each individual is brought to it and initiated into it as a relatively "passive" recipient of the timeless charm of the magic mountain atmosphere. In Tolkien's *The Lord of the Rings*, Frodo, who shares various personal qualities with Conway in *Lost Horizon*, especially an appreciation of natural beauty, harmony, and serenity, an inner energy and a capacity for spectatorship, is destined as the heir of Bilbo (not only the heir to the revered hobbit's material possessions but also his emotional and spiritual heir) to participate in the quest which involves the experience not only of such ethereally beautiful places as Rivendell and Lothlórien but also of such horrific sites as Mordor. It is especially noteworthy that as Bilbo shows pity towards Gollum on an earlier journey, so the pity which Frodo shows Gollum on his quest allows for its ultimate success—perhaps Frodo, as the individual destined to bear the ring, even sensed that Gollum had an important part to play in the ultimate fate of the ring.

The physical remoteness of Shangri-La and its seeming impregnability by foreign, unguided elements proclaims and reinforces the otherworldly, timeless quality of this environment. Yet, from the beginning of the description of Shangri-La, it is clear (the manuscript's narrator wishes, perhaps less consciously than unconsciously, to make clear to us) that the feeling of permanence and timelessness is qualified by a realization that a natural catastrophe might, at an unexpected moment in the future, undermine this seemingly eternal domain. After thinking that this distinctive space represented a most frightening mountainscape, Conway imagines that the great strain of snow and glacier might someday cause the mountain to split, sending threatening avalanches into the valley below. Moreover, the narrator is aware that the existing cleft below the mountain wall is a likely consequence of a past natural upheaval. This apparent fragility merely enhances the unique, ethereal beauty of the Shangri-La ambience. This ambience of a fragile beauty is also present in Rivendell and in Lothlorien, for even though they seem to signify secluded sanctuaries, there is also the sense that the forces of evil, if gathered together, could exert a deleterious and destructive influence on these lovely and effulgent places.

The description of the library reinforces the serenely wise atmosphere and tone of Shangri-La. The library is a sanctuary characterized by and infused with an ambience of lofty spaciousness as well as of good manners and profound wisdom. This library offers a balance of the world's best literature in addition to a variety of more abstruse material. As the material, physical qualities of the lamasery, which have a cosmopolitan aura, the Shangri-La library represents a harmonious balance of

Western and Eastern texts. Conway, because of his capacity for seriousness and studiousness in private and public activity and because of his global inclinations, feels very much at home emotionally, intellectually, and spiritually in this environment of quiet erudition. The library of Shangri-La in *Lost Horizon* is analogous in function and scope to the exceedingly rich collection of lore, stories, and cultural information in Rivendell about the history of Middle-earth and about various important individuals and peoples. The House of Elrond and a number of heroic, intelligent, and prominent characters intimately associated with it such as Elrond represent a treasure-trove of wisdom and knowledge about the world of Middle-earth. Rivendell signifies a cultural oasis which cherishes and preserves extensive sources and texts of myth, music, language, and song, a golden heritage of the lore of the Elves and of other significant and noble races. It is noteworthy that Rivendell is a place of profound reflection and tranquility where Bilbo feels comfortable enough to complete the significant book on which he has been working.

As Frodo and his companions leave the ambience of Rivendell, they travel southward along the western side of the Misty Mountains. It is sadly evident that many lands are noticeably barren and empty of people and of animals. In Hollin, for example, Aragorn observes the absence of many animate creatures, especially birds, which used to be prevalent there. This is a sign of an evil presence beginning to overtake this region. Because of terrible winter weather the Company is thwarted in their attempt to traverse the heights of Mount Caradhras. Their only other option is then to attempt to go under the mountains through the Mines of Moria. This proves to be a very dangerous and tragic route for the members of the Company, especially because of their discovery of the vanquishing of Balin, the lord of Moria, and his Dwarves by swarms of orcs, because of their own encounter with the horrific orcs, and because of the apparent loss of Gandalf in the conflict with the balrog.

However, after escaping the perils of Moria the remaining members of the Company are led by Aragorn, who states that he will follow the road which Gandalf had chosen—they will follow the Silverlode for many miles and hope to eventually reach Lothlórien. Of the beauty of Lothlórien, Legolas says that it is the most lovely of all the dwellings of his people. One of the most delightful aspects of this Elven domain is that in the autumn the leaves of the special trees do not fall, instead turning to gold. When the travelers reach the eaves of the Golden Wood, Legolas and Aragorn both speak of the enchantment of Lothlórien. After they have gone a short distance in the forest, Legolas is delighted to find Nimrodel, the lovely stream of which the Elves sing, praising the rainbow on the falls and the golden flowers on the waters. After crossing the stream the travelers feel refreshed as if much of their weariness had been washed away. The sense of Lothlórien's beauty is further enhanced before they actually observe its central area not only by the tales of this special place and of its sunlight and starlight which Legolas and the other elves of Mirkwood carry in their hearts but also by the song of Nimrodel which Legolas softly sings. It is a beautiful and yet sad song, for Nimrodel was lost in the White Mountains. Legolas also recalls that the Elves of Lórien dwelt in large and beautiful trees and were thus called the Galadrim, the Tree-people.

When Legolas, Frodo, and the other members of the Company first encounter some of the Elves of Lothlórien, they are told that these Elves live in the heart of the forest in relative seclusion away from other peoples, even separated from the Elves of the North. As they proceed further towards the heart of Lothlórien, Haldir, one of the Elves they initially meet, speculates that the world which will emerge in the future will never be like the more congenial and luminescent one of old and that the Elves will ultimately decide to travel to the sea from where they will leave Middle-earth forever. Haldir is especially melancholy as he ponders this possibility for he cannot imagine a life without the beautiful mallorn-tree which is so prevalent in Lothlórien. When Frodo reaches the far bank of the Silverlode and continues on into the Naith he experiences an epiphanic moment, for he feels as if he had walked "over a bridge of time into a corner of the Elder Days, and was now walking in a world that was no more" (I, 453). This vision leads to an interesting distinction which is made between Rivendell and Lothlórien. While in Rivendell there is a profound rememberance of ancient individuals, beings, and legends, in Lothlórien the ancient and mythical individuals and beings still live in the present.

On the next day Frodo and the Company reach Cerin Amroth, which Haldir describes as the heart of the ancient realm of the Elves as it existed many generations ago. This is a place of great natural beauty containing a considerable mound of green grass on which are two circles of trees—the outer trees are snowy white and leafless and the inner trees, the great mallorn-trees, are decorated in pale gold. And beneath the lovely mallorn-trees glisten and shimmer the yellow *elanor* and the pale *niphredil*. As Frodo looks about him and contemplates the extraordinary loveliness of the scene he experiences another epiphanic vision, for he seems to be looking through a lofty window upon a "vanished world" (I, 454). The natural ambience is pure and splendid in its colorful array. As Frodo observes the pristine gold, white, and green, which appear in different manifestations (and often as gold, silver, and green) throughout the narrative, he expresses a sense of enchantment. This wonder is intimately connected to the power of the word, for Frodo feels, in this moment of perception, as if he had conceived new names for such luminescent aspects of nature. The enchantment which Frodo reveals here is echoed by Sam who declares that he feels as if he were a character in a song, in an epic ballad. As Frodo walks with Haldir up the grassy slopes of Cerin Amroth with the delightful flowers he feels as if he is in a timeless domain "that did not fade or change or fall into forgetfulness" (I, 455). Such a sensation or vision is motivated not only by the beauty of the place but also by the affirmative and effulgent power of Galadriel and Celeborn. It is noteworthy that this passage in the text which describes the ascent of Cerin Amroth also declares, in the sense of Wordsworth's "I Wandered Lonely as a Cloud" and Eichendorff's "Abschied," that when Frodo is once again in the outside world he will recall this beautiful place and his spirit will walk upon the grass of Lothlórien and find considerable comfort there.

For Frodo at least the entrance into the world of Lothlórien represents a heightening of his senses and of his sensory awareness. When Frodo is blindfolded with the other members of the Company as they enter the threshold of Lothlórien, he was not only able to smell the grass and feel the warm sunlight but he was also able to hear the river murmuring in the distance and the song of birds in the sky. And when Frodo enters the circle of white trees upon Cerin Amroth in the presence of the south wind, he can hear the murmuring of the waves of ancient seas upon beaches which had been washed away a long time ago and the crying of sea-birds whose race had vanished many years ago. As Frodo is about to climb up to the high flet he touches the tree next to the ladder and has a profound sensation of the delightful texture of the skin of the tree. The power of extraordinary perception and vision is also evident in Aragorn for when Frodo climbs down from the tree, he sees his friend with a bloom of *elanor* in his hand and seemingly rejuvenated by a congenial memory of a previous experience in Lothlórien. The inevitable connection of beauty and transience is evident even in this lovely place for the text proclaims that Aragorn, after exclaiming that the heart of Elvendom is in Lothlórien where his heart is, will never return to Cerin Amroth in mortal form. Matthew Dickerson and Jonathan Evans interpret the power of the enchantment of Lothlórien thoughtfully in *Ents, Elves, and Eriador: The Environmental Vision of J. R. R. Tolkien*: "In this enchanted place whose floral and arboreal beauty is preserved, cultivated, and enhanced by the Elves' care over it, those who enter Lothlórien are vouchsafed a taste of both the ideal perfection of the natural order and the sensory capacity to appreciate its qualities" (112).

In Chapter 7 of Book II of *The Fellowship of the Ring* Frodo and his companions arrive at Caras Galadon where the Lady Galadriel and Lord Celeborn reside. The natural architecture which Frodo initially observes is impressive. The green hill contains mallorn trees which are taller than any which he had previously seen and are depicted as "living towers" (I, 457). The beauty of this architectural ambience is further described: "In their many-tiered branches and amid their ever-moving leaves countless lights were gleaming, green and gold and silver" (I, 457). A reverence for trees, for lovely trees, has an extensive cultural history. For example, Seneca, the Roman philosopher and writer, said:

> When you find yourself within a grove of exceptionally tall, old trees, whose interlocking boughs mysteriously shut out the view of the sky, the great height of the forest and the secrecy of the place together with a sense of awe before the dense impenetrable shades will awaken in you the belief in a god.

The abode of Galadriel and Celeborn is a noble and lofty space which is reached by climbing various paths and many stairs—this high place is distinguished by a wide lawn with a rippling fountain and a giant mallorn-tree. High up in this amazingly extensive tree was a wide *talan* on which was built the royal house. Lady Galadriel is portrayed as lovely, ageless, and regal. In *J. R. R. Tolkien's Sanctifying Myth: Understanding Middle-earth* Bradley Birzer makes an analogy between Galadriel and Mary: "The most obvious Marian figure is Galadriel. The Elven queen of Lorien, a timeless realm she created and sustained with the ring Nenya, Galadriel spent much of the Second and Third Ages resisting the power of Sauron. She also created the White Council, which was dedicated to overthrowing the darkness" (64).

Lothlórien is an exceptionally beautiful place in Tolkien's *The Lord of the Rings*. The emotional and spiritual heart of this realm is Caras Galadon, the city of the Galadrim where the Lady Galadriel and Lord Celeborn reside. After crossing a white bridge and after being allowed to enter the gates of the city which face south-west, the members of the Company travel on various paths and climb numerous stairs until they reach a high place with a wide lawn and a fountain, lit by silver lamps. On the south side of the lawn is a giant and impressively massive mallorn-tree. The lower levels of this great tree contain flets on both sides; and in the heights of this towering arboreal magnificence is the residence of the Lady Galadriel and the Lord Celeborn. The chamber in the high flet where the presence of the Lady Galadriel and Celeborn is initially revealed is softly luminescent, with walls of green and silver and a roof of gold. These two elegant and graceful monarchs seem ageless and do not show any sign of the passage of time, except in the depths of their profoundly wise eyes. The domain of Galadriel and Celeborn is characterized by great natural beauty, enhanced by the presence of the yellow *elanor* and the pale *niphredil*. In *Master of Middle-earth: The Fiction of J. R. R. Tolkien* Paul Kocher emphasizes the absolute significance of Galadriel saying that "the whole enchanted region is created by the power of Galadriel focused through the elf ring Nenya, which she is wearing" (94). Kocher describes Lothlórien as a place of mythical vitality and light: "In Lórien is the purest essence of faery, resembling the light of the Two Trees in Valinor, whereby Galadriel has made for herself and her people a region and a life as close to that of the Undying Lands as she can contrive on Middle-earth. In keeping with the nature of the elf ring from which it springs, Lórien the fair is a land of peace and healing" (94–95).

When the remaining eight members of the Company are present before Galadriel and Celeborn, who are very distressed to hear about the apparent fall of Gandalf in Moria, Aragorn narrates the story of their recent adventures. After saying that she had first called together the White Council, Galadriel declares that despite the appearance of recent events she still maintains a sense of hope. As she concludes her concise statement Galadriel reaffirms that a glimmer of hope will remain as long as the members of the Company are true. The members of the Company sleep very peacefully on their first night in Lothlórien. They are fortunate in being able to spend thoroughly serene and relaxing days in this beautiful place—the sense of rejuvenation which they feel is enhanced by the fact that they do not know how many days pass during this halcyon sojourn. The aura of timelessness heightens their sense of revitalization. It is interesting that Frodo is inspired by the loveliness of Lothlórien, and especially by the fountain and by the Elven-voices, to create a song about their experiences so far on the quest. It is also noteworthy that Frodo, when he tries to repeat the song in its entirety to Sam is only able to express a handful of stanzas, as if implying perhaps that in the extraordinary and ethereal ambience of Lothlórien his language cannot adequately capture the beauty and the spirit of Elven words and melodies. That Frodo is only able to articulate some of the stanzas could also reflect his deep sadness about the apparent demise of Gandalf, which is one of the primary themes in the song. Such sadness is also manifest in the melancholy laments of the Elves in response to the news that Gandalf has fallen. In a conversation between Sam and Frodo one evening when Frodo senses that their departure from Lothlórien is imminent, Sam makes the interesting observation that the Elves in Lothlórien seem to belong there even more than the Hobbits in the Shire. His statement suggests an intimate interconnectedness between the Elves and the area in which they live, the natural environment which they love and cherish. The aura of Lothlórien, the heart of the Elves in Middle-earth, is further described as one of great serenity and of a profound and peaceful appreciation of and sensitivity for nature.

As if in response to Frodo's expressed hope that he will see the Lady Galadriel before their departure she appears and leads him and Sam through a high hedge into an enclosed garden. They climb down into a green hollow through which runs a silver stream. On a pedestal is an extraordinary silver basin, the Mirror of Galadriel. Galadriel fills the basin of silver with water from the stream and invites Frodo and Sam to look into the Mirror if they wish. When Sam looks into the mirror he presumably sees visions of the future: the first image foreshadows the apparent death of Frodo when they are misled by the deceitful Gollum and the next image projects the moral and physical destruction of the Shire, which may yet be averted if the quest is successful.

When Frodo asks whether Galadriel would advise him to look into the Mirror, she states that she does not give such counsel one way or the other, for seeing can be either good or dangerous. However, Galadriel also says that she believes that Frodo has the courage and the wisdom to gaze into the Mirror, or she would not have thought of bringing him to this special sanctuary. The first vision which Frodo experiences is that of a twilit land with mountains and of a figure robed in white walking slowly on the long road—Frodo appears to interpret this individual as Gandalf. The next vision which Frodo sees is that of Bilbo working in a room filled with papers strewn all around. After a series of scenes which reflect parts of the historical events which are unfolding in the world, the mist clears and Frodo observes a natural environment which he has never directly experienced in his life, namely, the sea. At the end of this vision, which incorporates images of the sea, of a storm, of the sun, of a river flowing through a city, of a white fortress with towers, of a ship with black sails, of battle, of a banner with the sign of a white tree, a small ship passes away into the distance. Such a vision could foreshadow Frodo's ultimate departure from Middle-earth from the Grey Havens at the end of the novel. The final vision which Frodo sees is the most dangerous and the most disturbing—for he sees the eye of the dark lord searching for him. However, Frodo is able to prevent his being seen, although the ordeal is very draining for his inner being. The presence of Galadriel is vital here, for when Frodo seems to be falling forward, her soft voice exhorts him not to touch the water and the vision vanishes.

Galadriel says that she is aware of the dark lord and of his attempt to infiltrate the realm of Lothlórien. Galadriel then explains what Frodo seems to feel intuitively: that the lovely ring on her finger, which "glittered like polished gold overlaid with silver light" (I, 472) and which appears to contain the light of Eärendil, the Evening Star, so beloved among the Elves, and reflects its luminescence, is one of the three special Elven Rings. For Galadriel is the keeper of Nenya, the Ring of Adamant. The Lady Galadriel then articulates with quiet melancholy the dilemma of the Elves of Lothlórien. If the quest to destroy the one ring of the dark lord fails, then the Elves will be exposed to the destructive caprice of the enemy. And if the quest succeeds and the one ring is destroyed, then the power of the Elves will be weakened and Lothlórien will diminish and eventually be washed away by the tides of mortality. For the vitality of Lothlórien is directly and inextricably connected to the power of Galadriel's lovely ring, Nenya. Michael N. Stanton effectively says of this ring in *Hobbits, Elves, and Wizards:* "It is this Ring's power that is preserving Lothlórien and keeping Sauron both baffled and at bay" (42). And, of course, Galadriel's honor, nobility, and will are guiding and motivating the ring's presence. Galadriel is saddened because she knows instinctively that the Elves will inevitably have to leave Lothlórien, their beautiful home and the natural environment they love, in the future and depart for the West. It is noteworthy that Galadriel, as Gandalf before her, is wise enough to decline Frodo's offer to take the one ring which he bears if this would enhance her existential position. For she knows that this ring, forged originally by the dark lord, is instinctively and ultimately a ring of evil. The Lady Galadriel shows her greatness by resisting this temptation and proclaiming that she will be content to ultimately go into the West, to the ancestral home of the Elves, remaining herself and retaining her integrity.

Throughout *The Lord of the Rings* and especially in *The Fellowship of the Ring* a capacity for goodness and an appreciation of nature are intimately connected. Patricia M. Spacks discusses this theme very thoughtfully in her essay "Power and Meaning in *The Lord of the Rings,*" citing the Rangers, Tom Bombadil, and the Elves as exemplifying such a connection. For example, of the Elves of Lórien, Spacks writes that the "power of the noble Elves gives Frodo new awareness of trees" (84). And one of the reasons for the success of Aragorn, despite all of the hardships and sufferings which he experiences in the course of his life, is that he, like other Rangers, who represent the force of goodness, understands "the languages of beasts and birds" (Spacks 84).

Chapter 8 of Book II, "Farewell to Lórien," is permeated by a heightened aura of melancholy as the members of the Company say goodbye to Lothlórien and to Galadriel and Celeborn. The speech of Celeborn to the Company on the night before their departure intensifies the sense of melancholy and sadness for he speaks of the uncertainty of achieving peace and of the fragility of the world which they now cherish. Celeborn says that he will provide the Company with boats to journey upon the Great River. Aragorn is especially pleased with this for this will give the Company more time to decide their future course. The Elves are very generous and provide the members of the Company with various gifts of food and clothing, including lembas and special cloaks for their perilous journey. The "magic" cloaks represent a rare gift for they were made by the Lady Galadriel and her maidens. As the members of the Company prepare to depart and say goodbye, it is noteworthy that they feel as if this lovely place had become a home to them and as if time had passed so smoothly that they are not sure how many days and nights have been spent in Lothlórien. For there is a timeless aura at the heart of Lothlórien and permeating this beautiful place which at least several members of the Company deeply appreciate and value.

In *Tolkien's Art: A Mythology for England* Jane Chance Nitzsche emphasizes thoughtfully the redemptive quality of Galadriel and Lothlórien saying that "the spiritual form of death represented by sin stems from within the individual but is redeemed by the 'new life' of wisdom and virtue counseled by Galadriel, the supernatural equivalent of Tom Bombadil who resides in the paradisal Lothlórien" (108). Lothlórien is characterized by and permeated by an eternal present "where all remains new and young, and filled with the healing spirit of elven mercy and *caritas*" (108). Jane Chance Nitzsche proceeds to emphasize the rejuvenating beauty of the lovely Lothlórien: "Lórien of the Blossom boasts an Eternal Spring where 'ever bloom the winter flowers in the unfading grass' (I, 454), a 'vanished world' where the shapes and colours are pristine and new" (108). She also suggests that there is an aura of timelessness in Lothlórien: "In this paradise of restoration...time almost ceases to pass and seems even to reverse so that 'the grim years were removed from the face of Aragorn, and he seemed clothed in white, a young lord tall and fair' (I, 456)" (108). It is also noteworthy that at this moment of rejuvenation Aragorn speaks words in the Elven tongue to the spirit of Arwen. It is as if the sense of physical revitalization motivates and inspires an emotional and a spiritual rejuvenation as well.

In his essay "Tolkien and Frodo Baggins" Roger Sale speaks of the power of the light in Lothlórien and argues insightfully that "'light' has the effect here of being a name for the moral power of goodness" (259). Sale proceeds to describe the luminescence of Lothlórien further: "The light of Lothlórien shines from a vanished world, and the light which Aragorn once saw when all Lothlórien was alive shines now only as a memory. Yet he was there so he now is wrapped in the memory that shines in his eyes" (260). Yet this light is still so powerful that it can, through the beauty and the vitality of Galadriel, illuminate the world of Middle-earth and sustain at least some of the members of the Company in memory and in spirit as they journey on the quest to destroy the ring of power. The phial of light which Galadriel gives to Frodo as a parting present is of supreme significance in enabling Frodo and Sam to survive in the ambience of Mordor.

In *Tolkien's Art: A Mythology for England* Jane Chance Nitzsche also discusses very effectively the importance of lembas as a sign and a symbol of regeneration: "The physical and spiritual regeneration or 'life' characteristic of these elves is embodied in their lembas, a food that restores spirits and lasts exceedingly long—a type of communion offered to the weary travelers" (108). Jane Chance Nitzsche also emphasizes the spiritual importance of other gifts of the Lady Galadriel for the members of the Company: "Other gifts of the Lady Galadriel—the rope, magic cloaks, golden hairs, phial of light, seeds of elanor—later aid them either physically or spiritually at times of crisis in their quest almost as Christian grace in material form" (108–09).

As they leave the city of the Elves they can hear various voices singing in the trees. The Elves have prepared three small grey boats for the use of the travelers. As they move down the stream they perceive an extraordinary boat in the shape of a great swan—Galadriel and Celeborn have come to say farewell. Galadriel sings a lovely and melancholy song of golden leaves and of a golden tree in a place beyond the reach of time and mortality. This song also mentions Elven-tears which flow because of the awareness of the presence of falling leaves and winter, because of an intuition that Lórien will not be able to preserve its past glory, and because of a quiet longing for the immortal realm. The lyric ends with the persona wondering whether there is a ship which would take her back to the beautiful, timeless place which she cherishes in her heart. As Frodo gazes at Galadriel in great admiration during the feast which is held upon the green grass, she seemed "present and yet remote, a living vision of that which has already been left far behind by the flowing streams of Time" (I,483).

After Galadriel and Celeborn drink the cup of farewell with their guests they give special gifts to all of the members of the Company. The gifts which they bestow are important because they bear the spirit of Lothlórien in them and will be of great benefit to the recipients. To Aragorn, for example, Galadriel gives a special sheath with elven-runes for his sword and a clear green stone set in a silver brooch which has an effulgent power. To Legolas Galadriel gives an important bow and a quiver of arrows. To Boromir the Lady offers a belt of gold; and to Merry and Pippin she offers silver belts with golden clasps. To Sam the Lady gives a small box of earth from her orchard with her blessing. At the end of the narrative this gift will aid considerably in the rejuvenation of the Shire after the deleterious aspects and malevolent individuals have been removed. This aura of rebirth is discussed effectively by Jane Chance Nitzsche in *Tolkien's Art: A Mythology for England*: "Once Sharkey and Worm have disappeared, Sam the new Mayor as gardener can replenish its natural stores as well. After he plants the seed given him by Galadriel, new trees, including a mallorn with silver bark and gold flowers, burst into bloom in the spring" (125). This new growth initiates a period of personal and natural rejuvenation in the Shire. The gift of three of her golden hairs which the Lady Galadriel gives to Gimli in response to his request is accompanied by her statement, in tacit acknowledgement of his chivalric courteousness, that he will be rewarded with considerable material wealth in the future if the quest does not fail. And to Frodo, the Ring-Bearer, the Lady Galadriel gives a phial which contains the light of Eärendil's star in the aura of the waters of her fountain. This lovely light will be a comforting and potently luminescent guide in the darkness and during the bleak moments of the dangerous and arduous journey.

As the Company enters their boats and moves down the stream, they say a quiet and melancholy farewell to Galadriel, Celeborn, and the Elves. As they pass the Lady Galadriel it seemed to the travelers that she was floating away from them. This sensation is extended to include the entire aura of Lothlórien, for it seemed to the Company as they proceed down the river that Lórien was slipping backward in time, in the stream of mortality, and flowing towards distant and primordial shores. Such an image affirms the inevitable disappearance of Lothlórien into the mists of memory and timeless visions for this beautiful place creates and participates in its own sense of time. In seeming to move backward, the Elves of Lothlórien, that is, the Lady Galadriel and some of her kindred, are actually anticipating and aspiring to achieve a return to their blessed, immortal realm beyond the sea.

As the travelers on the quest flow down the stream, the figure of the Lady Galadriel becomes increasingly distant, yet still revealing a potent refulgence, shining like "a window of glass upon a far hill in the westering sun" (I, 488). Appropriately, Galadriel, even as she fades from the sight of the Company, appears as a lovely effulgent image, a vision of natural beauty. This luminescent image is accompanied by the sound of her voice singing a profoundly sad song about a sense of loss and about the inevitable passage of time, ending with the very faint glimmer of hope that perhaps a sense of the beautiful may be found again someday. As they follow the river around a bend, the light of Lothlórien becomes hidden. Although Frodo preserves in his heart forever the spirit of this meeting with Galadriel, he will never see Lothlórien again.

There are interesting parallels between Lothlórien in *The Fellowship of the Ring* and Shangri-La in Hilton's *Lost Horizon*. For Lothlórien is a special space of exquisite aesthetic beauty and natural vitality. In Hilton's *Lost Horizon* Conway's quest for timelessness and for a peaceful sanctuary is simultaneously a search for aesthetic enrichment. Conway's experience of Shangri-La will not only develop his sense of time and potential timelessness and his appreciation of the sanctuary environment— it will also enhance his aesthetic awareness. Perhaps these features are inevitably and inextricably linked. The aesthetic education of Conway in this serene sanctuary is strengthened in his perception of treasures that museums and wealthy individuals would be interested in. These impressive objects include pearl blue Sung ceramics, paintings in tinted inks, and beautiful lacquers.

The exquisite and exquisitely fragile beauty of the artistic objects in this sanctuary is reinforced in the following description in *Lost Horizon* of the Shangri-La aura: "A world of incomparable refinements still lingered tremulously in porcelain and varnish, yielding an instant of emotion before its dissolution into purest thought" (97). In this ambience the aesthetic image (in Pound's sense of the image as an emotional and intellectual complex in an instant of time) is transformed into an aura of ethereal, contemplative harmony. By appreciating the delicate beauty of such delightful art objects, Conway participates aesthetically and emotionally in the world of Shangri-La and instinctively enhances his sense of belonging in this lovely sanctuary. Lothlórien and Rivendell are similarly characterized by and permeated with beautiful aspects of nature and with aesthetically interesting objects of considerable loveliness. When a member of the Company in *The Lord of the Rings* such as Frodo, for example, appreciates profoundly and sensitively the beauty of Lothlórien and of Rivendell, this reinforces his feeling of being forever a part of such extraordinary and mythically vital landscapes.

It is also interesting that Bilbo and Frodo in *The Hobbit* and in *The Lord of the Rings*, as Father Perrault, the High Lama, in Hilton's *Lost Horizon*, all have their important adventures when they are around the age of 50. The character, strength, motivation, and mythical vitality of Gandalf, Bilbo, Frodo, Elrond, and Aragorn in Rivendell, and Galadriel, Aragorn, and Frodo in Lothlórien in Tolkien's work are similar to that of Conway and the High Lama in Hilton's *Lost Horizon*. Gandalf, Aragorn, Bilbo, and Frodo, as the High Lama and Conway, have an instinctive Wanderlust, a capacity and a desire to travel in and explore regions beyond their accustomed and familiar existential context which complements and affirms their devotion to the cause of goodness and truth and their commitment to the acquisition of greater knowledge and to achieving a vital awareness of their contemporary world. In fact, for many years and decades Gandalf and Aragorn have travelled widely and extensively and in a spirit of exemplary self-sacrifice and selflessness throughout Middle-earth on various errands and missions of the utmost importance to the preservation and well-being of that realm. Whereas some of these extraordinary individuals, such as Galadriel and Elrond, are immortal, others, such as the High Lama, are aware of their mortality. Yet, all of these individuals have led exemplary lives of nobility, generosity, aesthetic sensibility (in the sense of a profound appreciation for the beauty of nature, language, myth, and music), and humanitarian sensitivity. The experience of Conway in Shangri-La in Hilton's *Lost Horizon* and the experience of Elrond, Aragorn, Bilbo, Frodo, and Sam especially in Rivendell and of Galadriel, Aragorn, Frodo, and Legolas especially in Lothlórien in Tolkien's *The Lord of the Rings* represents a culminating moment of their lives for such magnificent places signify sanctuaries of natural beauty, emotional and intellectual vitality, oases of cultural awareness and knowledge, which are permeated by an aura of cosmic serenity and harmony and an apparent timelessness beyond the flux of mortality.

In Part Two (Books 3 and 4) of *The Lord of the Rings*, *The Two Towers*, one of the most splendid architectural creations is Meduseld, the hall of Théoden, King of the Mark of Rohan. From a distance the hall seems to Legolas to shine like gold. The land of King Théoden, Rohan, has a vitality about it, especially seen in the abundant greenness, the willow trees, and the blossoming white flowers. The interior of the hall of Theoden is aesthetically dynamic and interesting, for it is long and wide with great carved pillars upholding the high roof. And the floor of this impressive hall is paved with stones of varying colors and runes. The hall also contains various tapestries or cloths upon the walls with important figures of mythical and legendary vitality.

Two other impressive architectural creations in Book 3 of *The Lord of the Rings* are the Hornburg, containing lofty walls of ancient stone and a high tower, and Isengard, formerly the fortress of great lords, the wardens of Gondor upon the West. Yet, for a long time now this had been the dwelling-place of Saruman, whose citadel was Orthanc. Through his cunning inclinations and malicious devices Saruman thought he was improving Isengard, delving deep into the earth as he obliterated the natural beauty of the area—yet, in fact, as the narrative makes clear, Isengard became merely a copy of the Dark Tower of Sauron. When Gandalf, Aragorn, Legolas, and Gimli, Théoden, and the others arrive at Isengard they are astonished to see it in ruins, having recently been the recipient of the frustration and the wrath of the Ents, who had for a long time observed and experienced the mistreatment and disdain of Saruman. Isengard exemplifies a building which once existed in harmony with its natural environment. However, Saruman's abuse of nature and his destruction of trees and plants for his malevolent purposes undermined not only the physical but also the spiritual foundation of Isengard. Michael N. Stanton describes this situation effectively in *Hobbits, Elves, and Wizards*, saying that Saruman has produced "an industrial wasteland (58) characterized by "pollution, disorder, noise" (58) and by a replacement of the natural by the mechanical (58). The power of Treebeard and of his fellow Ents, once inspired, initiated and completed the constructive, life-affirming transformation of Isengard and infused this bleak region with a spirit of renewal. Treebeard even speaks of allowing the waters of the stream which pours through the polluted Isengard to begin a cleansing process.

One might view Saruman's destructive inclinations as a manifestation of his greed for power. An individual who is so utterly motivated by a desire for power would also be thoroughly tempted by the lure of the one ring. This is manifest in the character of Gollum, whose existence has become completely driven by and morphed by his possession of the ring and by his desire to possess it again. Boromir, too, becomes overwhelmed by a sudden lust for the ring which is his undoing. The one ring of Sauron can be used by others, for a while, at least, if they do not let it control their entire existence and if they do not let it generate within them an obsession with power. As Tom Shippey states in *The Road to Middle-Earth* there are various characters who are or who seem to be indifferent to the lure of the ring, for example, Sam, Aragorn,

Legolas, Gimli, Merry, and Pippin; however, for others, the ring is 'addictive' (126). The invisible aspect of the ring is effectively addressed by Robert Eaglestone in his essay in *Reading The Lord of the Rings: New Writings on Tolkien's Classic*. Eaglestone argues that "Invisibility, ironically, is a highly visible form of evil" (74) and cites the story which Glaucon tells in *The Republic* of the ring of Gyges. In this story a shepherd finds a ring which makes him invisible—he uses this invisibility "to seduce the king's wife, kill the king and seize the throne" (Eaglestone 74). Eaglestone proceeds to say that "Invisibility, for Glaucon, is a way of avoiding the need to 'seem moral'—-reputation—which, in turn, even for the 'iron willed,' allows immorality to flourish" (74–5) and that such a description is applicable for Gollum, Sauron, and even to some extent Bilbo and Frodo (Eaglestone 75).

At the beginning of her essay "Men, Halflings, and Hero-Worship" Marion Zimmer Bradley speaks of the importance of love as hero-worship in Tolkien's *The Lord of the Rings*: "Love is the dominant emotion in *The Lord of the Rings*, and love in the form of hero-worship is particularly evident in the relationship between Aragorn and the other characters and between Frodo and Sam" (109). Bradley also discusses effectively heroic qualities of Aragorn and Frodo, stressing that Aragorn, descended from a line of kings, is destined to accomplish great things, while Frodo is compelled by circumstances to be heroic (117). Marion Zimmer Bradley elaborates on the distinction between the heroic inclinations of Frodo and Sam, saying that Frodo accepts the extraordinary responsibility of bearing the ring which has seemingly come to him by chance, while Sam is not consciously interested in heroism and just wants to protect Frodo in the adventure (117).

One of the reasons why the quest of Frodo and his companions is successful is because of the inherent weakness of the evil of Sauron. Of this weakness W. H. Auden writes in his essay "The Quest Hero": "His primary weakness is a lack of imagination, for, while Good can imagine what it would be like to be Evil, Evil cannot imagine what it would be like to be Good" (57). W. H. Auden proceeds to mention various characters who represent vital goodness and who have the capacity to imagine themselves in other guises. Auden says, for example, that Elrond, Gandalf, and Aragorn can imagine how Sauron would be and think and are thus able to overcome the temptation to use the ring (57). Auden proceeds to state that Sauron, in contrast, cannot believe that anyone who is aware of the power of the ring would not wish to use it—Sauron certainly does not think that anyone would desire to destroy it (57).

The element of evil in *The Lord of the Rings* is associated with a disdain for nature and a desire to destroy the beautiful natural environment. Patricia M. Spacks describes the development of the narrative effectively in terms of this disregard for nature, stating that the "progress toward the heart of evil…is from natural fertility to the desolation of nature" (84). Spacks proceeds to describe the domain of the enemy as "physically and morally a Wasteland" (84), concluding that "the implication is strong that the barrenness of nature here is a direct result of the operations of evil"

(84). The narrative of *The Lord of the Rings* concludes with a celebration of goodness over evil, for the ring is cast into Mount Doom and Sauron is defeated, and with a spirit of revitalization for various major characters and races which have suffered in their battle against evil and against the forces of Sauron. It is noteworthy that Frodo, having reached the Crack of Doom after an immensely heroic effort, appears to change his mind about casting the ring of power away. Sue Zlosnik writes in "Gothic Echoes" of the destructive power of the ring: "The Ring's power to disintegrate the subject and transform it into something abject is most powerfully demonstrated in Gollum but remains a constant threat to the identity of Frodo as long as he remains the Ring-bearer" (56). Yet Gollum, or perhaps a manifestation of fate, intervenes, attacks Frodo, and after biting off the finger with the ring falls into Mount Doom so that the destruction of the ring is accomplished. Patricia Spacks makes a very important point about the relation of the individual to fate: "Free choice of good by the individual involves his participation in a broad pattern of Good; individual acts become a part of Fate" (95). Spacks proceeds to say that Frodo's "merciful acts determine his fate" (95).

Orthanc and Mordor are industrial and mechanical blots and pits with no appreciation for the beauty and vitality of nature. When Saruman was in control of Orthanc he used and exploited various aspects of nature, and especially trees, for his military and industrial purposes. Saruman and his orcs assaulted and mistreated the trees in Fangorn. What makes Saruman's abuse of the natural environment so terrible is that he not only practiced blatant deforestation for the purpose of using the trees to provide fuel for his nefarious plans but he also merely destroyed trees as a caprice—the uprising of the Ents represents a dynamic attempt to halt this abuse of the natural environment. Tom Shippey argues very effectively in *J. R. R. Tolkien: Author of the Century* for the strong relevance of Tolkien's environmentally motivated critique of Isengard:

> The 'applicability' of this is obvious, with Saruman becoming an image of one of the characteristic vices of modernity, though we still have no name for it—a kind of restless ingenuity, skill without purpose, bulldozing for the sake of change…the Sarumans of the real world rule by deluding their followers with images of a technological Paradise in the future…but what one often gets…are the blasted landscapes of Eastern Europe, strip-mined, polluted, and even radioactive. (171)

Treebeard and the other Ents are committed to the preservation of nature, and especially of the forests. The Ents are the shepherds and the protectors of the trees. Matthew Dickerson and Jonathan Evans write in *Ents, Elves, and Eriador: The Environmental Vision of J. R. R. Tolkien* that "the word *Ent* is a modernization of two apparent Old English synonyms found in *Beowulf*: *ent* and *eoten*" (126). The Old English word means "giant." It is noteworthy that Treebeard, as his creator, has a great interest in language and in names. Tolkien had a lifelong interest in and appreciation for trees. In a 1955 letter Tolkien writes: "I am…much in love with plants and above all trees, and always have been; and I find human maltreatment of them as hard to bear as some find ill-treatment of animals" (*Letters*, 220). The Ents, devoted preservers and protectors of the natural environment, assist considerably in and ensure the dramatic overthrow of Saruman, for they are very upset by his willful destruction of and disdain for nature, its beauty, and its vitality.

Treebeard, or Fangorn, as many other Ents, has a physically powerful, intellectually aware, and emotionally vital presence in the world of Middle-earth. As the heart of the forest, Treebeard is not only a caretaker and preserver of the beauty of the natural environment but also an individual who creates and nurtures his own sense of time. Treebeard's appreciation of nature is intimately connected to his linguistic awareness and his sensitivity for names, especially of various objects in the natural environment. He seems to proceed with various activities in a slow manner, in part because this is his instinctive life-philosophy and in part because of his reverence for the mythical presences in the natural environment around him. Treebeard is himself aware of this slowness, especially in contrast to the more hasty responses of Merry and Pippin—but such a sense of time is not only his own, it is also a source of his strength and his vision. Moreover, Treebeard, as Tom Bombadil in his own right, is a figure of ancient mythical vitality who has been in existence since the youthful days of the world when the forests were more prevalent and expansive.

The exploitation of the natural environment in the ambience of Isengard which is caused by Saruman is even more horrific and intensified in Mordor as Sauron displays a blatant disdain for nature in his all-consuming search for the one ring which will coalesce his evil powers. Mordor shows a terrible abuse of the natural environment—it is a place permeated with conspicuous images of decay and death and enveloped in an aura of physical and spiritual darkness, gloom, and wretchedness. There is little, if any, sign or indication of life or of green things in Mordor where the natural landscape has been mistreated for so long under the violent grasp of Sauron's lust for power and absolute hegemony. Such an abused natural ambience also shows the inherent fragility and weakness of Sauron's enterprise, which he fails to observe or realize. Sauron is so self-absorbed and self-directed in his search for absolute power that he ignores or misinterprets the signs of death and desolation permeating his realm—for such signs foreshadow an inevitable end to this greedy maliciousness. Various critics have mentioned literary precursors to Tolkien's description of the ravaged environment of Mordor, especially several poems by William Blake and novels of Charles Dickens such as *Hard Times*, in which the spirit of Coketown bears a distinct resemblance to Mordor.

While neither Orthanc of Saruman nor Mordor and Mount Doom of Sauron are magnificent, beautiful, or splendid, they are architectural "creations" in a sense and their destiny shows the negative aspect of how such "creations" can be affected and shaped by the misguided, destructive inclinations of their owners and by mortality. Orthanc is, in a sense, an artificial building of Saruman for he ravages and destroys the surrounding natural environment in his quest for power. Orthanc is doomed by the destructive motivation which has created and developed it and its hordes of evil individuals, orcs and others. Mordor is depicted as even more of a bloated and unpleasant wasteland than Orthanc and its environs. The barrenness of the landscape reflects and reaffirms the emptiness of Sauron's inclinations and lust for power. The fragility of this place is especially manifest in its final destruction as Gollum falls with the ring into the Crack of Doom—structures, towers, and walls fall down and are vanquished in an atmosphere of horrific chaos and smoke. The magnitude of this destruction is a reflection of the power which had been infused into the ring. The passage describing the end of Mordor and of Sauron displays the frailty of building which is not cognizant of and sensitive to the environment in which it is developed or in which it exists. In contrast, the architectural creations of Rivendell and Lothlórien thrive because they are aesthetically, emotionally, physically, and spiritually at one with their natural environment and with the ambience of history and lore with which they are connected and which encompasses and infuses them. Both Rivendell and Lothlórien exemplify and symbolize the spirit of Frank Lloyd Wright's notion seen in various of his houses that the building should exist in a harmonious relation with its environment and that the building should affirm and elaborate significant features of its environment. Wright's Robie House is a good example of this philosophy of architecture, as is Nansen's Bleekenwarf in Siegfried Lenz's *Deutschstunde, The German Lesson.*

In his essay "The Appeal of *The Lord of the Rings*: A Struggle for Life," Hugh T. Keenan emphasizes the importance of the theme of the struggle for life against death. Keenan highlights examples from *The Lord of the Rings* which exemplify the use of elements of the Wasted-Land-and-the-Wounded-King theme as emphasized in Jessie L. Weston's *From Ritual to Romance*: "Gandalf comes to Théoden's court, rouses the old king from illness, drives out Wormtongue, and thus restores the leader to his people and the land to its former vigor" (72–3). Keenan also mentions Aragorn's revitalization of Gondor which encompasses such significant thematic elements as the return of the kingdom to the rightful owner and the resurgence of the city and its residents (73). The ultimate rejuvenation of the White Tree in Minas Tirith symbolizes the rebirth of Gondor.

In "The Shire, Mordor, and Minas Tirith" Charles Moorman discusses insightfully the regeneration of Minas Tirith, asserting that with the defeat of Sauron this city assumes once again its "proper order and glory" (208). As a most vital dimension of this renewed order Aragorn takes his "true place as King Elessar and marries Arwen, the daughter of Elrond" (208). The positive transformation of Minas Tirith which the presence of King Elessar initiates and nurtures is effectively depicted in Book VI of *The Lord of the Rings*, in the chapter of *The Return of the King* entitled "The Steward and the King" which describes the city as becoming even more beautiful than it had been during its glorious past: "it was filled with trees and with fountains, and its gates were wrought of mithril and steel, and its streets were paved with white marble...and all was healed and made good" (III, 304). It is also noteworthy that the reign of Aragorn, King Elessar, while initiating a new age, preserves and cherishes the memory and the glory of the past age. The aura of rejuvenation which pervades Middle-earth after the destruction of the ring and the defeat of Sauron is also manifested in the reconciliation of the Elves and the Dwarves, symbolized by the friendship of Legolas and Gimli. The Elves under the leadership of Legolas in Ithilien and the Dwarves ruled by Gimli thrive not only in their own right but also in their supportiveness of the enterprises and projects of their neighbors. In *Master of Middle-earth: The Fiction of J. R. R. Tolkien* Paul Kocher affirms the vitality of Aragorn as a king and a savior and the splendor of the celebration which acknowledges this:

> The ceremonies by which Aragorn ascends the throne are just what they should be. Magnificent in themselves, they reenact and refer back to the historical events from which he derives his title, and they unite all the elements of the kingdom in a common consent which will assure its future political stability. (158)

The coronation ceremony culminates in Gandalf's placing the crown, the ancient crown on the summit of which was set a single effulgent jewel, on the kneeling Aragorn. In the ceremony Aragorn repeats the promise made by Elendil so many, many years ago: "Out of the Great Sea to Middle-earth I am come. In this place will I abide, and my heirs, unto the ending of the world" (III, 303). The physical presence of Aragorn, King Elessar, is regal and impressive, for his tall stature exudes an aura of ageless vitality, wisdom, healing, constructive willpower, and a potent luminescence. Aragorn is destined to be the King of the reunited kingdom fusing Gondor and Arnor, not only by virtue of his being Elessar of the line of Valandil, Isildur's son, Elendil's son and victorious Captain of the Host of the West, and bearer of the Star of the North, but also because Galadriel has given him her blessing, because Gandalf believes that Aragorn should be the ruler of this renewed realm, and because Elrond finally adds his support as well, for Arwen Evenstar, Aragorn's love, is his daughter.

Before Gandalf leaves Aragorn, King Elessar, and Gondor, they ascend a path up Mount Mindolluin which had formerly been used by kings. As they look over the lands beneath them, Gandalf proclaims that this is Aragorn's realm and that it signifies the beginning of a new age. Gandalf directs Aragorn towards a sapling of the white tree, which already displayed one cluster of white flowers. When he returns to the Citadel, Aragorn removes the dead tree which is there, gives it a proper burial and plants the new sapling in the court by the fountain. This new white tree symbolizes the revitalization of Aragorn and his lineage on the throne—Gandalf even says of the precious sapling that it has been concealed on the mountain as the race of Elendil has been hidden in the northern realms. The importance of an appreciation of the natural environment is again emphasized in this context, for Gandalf adds that the line of this sapling, a descendant of the eldest trees, is much older than the line of Aragorn, King Elessar. And then as an affirmation of this sense of continuity

Aragorn and Arwen Evenstar are married on Midsummer's day—and the sapling of the white tree has blossomed. It is interesting that when Frodo sees Arwen on the occasion of her arrival on Midsummer's Eve he says to Gandalf that now both day and night will be beloved and blessed, as if suggesting that the union of Arwen and Aragorn will create a realm of complete and profound happiness.

In Part Three of *The Lord of the Rings*, *The Return of the King*, another important theme, which is connected to the theme of revitalization, is that of sacrifice. All of the members of the Company have sacrificed greatly in the quest to destroy the ring of power. Gandalf, Aragorn, Frodo, Sam, Legolas, and Gimli especially have shown an immeasurable capacity for sacrifice in the service of goodness against evil. They have endured terrible physical strain and suffering as well as considerable emotional travail on their quest, while confronting perilous dangers—yet they have born and confronted such hardships and miseries with a nobility of character rarely seen in the annals of world literature. They have encountered and experienced doubt, despair, and hopelessness on numerous occasions and yet have still preserved a sense, or a glimmer, of hope and faith that their quest would achieve an affirmative conclusion. It is also noteworthy that the members of the Company, as well as various other individuals in the narrative, endured great suffering and misery in their devotion to the cause of goodness knowing that their efforts were not for themselves alone but were for the sake of all of the free peoples of Middle-earth.

Perhaps the one who sacrificed and suffered the most, in part because he would have preferred a more quiet and less heroically vital existence which would not have involved a trip to Mordor, is Frodo. As the Ring-bearer Frodo was given by the Council of Elrond the tremendous responsibility of returning the most potent ring to its place of origin in Mount Doom. However, even though this might seem to have imposed a great strain on Frodo, it is noteworthy that even before he left the Shire, this extraordinary hobbit intimated that he was aware of the special burden which he would have to wield, and he was not unwilling to do this. And Frodo was even willing to leave because he did not want to endanger the Shire in any way—he was willing to sacrifice his enjoyment of the Shire so that others would be able to cherish the beauty and peacefulness of this domain. At the end of the novel Frodo expresses a similar sentiment saying to Sam that when things are in danger, someone has to give them up so that others may keep them. Moreover, Frodo encourages Sam not to suffer from a sense of divided loyalties and to enjoy a blissful and productive future in the Shire. Marion Zimmer Bradley effectively says of Sam in "Men, Halflings, and Hero-Worship": "Sam, in becoming Frodo's heir, retains and passes on and keeps alive the memories of the days that are gone" (126). Frodo's sufferings have been too intense and too extensive for him to return to a normal life in the Shire. Verlyn Flieger in "Gilson, Smith, and Baggins" contrasts the secure return of Sam to the Shire with the painful return of Frodo: "Frodo, of all of them the one who most deserves to be 'back,' is never back in the way that Sam is. Unwelcomed, unappreciated, wounded, recurrently ill, recurrently in pain, he cannot stay in the Shire, for it no longer has any place for him" (91). The three wounds which Frodo endured, the knife-wound of Weathertop, the attack of Shelob, and the finger lost with the ring, have been too much for his physical well-being and for his sense of nurturing and sustaining a relatively peaceful existence in the Shire—Frodo leaves for the domain beyond the Grey Havens to be healed more completely. Moreover, as a past ring-bearer with a deep appreciation for and connection to the Elves, Frodo realizes that he cannot remain in the Shire. As Patricia Spacks insightfully says in "Power and Meaning in *The Lord of the Rings*," Frodo "gives up his beloved Shire, and goes into the unknown West, to a land equivalent to Arthur's Avalon" (92). Marion Zimmer Bradley discusses thoughtfully in "Men, Halflings, and Hero-Worship" the greatness of Frodo's suffering, saying that Frodo's dream of peace is not achieved because "he has given too much of himself to the struggle to cast away the curse, suffered too much in the achieving of this peace for others" (125). Yet Frodo has attained an exemplary nobility of character through his heroic efforts for the advancement and preservation of goodness.

In "Moral Vision in *The Lord of the Rings*" Rose A. Zimbardo addresses a related issue, the effect which bearing the ring and of self-sacrifice have on Bilbo and Frodo: "In losing their hobbit nature they have changed their position in being as well as in time; they become part of the elvish aura that must fade from the earth" (106). For someone as sensitive to the beautiful aspects of nature and as appreciative of the aesthetic, linguistic, and emotional inclinations of Elves as Frodo this is not an unnatural transformation. In fact, considering Frodo's love for the Elves and for the world of the Elves and the loveliness which it represents, which is manifest from his days in the Shire when he would walk in the moonlight and starlight and from the early phase of his journey from the Shire when he encounters Gildor and is shown to have a capacity to understand and appreciate the language of the Elves and is viewed as an Elf-friend, one could say that Frodo feels at home with the Elves—and one can imagine that with the passage of time he, as Bilbo who has cherished an extended and happy connectedness with Rivendell and with the Elves, will feel an increasingly greater sense of consanguinity with Elrond, Galadriel, and numerous other Elves in the West.

At the end of *The Lord of the Rings*, Elrond, Galadriel, the Elves, Frodo, Bilbo, and Gandalf leave Middle-earth from the Grey Havens: "And the ship went out into the High Sea and passed on into the West, until at last on a night of rain Frodo smelled a sweet fragrance on the air and heard the sound of singing that came over the water. And then it seemed to him that as in his dream in the house of Bombadil, the grey rain-curtain turned all to silver glass and was rolled back, and he beheld white shores and beyond them a far green country under a swift sunrise" (III, 384). This passage is similar in language and spirit to a statement which Nick Carraway makes at the end of (in the fourth-to-last paragraph of) F. Scott Fitzgerald's *The*

Great Gatsby about his awareness of the pristine condition of Long Island which would have been experienced by the first Dutch sailors:

> And as the moon rose higher the inessential houses began to melt away until gradually I became aware of the old island here that flowered once for Dutch sailors' eyes—a fresh, green breast of the new world. Its vanished trees, the trees that had made way for Gatsby's house, had once pandered in whispers to the last and greatest of all human dreams; for a transitory enchanted moment man must have held his breath in the presence of this continent, compelled into an aesthetic contemplation he neither understood nor desired, face to face for the last time in history with something commensurate to his capacity for wonder. (189)

Both Frodo and Nick Carraway have visions at night in their respective passages of a world that is new and pristine which has the capacity to revitalize the self. Each vision is a prelude to a new life, for Frodo leaves his old home, his beloved Shire, for a new home, the blessed realm of the Elves, and Nick has his vision before departing for his new residence, which is actually his prior home landscape in the middle-west. That the "aesthetic contemplation" which Nick mentions in his vision is neither "understood" nor "desired" is at least somewhat comparable to the experience of Frodo as he ventures westward. For the "far green country" to which Frodo is travelling represents a completely novel place for him which he has never personally seen—and while Frodo certainly desires this trip to some extent, he also leaves something of himself back in the Shire. The "capacity for wonder" which characterizes and infuses not only the first view which the Dutch sailors had of the new world but also Nick's vision of the old island and Gatsby's attempt to recreate his personal past with Daisy is instinctively present in Frodo's vision as well. For Frodo's capacity for wonder, for imaginative thinking, and for appreciating the extraordinary in the world around him have motivated his past life in the Shire and his heroic endurance on the quest and will enhance his existence in the realm of the Elves in the West. As Gatsby's dream is "somewhere back in that vast obscurity beyond the city, where the dark fields of the republic rolled on under the night" (189), so one might claim that Frodo's dream which seems to be ahead of him as the ship leaves the Grey Havens is at least to some extent somewhere back in his past, in the hills, forests, and meadows with which he had felt such spiritual connectedness and which he had cherished with such elvish delight.

When one thinks of the phrase "green country" in the statement about Frodo's dream one might also reflect upon the greenness, the vernal vitality, which will be achieved, sustained, and cherished in the future in such realms as Gondor, through the leadership of Aragorn and Arwen, Ithilien, through the guidance of Faramir and Eowyn, Isengard, with the nurturing supportiveness of Treebeard and the Ents, and the Shire, with the lovely gift of Galadriel and through Sam's guidance. Yet, this greenness which will flourish in the world of Gondor, Ithilien, and the Shire is somewhat different from the "greenness" of the "far green country" in Frodo's vision. There is a religious aspect to *The Lord of the Rings*, which, as Tolkien himself admitted in a letter to Fr. Robert Murray is absorbed into the story and the symbolism—one might say that this aspect is especially manifest in the extraordinary place to which the several ringbearers and numerous Elves are travelling which signifies perpetual "greenness" and immortality for the Elves. Yet, this is not necessarily a perpetual heavenly paradise for all. For Frodo and the other mortals who travel with him and who may take the ship from the Grey Havens in the future, the realm to which they are going is a lovely domain where they may enjoy an extended period of rest and serenity in the natural beauty of "Arda," of the pristine aura of the earth untainted by evil. Although the hobbits leaving with the Elves from the Grey Havens are apparently mortal, they will always be remembered in the world of Middle-earth which only survived through their generous and noble efforts. The statements which Queen Arwen makes to Frodo before his departure for Rivendell and for the Shire in Book VI, Chapter 6 of *The Return of the King* are of special relevance with respect to the issue of Frodo's future. First, it is interesting that when Frodo comes to King Aragorn and Queen Arwen to raise the issue of his departure, Arwen is singing about Valinor, the blessed realm, as if to imply that Frodo will have a connection with such a realm in the future. Arwen also proceeds to predict that Frodo, if he is burdened by his sufferings from the quest, may go into the West where his wounds will be healed. Arwen even says that as she has chosen the mortal path of Lúthien and will remain with King Elessar, Aragorn, in Gondor, she considers Frodo as the individual who will go instead of her with Elrond into the West. Arwen also gives Frodo a special necklace with a gem which will comfort him if his memories of the horrific moments of the quest assail him.

It is also noteworthy that not all of the Elves are planning to leave from the Grey Havens and travel to the west. For example, it is said in the "Note on the Shire Records" prior to the beginning of Book I, Chapter 1 of *The Fellowship of the Ring* that after Elrond's departure from Rivendell his sons remained there for a long time with some of the High-elven folk. Moreover, Celeborn went to Rivendell for a while after Galadriel's departure, although it is not known when he, too, decided to go to the Grey Havens. In the future Aragorn, King Elessar, assures that the Shire will always be held in high regard. And Sam will always, as Frodo encouraged him to do, read passages out of the Red Book, and cherish and preserve the memories of the quest and of the age which has just passed. The "Note on the Shire Records" declares that the Red Book of Westmarch represents the most significant source of information about the history of the war of the ring—this text was originally Bilbo's private diary which he took to Rivendell and which Frodo eventually brought back to the Shire adding much important material after his return from the quest. In the "Note on the Shire Records" we learn that while the original Red Book did not survive, various copies were made. Such texts as the Red Book, with the vital contributions made to it by Bilbo and Frodo, as well as numerous other texts in the libraries at Rivendell, Gondor, Bucklebury, and Tuckborough, in particular, which preserve a sense of the importance of myth, of the fairy story, and of language (especially of the power of words with their historical resonances) are at the heart of and affirm the significance of *The Lord of the Rings*. J. R. R. Tolkien once wrote: "It was in fairy stories that I first divined the potency of words and the wonder of all things, such as stone, and wood, and iron; tree and grass; house and fire; bread and wine" (C. Tolkien 109). The stories of Bilbo and of Frodo, the ring-bearers, are permeated with an aura of mythological vitality and with a strong sense of the importance of words and of language which is profoundly shared by their companions in the quest. Of the myth makers J. R. R. Tolkien wrote in "Mythopoeia":

> They have seen Death and ultimate defeat,
> and yet they would not in despair retreat,
> but oft to victory have turned the lyre
> and kindled hearts with legendary fire,
> illuminating Now and dark Hath-been
> with light of suns as yet by no man seen. (100)

One might interpret Frodo's journey at the end of *The Lord of the Rings* as an implicit aspiration to reach the land of Valinor, the lovely ancestral realm of the Elves permeated by a magnificent radiance. In Tolkien's *The Silmarillion* it says that "the land of Aman and Eressëa of the Eldar were taken away and removed beyond the reach of Men for ever…and the world was diminished, for Valinor and Eressëa were taken from it into the realm of hidden things" (279). Valinor represents a blessed and ethereal realm of profound beauty with its effulgent flowers and luminescent trees, a radiant paradise with an aura of heaven. While Valinor shares with Rivendell, Lothlórien, and Shangri-La (in Hilton's *Lost Horizon*) a profound sense of natural and architectural beauty, cultural vitality and stewardship, and the aura of a spiritually transcendent realm, it is distinguished from these by its absolute physical inaccessibility, except for those individuals who are destined to travel or to wander there. Valinor preserves and nurtures the seeds of a potentially vital future in the Two Trees and their gold, green, and silver lights, which Yavanna created, for "about their fate all the tales of the Elder Days are woven" (*The Silmarillion*, 38). In the chapter entitled "The Field of Cormallen" in *The Return of the King* Legolas expresses in song his hope that some of his Elven-folk may come for a while, whether for a month, a life, or a hundred years, to the realm where Aragorn rules as King Elessar to make a productive contribution to society before their inevitable journey to the sea and to the blessed realm which is their ancestral and mythically vital home, where Galadriel, Gandalf, Elrond, Bilbo, and Frodo will eventually travel or venture:

> Long are the waves on the Last Shore falling,
> Sweet are the voices in the Lost Isle calling,
> In Eressëa, in Elvenhome that no man can discover,
> Where the leaves fall not: land of my people for ever! (III, 289)

The beauty of magnificent natural places and architectural spaces in Middle-earth, the mythically vital narratives generated and inspired by them, and the memories and visions of such loveliness will be perpetually cherished, preserved, and treasured not only in Rivendell, Gondor, and the Shire but also in Valinor, in Eressëa, where the luminescent peacefulness and serene wisdom of the Elves will endure and prevail forever.

CHAPTER 4

Siegfried Lenz

The first sentence of Siegfried Lenz's *Deutschstunde, The German Lesson* (1968) effectively sets the scene of the novel for the protagonist says that he has been kept in to write an essay. The protagonist, the first-person narrator, does not write the assigned essay, 'The Joys of Duty,' in his class and is consequently put into solitary confinement in the reformatory where he then produces a series of thoughtfully written and personally revealing essays. The interconnected themes of imprisonment within one's self, within one's past, and within one's environment are all important here. Siggi Jepsen, the protagonist, is able to confront, challenge, and ultimately transcend his imprisonment through his writing. The endeavor of writing does not come easily to Siggi, for he is distracted by various features of his immediate ambience and by reflections on the past so that he cannot seem to find an effective starting-point.

The issue of duty is arguably the central theme of the novel for it permeates the lives not only of the major characters but also pervades the landscape which they inhabit and the atmosphere in which they work and strive. Claus Nordbruch discusses the importance of this theme in the novel in *Über die Pflicht: Eine Analyse des Werkes von Siegfried Lenz*: "…ist es primär die Auseinandersetzung des Erzählers mit den Pflichtauffassungen Jens Ole Jepsens, Max Ludwig Nansens, Siggi Jepsens und auch Karl Joswigs, die den Aufbau, die Handlung und die Aussage des Romans bestimmen" (85–6). While most critics interpret Jepsen's sense of duty in a negative manner and Nansen's sense of duty in a positive way, Siggi's relation to duty is often viewed as "die aktuelle Problematik der denkenden, 'vergangenheitsbewältigenden' Nachkriegsgeneration" (86).

In his essay "Pflicht und Verantwortungsgefühl: *Es waren Habichte in der Luft, Deutschstunde* und *Ein Kriegsende*" Gordon J. A. Burgess speaks of the complex discussion of the theme of duty in *Deutschstunde*: "In der *Deutschstunde* ist der Pflichtbegriff komplexer ausgearbeitet als in jedem anderen Lenzschen Werk, nicht zuletzt weil der Hauptvertreter eines blinden Pflichtgehorsams, Siggis Vater, seine Konzeption von dem, was er für seine Pflicht hält, im Laufe des Geschehens ändert" (30). Burgess, as other critics, emphasizes the fact that Siggi's father eventually, even after the war, becomes completely obsessed with his initially designated war-time "duty" of ensuring that Nansen follows the order from the Nazi authorities and does not paint: "Aber allmählich wird seine 'Pflicht,' das Malverbot zu überwachen, zur fixen Idee, so daß er am Ende die Überwachung weder aufgeben will noch kann, obgleich sich die politischen Verhältnisse geändert haben" (31).

For Siggi Jepsen there are three distinctive spaces of special importance in his life—Bleekenwarf, the home of the painter Max Nansen, the mill, and his parents' home. These are the landmarks which determine and define the spatial parameters of the novel. The narrator re-creates images of the past to help him find a good starting-point for his narrative. He reflects on his father's attempt to enforce the ban on Max's painting, suggesting that his father was so obsessed with the ban that he tries to enforce it not only during the war when the Nazi authorities established it but also in peacetime, when it should no longer have been applicable. The presentation of various images is important not only because this shows the struggle which Siggi is going through to begin the narrative but also because it introduces us to the images which will become increasingly important as the novel progresses. As other twentieth century writers Siggi offers the image of descending into his memories as if descending into the abyss, which could be the abyss of memory or the abyss of the self.

Of the realistic dimension of the novel Hans Wagener writes in *Siegfried Lenz*: "Das Milieu stimmt, die Landschaft stimmt, die Topographie ist imaginär: Rugbüll wird man auf der Landkarte vergeblich suchen, auch wenn es nicht weit von der oft erwähnten größeren Stadt Husum zu finden sein müßte" (52–3). Wagener proceeds to make an appropriate parallel between the approach of Lenz and Theodor Storm: "Eine karge, düstere, wenig farbenfrohe Landschaft, in der Lenz seine Handlung ansiedelt, die er mit genauem Realismus so stimmungsmäßig richtig beschreibt, wie es seit Theodor Storm selten in der deutschen Literatur geschehen ist" (53). Both Storm and Lenz are very adept at capturing the atmospheric beauty of the north German landscape and the capacity of certain individuals to appreciate this landscape intuitively and deeply.

As Siggi is excused from all of his duties at the reformatory he can devote himself unreservedly to his narrative endeavor, a seemingly optimal environment for an artist. Siggi believes that he has a duty in writing as his father felt that he had a duty in forbidding Max to paint as Max felt that he had an inner obligation to express himself through his painting. Siggi feels that he must describe the joys of duty in full if he is to do justice to them. Despite the occasional noisy interruptions which distract or delay him Siggi is ultimately able to start writing not only because he has the essential solitude he requires but also because he has found the appropriate place, sitting at the table with "angular initials, dates, patterns that are reminders of moments of bitterness, of hope and of stubbornness passed and gone" (18).

The narrator is an extremely sensitive observer of atmosphere and of the nuances of the natural environment around him. Chapter 2 begins with an emphasis on the importance of the powerful, the mystical wind. The wind is so potent that it "shaped the landscape" (19), "made the roofs keen of hearing" (19), and "made the trees prophetic" (19). Such a sensibility for nature is shared by Siggi and Max Nansen, who is a very sensitive portrayer of the beauty and dynamism of nature. Although nature seems to be the ultimate controlling force as "the wind…played havoc with a newspaper, with a victory in Africa, a victory in the Atlantic" (20), as if the wind could influence and override any events in the human domain, Nansen seems very much at home in an isolated natural landscape. Nansen and his house, Bleekenwarf, exist in a state of aesthetic, emotional, and spiritual communion with nature. One might say that this splendid house represents an extension of or a manifestation of the surrounding natural environment.

The living-room at Bleekenwarf is depicted as being as symbolically spacious as the North German plain for it has numerous windows and "room for at least nine hundred wedding-guests" (23). The "ponderous chests" (23), the "cupboards with rune-like dates carved in them" (23), and the "dark, clumsy tea-set" (23) all contribute to the venerable atmosphere of the room. The interior of this living-room, as the interior of some of the rooms in the house of the Archivarius Lindhorst in E. T. A. Hoffmann's *Der goldne Topf,* has an extraordinary spatial expansiveness. The expansiveness of the interior is reinforced by the description of Bleekenwarf as being surrounded by a moat (still water bordered by reeds), as if it were a fairy-tale castle or even a bewitched castle or a castle which has the capacity to bewitch those who come into contact with it.

On the occasion when Jens comes to inform Max of the ban on his painting imposed by the Nazi authorities Max is working on his painting of the mill, placing the mill in a different context and giving it new life and light. When Max paints he talks constantly with his aesthetic confidante, Balthasar, who might also be interpreted as his artistic alter-ego. Although no one else can see or hear Balthasar, he is portrayed in at least one picture by Nansen as an embodiment of color dynamism with his "bristling purple coat" (27) and his "beard of boiling, bubbling orange" (27). Balthasar, interestingly enough the name of one of the three wise men from the East, one of the three kings who came to adore Jesus, could be interpreted as Nansen's confidante, his artistic partner in discussion, or even a manifestation of part of the power of nature, an aspect of natural vitality come to life in the presence of an individual who has a profound appreciation for nature. That Nansen quarrels with Balthasar could also reinforce the notion of a conflict with the self. The close connection of Nansen to the natural environment, for he is a devoted landscape artist, is reaffirmed by the fact that his "body's behavior simply bore witness to and confirmed whatever he was creating" (27). For example, when he paints the wind on a tranquil day, one could hear the wind rustling through various aspects of the environment and one could even see his overcoat blowing gently.

After Nansen and Jens recognize each other in the mirror of the moat the painter works on his *The Big Friend of the Mill* despite the attempt of Jens to get his attention. The sensitivity for nature which is apparent in this painting is reaffirmed in the depiction of Nansen's studio which represents a resting-place for the various interesting figures he creates in his works and which contains numerous vases of colorful and resplendent flowers. The life of Max Nansen in the narrative represents a fictionalized biography of Emil Nolde. Hans Wagener states in *Siegfried Lenz* that the first names of Max Nansen, Max Ludwig, could also refer to other persecuted or struggling expressionist artists such as Max Beckmann or Ernst Ludwig Kirchner (53). Hans Wagener affirms that Nansen's philosophy of art is exceedingly similar to that of Emil Nolde and that various works of art by Nansen correspond to art works by Emil Nolde: "Auch die einzelnen im Roman beschriebenen Bilder Nansens sowie seine Kunsttheorie entsprechen Bildern und Anschauungen Noldes, der im August 1941 ein periodisch, wenn auch großzügig überwachtes Malverbot erhielt und nun vor allem kleinere Aquarelle, seine 'ungemalten Bilder' malte—wie im Roman Nansen seine 'unsichtbaren Bilder'" (53). Nansen's youth also shows distinctive similarities to that of Nolde. Claus Nordbruch describes Nansen's youth as follows: "Als Sohn friesischer Bauern geboren, wächst Nansen—wie Jepsen—im ländlichen Glüserup auf und beginnt bereits als Jugendlicher, sich dem Malen und Zeichnen zu widmen" (91). Nolde also showed aesthetic inclinations in his youth.

Nansen's paintings of flowers and the presence of an abundance of flowers in his studio are very reminiscent, not surprisingly, of Emil Nolde's love for flowers, manifested in his own garden and in such watercolors as *Rote und Gelbe Sonnenblumen, Lilien,* and *Mohn.* It is as if the garden has come indoors or has been recreated indoors—one might even say that the lovely natural environment of Nansen's paintings has manifested itself in the everyday world of the studio. Moreover, the studio with its "skylight and fifty-five nooks and crannies" (31) has an inner spatial expansiveness comparable to that of the house to which it is attached. The studio not only reveals painterly qualities but seems to signify a painting in its own right. The love for flowers which is abundantly manifest in the work of Nolde, and naturally also in the work of Nansen, derives at least to some extent from the influence of the lovely flower gardens which Nolde's mother kept at Geesthof. Several paintings by Nolde which show a deep love for nature and for the beautiful colors of a garden are *Blumengarten* (1908), *Sonnenuntergang* (1909), *Vorabend—Marschlandschaft* (1916), *Blumengarten—Utenwarf* (1917), *Blumengarten* (1926), *Steigende Wolken* (1927), *Große Sonnenblumen* (1928), and

Gelbe und hellrote Dahlien (1937). In *Blumengarten* (1908), for example, a circlet of red flowers represents the focus embraced by the radiantly green leaves of an overhanging tree as splashes of yellow and blue lead the viewer on a path into the distance. And in one of Nolde's paintings of zinnias and yellow sunflowers, for example, a lovely array of red, purple, yellow, and white zinnias display themselves in the foreground in pleasant consanguinity with two prominent sunflowers beaming their radiant faces over the space of the composition.

In his *Jahre der Kämpfe*, Emil Nolde wrote of his great and abiding love for flowers and their lovely colors:

> Die blühenden Farben der Blumen und die Reinheit dieser Farben, ich liebte sie. Ich liebte die Blumen in ihrem Schicksal: emporschießend, blühend, leuchtend, glühend, beglückend, sich neigend, verwelkend, verworfen in der Grube endend. Nicht immer ist ein Menschenschicksal ebenso folgerichtig und schön. (68)

The purity, the pristine dynamism, and the effulgent radiance of the flowers which Nolde so deeply appreciates is conspicuously manifest in his beautiful paintings of them.

Emil Nolde spent several especially happy and productive years at Utenwarf—during this period he nurtured a lovely flower garden. When Nolde moved with his wife to Seebüll (near the border of Germany and Denmark) in 1927 he created there another very beautiful flower garden. Martin Urban describes Nolde's garden at Seebüll thoughtfully in *Emil Nolde—Flowers and Animals*: "The garden, with its splendid luxurious blossoms, has remained unchanged, like a magic garden in the green marsh landscape" (45). The garden which the painter Nansen in *Deutschstunde* creates is characterized by a similar spirit of beauty, colorful abundance, and inner vitality.

The power of art and of the artist is implied in *The Big Friend of the Mill* for Nansen says defiantly to Jens that the mill, that the sails of the mill, will be turning long after they are gone. The mill, symbolic of the creative artist, will continue its productivity, despite attempts to diminish, undermine, or stop it. The mill is in its own way as vital as the sea or the gulls, aspects of nature described in chapter three which have an eternal presence in contrast to the transience of human endeavor. In Bleekenwarf Nansen also painted the cycle called *Stories told by an Old Mill on the Sea Coast*. The power of Nansen's works, *The Big Friend of the Mill* and *Stories told by an Old Mill on the Sea Coast*, are reminiscent of and similar to several vital creations by Emil Nolde and especially the following watercolors: *Die Mühle* which contains a mill, adjacent to a house, which represents an integral part of the lovely landscape with a colorful orange-red-blue-gray sky; *Marschlandschaft*, in which a house is snugly nestled into the flowing and rolling green marsh landscape as storm clouds gather overhead to challenge the luminescent presence of the sun; and *Windmills on the Marsh* which displays two prominently positioned windmills which share the dark gray color of the sky and which are intimately connected to the earth and sea by the splashes of color around them. Of this landscape M. Gosebruch writes: "In *Windmills on the Marsh* we find the true Nolde landscape.... Two windmills, jutting sharply out of the marsh, provide a stabilizing framework for the watercourse and the swaying lines of the landscape" (27). Gosebruch proceeds to describe the heroic power of the windmills: "If the lord of these flats is the wind, beneath which the farmhouses on the horizon crouch with gently rounded corners, its only heroes are the windmills,...They perform the same function in the landscape as church towers" (27). Other vital aesthetic representations of the marsh landscape by Nolde are *Bauernhaus in der Marschlandschaft* (1920), *Marschlandschaft mit Mühle* (1920), *Abendliche Marschlandschaft* (1935), *Marschlandschaft mit Hof* (1945). Siggi's sensitivity for nature and for the subtleties of the natural environment is seen not only in his writing and in his reflections about writing but also in his capacity to appreciate the profundity of Nansen's closeness to nature and to understand sympathetically when Nansen is discussing a point with Balthasar or when he is communing with or imagining the nature-spirits such as the "rain-kings, cloud-makers, wave-walkers...and mist-men, those big friends of the mills" (51) which are so prominently present in his paintings. And, of course, Siggi produces his own painterly descriptions of his familiar North German landscape which are certainly influenced by his connectedness to Nansen, his aesthetic presence, and his vibrantly colorful studio.

The sixtieth birthday party of Doktor Busbeck described in chapter 4 is a very important event. In his speech emphasizing the importance of Doktor Busbeck to him and Ditte, Max Nansen mentions a time thirty years before when he was very impoverished and Ditte was ill. On a certain day in March Busbeck came to Max's poor apartment in Cologne, bought various art works and gave him four hundred marks in gold. Nansen also speaks of times since then when Busbeck was extremely supportive and expresses the deep gratitude of himself and his wife. Doktor Busbeck's reply is equally positive, praising Nansen as being one of the greatest painters of light and how honored he was to be associated with him. The birthday present which Nansen gives to Busbeck is the painting *Sails Dissolving into Light*, which represents a union of sea and sky and an exuberance of luminescence. The spirit of this painting is reminiscent of and similar to Emil Nolde's *Abendliche Marschlandschaft* (1935) and *Meereslandschaft mit roten Wolken*.

As the chapter progresses Max and Jens have a tense discussion about the decision which the Nazi authorities made to confiscate all of the work which he has done during the past two years. Max stresses that the authorities are afraid of art and that the lighted match is their only way of evaluating art. Max makes two especially important points: 1) that even if the authorities confiscate and destroy his pictures, the achievement of their beauty remains; and 2) despite the ban on his work he will continue to paint, indeed, he will paint invisible pictures which will contain such an abundance of light that the authorities will not be able to see anything. The devotion of the individual to a sense of duty, whether socially and outwardly imposed or self-imposed or both, is a central theme of the novel. As Max is dedicated to his painting, so Jens is focused on the ban which he feels compelled to impose on Max—similarly, Siggi is devoted to the writing of his essay. Hans Wagener speaks of the importance of Kant and Schiller in the historical development of the discussion of duty: "Kant und Schiller stehen am Anfang dieser Entwicklung: Kant mit seiner im kategorischen Imperativ zusammengefaßten Pflichtethik, Schiller mit seinem Versuch der Versöhnung von Pflicht und Neigung in Begriffen wie der 'schönen Seele' und dem 'Erhabenen'" (53). With respect to the notion of duty, the development of the relation of the individual to the state in nineteenth century society is also very significant. The sacrifice of the individual to the demands and obligations of the state would become especially pronounced during the period of the Nazi hegemony. Claus Nordbruch emphasizes in *Über die Pflicht: Eine Analyse des Werkes von Siegfried Lenz* that Nansen's resistance to the painting ban by the Nazi authority is motivated less by political concerns than by an unswerving devotion to an individualistic way of life (92). Nansen believes strongly in the freedom and in the integrity of aesthetic expression for an artist which should not be encroached upon by the state or by its representatives.

Heidrun Worm-Kaschuge also emphasizes in *Lenz—Deutschstunde* the historical background of the notion of duty: "Die Bestimmung dieses Begriffs geht auf Kants Moralphilosophie zurück, insbesondere auf die Schriften 'Grundlegung der Metaphysik der Sitten' und die 'Kritik der praktischen Vernunft.' Pflichterfüllung heißt seit Kant Aufgabe persönlicher Wünsche und Neigungen" (75). Worm-Kaschuge states that *Deutschstunde* does not attempt to provide a definition of the concept of duty, but instead shows different individual approaches and responses to the notion of duty: "Der Roman versucht nun keine Definition dieses Begriffs zu geben, sondern löst ihn aus einer einseitigen Dimension heraus, indem er verschiedene Pflichtauffassungen und daraus entspringende Verhaltensweisen und Handlungen vorführt und an einzelnen Personen demonstriert" (75–6). In her discussion of the concept of duty in the novel Worm-Kaschuge emphasizes that Siggi shows in his devotion to the writing of a thorough essay "eine Art Pflichtbewußtsein, daß sich durch das bereits aufgezeigte Bemühen um Totalität der Wahrheit auszeichnet und somit zu einem Teil Nansens Pflichtbegriff nahe kommt" (79). Worm-Kaschuge also stresses the antithetical approaches of Jepsen and Nansen to the notion of duty: "Der eine kennt nur Obrigkeit, der andere orientiert sich an sich selbst" (81). In thinking of himself as a "law unto himself" who should not be compelled by the domineering and interfering authorities to abandon his art, Nansen shows his capacity to nurture and develop the "invisible pictures" which represent aesthetic signs for the future, images which will blossom in a more hospitable climate and era not only for sensitive and appreciative individuals but also for communities and societies with humane values and humanitarian inclinations.

Another significant theme in this chapter is that of self-transformation. For example, Siggi envisions various people at the party as sea-animals. The association of individuals with different sea-animals might give insight into their characters as Siggi perceives them. This theme of transforming or modifying the self leads into the next chapter for Klaas returns secretively after having left the military prison-hospital in Hamburg where he was placed after his self-inflicted wound. Siggi tries to help his brother and conceals him in his special mill which contains his private collection of pictures of equestrian figures and horsemen. The seclusion of this place is affirmed by Siggi's statement that no one has ever been there. Eventually Siggi takes Klaas to Nansen to ask him for assistance. Nansen is working intensively on his painting *Landscape with Unknown People* and, while talking with Balthasar, makes the exceedingly important point, especially for a landscape-artist as himself, that "there's only one action in every painting, and that's the light" (111). Nansen's *Landscape with Unknown* People possesses the aesthetic spirit and poignant mystery of Emil Nolde's oil painting of 1912 which focuses on two priestesses and of his water-color which concentrates on a young couple with their effulgent faces, vibrant colors, and penetrating or even melancholy eyes. Disturbed by the sudden appearance of Klaas, and realizing how dangerous it is for him to be harbored at Bleekenwarf, Nansen nevertheless finds a place to hide the fugitive, perhaps not only because he sympathizes with Klaas' rebellion against the military authority but also because he has used the emotional simplicity of Klaas' face in several paintings. Nansen's house hides Klaas as his overcoat conceals various items.

Siggi's approach to nature reveals not only his own sensitivity but also the extent of the influence which Nansen has on him. For Siggi's descriptions of the natural environment are painterly. For example, in the opening paragraph of chapter five Siggi is describing the morning and says that he "must produce a slow dawn now, where an irresistible yellow has it out with greys and browns" (86) and that he "must introduce a summer with an illimitable horizon" (86). He proclaims that he must devote himself to capturing the subtle colors and the essential light of nature even though each memory may produce new meanings and may be characterized by transience.

During the meeting of the Glüserup Folklore Society described in chapter six Asmus Asmussen talks about "Sea and Homeland." Asmussen's statement that when one earns the sea's love "she reveals herself in all her moods and mysteries" (124) is significant because it could apply as well to Nansen and his devotion to nature. Nansen has a profound nature-sensibility and a connection to nature so that he understands the moods and mysteries of the natural environment—of course, the essential difference between the appreciation of Nansen and Asmussen for nature is that Nansen does not have to struggle against it as Asmussen does on the ocean.

The meeting of the Glüserup Folklore Society is interesting not only because of Asmussen's presentation but also because of the sudden observation by Jens that a certain boat will be bombed. This capacity of second sight in Jens is astonishing because it has never manifested itself before. However, such a capability is diminished in the scene when Max and Jens argue about invisible pictures. For Max has brought along a portfolio of invisible pictures, blank canvasses which he paints as he talks about them to Jens and Timmsen. Perhaps Max has brought the blank sheets to tantalize Jens and to encourage him to realize how foolish his endeavor is; or perhaps he truly believes that he is creating "invisible pictures," which will reveal their beauty and vitality in the future. In this scene, as in other scenes, Max tries, implicitly and explicitly, to affirm his intellectual superiority over Jens. Of this theme Claus Nordbruch writes in *Über die Pflicht: Eine Analyse des Werkes von Siegfried Lenz*: "Es steht außer Frage, daß Nansen Jepsen intellektuell überlegen ist; ein Faktum, das er gern sarkastisch-ironisch auszuspielen weiß. Er läßt Jepsen dadurch spüren, daß dieser zu tiefgehenderer Reflexion politischer Ereignisse nicht imstande ist" (108). Nansen's insinuation that Jepsen does not understand the notion of the invisible pictures also symbolizes his implication that the policeman does not comprehend the deeper ramifications of the authoritarian ban which he is trying to impose on the artist.

In chapter 7 Siggi meets with Governor Himpel who tells him that his punishment is over, as he has been writing for 105 days, a much longer time than would have been expected for such a task as completing the essay on the joys of duty. However, Siggi refuses to accept this, proclaiming that he must continue with his writing, for he considers the work inadequate unless he is able to complete it to his satisfaction. Siggi asserts not only that he wants to understand the joys of duty thoroughly but also that he is telling the story to himself because it has a comforting effect on his mind.

The selections from Wolfgang Mackenroth's study of Siggi, "Art and Criminality, a Study of the Case of Siggi J.," provide insights not only into Siggi's life but also into the personal development of Max Nansen as an artist. While Siggi does not completely agree with Mackenroth's interpretation of his life, and consistently adopts a critical demeanor towards the psychologist's analysis, Mackenroth does serve periodically in a narrative capacity in the novel, as Theo Elm states in his essay "Siegfried Lenz: Zeitgeschichte als moralisches Lehrstück": "Er überträgt die Erzählfunktion nicht nur Siggi, sondern auch dem Psychologiestudenten Mackenroth, der mit Hilfe begrifflich-analytischer und kausal-erklärender Überlegungen Siggis pathologisches Verhalten aus dessen Vergangenheit heraus zu entwickeln versucht" (111–12). The artistic development of Nansen is based on that of Emil Nolde, the Expressionist painter. Mackenroth's study emphasizes the need for solitude of the artist as well as the intimate connection between the artist and nature. That Nansen is described as representing in his work "all those legendary and imaginative elements that he discovered in nature" (163) affirms the range of distinctive figures and characters who inhabit his paintings and his studio. The isolation of Nansen, deriving in part from his solitary nature, in part from his disappointment at the many rejections which his art work received, and in part from his inclination to live in a secluded natural setting, is stressed in Mackenroth's study, which shows how very difficult Nansen's life has been. However, his faith in his artistic capacities helped him to persevere despite seemingly insurmountable obstacles. Another reason why Nansen is able to survive despite considerable suffering and devaluation by the world of everyday reality is that he is emotionally and spiritually grounded in his favorite places and landscapes. These various features of Nansen's life as depicted in Mackenroth's study are strikingly similar to aspects of Nolde's life, especially his solitude, isolation, the stoic faith in his abilities despite the numerous rejections of his artistic work, his love for the beautiful landscape in which he grew up. In chapter six of the novel Asmus Asmussen says that only those individuals "who are firmly rooted weather the great storms" (130). Max Nansen as an artist and as an aesthetically inclined individual is firmly grounded in the beauty of nature, in the beauty of the North German landscape, in the loveliness of a natural environment which he admires deeply and which is essentially a part of him as he is a part of it. Similarly, one might say that Emil Nolde was emotionally, aesthetically, and spiritually attached to and connected to his beloved and familiar North German landscape, the beauty of which he always enjoyed capturing and representing in its different moods and nuances. One can see Nolde's love of nature and his sensitive devotion to nature in serene or relatively serene paintings of gardens such as *Blumengarten* (1908) and *Anna Wieds Garten* (1907), in paintings of individual flowers and in groupings of flowers such as *Blumengarten: Stiefmütterchen, Große Sonnenblumen* (1928), and *Gelbe und hellrote Dahlien* (1937), in representations of a harmonious connection between different aspects of nature such as *Figur und Blumen* (1915) and *Blumen und Wolken* (1933), and in more tempestuously luminescent portraits of nature such as *Hohe Wogen* (1940) and *Bewegtes Meer* (1948).

Max Nansen is depicted in chapter eight as being an important source of light and a symbol of light. Jens, in contrast, in his approach of blindly doing his duty as ordered by the Nazi authorities and persecuting Max, is portrayed as a sign of darkness, of the contemporary cultural and intellectual darkness pervading the country. Hans Wagener describes the absolute commitment of Jens to his "duty," to his own myopic sense of what that duty should be, as exemplifying ultimately a type of insanity (54). The ray of light which emanates from the studio showing that Nansen is working despite the ban by the authorities also signifies a symbolic beam or beacon of light which illuminates the surrounding darkness. Nansen believes that the artist must search for the truth, as disturbing and problematic as it may sometimes be or seem to be. The painting of the man in the red cloak, on which Max is working when Jens comes to persecute him, displays an individual of primordial creative power, an archetypal artist. One might also argue that the artist, and Nansen certainly exemplifies this point of view, has the intellectual capacity to preserve in his mind images or paintings which are absolutely secure in such an inner sanctum from the encroachment or intervention of an authoritarian or autocratic government. Claus Nordbruch stresses this capacity of Nansen, a capacity intimately connected to his feeling of intellectual superiority over the Nazi authorities, to maintain in the landscape of his mind images of his artistic creativity (110). The images and landscapes of the mind are safe from the examination and persecution by the Nazi authorities.

Yet, despite the fact that Jepsen ultimately becomes obsessed with his sense of duty and with the necessity of imposing the ban on Nansen's work, some critics have argued effectively that this obsession developed gradually and was not present when the Nazi authorities first required the imposition of the ban. Claus Nordbruch states, for example, that Jens does initially show some sympathy, implicitly and explicitly expressed, for the plight of Max in struggling with the ban (105). Nordbruch makes the important point that Jepsen passes some information about Nansen's disregard for aspects of the ban to the local authorities and not to the more powerful governmental figures in Berlin who might have imposed harsher and swifter punishment on the painter (105). As Nordbruch correctly points out, when Nansen increases his insulting demeanor towards Jepsen, then the policeman's sense of following the regulations of the Nazi authorities is intensified to a personal vendetta (147). Jepsen also becomes so dedicated to pursuing his duty perhaps because he feels that this affirms his capacity to be an effective administrative official who is worthy of a higher appointment and perhaps because he feels that this is his available means of expressing his creativity. As this personal conflict between Jepsen and Nansen is heightened and exacerbated, their friendship is dissolved. Claus Nordbruch discusses effectively the apparent inevitability of the conflict between Nansen and Jepsen, for each is tenaciously committed to his way of life: "Es ist ein Rollenspiel, dem keiner der beiden entrinnen kann: Hört Nansen auf zu malen, stirbt der Maler in ihm, verzichtet der Polizist auf die Durchsetzung des Malverbots, riskiert er seinen Beruf" (109). Each individual feels that if he were to compromise or modify his approach, then he would challenge, diminish, or undermine the essence of his existence and the purpose of his life.

The importance of hearing is emphasized in the description of the dynamic natural environment. It is said that when one listens in the evening, in the autumn, and in the wind one, that is, presumably, a sensitive observer of nature, can hear murmurings in the hedges and voices in the wind. Nansen and Siggi are certainly such individuals of extraordinary nature-sensibility who appreciate the nuances of the beauty of nature as few others do. One of Nolde's works which exemplifies such a sensitive appreciation for the natural environment is *Marschlandschaft*, a watercolor of a marsh landscape in which a dynamic stream of light emanates from a dark swath of cloud over the horizon. As the deep yellow stream of light spreads over the earth and sea it transforms the darkness of the sky into lovely patches of green and blue and encompasses the earth in effulgent shades of green. There are several farmhouses present in the landscape, one of which is especially prominent on the left side of the painting—this solitary farmhouse in red and black is bathed in the softly dynamic luminescence which embraces the atmosphere. Another of Nolde's watercolors which exemplifies the same profound admiration for nature and for the spirit of nature as

Nansen expresses presents a wanderer among the stars—in this watercolor a solitary individual cloaked in gray with a green face is surrounded by yellow shining stars and a blue sky. Such a melancholy, sensitive, vitally introspective individual could be a self-portrait or even a representation of one of the spirits of nature which so delightfully inhabit his landscapes. Other works by Nolde which display an appreciation for the beauty of the individual or present an interesting or provocative portrait are *Lesende Dame* (1906) which shows a woman who seems in a state of congenial harmony with the surrounding natural environment, *Der Prophet* (1912), *Die Priesterinnen* (1912), *Herrenbildnis* (1915), and various self-portraits. The individuals in these works, as the one in *Figur und Blumen* (1915), appear to attain an emotional and a spiritual union with the natural environment surrounding them. Nolde's great capacity to paint sensitive portraits and representations of individuals is also manifest in his religious paintings, such as *Abendmahl* (1909), *Anbetung—die heiligen drei Könige* (1911), and *Heilige Nacht* (1912).

Siggi's admiration of Nansen and his art inspires him to save the shreds of the painting which was torn up when Jens disturbed Max earlier in the chapter. With Hilke's assistance Siggi tries to reconstruct the painting and then takes it away for safe-keeping. It is noteworthy that Siggi even states that he wishes to begin an exhibition, presumably composed of various paintings which he will gradually collect and save from the grasp of the Nazi authorities, which he will dedicate to the countryside. The imaginative vitality of Siggi is stressed in this chapter as well, for he conceives of various images and objects as he reconstructs the painting according to color formations. When Siggi says at one point in the process of revitalizing the painting that he can only see red and green, symbolic of fire and water, he affirms Nansen's declaration, made earlier in the chapter, that no color is neutral for a color is always assertive and revealing.

The significance of the specific North German landscape with which Siggi is familiar is emphasized in chapter nine. As a self-aware and self-conscious narrator who is always thinking about his approach to his work and his narrative strategy Siggi proclaims that he is speaking about his own landscape and telling his own story. He wants his story to be appreciated as an individualized narrative, as a representation of his own misfortune and of the particular natural environment in which it takes place. Siggi's stress on personal commitment in his writing is analogous to Max's commitment to his artistic endeavor. Such devotion is manifest at the beginning of chapter 10 when Siggi states that he feels instinctively obligated to write something down if he is aware of it, even though he senses that it might be transient or fleeting or "washed away the next time it rains" (216). This is precisely the same devotion to aesthetic truth and aesthetic sensibility which Nansen shows in his approach to painting. The artist feels so devoted to his home landscape that he wants to paint various aspects of it even though he senses or knows that such aspects or features of the natural or human environment are ephemeral, and even sometimes as ephemeral as they are beautiful.

Personal misfortunes appear to increase for Siggi at this point of the narrative. In chapter nine Klaas is brought wounded to his family's house in Rugbüll, the doctor is called, but says that Klaas has to be taken to the hospital as quickly as possible. And in chapter ten Nansen suffers the plight of the imaginative people in the world of everyday reality and is taken away by the authorities to be questioned. Before he is removed from his residence Nansen returns to his studio to look at his paintings and to find a hiding-place for *The Cloudmaker*. As no place seems suitable Nansen asks Siggi to take the painting, hide it, and then return it to Ditte. Siggi seems surprised that Nansen simply accepts his fate and walks with his suitcase towards the leathercoats in the car instead of trying to escape into the familiar natural environment. However, one might say that Nansen decides not to try to escape from the Nazi authorities who await him for the same reason that Siggi remains devoted to his essay writing, although he is given the opportunity to liberate himself intellectually from this task by accepting Himpel's assertion that he has been punished enough and is finished. For Nansen the painter, as Siggi the writer, has already initiated and developed an inner escape, an inner quest for freedom, a liberation of the soul which manifests itself within.

Perhaps Jens resents Max because he feels that the painter thinks of him merely as a common village policeman, while he believes that he is more than that. Perhaps Jens pursues the ban against Max so adamantly and relentlessly to prove to Max and to himself that he is a capable and special individual in his own right. Jens might even want to try to prove his vitality, especially psychological and physical, which he feels is not properly appreciated by those around him and even by the authorities whom he is supposed to serve. It might seem too generous to state that Jens shows a kind of creativity in trying to catch Max painting and in trying to discover the painter's hiding-places. Yet, Jens does proclaim his sense of his imaginative vitality when he declares that he is going to find Nansen's pictures, whether they are visible or invisible. One might even say that Jens becomes more confident in his persecuting strategy when he realizes that he has the power of second sight.

Chapter 11 begins with a depiction of the primordial ooze of the shore along the sea, where Siggi reflects that life is supposed to have begun. The cool mud of the shore is described, as well as the sand, the clouds, the wind, and in the distance the painter's hut on the dunes. The image is one of the vitality and spatial expansiveness of nature which is affirmed in the presence of Max Nansen and his artistic work.

Later in the chapter Busbeck explains to Siggi the importance of the invisible pictures: "They are small hints, pointers, allusions.... But what is most important, the things that matter, that's invisible.... Some day, I don't know when, at some other period, it will all be visible" (247). These paintings are important because they contain suggestive and potent images, or the implication of such images, which will blossom when the time is right for them and when they can be properly valued. In the current period of conflict and war in which Nansen is working these images are not appreciated, so they remain "invisible." Busbeck's statement about the significance of invisible pictures is also noteworthy because it possesses an inherent optimism, a conviction that there will be a time in the future when these images, and when the aesthetic motivations which produced them will be valued and admired by contemporary culture and society. Busbeck also emphasizes that if a painting is invisible, then it cannot be found and seized by the Nazi authorities—a painting that is invisible is safe from the encroachment of the devaluing regime.

When Jens discovers a packet of oiled paper with the heading "Invisible Pictures" hidden under the floorboards where Siggi had suggested it might be, he brings it to his house to examine it carefully. On one sheet there was a paddle-wheel surrounded by swirling water, on another the eyes of an old man. On another sheet there was a sunflower, somewhat drooping, yet still relatively luminous. Nolde's creative representation of a ripe *Sonnenblume* could be viewed as analogous to Nansen's painting of this sunflower which maintains its aura of effulgence despite its fleeting outward appearance. Other individual sheets contained images of part of a tree with an unusual beam of light, the carved back of a chair with crosses and garlands, a jacket in shreds, a curved flying-fish, old-fashioned anchors nailed to the sky, two darting swallows, an exploding haystack, and tracks in the snow, returning from nowhere, among various other distinctive images. Nansen had once said that his invisible paintings contained everything he wished to say about his contemporary society, including a personal confession of his own experiences in and observations about the world of everyday mortality. Some of these images in the invisible pictures are characterized by or pervaded by doubt, darkness, and despair, as if they were aesthetic symbols or symptoms of a decaying civilization, while others have a semblance of hope, a touch of inner light, an insinuation of effulgence, as if they were the seeds of the future, of a more vital and congenial future aesthetic development.

In Chapter 12 Mackenroth, the psychologist, gives Siggi part of his thesis manuscript, entitled "Art and Criminality, The Case of Siggi J.," which contains various interesting details about Siggi's childhood and youth which are not presented or so explicitly described in Siggi's own account of his past. One of the points which Mackenroth makes is that because Siggi did not have any playmates of his own age he created a realm of imaginative existence for himself. Siggi was portrayed as a relatively quiet, modest child who excelled in school, especially in writing and drawing. As often happens to superior and talented children, Siggi was admired by some of his classmates and persecuted by others who were jealous of his abilities and success. Because of this situation Siggi became increasingly isolated and lonely. Mackenroth also discusses the burgeoning friendship between Nansen, the painter, and Siggi. Although Nansen typically did not want anyone to be near him when he painted, he allowed Siggi to be present. When Siggi ran away from his persecuting classmates he would often conceal himself in Nansen's studio.

Mackenroth also mentions Siggi's interest in collecting various objects, including the equestrian paintings, and keeping them in safe places. Mackenroth also affirms Siggi's account in his essay that he helped Nansen in various ways, including saving his paintings, while also acting as a spy for his father who was trying to enforce a ban on the painter's work. The separation of Siggi from his parents was caused, according to Mackenroth, by the fact that Klaas, his brother, when returning home after his escape from a military hospital was not accepted by his mother and was given by his father to the authorities.

After Siggi reads Mackenroth's observations, he says that this account is correct in its own way, but adds that if someone wants to learn more about the people and places in the study, he should consult other sources. Siggi also stresses the process of writing, perhaps directing such a remark not only indirectly to Mackenroth but also directly to himself, for he asserts that nothing is ever really finished, and that even though he has already written so much about his past, he would like to narrate his own story over again and in a different way. But Siggi feels pressured because he knows that Himpel would like him to finish his essay on the joys of duty in a reasonable amount of time.

The death of Ditte, Nansen's wife, in this chapter seems to bring many members of the community together. Yet, the passing of Ditte, emaciated and gaunt from a disease which Doctor Gripp could only diagnose as pneumonia, also takes something away with her—it is as if a phase of the life of this community has ended forever. Pastor Bandix movingly and thoughtfully reviews the stages of Ditte's life, from her life of relative wealth in Flensburg to her meeting Nansen to the struggles which characterized the life of a committed and devoted artist. Bandix also implies that Ditte and Max were kindred spirits, which made all of the hardship and suffering which they were compelled to endure bearable and which enhanced the joys which they shared together. This is another aspect of the life of Emil Nolde which is biographically fictionalized here. For around 1900 when Nolde rented a studio in Copenhagen, where he felt very lonely, he happened to meet the Danish actress and musician Ada Vilstrup, who became his lifelong companion. She gave up her career for Emil, who at the time of their marriage changed his name from Hansen to Nolde. In their early years together the couple took a fisherman's cottage on the island of Alsen and spent the winter in a studio in Berlin. In 1909 Nolde and his wife moved to the west coast of Friesland which had a less serene climate than Alsen. After spending some time in a farmhouse in Utenwarf, Nolde purchased the farm of Seebüll (near the German—Danish border) in 1926 where he spent many years for the remainder of his life. One especially interesting portrait by Nolde presents a lovely face in yellow, blue, and light gray with dark eyes which looks out in a spirit of expectation, yet perhaps not of hope or of an underlying optimism. The most vibrant yellow colors in the painting are in the shoulders and upper part of the dress which the woman is wearing and which reflect or connect to the colors in her face. The red lips suggest youthful vitality, but there is an aura of sadness in her face which permeates the entire composition. Such a portrait signifies the spirit of Ditte as well as of Ada Vilstrup. One might even say that the aura of this very sensitive portrait is similar to that of Nolde's presentation of the ripe *Sonnenblume* in its melancholy undertone. In one moving letter which Nolde wrote to his wife Ada on September 7, 1910 he describes his profound appreciation for nature, his sense of achieving a physical and spiritual harmony with nature, which she certainly also deeply appreciated: "An old toad lives in one of my pockets, and wild bees have chosen my hat as a place to make honey in. My hands and fingers are taking root deep down in the sand, my toes have grown to about twice their length and will soon turn into great trees, flowering in strange colours" (Urban 64).

The tension between Max and Jens flares up again in chapter 13 when they are activated as part of the gathering of the local Volkssturm as the war comes to an end in northern Germany. During the anxious period when the local members of this group are awaiting and preparing for the advance of the military opposition, Siggi manages to escape temporarily to his mill, to his hiding-place. Jens is able to burn various files and invisible pictures before he is taken into custody by the English soldiers. As Max in a similar previous situation, Jens makes no attempt to escape. Even though Jens is clearly trying to destroy vestiges of the past and traces of the present, one might ask whether anyone with second sight, or with the semblance of second sight, can really destroy such images?

In chapter 14 the narrator is in a captive situation with the other local residents for the war is finished for the Germans. Nansen soon returns to his home and studio and paints an interesting self-portrait. This painting is important not only because it is depicted as Nansen's last self-portrait but also because the artist suggests that everything keeps changing and that he cannot resolve or harmonize the tensions and contradictions. The self-portrait which Nansen produces shows a face with two halves, each permeated by different colors: the left half of the face was reddish-grey and the right half greenish-yellow. As he argues with his aesthetic alter-ego, Balthasar, Nansen stresses the importance of seeing and suggests, especially in the spirit of a community which has just suffered through the world war, that it is necessary to start learning to see and observe again. Nansen proceeds to elaborate on the significance of seeing: "Seeing means penetrating and enhancing. Or inventing. In order to get your own likeness, you have to invent yourself, over and over again, with every glance. Whatever is invented turns into reality" (335). One might also apply this statement to Nansen and his creation of various interesting figures—Nansen in a sense becomes one of the nature-spirits, one of the kobolds, one of the nature-prophets which he creates so imaginatively and so readily in his paintings. He becomes the manifestation of nature, of the spirit of nature, which he is trying to conceive and convey in his paintings. Or perhaps one might say that the spirit of nature is working through Nansen, through the art of Nansen, to portray and exemplify its dynamism and its vitality in evocative aesthetic representations of color and character. It is as if Nansen embodies a nature-spirit come to life, an individual who exists in close emotional and spiritual communion with the surrounding natural environment and whose life inspires an appreciation and an admiration of the lovely landscape. Nolde's portrait of the wandering figure among the stars signifies such a nature-spirit who is at one with the surrounding natural environment, whether one interprets this watercolor as representing a lyrical soul wandering through a field of marigolds and zinnias, or through a sea of sunflowers, or through a meadow of golden stars. Some of Nolde's self-portraits also represent an individual who appears to be a nature-spirit, a bringer of light, a harbinger of novel and dynamic color emanations, a prophet of the aesthetic effulgence and vitality of the future.

In continuing his discussion of the importance of seeing Nansen says that seeing can also mean waiting for a situation to change or investing for the future. Such an approach and a philosophy of aesthetic expression is precisely what the invisible pictures signify. He especially stresses the possibility of change in saying that one may create an image, an idea, or an ambience, then leave or be at a distance from it for a while, and when one returns something in or about the creation has been transformed or has transformed itself. As a corollary to this point Nansen declares that when one makes an image, one has to create its inherent potentiality as well. For example, a face which exemplifies such a philosophy of art would show not only the present condition of the individual but also provide hints about his past experiences and perhaps even indications about his future as well.

When Maltzahn appears Nansen asserts that he prefers to work in isolation, in the "chamber of horrors" to which an art periodical had once relegated him. Even though the art critic wants to look at the painter's invisible pictures, Nansen states that he just wants to be left alone. When Busbeck comes into say good-bye Nansen makes it evident that Maltzahn, who had once treated him so wretchedly, is no longer welcome. In leaving Bleekenwarf, Busbeck explains that he feels he must start his life anew, but that he plans to return every summer to see Max. Busbeck also suggests that the countryside is too solemn and austere for him, even when the sun is shining. After Nansen and Siggi have said farewell to Busbeck at the Glüserup station as he boards the train with numerous other passengers, they walk back home. Siggi, watching two people moving into the distance under the immense sky of this region, observes the powerful presence of the horizon. As Siggi walks with Nansen he speaks of appreciating his kindly and generous presence and of having a sense of anticipation and expectation, as if something interesting were going to happen or as if something distinctive would be expressed. Even though Siggi is much younger than Nansen, the artist treats him with appreciation, consideration, and respect. Each character values the presence of the other not only because they both have potent nature-sensitivities and profound aesthetic sensibilities but also because they have shared important experiences during the period of the second world war. Both Nansen and Siggi also have a deep appreciation for the beauty of the north German landscape, for the wind, for the shore, for the sand and the various creatures in and on it, for the ocean and its immensity, for the sky and its spatial expansiveness, for the horizon, and for the multifarious lovely colors of nature.

When one thinks of Nansen's statement that to get your likeness you have to invent yourself over and over, one might view Klaas, Siggi's seemingly lost brother, as a manifestation of this. For Klaas, having had experiences such as entering the military hospital with a self-inflicted wound, escaping, being shot in the bog, returning home only to be returned by his parents to the authorities, then emerging later as the figure of Brother Martin in the theatrical performance at the prison-camp, and finally having a personal connection with Jutta, has gone through various transformations. Perhaps Klaas was able to endure and survive the various painful experiences in his life because he was rooted in some way in his past, in the landscape of his past. That he is able to rejuvenate himself in this landscape would seem to affirm this notion—moreover, one might claim that the rootedness of Klaas in the landscape of his home environment is generated at least to some extent by the portraits which Nansen has done of him over the years. One might even say that the presence of Klaas in these paintings done in and of the north German landscape which Nansen knows so well and appreciates so intuitively reinforces his emotional and spiritual groundedness. That he is present in these paintings enables him to return with a feeling of well-being to his native landscape.

Chapter 15 begins with Siggi's statement that today, September 25, 1954 is his birthday and that he is twenty-one years old, an age when Joswig says that one begins to commit oneself, to make decisions, and to ask oneself questions. As Siggi becomes aware of a birthday mood spreading over him, he asserts that he has to go back into the past and explore his personal Atlantis. As Siggi reflects on his past he says that when Jens returned from his interment, he forbade the family from having anything further to do with Klaas and he continued to burn Max's paintings. When Siggi bravely tells his father not to confiscate or burn any more of Nansen's art, he responds harshly that he can treat Siggi in the same manner as he treated Klaas. One of the notable events of this chapter is the arrival of the Landeskommissar at Bleekenwarf along with several other people, including General Tate, to present the Diploma of Honorary Membership of the Royal Academy in London to Nansen in appreciation of his contributions to the world of art. In the ensuing discussion Nansen is pleasantly surprised to learn that a number of his paintings which had been confiscated by the Nazi authorities and which he thought had been destroyed had actually been sold and were beginning to recirculate. General Tate says that he admires Nansen's work and possesses several of his paintings.

In response to the question how Max had survived the ban, he states that a painter simply has to adapt and has to keep painting, despite the threats of the restrictive authorities. Max also stresses that a genuine painter is always a painter, even in his dreams, and cannot stop painting because of artificial limitations. Max also shows his tactfulness by not criticizing Jens for enforcing the ban mindlessly, although he could easily have done so when asked how the ban was enforced.

As Max Nansen is portrayed as a painter of light, it is readily understandable that he would have the greatest appreciation for the works of J. M. W. Turner. In response to the General's question why he wants to see Turners, Nansen says that this great artist achieved everything, whether substantive or elusive, with light. Nansen also admits that he does not really like big cities and, despite his great admiration for Turner's work, doubts that he would ever travel to London to see an art exhibition. While Nansen enjoyed travelling in earlier days, he no longer wishes to make long journeys and feels that there is still a great deal for him to experience and observe in the natural environment between Glüserup and the main road to Husum. In response to the General's query whether there is a big city or an aspect of an urban milieu which inspired him, Max says: "The big cities we need are within ourselves. My own metropolis is here. I have everything I need, indeed even more" (377). Max concludes by saying that even in the several years which are left to him as an artist he will not be able to express and communicate everything that is interesting and worthwhile about the nearby countryside. As Nansen emphasizes the importance of his familiar landscape, the natural environment which he has come to admire and love, one might think again of the statement made earlier in the novel about groundedness, namely, that those individuals who are firmly rooted can effectively confront, endure, and survive the tempestuous times and storms. Nansen as an artist and as an individual is firmly rooted in his beloved north German landscape which inspires him aesthetically and to which he feels deeply and eternally connected.

Siggi's painterly and sensitive appreciation of and admiration of the landscape in his home area is again seen at the beginning of chapter 16. As Siggi rides his bicycle to the Theodor Storm Grammar School in Glüserup, he observes various subtleties in the sea, the farmsteads, and the wind, affirming that there are hourly and daily changes in the world around him. Siggi's statement that the journey to and from this grammar school in Glüserup never bored him not only affirms his love of the local landscape but also implies in its awareness of the capacity of the light to present each day the aspects of nature differently the possible influence of Nansen, who is, like Turner and Nolde, a painter of light.

In chapter 16 the old mill, Siggi's hiding-place which contains not only his own private exhibition of equestrian pictures but also a number of Nansen's works, burns down. Nansen brings Siggi into the studio where he tries to comfort him. When Nansen steps out for a moment, Siggi, who feels very much at home among the various figures and faces in the paintings, the Slovenes, the market-people, the dancers, and others, has a vision that a light is moving towards the picture of the money-changers. Afraid and anxious for the painting, Siggi takes it down and removes it from the frame, ultimately putting it next to his body to protect it. Siggi admits that he had no interest in keeping this painting, nor the various other paintings which he tried in the future to save in the same way—he only wanted to protect them from the danger of confiscation and burning which he knew that his father was subjecting them to. In the ensuing discussion which Siggi has with Nansen he tells the painter that he is certain that his father burned down the mill, for he is continuing to do his "duty" by destroying although the war is over, just as Siggi will perform his "duty" by saving the paintings. Max tries to comfort Siggi by saying that traces of one's accomplishments and collections remain for longer than one thinks after they have outwardly passed away. At the end of the chapter Max also gives Siggi special advice, saying that in life things inevitably get lost and that it is important always to try to make a new start. Such a life-philosophy, as hard as it may sometimes be to develop, certainly sustained Max Nansen and gave him a sense of hope or a glimmer of hope during the periods when his work was rejected and undervalued and when his paintings were confiscated by the Nazi regime.

In chapter 17 a reproduction from a magazine of Nansen's painting *The Dancer on the Waves* is sent anonymously to Siggi's parents. The image causes an uproar because the dancer in the painting, mostly naked and wearing only a short skirt, is their daughter Hilke. When called upon to defend herself Hilke states that she only posed once for Nansen, while also asserting that she feels very much like the dancer in this picture, exhausted and yet perhaps gaining some consolation from her closeness to nature. Jens and Gudrun Jepsen are exceedingly upset with their daughter for having posed naked for this painting. Nansen is also disturbed because he believes that someone stole the painting from him and is trying to get it back from the Jepsen household, which he thinks has concealed it somewhere. Actually, Siggi has concealed this painting with various others in his new hiding-place, in the attic of the house of his parents which is filled with numerous objects.

As chapter 17 progresses Siggi is given more pages of Mackenroth's study of him to read. This study says that Siggi removed paintings from various places in Glüserup, Husum, Schleswig, Kiel, and Hamburg to protect them from his father's obsessive desire to burn them. When Siggi was caught doing this his defense was that he was trying to save endangered paintings. Siggi, who had for a long time nurtured a desire to collect objects, even proclaims that he was "predestined" to gather various objects in his personal collection. We also learn in this section of Mackenroth's account of Siggi's life that at one point his father, after a violent argument with him, cast him out of the family. When Siggi finishes this section of Mackenroth's manuscript, as when he completes the reading of other sections of this work, he seems to agree and disagree with the tone and with various details. On the one hand, he says that Mackenroth was correct; yet, on the other hand, he says that Mackenroth did not present the material correctly. Such a response reflects Siggi's own emphasis on the process of writing, that one must continually try to reflect on and refine one's work. Such a statement also reflects Siggi's belief that if he could tell his own story over again, he would present it differently. The response of Siggi to Mackenroth's account could also reflect Max's influence on him in the spirit of the painter's statement that when you return to an image or a situation, sometimes everything has been transformed.

In chapter 18 Siggi, declaring that he is always punctual at various personally and publically important events, arrives early at the exhibition of Max Nansen's paintings at the Schondorff Gallery in Hamburg. Nansen, in the company of Teo Busbeck, seems to be pleased by the very positive comments made about his work by Rudolf Schondorff and by the art-critic Hans-Dieter Hübscher. Nansen appears to agree especially with what Hübscher says about the experimental color-schemes which he used to try to fuse them in a universal chord, an approach which he shares with Rembrandt. It is sad and ironic that at this point in his career when Nansen finally seems to be receiving some considerable public acclaim he has broken off his connection to Siggi. For we learn that Nansen had a while ago forbidden Siggi to come to his studio, perhaps because he senses that Siggi is in some way helping his father with the surveillance of the painter's work. Even though Nansen is praised by some at the exhibition, there are also those individuals who criticize him, laughing behind his back and saying that with his clothing he seems to have emerged directly from one of his paintings.

The painting *Garden Masks* is significant not only for its depiction of the glowing colors in the garden but also for the three masks dangling from a tree and perhaps posing a threat to the natural forms. Siggi feels instinctively that the faces of these masks, two male and one female, are familiar. As he reflects on this image of intense growth and on the masks symbolizing the strategy of self-concealment, Siggi is accosted by the two men in trench-coats. By running for a long time Siggi manages to escape from their grasp and goes to the rather dingy apartment in a relatively deserted part of Hamburg which his brother Klaas, now a photographer, shares with Jutta. In an intense discussion which Siggi subsequently has with Klaas' rowdy neighbor he defends Nansen and his work saying in particular that he always achieved a perfect sense of perspective. Yet, the implication of this passage, as of the depiction of Nansen at the exhibition in Hamburg, is that he has become, at least for the younger artists, "äusserlich...wie ein Relikt aus einem Heimatmuseum" (Wagener 58). Siggi's life reaches a painful nadir as the chapter draws to a close, for not only has he been exiled from the paradise of Nansen's studio, which used to be a place of such aesthetic stimulation and emotional comfort for him, but he even felt that he had to conceal himself from Nansen at the exhibition because of the painter's criticism of him. Moreover, Siggi has been cast out from his parental home and has become a wandering and lost soul as some of the figures in Nansen's paintings and is not wanted by Klaas who says that he can only stay briefly in his apartment because the authorities will likely know where to find him. Siggi's situation is even more poignantly painful than that of the lost and wandering figures in some of Nansen's paintings because they may be located in the natural landscape to which they feel connected, whereas Siggi is not at home in Hamburg. He belongs in his native shore landscape and heath and is completely isolated emotionally and spiritually in the city, even though he is able to locate his brother. This mournful episode in Siggi's life ends when he is recaptured by the trench-coats at the conclusion of the chapter. When one reflects on the image of Hilke dancing along the shore in one of Nansen's paintings, one might even assert that she, too, seems to be at one with the natural environment around her—her dynamism is generated by her presence in nature. As in several of Nolde's paintings of dancing figures, they are sometimes portrayed as gaining their identity and integrity through their closeness to the natural environment around them. Some of the figures might be dancing wildly, as Nora in Ibsen's *A Doll's House*, to distract from, forget, or sublimate the anguish or difficulty of the present, while others might signify characters who have achieved a holistic awareness of the world, a sense of the eternal harmony which, as E. T. A. Hoffmann says in *Der goldne Topf*, underlies the universe.

In chapter 19 of *Deutschstunde* Siggi is back at the beginning and explains how he was initially brought to the reform school. In response to a question from Governor Himpel who is visiting the rookie inmates of the institution with several psychologists Siggi declares that he is here in place of his father, the Rugbüll policeman, who is considered by society as too old to be rehabilitated despite his obsessive addiction to his duty of confiscating Nansen's paintings which should have ended with the conclusion of the world war. In his conversation with Himpel and the psychologists Siggi also reaffirms his previous revelations in the novel that he took paintings from galleries and from other locations to keep them safe from the prying obsession of his father. Siggi also proclaims once again his belief that his father burned down the mill with various art works and that his father also eventually discovered his new hiding-place in the attic. It is especially melancholy to reflect on such statements because Siggi, perhaps more than anyone else in his home area, really loved the local natural environment. And yet, because of his devotion to saving aesthetic representations of that environment and of the spirit of that environment, he is compelled to be distant from it and is even forbidden by the two owners, namely his father and Nansen, of the places he most often lived in and frequented, to return and to continue to be a part of such important places in his life. Siggi is struggling because he has been emotionally, aesthetically, and spiritually uprooted from his beloved home landscape— what makes this situation the more painfully poignant is that he has been forced away by the two individuals who should have nurtured his presence and who should have been supportive of him and of his interests.

Perhaps Siggi as a literary artist needs the physical detachment from his home landscape in order to write about it effectively. Perhaps one of the advantages to being isolated in this reform school is that Siggi may devote himself to the essay on the joys of duty, which is the story about his own past life, without the multifarious distractions of everyday mortality. In chapter 20 Siggi appears to have reached the conclusion of his literary endeavor; moreover, Himpel says that Siggi must now stop his writing and submit his work and he would then be released. Even after Siggi finishes the writing the fact that he keeps the copybooks for five days in his cell is another indication of his collecting passion. Himpel even declares that the punishment which Siggi imposed on himself to complete the writing task was greater than that which the institution had imposed upon Siggi.

Siggi wonders what he will do when he is released from the reform institution. He says that even though he may be physically distant from Rugbüll, he is inevitably and inextricably linked to it forever. The notion of being perpetually connected to the past and of learning from it effectively and thoughtfully, or less vitally so, is addressed by Theo Elm in his essay "Siegfried Lenz: Zeitgeschichte als moralisches Lehrstück" when he distinguishes between the relation of *Deutschstunde* (1968) and *Heimatmuseum* (1978) to the past and to history: "Während Siggi Jepsen über das Ende seiner Strafarbeit hinaus an die Vergangenheit und deren Traumata gefesselt bleibt,...entrinnt Zygmunt Rogalla dem Bann der Vergangenheit, weil er in emphatisch aufklärerischem Sinn aus ihr lernt und das Erlernte—seinen neuen Heimatbegriff—als Halt für die Zukunft versteht" (122). I would say that even though Siggi seems so consistently or even constantly drawn to his past and to reflections about past events in his home landscape, he achieves a dynamic aesthetic and literary connection to his youth and childhood which will inspire further artistic expression. For in the process of narration Siggi develops and refines his aesthetic sensibility and his sensitivity for nature, two qualities which have always been of the utmost importance for him. Just as Max Nansen can focus effectively and legitimately as an artist on images and visions relating to the natural environment where he lives, so Siggi can affirm and strengthen his capacity as a literary artist by reflecting on, describing, and elaborating on objects, individuals, and events from his past, whether recent or more distant. While both of these aesthetic focal points might seem to some people to be confined or might seem to some to suggest an intellectual or aesthetic limitation of the artist who concentrates on them, on the other hand one might readily claim that these artists are merely working on a specific area which is of the greatest personal significance and interest to them. As Dorothy van Ghent says in *The English Novel* in her essay about Jane Austen's *Pride and Prejudice*, what Austen "excludes from her fictional material does not, then, reflect a personal obliviousness, but, rather, a critically developed knowledge of the character of her gift and a restriction of its exercise to the kind of subject matter which she could shape into most significance" (99–100). What Dorothy van Ghent proceeds to say about Austen's thematic focus is equally applicable to the narrative concentration in Lenz's *Deutschstunde* of Max and Siggi on the familiar landscapes to which they are so attached: "This 'two inches of ivory' (the metaphor which she herself used to describe her work), though it may resemble the handle of a lady's fan when looked on scantly, is in substance an elephant's tusk; it is a savagely probing instrument as well as a masterpiece of refinement" (100). Both Max Nansen and Siggi Jepsen use their art as an instrument to reflect on, examine, and probe the past while simultaneously achieving masterpieces of aesthetic vitality and refinement in their quest for aesthetic richness, emotional sensitivity, and understanding.

Whenever Siggi starts listening and reflecting he can imagine his home area, hear its sounds, and feel the memories flowing back. In the interest which he shows in Rugbüll and in the questions that he raises, such as who is it that knocks on the doors in thunderstorms and who brings the darkness and the gray days, who generates the mist on the shore, and why is it that the stranger is left outside without help and comfort, Siggi is very much like Nansen. For Nansen had said that what he wanted to do as an artist was to focus aesthetically on a part of his home landscape for the rest of his life—Siggi, too, realizes instinctively the inspirational richness of this environment for he is constantly drawn back to it as well, if only in memories and visions as colorful and as poignant as Nolde's *Blumengarten—Utenwarf* (1917), *Garten im Sommer* (1923), and *Gelbe und hellrote Dahlien* (1937).

Hans Wagener says appropriately and insightfully in *Siegfried Lenz* that Lenz, whose work implies a connection between the provincial and the ideology of the Third Reich, is not the only writer after 1945 "der seine erzählerischen Werke in der Provinz angesiedelt hat" (61). Wagener proceeds to say that Günter Grass "zeigt die ideologische Affinität der Provinz nicht zufällig ähnlich in seinen um Danzig und die Weichselmündung spielenden Romanen und Novellen" (61). Wagener also speaks of the metaphorical value of Rugbüll: "Rugbüll wird so zur Metapher für Deutschland. Siggis Auseinandersetzung mit seiner Vergangenheit in Rugbüll ist Auseinandersetzung mit der deutschen Geschichte des Dritten Reiches" (61–2).

Siggi also thinks about Himpel's statement that what really matters is not the result but rather one's attitude and one's tenacity. Siggi wonders what could be done with his copybooks, whether he might give them to Hilke or to Mackenroth or throw them in the Elbe. Siggi also ponders the possibility of selling them for publication after this release, which definitely suggests that he views himself at least to some extent as a future writer. The last paragraph of the novel presents an image of what will happen when Siggi and Himpel meet for the last time: "He will make a gesture and we shall both sit down, shall sit facing one another without stirring, each of us thoroughly pleased with himself because he feels he has won" (471). Such a scenario represents not only the tension between Siggi and Himpel but also the outcome of the conflict between Max and Jens. Even though Siggi might wish to proclaim in some sense that he has "won" this conflict with Himpel, it is also noteworthy that he believes, as he has stated before, more in the importance of the process, the means, of producing the work than in the "finished" product. Siggi, despite having completed the required essay in the copybooks, is still searching for his personal Atlantis, for his personal ideal, and for a vital vision of his past. It is the search itself that is of the utmost importance, that justifies and motivates Siggi's attempt to appreciate, to understand, and perhaps even to overcome his past. John Dewey once wrote: "Not perfection as a final goal, but the ever-enduring process of perfecting, maturing, refining is the aim in living.... Growth itself is the only moral 'end.'" Both Siggi Jepsen and Max Nansen exemplify and fulfill the challenge and the aesthetic promise of Dewey's statement. One might even say that Siggi, in trying to escape not only from his past and from the reform school environment but also from the prisonhouse of language, creates his own invisible pictures. Siggi's words and phrases, his reminiscences and visions of the past, motivated by his manifold experiences in his familiar and frequently beloved north German landscape, are his "invisible pictures," hints and pointers towards a future when various emotional conflicts and complicated events from his past might or even will be more comprehensible and "visible." These "invisible pictures" are also significant because they will continually inspire and motivate Siggi to new artistic endeavors. Although seemingly separated from Max Nansen forever, from any future contact with the painter, Siggi will, as an artist and as an individual of heightened aesthetic sensibility, always keep in his heart and mind, whether consciously or subconsciously, the spirit of Max's statements that seeing involves penetrating and enhancing, that to depict your own likeness you have to create and invent yourself, over and over again, and that when you create an image or an object, it is necessary to provide the inherent potentiality of such an image or object as well. Siggi's quest for his personal Atlantis, generated by the internalized images and visions of the most significant architectural spaces in his life, his childhood home, Bleekenwarf, and his mill, and motivated by various experiences associated with and connected to those architectural spaces, will be an arduous and continuous process of aesthetic development, emotional refinement, and intellectual enrichment which may ultimately come to terms with the manifold individuals, nature-spirits, prophets, goblins, apostles, radiant flowers, mills and other phosphorescent beings and creations which haunt his memory and vision of the landscape of Rugbüll and Bleekenwarf and which may perhaps in the future even become a luminescent focus of narrative energy as vital as the radiant unity of Nansen's *Sails Dissolving into Light* or *The Big Friend of the Mill* and of Nolde's *Blumengarten* (1926) or *Blumen und Wolken* (1933).

Conclusion

In this book I have discussed various magnificent houses and mansions in twentieth century European literature. In examining diverse works of Thomas Mann, Evelyn Waugh, J. R. R. Tolkien, and Siegfried Lenz, I have shown that the protagonists in these novels and short stories are often able to preserve the spirit of or a sense of the beauty and splendor of their favorite architectural places in their hearts, minds, and souls when they are separated, either temporarily or more permanently, from such lovely spaces. The socioeconomic environment, the cultural background, and the emotional, intellectual, and spiritual development of these protagonists may be different from their earliest childhood and youth, but what they all share is a belief in the importance of a beautiful architectural domain, a space often connected to or surrounded by a natural loveliness and luminescence, which has the capacity to comfort, inspire, heal, and revitalize. Each of these protagonists is associated with a magnificent or aesthetically interesting house which signifies the central architectural experience of their lives.

In Thomas Mann's *Buddenbrooks* Tony Buddenbrook develops from her childhood a deep admiration and love for her childhood home on Meng Strasse. She thinks of this delightful house as a place of sanctuary, security, and stability. These qualities are also essential to and appreciated by other family members such as Johann Buddenbrook, his son, and his grandson, Thomas. Yet, it is Tony Buddenbrook, perhaps because she is not directly connected to the mercantile and commercial aspects of the house and family business, who cherishes the fondest attachment to the house and who is the most profoundly saddened when the house ultimately has to be sold. Tony is fortunate that she was able to experience a mythological, a mythologically vital, ambience in her family's house in Meng Strasse for many years. When the house diminishes in significance for the family and for the existence of the family business and is eventually sold, Tony transforms the mythological atmosphere to a mythical aura, which she carries around with her, making it an integral part of her emotional and spiritual life. The mythological dimension of the family mansion on Meng Strasse with its devotion to gods and goddesses, is transfigured to a focus on Tony and her mythically vital capacity to nurture and preserve a Cinderella-like existence in a world of everyday mortality which is generally too harsh or coarse to appreciate her inner beauty and her nobility of character.

Tony Buddenbrook is a noble-spirited individual who internalizes the beauty, the magnificence, and the serenity of the house which she enjoyed and loved in her childhood and youth so that as she grows older the internalized images, reflections, and visions sustain her emotionally and spiritually. In Thomas Mann's *Tonio Kröger* Tonio does this to a considerable extent as well. As Tony Buddenbrook, Tonio Kröger loved his childhood home with its aura of seclusion, splendor, and tranquility. As an artist Tonio feels later in his life that a return to his home area would inspire and revitalize him aesthetically and emotionally. While the return to his hometown and his past has its difficult moments, especially when he is questioned by the authorities in his hometown as a potential criminal, Tonio does experience a moment of considerable pleasure when he finds one of his own literary works in the town's public library. Although Tonio is somewhat disappointed to see that his former home has been transformed into a public venue, the fact that his work is present there suggests not only the significance of his artistic enterprise but also the idea that he has attained a sense of continuity which his other family members were unable to achieve. In cherishing and savoring the cultural and the linguistic ambience of his hometown area once again and in experiencing the presence of the Hans- and Inge-like figures at the dance at the resort hotel Tonio is able to establish a renewed connectedness to his artistic and emotional roots which he believes, as he declares at the end of the narrative in his letter to Lisabeta, will ultimately rejuvenate his aesthetic sensibility.

In Mann's *Tristan* there is little direct evidence about the socioeconomic background of Spinell, the aesthetically sensitive author at the sanatorium. That Spinell can afford to stay at this sanatorium without any vocation or notable source of financial support could imply that he comes from a relatively well-to-do family or that he has recently received an inheritance which has enabled him to stay in this ambience permeated by the Empire style. Perhaps Spinell grew up in a house or in an environment with a similar architectural style for which he developed an attachment. Spinell reenergizes himself aesthetically and emotionally in his conversations with Gabriele about her past and in his attentive listening to her musical virtuosity on the piano. It is as if Spinell is using Gabriele to recreate his own forgotten, lost, or sublimated past (or perhaps even to create a past which he had wished for but had not directly experienced)—in envisioning for Gabriele a more glorious past than she herself remembers having and in interpreting or reinterpreting her own past in her childhood garden when she was "wearing the golden crown," Spinell might be attempting to refine his own aesthetic and imaginative capacity or he might even be trying to recapture the spirit of a similar event in his own life. Perhaps he had a sister or a family member who resembles Gabriele and in recreating the garden moment he revitalizes a sense of attachment to such a pleasant memory. Or perhaps Spinell envisions himself by proxy as the one who is the focus of the attention in the garden and thinks of himself as a regal figure. While Spinell seems to admire Gabriele, he also sadly seems to undervalue her well-being in encouraging her to play the piano despite his awareness or sense that her physical health will be negatively effected. In participating in and in sharing the vitality of the moment of musical rapture which Gabriele creates, Spinell attains a semblance of mythical vitality and a renewed appreciation for the architectural space which he cherishes.

In Mann's *Der Zauberberg* Hans Castorp, because of the death of close family members in his early youth and because he never developed or had the opportunity to develop a profound relation to an architectural ambience, does not have the same direct feeling of devotion to a childhood home as Tony Buddenbrook, Tonio Kröger, or Sebastian Flyte. However, as a child Hans Castorp did have an appreciation for and a reverence for death and its solemnity—thus, one might say that his attachment to the Berghof environment represents a continuation of this interest in and curiosity about death. It is noteworthy that Castorp is portrayed as being a good patient at the Berghof Sanatorium, as if he had an instinctive sense of appreciating and belonging in such an environment. Castorp's experience of the Berghof Sanatorium signifies the central architectural experience of his life—his intellectual, emotional, and aesthetic inclinations and sensibilities are nurtured, expanded, and refined by this adventure on the magic mountain. Castorp shows a special affinity for the various aspects of the Berghof environment, from the challenging and provocative conversations with Settembrini and Naphta which enrich and stimulate his life to the aesthetic beauty of the architectural features of the sanatorium to the lovely, and sometimes intriguing and threatening, natural landscape surrounding the Berghof.

In Waugh's *Brideshead Revisited* Sebastian Flyte feels a great emotional, aesthetic, and spiritual intimacy and attachment towards Brideshead Castle, his childhood home and a magnificent mansion with extensive grounds surrounding and encompassing it. More than any of the other members of the Flyte family Sebastian has a genuinely profound appreciation of and admiration of this glorious house which has developed through the course of time. That Sebastian returns fondly to visit Nanny Hawkins represents not only an attempt to revitalize the spirit of his childhood; such a return also signifies Sebastian's deep attachment to the beauty of Brideshead. Sebastian's attachment to the congenial spirit of his childhood and youth is intimately and inextricably connected to his love for Brideshead Castle.

It is a melancholy reality in the novel that Sebastian eventually becomes permanently separated from Brideshead Castle, the mansion which he loves so much. When he is compelled by external circumstances (especially by the mistreatment of others) or when he feels compelled to leave this splendid castle to find a more congenial place of residence, Sebastian internalizes the spirit of its beauty and radiance and takes it with him as an integral dimension of his own mythical vitality. For he, like Tony Buddenbrook in Mann's *Buddenbrooks*, is a Cinderella-like individual whose kindness, humanity, nobility, and generosity of spirit are almost completely undervalued and devalued by his peers and by contemporary society, whether because of envy, jealousy, their own inadequacies, or their lack of sensitivity.

It is also very sad that Sebastian and his mother, Lady Marchmain, never have a reconciliation before her death and that two of Sebastian's siblings, Bridey and Julia, make no attempt to visit, to console, or to help him. The insensitive and selfish behavior of Bridey and Julia is to some extent mitigated by the appreciation and the love which Cordelia certainly has for Sebastian. Perhaps even in his childhood and youth Sebastian sensed that Bridey and Julia, and certain other family members, never truly appreciated him so he turned his attention to those aspects of his environment, such as Nanny Hawkins and the house, which he felt intuitively cared for him and allowed him to show and share his love and his capacity for emotional attachment. The important conversation which Cordelia, the most pious and genuinely religious child of Lord and Lady Marchmain, has with Charles later in the novel after her return to Brideshead Castle shows how considerably she values the inner nature of Sebastian and his capacity for holiness. It is ironic that someone like Bridey, who seems outwardly religious (and who wants to be seen outwardly as religious) displays such unkind and insensitive behavior towards his brother, paying no attention to him in his despair and making no attempt to comfort him or to revitalize him. Similarly, Julia typically has a formal, public, and showy sense of religion and does not demonstrate any interest in helping or in trying to alleviate the suffering of Sebastian. Cordelia's statements to Charles regarding her trip to Morocco to visit her brother are very important because they affirm the notion that there are various people who are able to look beyond the struggles with alcoholism which Sebastian experiences and who appreciate or who sense the holiness and piety in his character.

The hall at Brideshead Castle with its tapestries shares the sense of Baroque magnificence and radiant splendor which permeate the great hall at Castle Howard designed by John Vanbrugh. Other architectural spaces of similar orphic magnificence and inner harmony are the Double Cube Room at Wilton House (created by Inigo Jones and containing portraits of the Herberts by Van Dyck and gilt furniture by William Kent), the Blue Drawing Room at Chatsworth (the decoration of which was largely designed by Carr of York for the 5th Duke of Devonshire), the Throne Room and the White Drawing Room at Buckingham Palace, the Minstrel Hall and the Throne Hall at Neuschwanstein Castle, Frederick the Great's picture gallery at Sans Souci, the Hall of Mirrors at Versailles, Ludwig II's Spiegelsaal (Hall of Mirrors) at Linderhof, the Large Gallery in Catherine's Karskoe Selo, the Great Gallery in the Castle of Schönbrunn, the White Sea Ballroom in the Royal Palace in Stockholm, and the Golden Gallery in the new wing of the Schloss Charlottenburg. These are some of the many lovely architectural interiors in palaces and castles which share a sense of extraordinary beauty and spaciousness with various parts of Brideshead Castle.

Lady Marchmain certainly appreciated the beauty, secular and religious, of Brideshead, as did Lord Marchmain, despite the fact that he felt that he must live abroad for so many years for personal reasons. And Sebastian, although he eventually departs from his cherished England for another country, possesses a most profound appreciation of the architectural beauty of Brideshead Castle. Sebastian's aristocratic bearing, which is especially noticeable during his early days at Oxford, is an important part of his private and public persona, both of which are enhanced by his admiration of the magnificence of Brideshead Castle. For only a true aristocrat would appreciate such a beautiful house not merely as a place to give parties, social events, and social gatherings, but even more importantly as a space for the development and nurturing of the heart, mind, soul, and spirit of the noble individual and of other individuals of similar kindness, temperament, and wisdom. With the proper affection and support from his family and "friends" Sebastian could have become a model aristocrat in British society—he could have exemplified the spirit of the wealthy noble described in Alfred, Lord Tennyson's *The Lord of Burleigh* as well as the kindhearted nobility and humane serenity of the Earl of Emsworth at Blandings Castle in the stories by P. G. Wodehouse. Sebastian's return to Brideshead in the first part of *Brideshead Revisited* represents an attempt not only to reestablish an emotional and a spiritual connection with his glorious past, to visit Nanny Hawkins as a symbol of such a past, and to show Charles this gorgeous house, which he senses his friend would appreciate, but also to affirm, or perhaps even to reaffirm, his aesthetic capacities by being in the presence of so much architectural and natural magnificence.

In J. R. R. Tolkien's *The Lord of the Rings* there are various important architectural creations, including not only the house of Bilbo and Frodo Baggins, the house of Tom Bombadil and Goldberry, Rivendell, and Lothlórien in *The Fellowship of the Ring*, but also Meduseld and The Hornburg in *The Two Towers* and a revitalized Minas Tirith in *The Return of the King*. The serene and seemingly timeless worlds of Rivendell and Lothlórien are admired by many individuals, not only by the Elves but also by visitors to these extraordinary places such as Bilbo, Frodo, Aragorn, Legolas, and Gandalf. Rivendell and Lothlórien each represent an exceptional ambience of aesthetic delight, architectural beauty, cultural vitality, and peacefulness. This signifies an ideal, or idealized vision, in which various individuals are thrilled to participate, if only temporarily. Elrond and Arwen belong to Rivendell as Celeborn and Galadriel belong to Lothlórien. A similar place of relative timelessness and serenity is Shangri-La in James Hilton's *Lost Horizon*. Hugh Conway, the protagonist of *Lost Horizon*, belongs as intuitively to this sanctuary as Galadriel to Lothlórien. Elrond,

Galadriel, Gandalf, Aragorn, and Hugh Conway all share important qualities such as a vital appreciation of natural beauty and aesthetic creativity, a patient intellect, a strong sense of humanitarian vitality, a serene wisdom, and a capacity for visionary thinking. Conway instinctively belongs to Shangri-La—the High Lama senses this and sees in Conway his heir and an exemplary person who has the capacity to guide Shangri-La into a congenial future. The world of Shangri-La is similar to some extent to the philosophical utopia governed by a relatively monastic elite which Hermann Hesse creates in *Das Glasperlenspiel, Magister Ludi: The Glass-Bead Game* (1943).

Even though Galadriel and the Elves will have to leave Lothlórien in the near future after the power of the Elven ring is diminished, one might claim that their spirit remains a perpetual and integral dimension of their beloved home with the golden mallorn-trees. And even though Elrond and Arwen will leave Rivendell on their different personal journeys their spirit will always be an important part of the loveliness of Rivendell, regardless of who the future owners might be. Similarly, in Hilton's *Lost Horizon*, once Conway has been a part of Shangri-La, once his noble and humane spirit has experienced, contributed to, and participated in the beautiful ambience of Shangri-La, it is as if he has always been there—it is as if his spirit represents an eternal part of Shangri-La's beauty.

Indeed, one might make a similar argument for a number of the other major characters discussed in this book. Tony Buddenbrook, Thomas Buddenbrook, in particular among the Buddenbrooks, and Tonio Kröger will always be an integral part, even if only in a quiet, unobtrusive, or symbolic manner, of the spirit of the Lübeck society in which their families once played such a prominent and dynamic role. One might even assert that the noble and generous spirits of Tony Buddenbrook, Thomas Buddenbrook, as well as of other Buddenbrook family members and of Tonio Kröger will always be present in the emotional and aesthetic aura of Lübeck society, whether such nobility and generosity are remembered and appreciated or whether the great houses which the Buddenbrook and Kröger families once possessed are admired and remembered as being part of those family legacies. Sensitive and thoughtful individuals like Tony Buddenbrook, Tonio Kröger, Sebastian Flyte, Lady Marchmain, Lord Marchmain, Cordelia Flyte, Bilbo Baggins, Frodo Baggins, Gandalf, Elrond, Arwen, Aragorn, Legolas, Galadriel, Celeborn, Siggi Jepsen, and Max Nansen who try to have a positive, humane, noble, and luminescent effect on the world of everyday mortality will always be a part of the aesthetic aura and of the architectural ambience which they loved, admired, and influenced (even if the house or residence which they valued is slightly modified, considerably changed, or even significantly transformed in the course of time).

Some families, especially those who are an essential part of an hereditary aristocracy, are fortunate in their possession of great wealth and in their ownership of a magnificent house or splendid mansion which has been passed down from one generation to the next. The individual members of exceedingly rich families, such as the members of the Flyte family, are fortunate in that they may typically live in such a splendid mansion (or in multiple imposing houses) for the duration of their childhood and youth and for some or many years after that as well, that is, until they move away to get married or for other personal reasons. Such individuals usually have periodic or consistent access to the family mansion for the duration of their lives, unless there is a conflict with the family member who is the owner of the house, or unless they have moved to a distant place which makes a return to the house difficult, or unless they choose not to visit the house regularly or very often. The individual who inherits the great house is the most fortunate and blessed of all, especially if the family's financial and socioeconomic situation is excellent and secure. Mr. Darcy in Austen's *Pride and Prejudice* exemplifies such a character in literature who is the undisputed heir of his family's great house, Pemberley. Moreover, his very congenial relation with his sister, Georgiana, will enable her to live at Pemberley for as long as she would like to. As many of the great houses of the British aristocracy and as many other splendid mansions around the world which are passed from one generation to the next, Brideshead Castle has been in the family of Lord Marchmain for numerous generations and signifies a relatively perpetual sanctuary of beauty, serenity, and stability (except during wartime when it is taken over by the military) for family members who admire and appreciate its magnificence and who wish to reside there and to maintain a consistent or permanent connection with it. In contrast to the radiantly and uniformly positive feelings which Darcy and Georgiana have for Pemberley House in Austen's *Pride and Prejudice*, it is noteworthy that each of the children of Lord and Lady Marchmain has a conflicted approach to and a different appreciation for Brideshead Castle. Ironically, Julia, who does not have the profound appreciation for Brideshead which Sebastian does, is the one who will presumably inherit the family estate. Yet, perhaps in time she will come to admire the castle with a measure of the love which Sebastian has nurtured for it. In Mann's *Buddenbrooks* fate, chance, and the vicissitudes of mortality intervened to undermine the legacy of the Buddenbrooks and to prevent a potential inheritance from being fulfilled. If the Buddenbrook house on the Meng Strasse in Mann's novel had been part of an hereditary legacy and if the family had not experienced the tragedies and financial losses which precipitated its decline, an individual such as Tony Buddenbrook would have loved to spend the duration of her life there.

With respect to the issue of the continuity of possession of a splendid house in a family for many years and successive generations one might wonder about the nature of the relationship between the house and the family. For example, if one assumes that a magnificent house or a splendid mansion has a soul or a spirit, the following interesting questions are worth considering: does the soul or spirit of the house esteem the family with which it is so intimately associated, does the house favor certain individuals in this family who appear to value it deeply, does the house cherish its geographical location and natural ambience or does it quietly and tacitly encourage the owners to move it to a more congenial spot (as seems to have happened in the case of Brideshead Castle), does the house appreciate the fact that it is the centerpiece of a family legacy, is the house a passive recipient of the vicissitudes of fate or chance or does it have the capacity to exert its will in subtle ways to ensure its existence, stability, and longevity, and does the house have the ability to shape the destiny of its owners? Does the house in Meng Strasse, for example, remember the love which Tony Buddenbrook and other Buddenbrook family members had for it, does it preserve in its own aesthetic memory this affection, especially if other owners are not as appreciative of its beauty? One might also wonder whether a once splendid castle or prominent mansion which is now in partial or considerable ruin and which is currently either treated as a tourist attraction or seems to be forgotten by the world still preserves a semblance of its former greatness and whether the architectural spirit of the house is still extant, merely waiting for the possibility of a future reconstruction? For example, one might think of Kenilworth Castle in England, now in ruins but which was once a lovely structure with an extensive history. Originally built in the eleventh century, Kenilworth evolved through the centuries—in the late fourteenth century its owner built a great hall which was reputed to be the most splendid in the country after that of the royal residence. Does the spirit of this great hall linger in this lovely romantic ruin or has the inevitability of mortality compelled it to flee to more congenial haunts? Perhaps the spirit of a ruined great house moves or is eventually forced to flee by the passage of time to a new location, to a new house of similar architectural beauty and comparable natural loveliness. And in some instances one might even claim that the spirit of a magnificent house is waiting, as Minas Tirith is in some sense awaiting the arrival of the King Elessar, and as the High Lama in Hilton's *Lost Horizon* is anticipating the arrival of Hugh Conway, for an owner or leader of great sensitivity and vision who will profoundly appreciate and admire its beauty and its presence. Such an individual is also Max Nansen in Lenz's novel who in his artistic devotion and inclination seems perfectly suited to Bleekenwarf and its radiantly colorful ambience.

In Siegfried Lenz's *Deutschstunde* the profound sense of connectedness which both Siggi Jepsen and Max Nansen nurture and develop towards their familiar north German landscape and towards a personally significant building in that environment reflects a shared love for this beautiful landscape which was also so important and inspirational for the Expressionist painter Emil Nolde. Siggi, who shows an instinctive aesthetic sensibility in his youth, appreciates the presence of Nansen and develops a close friendship with the painter. That Siggi is in a "reform" institution is because he has stolen a number of paintings, ironically, not for personal profit but to save them from being confiscated and burned by his father, who is overzealous in the performance of his duty to prevent Max from painting. Even though Siggi does feel a personal connection to his home landscape, he is also ambivalent and troubled about it because of the suffering in his own life caused by his father's extreme sense of duty and by Nansen's ultimately negative treatment of him. Siggi, writing in 1954 about the present as well as about events which occurred in his home area during the second world war, is sadly estranged from his familiar landscape. Although Siggi finds it difficult to write about his past and although he is inwardly distressed about such an estrangement, he does find personal rejuvenation through writing. As Siggi is commited to his writing, to the exploration and the investigation of the past in the process of writing his essay on the pleasures of duty, so Max is committed to his art, to his painting and to personal artistic expression regardless of the encroachment on his life and the mistreatment which he endures at the hands of the Nazi authorities. Even though the friendship between Siggi and Max is ultimately severed, both individuals feel perpetually and inextricably connected to their home landscape. Max Nansen, as the fictionalized embodiment of the German Expressionist painter Emil Nolde, has internalized the beauty of the natural environment he knows and loves so well so that whether he is physically or psychologically distant or separated from it, he still feels emotionally and aesthetically attached to it. One might say that Nansen feels perpetually and harmoniously connected to his home landscape in the spirit of the persona in Joseph von Eichendorff's "Abschied" who, although compelled to leave his beloved forest, will always be able to revitalize himself as long as he can imaginatively carry with him congenial memories and visions of that lovely ambience to guide and illuminate his future path. The importance of such visions is comparable to the significance of the invisible pictures of Nansen (and the "ungemalte Bilder" of Nolde) for they anticipate a more refulgent and pleasant future when the aesthetically sensitive individual will feel a greater sense of emotional healing and spiritual wholeness than the present world of everyday mortality can offer with its manifold vicissitudes of chance and fate.

I would like now to discuss several other important architectural interiors and significant architectural contexts in twentieth century European and American literature, focusing especially on lovely houses and distinctive aesthetically vital spaces in works by Heinrich Böll, Hermann Hesse, F. Scott Fitzgerald, Anton Chekhov, E. M. Forster, Virginia Woolf, Edith Wharton, and Boris Pasternak.

In Heinrich Böll's *Billard um halbzehn, Billiards at Half-Past Nine* (1959) there is an attempt to create an inner sanctum of hermetic and seemingly timeless vitality in an important building, in a significant public architectural space. Robert Faehmel, the protagonist of *Billard um halbzehn*, strives to transcend mortality and the flux of time not only by creating an ordered and orderly life but also by achieving a timeless "moment" of aesthetic and intellectual enchantment (from half-past nine until eleven in the morning) in the billiard-room at the Prinz Heinrich Hotel. Robert Faehmel creates a timeless enchanted moment through and in the formulaic, geometric configurations of the billiard balls which comprise a "starry heaven" (31). The movements of the colored balls over the green felt are vital expressions of hermetically cosmic energy which develop their own sense of time. Even though there are no lasting and permanent forms which result from the "mere rolling of spheres" (31), there is the sense that the aura of the interactions is infused with and guided by the laws of geometry and physics. Faehmel often plays for periods of time "with only one ball, white over the green surface, a solitary star in the sky" (31). The phrase, "a solitary star in the sky," could apply with equal effectiveness to the billiard-ball or to the novel's protagonist, who appears to establish such a solitary existence. The result of this playful endeavor is described as follows: "Light, faint music without melody, painting without likeness. Hardly any color. Mere formula" (31).

Heinrich Böll seems to share the view of Ezra Pound that the image (which Pound defines as "an emotional and intellectual complex in an instant of time") signifies the heart of poetic experience, that from the vibrant centers called "images" the poem or literary work will gain its significant form and rhythm. Such images, such centers of aesthetic dynamism, are exemplified by the passages quoted above from the beginning of chapter three of *Billard um halbzehn* and by the following passage about the nature of timelessness in the billiard-room ambience (from the perspective of Hugo, Robert's confidante): "Time here ceased to be a dimension making things measurable. Time was blotted out by that green rectangle of blotting paper. In vain hours chimed, hands moved in vain.... Airless rooms, timeless clocks, and he submerged here...reality not penetrating, its nose pressed against glass outside, as against shop or aquarium window" (47). Although Hugo occasionally has to get a double cognac for Robert Faehmel between nine-thirty and eleven, he still feels as if he were infused with and encompassed by an aura of eternity, for mortality and the exigencies of mortal existence are excluded from the billiard-room experience.

With a seemingly magical capacity Robert Faehmel escapes the negative, destructive images and memories of his past in this timeless moment of formulaic enchantment and formal detachment from everyday mortality: "Only the three billiard balls, rolling over green blotting paper, forming ever-new figurations, were real. Infinity in a thousand formulas, all contained within two square meters. He struck them forth, his cue a wand, while his voice lost itself in eons of time" (47). It is noteworthy that infinity is described as existing in a confined and limited space, as if space, a specific architectural space, has the capability to create its own sense of time and timelessness. Faehmel is presented as a potent character of wizard-like abilities who can wander through the corridors of time freely and then return to the context of the billiard-room at his convenience. As Hugh Conway in Hilton's *Lost Horizon* frees himself from the chaos of mortality in the aesthetic and cultural beauty of Shangri-La, so Robert Faehmel tries to escape the problematic past and the difficult present in the formulaic enchantment of the billiard-room ambience. Even though Conway leaves Shangri-La ultimately to help his friend, he is able to return, at least spiritually, not only because his soul belongs instinctively to its aura of timelessness but also because he retains in his mind an image, in the sense of Pound's conception of the image, of the lamasery world as an aesthetically enchanting emotional and intellectual complex in an "instant of timelessness."

Hugo is an appropriate confidante and participant in the billiard-room experience and in its aura of eternity for he, like Robert, has suffered and refused to partake of the "host of the beast." He says that he used to get beaten up regularly because he was "God's little lamb" (59). He was one of the significant individuals who believed instinctively in the importance of gentleness, kindheartedness, patience, meekness, all qualities which were antithetical to the life-philosophy of the brutal people like Nettlinger and the Nazi authorities. Hugo tries to get locked in the school overnight so he does not have to be beaten by his ruthless, evil classmates on the way home. Beaten and mistreated at school and at home, Hugo runs away and is taken in by a child-welfare center. Hugo, when telling Robert his story, says that even at the child-welfare center where no one knew him his countenance and demeanor inspired people to call him "God's little lamb." As Hugo describes the misery and suffering of his childhood and the good fortune which brought him to the child-welfare center where he soon at the age of fourteen was the only one selected by the manager of a prominent local hotel to go into service, there is the sense that this child, despite the mistreatment and torture which he endured, has a fairy-tale aura about him—it is as if he were a prince taken as a child abruptly from the kingdom over which he rightly should have governed. The comment which the hotel manager makes to Hugo at their initial meeting is very important: "All I hope is you never find out how much your looks are worth. You're the purest God's little lamb I ever laid eyes on" (61).

Not only in the billiard-room ritual but in his everyday life Robert Faehmel tries to liberate himself from the anguish of everyday mortality, from the ever-present reality around him and its encroachments, by creating and sustaining a formulaic and well-ordered existence. He goes to Mass every morning at seven, spends time with his daughter from seven-thirty until eight, and breakfasts alone from eight to eight-thirty. Robert Faehmel then works from eight-thirty until nine-thirty in the morning, from nine-thirty until eleven he plays billiards at the Prinz Heinrich Hotel, and from eleven until noon he is at the Café Zons. During these several hours Robert Faehmel is available only to his mother, father, daughter, son, or Mr. Schrella. The most crucial part of the day with respect to the issue of Robert's quest for the timeless moment or for timelessness is his billiard-playing ritual from half-past nine until eleven. During this time he does not wish to be disturbed—he wishes to be completely absorbed by his self-generated and self-revitalizing ritual and by the stories about the past which he and Hugo share.

Perhaps Hugo is so conscious of the continuity of time, of the existence of a temporal continuum, because he has been given a sense of eternity by participating in Robert's enchanted moment of timelessness in the billiard-room. From the perspectives of Robert and Hugo the billiard-room ritual from half-past nine until eleven does generate and sustain enchanted timelessness—only upon Schrella's return later in the novel does such a timeless moment assume a mortal dimension. Once Hugo has attained a sense of eternity he feels that he has always had it. One might make the same argument for Robert Faehmel—once the individual attains a sense of eternity he feels that it has always signified an integral and permanent aspect of his inner being.

After Hugo tells Robert about his experience as "God's little lamb," Robert relates some of his war-time adventures. In an undertone of profound sadness Robert explains that although he was trained as an architect his activity during the war was only as a demolition expert. Instead of building houses, churches, villas, and bridges, his talents were used by the military to destroy such architectural features. He laments that he was serving a general who seemed crazy and determined to blow up various objects in the environment, including St. Anthony's Abbey, an especially important work, just before the end of the war.

In *Frömmigkeit bei Heinrich Böll*, Manfred Nielen speaks of the significance, biblical and secular, of the figure of the shepherd in *Billard um halbzehn*, suggesting that eventually Robert Faehmel does fulfill his capacity to be a shepherd by adopting Hugo: "Am Ende des Buches erfüllt er symbolisch sein Hirtenamt, indem er den Liftboy Hugo adoptiert" (77). Hugo is one of the exemplary lambs in the narrative. It is the lambs, as Werner Janssen suggests in *Der Rhythmus des Humanen bei Heinrich Böll*, who have the capacity to challenge and transcend time through their self-sacrificial silence (132). The presence of Hugo, the exemplary lamb, is significant not only as Robert's confidante but also to reaffirm and preserve the humanitarian potential within contemporary society.

Robert Faehmel's exceptional self-control and emotional poise could suggest and indicate a strong capacity to stand above change and the flux of time. This capability of suspending or internalizing any outward sign of emotional concern or vitality is reinforced by Robert's own statement that he only needed the totals and estimates of his associates without comment for he was not interested in collecting confessions. Although outwardly Robert shows very little emotion, one has the sense that he is concealing a very sensitive and emotionally vital personality behind his devotion to formulaic expression. Ihor Prodaniuk affirms this point in *The Imagery in Heinrich Böll's Novels*, saying that "Robert is not...a cold, frigid human being who has no compassion, for he knows of the heart's bliss and grief" (91). Prodaniuk also analyzes insightfully the significance of the formulaic ritual for Robert Faehmel: "Therefore, his reduction of everything connected with life to the abstractness of a formula functions as an escape device which shields him from reality and at the same time allows him to recreate reality in an objective unattached way" (91).

For Robert Faehmel the notion of the enchanted moment, whether seemingly timeless or transitory, is crucial to his experience of timelessness. Faehmel would seem to share the approach of Kirilov in Dostoyevsky's *The Possessed* who believes that there are moments when time suddenly stops and becomes eternal—during such moments one feels the presence of an eternal and perpetual harmony. In *Epiphany in the Modern Novel* Morris Beja speaks of retrospective epiphanies, which result from consistent meditation on an individual's past to give meaning to childhood experiences. Robert Faehmel attempts to achieve not only a retrospective epiphany in trying to come to terms with his past—he also aspires to create a timeless epiphany of aesthetic vitality.

The approach to a sense of timeless or seemingly timeless enchantment which Faehmel tries to achieve in the billiard-room is similar to various aspects of the philosophy of art of Paul Cézanne. In his mature style Cézanne developed brush strokes like building blocks and simplified forms as he aimed to create an ambience of order and solidity. Robert Faehmel articulates explicitly and implicitly a similar aesthetic strategy—he is interested in achieving a sense of permanence, order, and structural precision in the billiard-ball configurations to counter the vicissitudes of everyday reality. One pictorial complement of Böll's timeless enchanted moment might be Cézanne's "Fruit Bowl, Glass and Apples," which presents an aura of timeless motionlessness in the midst of solid forms.

Heinrich Faehmel, like his son Robert, prepares himself to experience a sense of timelessness—he creates the enchanted moment in his mind before it happens, as a prelude to its ultimate fulfillment in everyday reality. Heinrich Faehmel possesses a relative self-confidence about the passage of time, proclaiming that the present seemed to him as if it were the past fulfilled. From the first day of his arrival in the city Heinrich, at age twenty-nine, strives to create a personal myth. Heinrich is impressed and inspired by the imposing architecture which he observes on his arrival, from the Prinz Heinrich Hotel and the solid bank buildings to the cathedral and the four churches. As he reflects upon his recent past, Heinrich thinks about the devotion which he showed to developing his architectural abilities, constantly drawing everything from clouds, angels, and trees to churches and chapels in various styles, including Romanesque, Gothic, Rococo, Victorian, and modern. Upon being chosen as the architect for the abbey in the Kissa Valley, Heinrich envisions his future more particularly, planning on marrying Johanna Kilb, the daughter of a prominent attorney. That Heinrich builds the abbey suggests that he, like Robert, has an instinctive interest in and an intuitive admiration of a place of sanctuary.

Johanna Kilb Faehmel, Heinrich's wife and Robert's mother, lives in a sanatorium, an existential context similar to that of Robert's billiard-room experience. That Johanna is described as "the kind of woman you only see in the old pictures in the museums" (21) and that she is a member of a prominent family which lived for several hundred years on Modest Street suggests that she has an instinctive appreciation for tradition, for continuity, and for architectural vitality, as well as a capacity for timelessness. The commitment to humanitarian fairness and justice of the Faehmel and Kilb families complements and represents another dimension of the quest for timelessness, for the timeless enchanted moment: Perhaps Robert is trying to recapture indirectly in the billiard-room ambience the spirit of devotion to the Kilbian motto "Their right hand is full of bribes," which affirms the incorruptibility of the family. Johanna is an important character for her humanity, her kindheartedness, her sensitivity, and her representing symbolically Heinrich's critically aware and active conscience.

While Robert signifies the epitome of Schiller's "sentimental poet," as he is too aesthetically conscious, emotionally sensitive, and too mindful of unforgettably painful war-time experiences to exemplify a desire for considerable sociability and worldliness, Heinrich may be said to manifest Schiller's "naïve poet," who is more at one with the world of everyday reality. Johanna represents important characteristics of both Heinrich and Robert and a delicate fusion of the qualities of the sentimental and the naïve poet. Of her present situation in the sanatorium Johanna says that one is allowed to be "crazy" in such a place without being beaten. Even though Johanna is permitted to go out when she wishes, for she asserts that she is harmless, she proclaims: "But I don't want to go out, I don't want to know what time is..." (139). Johanna refuses to accept the time of the present—this is not only an escape from an uncongenial reality and a protest against the ruthlessness and mercilessness of the authoritarian elements of contemporary society but also an attempt to transcend the flux of time.

Johanna shares her son's critical concerns about the value of personal monuments and of the "permanence" of buildings. She says at one point: "I never could take building seriously. Concentrated baked dust, dust transformed into a building" (145). Her concern is motivated by her observation that some creative individuals, as well as various other socially prominent figures, tried to "forget themselves in building things, it's like opium" (140). Her statement also suggests an undertone of environmental awareness, that she is disturbed by the violation of the natural environment which occurred to produce various structures. Johanna discourages Heinrich from trying to establish a concrete monument for she knows that his greatest "monument" is his humanitarian vitality which can never be simplified to or signified by a material object.

Johanna, Robert, Heinrich, Hugo, and Schrella all embody and symbolize the humanitarian devotion and vitality which is the thematic focus and ethical center of the narrative. Such a consistent emphasis on the eternal significance of profoundly humanitarian values is affirmed and strengthened by the repetition throughout the novel of the leitmotif from a poem by Hölderlin—"Firm in compassion the eternal heart."

The arrival of Schrella causes a disruption in the atmosphere of the billiard-room, for not only is Robert Faehmel's sublimation of feeling challenged but the precision of the forms in the billiard-room ritual is undermined. Schrella's return is analogous to Mallinson's persuasion of Conway in Hilton's *Lost Horizon* to leave the comfort of Shangri-La. The crucial difference between these two experiences is that whereas in the one novel the timeless enchantment of the billiard-room ritual seems to be forever broken, in the other novel Shangri-La remains a sacred place of relatively timeless sanctuary to which Conway strives eagerly to return.

Schrella's disruption of the timeless enchantment of the billiard-room ritual is mitigated by the fact that it encourages Robert to realize how important Hugo is to him, to his family, and to his sense of humanitarian vitality. When Robert and Schrella decide to cease playing billiards, Robert brings forth documents which Hugo may sign to become an official part of the family. In response to Schrella's question whether they still need the boy, Robert asserts that they certainly and urgently do because he has Edith's smile on his face and Ferdi's spirit, that is, the humanitarian spirit of the lambs. Schrella understands Robert's concern that people like Hugo and other humanitarian figures must be preserved, nurtured, and strengthened because there are so few of them in contemporary society. Schrella declares that he is not afraid because the people who partook of the 'Host of the Beast' still exist in contemporary society but rather because the other kind, those who rejected the 'Host of the Beast' and who are devoted to compassion, kindness, and mercy, exist only in small numbers.

The infinity of formulaically splendid isolation in the billiard-room ritual has been transformed into a perpetual devotion to humanitarian sensitivity and critical awareness. Such a transformation is affirmed by Johanna's self-liberation from the bewitched castle of the sanatorium, by Robert's abandonment of his billiard-room routine, by Schrella's metaphysical uncertainty about returning to his old haunts, by Hugo's decision to quit his job and join the Faehmel family, and by Heinrich's cancellation of his Kroner breakfast-routine and by his very expressive gesture of passing the cut-off abbey spire to Robert. Robert's voice, which had once lost itself in eons of time, is now directed towards a present of critical awareness and active social commitment, though still rather embryonic. The timeless enchanted moment of the Prinz Heinrich billiard-room has become the enchanted "moment" of ethical renewal and emotional revitalization of the Faehmel family which is now trying to understand more honestly its past and the relation of past to present but which will also commit itself to the creation of a new and exemplary humanitarian spirit.

Robert Faehmel's devotion to humanitarian vitality is comparable to the commitment of Käthe Kollwitz to humanitarian sensitivity. Many of her drawings and paintings, like the aesthetic activity of Robert, like the psychological maneuvering of Heinrich to create a personal myth, and like the presence of Johanna, are moments of profound critical awareness demonstrating the inhumanity of war. Although Kollwitz reveals a softer, gentler tone in her work than Böll in his, both share the conviction of Picasso in the importance of humanely sensitive aesthetic activity. Picasso wrote once that painting is not done to decorate apartments but is instead a powerful instrument against brutality and darkness.

Perhaps Robert Faehmel is readily willing to give up his billiard-room ritual and its aura of timeless tranquillity because he has created through his temporary commitment to aesthetically formulaic activity a renewed sense of Apollonian peace, of a serenity of soul which Lucretius considered as essential to the humanitarian, Epicurean philosophy of life. One might even claim that Robert, who in his own right is as romantic, rhapsodic, and mystical as Dylan Thomas, would concur wholeheartedly with this poet's strategy of composition and creative expression: "Out of the inevitable conflict of images—inevitable because of the creative, recreative, destructive, and contradictory nature of the motivating centre—I try to make that momentary peace which is a poem." The private serenity which Robert attained in the billiard-room ambience is transformed into both a privately and a publicly directed peace reaffirming the humanitarian potential of the present in the noble characters of Hugo and Schrella as well as members of his family who embody the intensity and the strength of Hölderlin's statement: "Firm in compassion the eternal heart."

The heart and soul of a hotel, such as the Prinz Heinrich Hotel in Böll's novel, whether historic, extensive, lavish, splendid, or quaint (or a combination of several of these qualities) in its loveliness can be a room or special architectural space or a series of rooms or even an image in the interior of the hotel. For example, a hotel may have a portrait or painting of itself located in a prominent or in a more secluded position in the hotel, in a particular room or along an important staircase—such a portrait may be said to represent the soul of the hotel and to capture its spiritual essence. The valued presence of such an important portrait ensures that the hotel will continue to maintain its congenial existence. The heart and soul of a hotel may also be represented in a room or rooms which contain lovely furniture, paintings, porcelain, and tapestries—such furniture, paintings, porcelain, and tapestries may date back to the founding period of the hotel or they may be of more modern origin. In either case a room in a hotel which contains such beautiful objects symbolizes the aesthetic heart and soul of the hotel and generates the loveliness which permeates its ambience. In historic hotels and inns such rooms with attractive furniture, exquisite porcelain, rich tapestries, and perhaps even interesting and colorful paintings are of exceptional importance, but such objects may be of seminal importance in more modern hotels and inns as well. While the spirit of a hotel may be present, at least partially, in its social places, in its restaurant or, if it is larger, in its restaurants and conference rooms, the heart and soul of such a hotel most often exists in its private and serene architectural spaces, in a room or series of rooms or an image which signify a condition of peacefulness and luminescent sanctuary.

Hermann Hesse's *Siddhartha* (1922) depicts various places of sanctuary and of architectural interest. From his youth Siddhartha reveals a Buddha-like capacity and character—in his younger days he shows not only a fine intellect, a profound spirituality, and a graceful presence but also a potential to devote himself vitally to a cause or mission. Even in his childhood there is the sense that Siddhartha is destined for greatness in his life. Siddhartha is brought up on the teachings of the wise Brahmins, but gradually begins to wonder why they are continually seeking and do not seem to have a sense of inner peace. Siddhartha leaves his childhood home to join the Samanas who are wandering ascetics practicing self-denial. His goal as a Samana is to conquer the desires of the self to achieve an inner peacefulness, to unify the self with the universality of being.

After being with the Samanas for a while Siddhartha begins to question the vitality of their approach—his doubts about the Samanas are reinforced by their coincidence with the appearance of a rumor about the existence of the Buddha, a profoundly holy individual. Siddhartha and Govinda then search for the Buddha. What is noteworthy about this character is his complete or seemingly complete peacefulness and the aura of tranquility which envelops him. Gotama, who epitomizes light and peace, emphasizes that his goal is salvation from suffering. As much as Siddhartha admires the Buddha, he feels that he cannot accept the doctrines and teachings of others, but must explore the world on his own. Siddhartha then leaves Govinda as a follower of Gotama and aspires to experience the complexity and versatility of life in his own way. Instead of trying to mortify or destroy the self, Siddhartha decides to consecrate himself to his own emotional, intellectual, and physical development and to the exploration of the depths of the self.

Eventually Siddhartha arrives at a town where he meets Kamala, the courtesan, and Kamaswami, the businessman. From these two individuals he learns about the world of pleasure, enjoyment, self-gratification, and acquisitiveness which they represent. After a while Siddhartha does not enjoy the sensual and material pleasures of Kamala and Kamaswami any longer, but feels that such pleasures and possessions which they offer are a burden and a strain on his spirit. The dream which Siddhartha has of Kamala's small songbird and its death and the fact that he throws it away suggests to him that his life in this world of material enjoyments has become meaningless and that he is demeaning his soul in the pursuit of such transient pleasures.

As he reflects on his past Siddhartha thinks about those moments when he truly experienced joy in his life. When he was praised in his youth for his excellent accomplishments, then he felt a sense of joy and believed that a glorious life awaited him. He also heard the inspirational voice within him urging him on to new and greater challenges. In acknowledging that he has not heard this inspirational and important inner voice for a considerable length of time, and especially not during his sojourn of sensual raptures and pleasures with Kamala and Kamaswami, Siddhartha encourages himself to revitalize a sense of his former vitality. In admitting that Kamala was dear to him at times, Siddhartha also asserts that their life together was just a game and that such a game has left him feeling emotionally and spiritually impoverished. Kamala is not surprised at Siddhartha's sudden departure for she sensed that he was instinctively a pilgrim and a Samana at heart.

In leaving the town and its material concerns, sensual pleasures, and spiritual malaise, Siddhartha aspires to achieve a sense of oblivion and to liberate himself from the stain on his soul. As he continues the journey to escape from the degenerate aura of the town, Siddhartha reaches a river in the forest, the same river which he had crossed in his youth. In reflecting upon his situation, Siddhartha contemplates the possibility of suicide. As he gazes into the river the emptiness in the water appears to reflect the emptiness in his soul. As Siddhartha is on the verge of falling into the river in an act of self-destructive frustration with the sordidness and wretchedness of life, he hears a sound emanating from a distant dimension of his soul. This is the "holy Om," the sign of perfection, which he seems to utter almost unconsciously, or which a part of his soul expresses within him. Suddenly, instead of striving for peace by a destruction of the body, he is reawakened to his innate conviction in the indestructibleness of life in the unifying power of Om. Physically exhausted from his wanderings and from his self-imposed confrontation with death, Siddhartha falls into a deep sleep which refreshes him considerably. Not only does he feel that ten years have passed during this sleep, but he senses that "his whole sleep had been a long deep pronouncing of Om, thinking of Om, an immersion and penetration into Om, into the nameless, into the Divine" (73).

Upon awakening Siddhartha, in a state of spiritual and emotional rejuvenation, notices a monk in a yellow gown sitting near him and recognizes his old friend Govinda. Govinda, now one of the followers of Gotama, was watching over Siddhartha (though initially he does not recognize Siddhartha and thinks he is just guarding a needy traveler). In the ensuing conversation both individuals admit that they are engaged in "pilgrimages," Govinda devoted to the nomadic lifestyle of the monks, Siddhartha asserting that he is also "on the way," on a pilgrimage of self-enlightenment. Before Govinda departs Siddhartha emphasizes the transitory nature of the material and physical world, of the world of appearances.

Siddhartha's experience of Om in his profound sleep has inspired him to feel a sense of love to various aspects of the world around him. He reflects upon his recent past when he proclaimed to Kamala that he possessed "three noble and invincible arts: fasting, waiting, and thinking" (77). In devoting himself during his sojourn in the town to numerous sensual pleasures and to the acquisition of wealth Siddhartha feels that he has devalued and lost these arts. Now he feels as if he were starting a new life. Siddhartha rejoices because he has survived his experience of hopelessness and despair and feels emotionally and spiritually rejuvenated. In extricating himself from his dependence on his proud, materialistically motivated self, Siddhartha has instinctively revived a sense of youthful, pristine innocence, which is further strengthened by his contemplation of the beautiful, peaceful river.

As Siddhartha looks lovingly at the river he admires its great beauty and serenity. The voice within him, a voice of ethereal tranquility, encourages him to remain by the river and learn from it and its profound wisdom. Siddhartha senses the significance of the continual flowing of the river which is always the same and yet at every moment new and replenished, but he does not yet fully understand this notion. The river in *Siddhartha* is analogous in significance to Walden Pond in H. D.

Thoreau's *Walden*. Both lovely natural places not only inspire and rejuvenate the personae emotionally and intellectually experiencing their respective beauty and vitality, but also create a spiritual context where each persona may contemplate the space of eternity.

Proceeding to the ferry, Siddhartha asks the ferryman, Vasudeva, whose life he admires, if he may stay as his apprentice. When Vasudeva invites him to remain, Siddhartha narrates his personal story. Vasudeva is an excellent listener, for he has the capacity to listen patiently and thoroughly, without offering either praise or blame on Siddhartha's narrative. Vasudeva knows that Siddhartha has developed a love for the river, that the river has spoken to him, and that a sensitive, spiritual connection exists between his new apprentice and the river. In praising the river in its all-encompassing presence as knowing everything, Vasudeva says that the source of his great inner serenity is the river, which has been his teacher. The ferryman says that of the thousands of people he has taken across the river only a few have treated the river as a congenial aspect of nature and not as an obstacle; only a few have heard the voice of the river, listened to it thoughtfully, and realized its holy beauty.

The hut which Siddhartha and Vasudeva share along the river exists in a condition of peaceful communion with the natural environment—they also attain an emotional and spiritual union with nature. In the spirit of a Frank Lloyd Wright dwelling, this hut is at one with nature and celebrates the beauty and tranquility of nature in its own lovely serenity. This special hut represents a space of architectural simplicity and quiet elegance. One might even say that this modest house or hut seems to be an extension of the individual, namely Siddhartha, as the individual, Siddhartha, is an affirmation and manifestation of it. Such consanguinity between an individual, especially a sensitive and thoughtful individual, and his house and between an individual and the surrounding natural environment is present in a similar spirit in Max Nansen's profound connection to his house, Bleekenwarf, and to nature in Lenz's *Deutschstunde*.

One thematic variation of the house which is or seems to be an extension and an affirmation of the individual who resides in it and who truly appreciates it is the house of the sensitive and thoughtful artist who genuinely appreciates his home and the surrounding natural environment. Nansen's Bleekenwarf in Lenz's *Deutschstunde* is a perfect example of this, as is, not surprisingly because of the various shared similarities, Emil Nolde's Seebüll. Another prominent example is Claude Monet's Giverny. Monet first discovered the house and garden at Giverny in 1883—initially, he rented this and eventually purchased it. He transformed the existing kitchen garden, orchard, and several flower-beds into an Impressionist sanctuary of resplendent light and color. In 1893 Monet bought another adjacent piece of land and created his water garden with its Japanese-style bridge and the lovely waterlilies. As Nolde at Seebüll and Nansen at Bleekenwarf, Monet loved his garden and the natural environment surrounding the house, spending many hours walking around and appreciating its beauty or planting various flowers from asters, nasturtiums, and poppies to irises, sunflowers, and waterlilies.

Siddhartha assists the ferryman in this ambience with everyday activities and is very contented. However, the greatest joy for Siddhartha is his experience of the river from whom (from which) he learns much and continually. Most importantly, he learns from it how to listen with a quiet heart, "with a waiting, open soul, without passion, without desire, without judgment, without opinions" (87). Moreover, Siddhartha learns from the river that there is no such entity as time. Vasudeva affirms this realization that the river is everywhere at the same time, at the source, in the ocean, and in the mountains and that only the present exists for it without the influence or intervention of the past or the future.

Siddhartha's emotional connectedness to the river is reinforced by his assertion that his life is like a river and that the different stages of his life are interwoven with one another and only separated "by shadows, not through reality" (87). Siddhartha has learned that his previous lives are not, or were not, in the past, just as his death and return to Brahma are not in the future and that everything in his life has reality and presence. As all negative emotions and experiences are in time, embedded in mortality, when one conquers time and liberates oneself from mortality, one overcomes the negative feelings and occurrences which are part of it. The unifying presence of the river is reaffirmed in the capacity of the great stream to encompass and represent the voices of all living beings. The river itself is said to pronounce the word "Om" when it presents all of these voices at the same time.

By virtue of his consanguinity with the ferryman and with the river Siddhartha gradually develops a smile comparable in radiance and vitality to that of his companion along the river—this is the smile of the Immortals which is very similar to the smile of Gotama. In listening to the water, the flowing water of the stream, both Siddhartha and Vasudeva feel that they are listening as well to "the voice of life, the voice of Being, of perpetual Becoming" (88). Through many days, weeks, and months of offering benevolent and thoughtful advice and assistance to various travelers these two individuals develop a reputation of being holy and wise men.

One day Siddhartha encounters Kamala, the former courtesan who has become a pilgrim to Gotama, on her deathbed, for on the journey she suffered a fatal snakebite. Her aim was to acquire a sense of inner peace by visiting Gotama—as she does not meet him, she notices that Siddhartha has the same appearance of inner peace. Before her death Kamala feels ultimately that what she had hoped to gain from the Illustrious One she has found in Siddhartha. As Siddhartha gazes at her face he thinks not only about their shared past together but also affirms "the indestructibleness of every life, the eternity of every moment" (93).

Even though Vasudeva knows that Siddhartha has developed a profound appreciation of and for the river, he encourages his friend to listen even more carefully to the river. As Siddhartha listens to the many voices of the river and sees manifold images from his own life, he hears a unifying sorrowful voice. All of these images of various aspects of his life flow together and become part of the river. As he continues to listen, the river flows to the sea and to the ocean, reaches its goals and transforms itself into vapor, rain, and back again into a vernal stream. Siddhartha finally feels that he has mastered the art of listening—the difference in his appreciation of the river at this point derives from his awareness of the dynamic unity of the various voices he hears. When Siddhartha feels that he has achieved a supremely serene self, a radiant inner peace, and that he belongs intimately to the unity of all things, Vasudeva believes that this is the moment when he should depart forever from his friend to go into the forest and into the unity of all things.

The final chapter of the narrative, "Govinda," begins with a conversation between Siddhartha and Govinda, who have not seen each other in a long time and do not seem to recognize each other initially. One of the points which Siddhartha makes is that time is not real. If it is true that time is not real, says Siddhartha, "then the dividing line that seems to lie between this world and eternity, between suffering and bliss, between good and evil, is also an illusion" (115). Siddhartha clarifies this idea by declaring that the world is perfect at every moment because "every sin already carries grace within it, all small children are potential old men, all sucklings have death within them, all dying people—eternal life" (116). During profound meditation it is possible to overcome and vanquish time and to perceive simultaneously the past, the present, and the future.

In the farewell scenario between these two holy men Govinda looks at his friend and suddenly no longer sees the face of Siddhartha. Instead he sees a variety of faces which seem to change and revitalize themselves and ultimately become or remain Siddhartha. All of these forms, seemingly transitory and yet also eternal for they changed and were then reborn in other images, are connected in the smiling face of Siddhartha, "this smile of unity over the flowing forms, this smile of simultaneousness over the thousands of births and deaths" (122).

Govinda even notices that the smile of Siddhartha is precisely the smile of Gotama, the Buddha. The connection between Siddhartha and Gotama is affirmed not only in the fact that "Siddhartha" is a name that is often given to the Buddha himself but also in the emotional and spiritual similarities between the two holy men. That Siddhartha is a kindred manifestation and a kindred spirit of the Illustrious One is noticed not only by Govinda and Kamala but also by Vasudeva. Siddhartha's peaceful and gentle smile, which is also perhaps somewhat gracious and somewhat mocking of or distant from the world of everyday mortality, illuminates the world around him, as does the laughter of the Immortals in Hesse's *Der Steppenwolf.* Such an extraordinarily sensitive and instinctively magnanimous smile is precisely "that which is left over when a true man has passed through all the sufferings, vices, mistakes, passions and misunderstandings of men and got through to eternity and the world of space" (*Steppenwolf* 176).

The most important qualities which a magnificent house can offer are a sense of peacefulness, stability, security, an inner beauty (both with respect to the architectural aspects and with respect to the soul of the house), an external beauty (with respect to the property or grounds surrounding and encompassing the house), and a sense of sanctuary. The existence of Siddhartha and the hut along the river in which Siddhartha resides signify all of these important qualities. The being, the existential essence, of Siddhartha exemplifies an aura of serenity, emotional stability, intellectual security, spiritual beauty, and a holy and wise physical presence. Siddhartha feels a profound sense of emotional and spiritual connectedness to the river and to his immediate natural environment—the house in which he resides represents a sanctuary of light and serenity because of his inner holiness, tranquility, and wisdom. The noble-spirited and generous-hearted presence of Siddhartha endows the house in which he resides with an aesthetic, emotional, and spiritual magnificence.

In Hermann Hesse's *Der Steppenwolf, Steppenwolf* (1927) the Steppenwolf, because of his heroic and Promethean capacity to explore the self, the depths of his soul, to appreciate the multiple possibilities of self-growth, to understand the potential for self-transformation, to develop a critical awareness of culture and society in the spirit of the Nietzschean "Übermensch," and to admire the pantheon of Immortals (and to participate in their aura), is a type of grail-seeker. The Steppenwolf also shows a capacity to share the laughter of the Immortals and to encompass the world and its complexity and diversity in a gesture of profound compassion and love in the spirit of St. Francis and Siddhartha. As other grail-seekers the Steppenwolf has to undergo various ordeals and trials before he can arrive at his sacred castle, which could be represented by the "magic theater." Or perhaps one might view the magic theater as the focus of the Steppenwolf's heroic struggles and tribulations and thereby merely a prelude to the exploration of the sacred castle of the self.

The Steppenwolf's quest for immortality evolves not only from his reverence for the great artists, poets, and creators such as Socrates, Jesus, Dante, Mozart, Goethe, Beethoven, and Novalis but also out of his conspicuous difference from middle-class society and his awareness of that difference. The Steppenwolf, Harry Haller, is distinguished from the rest of society emotionally, intellectually, and spiritually. He is portrayed as an emotionally sensitive individual of unusually delicate sensibility. Hermine, the Steppenwolf's alter-ego and complementary self, implies Haller's potential to participate in the realm of the Immortals and emphasizes the heroic dimension of his approach to life in contrast to the mundane expectations of everyday life: "…you were ready for deeds and sufferings and sacrifices, and then you became aware…that life is no poem of heroism.… And whoever wants more and has got it in him—the heroic and the beautiful, and the reverence for the great poets or for the saints—is a fool and a Don Quixote" (171).

The Steppenwolf deliberately chooses to live in respectable middle-class homes because he is fascinated by the ambience and because he enjoys emotionally and intellectually the contrast between his seemingly lonely existence and the middle-class aura of comfortable, congenial activity. A passage from the German Romantic poet Novalis captures the philosophical undertone of the Steppenwolf's emotional-spiritual suffering: "A man should be proud of suffering. All suffering is a reminder of our high estate." The Steppenwolf ultimately vanishes, leaving behind only his manuscript. The narrator saves the Steppenwolf's manuscript not only because he was somewhat acquainted with this remarkably distinctive individual with a genius for suffering who boarded with his aunt, but also because he sees it as a personally and socially revealing document of contemporary significance.

In reflecting on his youth, Haller remarks that he used to love the dark evenings of late autumn and winter for the moods of melancholy which they offered his poetically sensitive soul. He also mentions his love for music, for the kind of music which reveals the presence of a divine world. Haller's experience of a concert of lovely, old music represents for him a transitory enchanted moment of emotional and spiritual vitality. This music opens for him the door to another world where he felt a sense of heaven and the presence of the divine. Haller's search for such enchanted moments, such divinely epiphanic moments, makes him less able or even unable to genuinely appreciate the fleeting entertainments and ephemeral pleasures of everyday existence.

It is interesting that Harry Haller, the Steppenwolf, observes the sign for the magic theater for the first time after reflecting upon his solitude, which has an aura of spatial expansiveness, timelessness, and profound tranquility, as if fate were intervening to affirm or to engage in external reality the images, thoughts, or inclinations developing in his imagination. It is also noteworthy that the old stone wall upon which the sign for the magic theater eventually appears is initially described as a quiet and peaceful space beyond the commotion of everyday mortality (a space analogous to the space of eternity). As the persona of Walt Whitman's "Song of Myself," the Steppenwolf in the magic theater senses that he is august, that he does not need to vindicate his spirit, for he has known the amplitude of time. Like Whitman's persona, the Steppenwolf signifies a cosmos endlessly unfolding, who laughs at dissolution, at the elasticity of time. Yet, the Steppenwolf does not quite attain the powerful self-assurance of Whitman's persona who can claim that he is deathless and that the converging objects of the universe perpetually flow to him.

In contemplating the Immortals the Steppenwolf explores the abyss of the self with an intensity reminiscent of the Nietzschean strategy of self-overcoming. Such a strategy of overcoming is related to Hesse's notion of "magical thinking" which Theodore Ziolkowski defines as "Hesse's somewhat romantic term for the act of mental projection that permits us to escape the sphere of seeming polarities: it is a spiritual revaluation of life, proceeding from an uncompromising examination of the chaos in our own souls" (Hesse, *My Belief* xi). Ziolkowski proceeds to say insightfully that "'magical thinking' implies the acknowledgment of a meaningful totality beyond chaos, for chaos is 'chaotic' only from the standpoint of conventional concepts of order" (Hesse, *My Belief* xi).

In one of the most important passages of the novel the following statement is given from the Steppenwolf treatise: "And these men, for whom life has no repose, live at times in their rare moments of happiness with such strength and indescribable beauty, the spray of their moment's happiness is flung so high and dazzlingly over the wide sea of suffering, that the light of it, spreading its radiance, touches others too with its enchantment" (51). One might make the same statement about various protagonists discussed in this book, especially Tony Buddenbrook, Tonio Kröger, Hans Castorp, Sebastian Flyte, and Hugh Conway. Such a capacity is also seen in the character of Gatsby in Fitzgerald's *The Great Gatsby*, for his luminescent happiness, although rare and transient, does effect the lives of others around him.

The possibility of finding peace, the peace of the inner soul, depends upon the capacity of the individual to fulfill the challenge and the promise of the richness of the self and to achieve the realization and internalization of a unified vision of inheritances and potentialities. This issue is addressed in the passage where the Steppenwolf is reminded that he will have to encompass more and more of the world into his painfully expanded soul if he is to attain a sense of peace. Every significant individual, and especially the Buddha, has realized this: "The return into the All, the dissolution of painful individuation, the reunion with God means the expansion of the soul until it is able once more to embrace the All" (73).

Eternity (and sometimes even an epiphanic moment of eternity) is the realm where the dimensions of the self may be unified in a dynamic whole. In the most significant appreciation and interpretation of eternity in the entire novel Hermine, who, in the tradition of Lisabeta Ivanovna in Thomas Mann's *Tonio Kröger*, is a more effective proponent of the universal importance of the thematic focus than the implied or presumed protagonist himself, describes the "kingdom of truth" not only as that domain which the pious call "the kingdom of God" (174) but also as the realm of "eternity at the back of time" (174). Hermine proceeds to elaborate on the importance of this kingdom: "The music of Mozart belongs there and the poetry of your great poets. The saints, too, belong there, who have worked wonders and suffered martyrdom and given a great example to men" (174). Hermine concludes this remarkable statement by saying that "the image of every true act, the strength of every true feeling, belongs to eternity just as much, even though no one knows of it or sees it or records it or hands it down to posterity. In eternity there is no posterity" (174).

As he develops his own capacities for self-development and as he aspires more sensitively to appreciate the realm of the Immortals, Harry Haller also understands the importance of Goethe's laughter, the laughter of the Immortals: "It was a laughter without an object. It was simply light and lucidity. It was that which is left over when a true man has passed through all the sufferings, vices, mistakes, passions, and misunderstandings of men and got through to eternity and the world of space" (176).

Eternity is then further described as "nothing else than the redemption of time, its return to innocence, so to speak, and its transformation again into space" (176).

This is the crucial sense of space that the Steppenwolf yearns for. Such a spatial domain exists beyond the frailties and vicissitudes of everyday mortality—it is a space pervaded by the atmosphere and ambience of eternity and eternal serenity. In the following paragraph, where the Steppenwolf reflects on the intellectual consanguinity between himself and Hermine and ponders the timeless space of the Immortals, passages of the music of Mozart and Bach come into his mind. As the Steppenwolf considers that this music is characterized by and permeated by a crystalline eternity and "cool starry brightness" (177), he concludes that in this music "there was a feeling as of time frozen into space, and above it...superhuman serenity, an eternal, divine laughter" (177). The Steppenwolf, hearing the laughter of the Immortals, is inspired to write about them. In the poem the Steppenwolf affirms the vitality of the realm of the Immortals in contrast to the transience and disorder of the world of everyday mortality. The special sense of space which the Steppenwolf experiences in the magic theater is similar in spirit to the inner sanctum of Ritter Gluck's room in E. T. A. Hoffmann's "Ritter Gluck," for this is a secluded sanctuary beyond the exigencies of the world of everyday mortality.

After the prolonged dance episode Harry, the Steppenwolf, is invited by Pablo to a special entertainment. Pablo prefaces the experience by saying to the Steppenwolf that his endeavor to discover a more congenial reality, "a world beyond time," is actually a journey into the self. The other reality for which the Steppenwolf longs exists only within himself. Pablo claims that all he can do for the Steppenwolf is to make his own inner world visible. The profound exploration of the self will enable the Steppenwolf to rejuvenate himself emotionally, intellectually, and spiritually as he discovers a special place of eternal vitality and abundant serenity where genuine music, joy, and the soul do matter immensely.

The smile of Jay Gatsby in F. Scott Fitzgerald's *The Great Gatsby* is similar in spirit to the laughter of the Immortals in Hesse's *Der Steppenwolf.* Gatsby, like the Immortals, possesses a solitary grandeur, a noble isolation, a mythological vitality, and an appreciation of the enchanted moment, whether timeless or seemingly timeless. Gatsby's smile of "eternal reassurance" (52) and his contentment to be alone in the world of everyday mortality which takes advantage of his generosity without truly making an attempt to appreciate him are qualities which he shares with the Immortals. A. E. Dyson in his essay "*The Great Gatsby*: Thirty-Six Years After" emphasizes that Gatsby views the world of everyday mortality around him with "benevolent detachment" (118). Such a capacity for "benevolent detachment" is another quality which enhances Gatsby's mythological vitality. As impressive as Gatsby's smile appears to be, it derives its potency to a considerable extent from the aura of the transitory enchanted moment. Nick Carraway is aware of the fact that this smile, like the entertainment at Gatsby's exuberant parties, reveals a transient radiance which is not sustained. Gatsby's enchanted moment—his attempt to revitalize the aura of his congenial past with Daisy—is grounded in a special space, in the context of his mansion. Gatsby's lavish house is the emotional and aesthetic source of his attempt to rejuvenate his past and to establish a personal reconnection with Daisy.

In chapter three of the novel the description of the lavish and exuberant summer parties at Gatsby's house suggests the presence of a mansion and grounds of considerable extent. The fact that very few of the many guests are formally invited to Gatsby's parties suggests that the house and Gatsby's aura have the power to attract and implies an impersonality to these affairs which may contribute to the mythical significance of his character. That Gatsby appears physically in the novel, even sitting at the same table with Nick and Jordan, without Nick being aware of his identity, reinforces the mythical presence of his host. That Gatsby chooses his words carefully could imply that he is not instinctively at ease and tries to appear to be more intelligent or thoughtful than he really is. Or, such linguistic attentiveness could parallel Gatsby's choice of architectural nuances in the creation of his house—Gatsby is merely being careful with the selection of words as he is with the arrangement of the architectural features of his mansion because he has a fine aesthetic sensibility. In chapter four when Gatsby tells Nick select aspects and events of his past, this could also suggest that Gatsby is careful about what he says and does for he wants to present a vital public image of himself and make a good impression in the public arena— for he instinctively feels that Daisy would be impressed and appreciative of such a positive appearance. Perhaps Gatsby also does this because he wants to imply that he has a capacity to shape or influence the creation of his public image and the awareness which society has or develops of him.

While the mansion with its architectural diversity could be said to symbolize Gatsby's cosmopolitan interests (which at times do seem rather parochial) it is noteworthy that Gatsby purchased the house not primarily for its architectural beauty but because of its proximity to Daisy. In explaining this to Nick at the end of chapter four Jordan also says that Gatsby would like Nick to invite Daisy to his house so he can meet her there. That Jordan also states that Gatsby told her that he would like to show Daisy his house is important because it suggests that he does admire its architectural dynamism and its splendor. Gatsby hopes not only that Daisy will be impressed by the loveliness of the house and by the ambience of wealth which the house exemplifies but also that the aura of richness which the house possesses and exudes will revitalize the past consanguinity between them, which had been considerably diminished and undermined, at least from the perspective of Daisy's family, by the fact that he was not her socioeconomic equal.

The rapture of the "transitory enchanted moment" is especially vivid in the encounter of Daisy and Gatsby at Nick's house, the emotional power and intensity of which is captured effectively in the following passage: "They were sitting at either end of the couch, looking at each other...there was a change in Gatsby that was simply confounding. He literally glowed; without a word or a gesture of exultation a new well-being radiated from him and filled the little room" (94). The success of this meeting is affirmed by the fact that Gatsby "literally glowed" (94) and that Daisy reveals an "unexpected joy" (94). Gatsby's feeling of considerable happiness, affirmed in the radiance with which he illuminates his immediate environment, is intensified when he shows Daisy his lovely house and when he observes that she genuinely admires its aesthetic richness.

Gatsby aims to create a prolonged and sustained enchanted moment in the ambience of his house, saying that he keeps "it always full of interesting people...celebrated people" (96). That Gatsby says that he aspires to have the interesting people in the house during the day and the night might suggest that he is instinctively lonely and needs the company to entertain or to distract himself. Or this might imply that Gatsby invites such celebrated people to the house in the hope that their presence, and their concomitant fame or importance, will attract Daisy. For Gatsby's primary aim in the purchase of this house and in the generous offering of numerous parties is to attract Daisy and to prove to her that he now has the wealth which was absent in the past and prevented her family from allowing any previous connection between them. Even though Gatsby acquires and develops his opulent mansion not primarily for the architectural beauty of the interior or of the exterior but rather to nurture and enhance his own personal myth and his aura of accomplishment and to attract the attention of Daisy, the house does have various interesting features. For example, Gatsby's house does possess a cosmopolitan and international aura encompassing different epochs, from "the feudal silhouette against the sky" (96) and the "Marie Antoinette music-rooms and Restoration salons" (96) to the "Merton College Library door" and the collection of fashionable clothes from England. The pleasant fusion of these aspects from different time periods implies that the mansion has the capacity to transcend spatial and temporal limitations. There is a timeless grandeur permeating Gatsby's house which seems to fulfill and strengthen the potential for mythological vitality in Gatsby's own character.

Daisy, in her tour of the marble house and the property, admires and is genuinely impressed not only by the mansion's exterior and the gardens but also by the loveliness and spatial expansiveness of the interior. That the interior of this splendid house possesses and is pervaded by an extensive spaciousness is affirmed in the description of the wandering journey which Daisy, Gatsby, and Nick undergo in their attempt to reach Gatsby's private apartment. They pass not only through the music rooms and salons but also through "period bedrooms swathed in rose and lavender silk and vivid with new flowers, through dressing rooms and poolrooms, and bathrooms with sunken baths" (96).

Even though Gatsby's dream of reestablishing a personal connection with Daisy does not succeed as he wishes it to, his attempt to revitalize the aesthetic and emotional dimensions of that dream and make it a reality against seemingly insurmountable odds gives him a heroic stature of mythical significance. Gatsby's dream possesses the same romantic longing and hope as the fragile dream of the early Dutch settlers as they confronted a new world. The romantic hopefulness and innocent optimism which permeates Gatsby's approach to life and to revitalizing his past with Daisy contributes, perhaps to some extent even unknowingly and silently, to the greatness of his house. For Gatsby's mansion, in its idiosyncrasies and intricacies, signifies and symbolizes his soul and his spirit. Gatsby, as most characters or figures of mythological vitality, creates and sustains his own myth and mythical significance to a considerable extent. As Nick says: "The truth was that Jay Gatsby, of West Egg, Long Island, sprang from his Platonic conception of himself" (104). This conception is developed, as Thomas J. Stavola emphasizes in *Scott Fitzgerald: Crisis in an American Identity*, from Gatsby's youth when he decided to create a new identity for himself: "With this decision Jimmie Gatz had already stripped himself of the past, the roots and history of his identity and given birth to a new romantic self, Jay Gatsby" (129).

The importance of Daisy's admiring presence in this scenario is confirmed in the statement that Gatsby seems to view or reconsider his possessions in the house in the light of her response to them. The wonder Gatsby feels in the presence of Daisy appears to culminate in his display of his clothes which he receives from England. Daisy's response to the very beautiful shirts which Gatsby owns is especially important because it implies and is infused with a sense of sadness that she did not wait, or more particularly that her family did not allow her to wait, for Gatsby to acquire this wealth. That Daisy did once have strong romantic feelings for Gatsby is affirmed even more vitally in her statement to him as she observes the billow of clouds in the west after the rain: "I'd like to just get one of those pink clouds and put you in it and push you around" (99). That Daisy never says something so romantic or sentimental to Tom implies that she did once have a deeper emotional attachment to Gatsby than to anyone else and that if it were not for Gatsby's lack of material wealth she might or would have married him.

One might argue that Gatsby's transitory enchanted moments—for example, the extravagant parties at his house or his attempt to revive his romance with Daisy—are most effectively illuminated by an inner light of profound love for Daisy, an inner radiance of Promethean proportions. Yet, they are also illuminated by an external light of Gatsby's creation. Of such light Dan Seiters writes effectively in *Image Patterns in the Novels of F. Scott Fitzgerald*: "Gatsby creates much light, but never matches the sun; he cannot really see his creation, cannot judge it" (69). Perhaps the light of Gatsby, as an "ecstatic patron of recurrent light" (94), is too centripetal and hermetic to revitalize the past and to transform reality. Yet, one might also say that such light is so hermetically powerful that it creates an enchanted moment of Gatsbyesque romantic hope which is too profoundly vital to be transitory. Gatsby has the aura, although not the mythological power, of an Apollo, for he is the "god of light" in this novel as he attempts to illuminate the world around him. When Gatsby is portrayed in chapter five of the novel as smiling "like an ecstatic patron of recurrent light" (94) as he communicates the news to Daisy that it has stopped raining, Gatsby serves not only as an individual who disseminates information about the light but also as a bringer of light, for the statement which he makes to Daisy gives her considerable joy.

Gatsby's quest for the transitory enchanted moment is not merely self-directed. He does want to give meaning to the lives of others and he aims to preserve a life-philosophy of hopeful romanticism which may be inspirational for others. Of Gatsby's romanticism Thomas J. Stavola writes: "Gatsby's romanticism, a product of the spirit, is relentlessly optimistic in its quest for fulfillment within a materialistic society that denies the power of the spirit and offers instead the...exhaustible, possibilities of success, money, and romance" (130). Gatsby may only experience the enchanted moment of his re-encounter or reunion with Daisy as transitory, but the strength and the profundity of his romantic vision will persevere. Of this vision Stavola writes: "It manifests itself in the rare quality of his faith in the goodness of creation and in his ultimate, although only partially recognized, refusal to compromise with the 'colossal vitality' of his dream" (130).

Of Gatsby's mythical aura Marius Bewley writes in "Scott Fitzgerald's Criticism of America" that he is "an embodiment...of that conflict between illusion and reality at the heart of American life; he is an heroic personification of the American romantic hero, the true heir of the American dream" (14). Bewley proceeds to say thoughtfully as a complement to Nick's statement that there was something "gorgeous" about his friend that Gatsby displays or wears such beauty "with an archetypal American elegance" (14). One might also say that the mythical aura of Gatsby is developed and sustained in his approach to Daisy. Marius Bewley effectively says that for "Gatsby, Daisy is only the promise of fulfillment that lies beyond the green light that burns all night on her dock" (20). The mythical capacity of Gatsby is affirmed in his belief in and devotion to the green light. Although the vitality of the green light is somewhat diminished when Daisy is actually in Gatsby's presence and when they speak about it together as they look out of a window of his mansion towards her home across the bay, this is a symbol of his dynamic and innocent hope that he can recapture the spirit of the congenial past.

An important feature of Gatsby's personal myth, and the vision or the illusion which complements it, is the mansion which is as impressive and splendid in its prime as it is ghostly and ephemeral in its loneliness. The large house, despite its emptiness at the end of the narrative, remains a significant feature of Gatsby's mythical vitality. For example, at the beginning of chapter five when Nick returns to West Egg one night everything seems to be ablaze—the source of this potent luminescence is Gatsby's house which is completely and ostentatiously lit up. Dan Seiters describes the lights of Gatsby's house as "artificial" (69) and seemingly transient, for the power of nature can readily "destroy artificial light" (69). The mansion with its cosmopolitan inclinations and its luminescence, which may appear either potent or fleeting depending on the time of day and the perceptual capacities of the individuals in its ambience, signifies a complement to Gatsby's own existence—the splendid house is the architectural and material manifestation of Gatsby's aesthetic and emotional essence.

Nick's vision of the old island "that flowered once for Dutch sailors' eyes—a fresh, green breast of the new world" (189) leads him to reflect on the comparable sense of wonder which Gatsby felt when he first noticed the green light on Daisy's dock. The enchanted moment, whether thoroughly or just partially transitory, which Nick experiences at the end of the narrative reveals his appreciation of and his vision of the sublime. Nick's sense of the sublime, which is intimately related to his experience of the enchanted moment, seems to concur with that of Longinus, whose ideas on the sublime are discussed effectively in Richard Payne Knight's *Analytical Inquiry into the Principles of Taste*: " The effect of the sublime is to lift up the soul; to exalt it into ecstasy; so that, participating, as it were, of the splendors of the divinity, it becomes filled with joy and exultation; as if it had itself conceived the lofty sentiments which it heard" (329). Nick is the heir to Gatsby's romanticism—he will take Gatsby's capacity for wonder back with him to his home domain in the mid-west and share this with others.

The mythical vitality of Gatsby's creative passion elevates his visionary dream (or dreamlike vision) to an existential level where it can never be touched or encroached upon by reality. One might claim that Gatsby is ultimately triumphant as Narcissus succeeds finally in Ovid's *Metamorphoses* in becoming a perennial, yellow-white symbol of mythological vitality and eternity. Although Gatsby dies on the altar of everyday mortality, a victim of a world which does not appreciate the profundity of his luminescent dream and his Apollonian capacity, his creative consecration to a romantic vision of light and hope will not only persevere but will prevail.

In the conclusion so far I have discussed several important architectural contexts—an inner sanctum in a public architectural space in Heinrich Böll's *Billard um halbzehn*, an inner sanctum in a private architectural space (which has the appearance of being in a public environment but which is really accessible only to a select few) in Hermann Hesse's *Der Steppenwolf*, a relatively small house which is given a stature of splendor by the noble spirit of the residents (Siddhartha and Vasudeva in Hesse's *Siddhartha*), and a grand house which is not truly appreciated for itself but which is used for a purpose beyond itself (namely, Gatsby's attempt to attract the attention of Daisy in Fitzgerald's *The Great Gatsby*) and which seems destined because of fate or existential circumstances to be a symbol of loneliness and transience.

Other interesting mansions and country estates in twentieth-century European literature which seem destined by fate or circumstances to exemplify a melancholy commentary on the isolation and ephemeral nature of the human condition while depicting an aura of architectural beauty are portrayed in Anton Chekhov's *Vishnevyi sad, The Cherry Orchard* (1904) and Boris Pasternak's *Doktor Zhivago, Doctor Zhivago* (1957).

In chapter one of Part One of Pasternak's *Doktor Zhivago, Doctor Zhivago*, Yurii Zhivago, after the tragic death of his mother, travels with his Uncle Nikolai to Duplyanka, the estate of Kologrivov, a silk manufacturer and patron of the arts. Yurii, or Yura, is allowed to wander around the lovely estate with carefree ease. As he listens to the beautiful sounds of nature in the meadows he always thinks that he hears his mother's voice. Feeling very sad and lonely in this isolated and inspirational place, Yurii says a prayer for his mother: "Angel of God, my holy guardian, keep me firmly on the path of truth and tell Mother I'm all right, she's not to worry" (11–12). Yurii also prays that his mother has been accepted into heaven because she was such a good person.

In chapter two of Part One the house of the Gromeko family in Moscow, where Yurii is ultimately taken to be brought up, is depicted as an interesting architectural creation. The top floor contained the bedrooms, the schoolroom, the study and library of Alexander Alexandrovich, the boudoir of Anna Ivanovna, and the rooms of Tonia and Yurii. The ground floor was used for receptions and evenings of chamber music, for the Gromekos were very cultured and social. It is also noteworthy that the father of Alexander's wife, Anna Ivanovna, was an ironmaster and owned a great estate in the Urals, near Yuriatin.

In chapter three of Part One Lara is able to spend three years as a governess at the estate of the Kologrivov family to escape the anguish of her relationship with Komarovsky. It is noteworthy that Lara loves Duplyanka, the estate of the Kologrivov family, even more than they do, and that the family is aware of this fact. The countryside between the railroad station and the estate appeals deeply to Lara with its infinite silence, its fragrant aura, and its spatial expansiveness. She feels personally connected to and revitalized by this lovely natural space.

In chapter eight (in Part Two) of Pasternak's *Doktor Zhivago*, the Zhivago family, including Tonia's father, after a long, grueling, and perilous train journey from Moscow to the vicinity of Yuriatin, reach their ultimate goal, Varykino, the old Krueger country estate which no longer officially belongs to the Gromeko family but which is now state property. As they travel on the road from the train station to Varykino their "hearts were at peace" (267). Varykino, as Brideshead in *Brideshead Revisited*, signifies a house with an architectural history which also represents an extension, sometimes symbolic and sometimes literal, of the aesthetic, emotional, and intellectual life of one or more of the individuals associated with it. For example, both Yurii and Tonia seem at times to be very intimately attached to Varykino and its ambience. Initially, Varykino appears to represent a sanctuary for Yurii, Tonia, and their family away from the chaos of the city and away from the political disorder and social turbulence pervading the contemporary Russian society. They can be close to nature, partially farm the land, enjoy the quietude of the country, and entertain themselves with serene reading and conversation. Varykino, based on Pasternak's home at Peredelkino, seems to be a picturesque and idyllic space. Yet, the Zhivago family's problematic sociopolitical position, given the Krueger family background, is an underlying concern, the persistence of which is mitigated at least to some extent by the considerable assistance which they receive from such individuals as Mikulitsyn, Samdeviatov, and Evgraf. The pleasantly quiet and productive life which the Zhivago family enjoys and cherishes there for a short while is permanently disrupted when Yurii goes into nearby Yuriatin and meets Lara again. Thereafter, the lives of various important characters in the novel will never be the same; and the fleeting nature of joy and pleasure is also especially reaffirmed in events such as the sudden capture and conscription of Yurii as a medical worker by partisans to a distant location which has the consequence that he never sees Tonia and his first family again.

The return of Lara and Yurii to Varykino in chapter fourteen on a gray winter afternoon revives some of the magical quality of the splendid isolation which this house and estate had represented earlier in the novel. To avoid potentially painful memories and to enjoy more spaciousness, especially for Katia, Yurii and Lara decide to stay not in the annex where Yurii had once lived with Tonia but in the Mikulitsyn's house. After they have removed the padlock on the door and gained access to the interior of the house, they notice that the house has recently been partially used. That someone else, presumably an unknown intruder, has been for a time residing in part of this house diminishes the sense of refuge which might have been expected there, but is also very understandable, given the wartime conditions which permeate the region of Yuriatin. In any region of military conflict no house, as vital an example of splendid isolation as it might seem, is safe and secure. Although both Yurii and Lara are aware that their shared happiness in this house is limited and transient, Yurii's heart is at peace and he is even inspired to write various poems, especially about Lara. The serenity and happiness which Yurii, Lara, and Katia enjoy at Varykino for about two weeks is suddenly undermined by the appearance of Komarovsky who declares that Lara and her child must, for the sake of their safety, leave on the next train from Yuriatin going to the Far East. The abruptness of Lara's departure is an extremely sad event, for she and Yurii are not even able to say a proper farewell to one another. As the late afternoon rays of the setting winter sun fall upon the scene, the aura of refuge in this once serene place is vanquished forever for Zhivago, reinforced by his poignant monologue: "Farewell, Lara, until we meet in the next world, farewell, my love, my…everlasting joy. I'll never see you again" (451).

In Chekhov's *Vishnevyi sad, The Cherry Orchard* (1904) the ancestral estate of Lyubov Ranevskaya is a lovely and an inspirational place. One of the most vital, if not the most vital, features and highlights of the estate is the beloved and famous cherry orchard which symbolizes for Lyubov the innocence and happiness of her childhood and youth. However, because of considerable financial problems the estate and the cherry orchard will have to be sold. Lopakhin's plan to save the estate by dividing it into summer cottages will inevitably cause the destruction of the cherry orchard. If Varya were to marry Lopakhin or if the family's great aunt in Yaroslavl were to be asked to provide financial support, then possibly the cherry orchard could be saved. However, neither of these plans comes to fruition. Lopakhin, the self-made business-man who has risen from serfdom to wealth, does purchase the estate and proceeds to cut down the cherry orchard. Ultimately, the melancholy departure of Lyubov and her family members signals the end of the estate, the demise of the cherry orchard, and the cessation of a way of life and of a sense of sanctuary. The sound of axes cut-ting down the orchard at the end signifies that the beauty which this country estate once represented is now thoroughly undermined. And yet, there is the sense that Lyubov, and perhaps even other of her family members, loved the country estate and the cherry orchard so dearly and so devotedly that the memory of this beautiful space will remain with them forever. As in Joseph von Eichendorff's "Abschied," wherever they will be in the world, whether in a rural, suburban, or urban setting, when they reflect upon the past beauty of the cherry orchard and the country estate, their hearts and souls will be uplifted and rejuvenated. Having internalized the experience of such a lovely place, Lyubov and the other family members who truly appreciated the cherry orchard will carry a congenial image of this delightful space with them in their hearts forever.

It is noteworthy that Chekhov, when living on a country estate outside Moscow in the latter phase of his life, became interested in gardening and planted his own cherry orchard, perhaps reminiscent of a pleasant cherry orchard which he had expe-rienced in his youth. After Chekhov moved to Yalta for health reasons he was very disappointed to learn that the person who had bought his former estate had destroyed much of the cherry orchard. Chekhov's drama was certainly inspired by such an inci-dent as well as by his deep environmental awareness. Chekhov greatly admired the trees and the forests and showed a strong appreciation for the preservation of the natural environment, reflected not only in this drama but also in the character of Dr. Astrov in *Uncle Vanya*.

There are also various architecturally interesting and innovative houses in litera-ture from the eighteenth century to the present which are depicted and developed as haunted, whether partially or thoroughly, temporarily or permanently. Notable exam-ples of such haunted houses in literature from the eighteenth century to the present are described in *The Castle of Otranto* by Horace Walpole, *The Mysteries of Udolpho* by Ann Radcliffe, *The House of the Seven Gables* by Nathaniel Hawthorne, *The Turn of the Screw* by Henry James, and *Rebecca* by Daphne du Maurier. Other interesting houses in literature which have an aura of being haunted are Misselthwaite Manor in Frances H. Burnett's *The Secret Garden* and the Professor's house in *The Lion, the Witch, and the Wardrobe* by C. S. Lewis. The aesthetically distinctive house which signifies the thematic focus of Hawthorne's *The House of the Seven Gables* possesses a rich history and numerous rooms containing personal and family mysteries. Misselthwaite Manor in *The Secret Garden* is an ancient house several hundred years old with an extensive array of rooms, many of which are presented as rather dark, gloomy, and concealing various secrets. The Professor's house in *The Lion, the Witch, and the Wardrobe* is described as containing not only numerous unexpected places and crannies but also many spacious and extensive rooms.

Another house in twentieth century European literature which possesses a rich family history (at least from the perspective of one side of the family) is Howards End in E. M. Forster's *Howards End*. It is especially interesting that Howards End is a recreated vision of Forster's childhood home, Rooksnest, in Stevenage, Hertfordshire which he loved. This lovely house, surrounded by a congenial natural ambience which included a pond and a meadow, represented a paradise for Forster until the age of 14 when he and his mother had to move to Tonbridge. One of the most salient features of the natural environment which Rooksnest and Howards End share is the presence of the wych-elm with its mythically vital potential.

In *Howards End* Mrs. Ruth Wilcox nurtures a profound love and appreciation for Howards End, a home which she has admired greatly for many years. Ruth Wilcox has the same kind of emotional and spiritual attachment to her beloved Howards End as Lyubov has to her ancestral estate in *The Cherry Orchard*. In chapter 10 of *Howards End* Ruth Wilcox wants to take Margaret Schlegel to see her cherished home not only because she sympathizes with Margaret's quiet and subtle lament that she will soon have to leave her London house, a house which she has known all her life, when the lease expires, but also because she senses that Margaret would instinctively appreciate it and would be able to describe the aura and aesthetic vitality of the house thoughtfully. Because of the passionate attachment of Ruth Wilcox to Howards End—expressed especially in her statement that if Howards End had been pulled down as was once planned, this destructive act would have killed her—she empathizes greatly with Margaret Schlegel's predicament and her awareness that she will inevitably have to leave her childhood home. Sadly, Mrs. Ruth Wilcox dies before she can show Margaret her beloved home and the lovely surrounding natural environment.

In chapter 23 as Margaret, as the fiancé of Henry Wilcox, visits Howards End she admires as if in a congenial vision the lilies, the tulips, the vine on the porch, and the fertility of the earth. Howards End, which was supposed to have been locked opens for her as the perilous hedge of briars in "Little Briar Rose" yields to the prince destined to encounter and fall in love with sleeping beauty after the interval of "a hundred years." Margaret does appear fated to have a personal and a profound connection to the special house which Ruth Wilcox loved so much. Although the interior of the house seems rather desolate Margaret is pleased with its sense of space and with the beauty of the natural environment which she observes from the perspective of the interior—as she looks out she sees not only the flowering cherries and plums in the garden but also the lovely meadow and the pines. Margaret especially appreciates the pleasant and quaint sense of space in the interior of the house.

That Margaret seems instinctively to belong in Howards End, that her presence in this house is exceedingly natural, is suggested not only by her spontaneous admiration of the beauty of the natural landscape around the house and by her appreciation of the idiosyncrasies of the interior space of the house but also by the fact that the house door, which was supposed to have been closed and which was thought to have been locked, opens at her touch. Moreover, Margaret's aesthetic and emotional sensibility seems perfectly suited for Howards End—she can even hear the heart of the house beating, which is a capacity only reserved for those individuals who are truly at one with their surroundings. It is also noteworthy that at the end of chapter 23 Miss Avery as she leaves the house says to Margaret that she has the same way of walking that Ruth Wilcox had—this is another indication of Margaret's consanguinity with the house and its aura.

In chapter 24 of *Howards End* as Margaret, having returned with Henry Wilcox to London, reflects on the exceptional house in the country which she has just visited, she revitalizes her awareness of and her appreciation of space which, as Forster says, "is the basis of all earthly beauty" (213). Margaret's experience of the beauty of Howards End has also given her a deep love of, or perhaps one might say has reaffirmed her instinctive love for, the natural landscape of England. Margaret also thinks about Henry's description of what he did financially and structurally to save the house and the surrounding farm from insolvency. Even though Henry saved Howards End "without fine feelings or deep insight" (214) and modernized it, the house and environs would seemingly not be appealing to the artistically inclined.

Margaret also reflects on the intimacy, the preternatural connectedness, of the wych-elm and the house thriving in the presence of each other. Each of these special entities, the house and the wych-elm, has its own mythology which contributes to and strengthens the vitality of the other. That Margaret mentions to Henry the story relating the importance of the pigs' teeth in the wych-elm, a tale told to her by Ruth Wilcox in London, is significant because it underscores her appreciation of the mythical capacities of the house and its natural ambience, qualities which are typically unappreciated by the supremely realistic and matter-of-fact Wilcoxes.

In chapter 33 of *Howards End* Margaret returns again by herself to the lovely house in the country. As Margaret reflects on the lives of the people who spend their lives in the country, in a relatively rural ambience, and on the beauty of nature in such an environment which has an aura of freedom inherent in it, she has a vision of the completeness of life which foreshadows the image of harmony at the end of the novel: "In these English farms, if anywhere, one might see life steadily and see it whole, group in one vision its transitoriness and its eternal youth, connect—connect without bitterness until all men are brothers" (281).

As Margaret walks with Miss Avery's niece to Howards End the vernal vitality of the hedge, of the celandines, of the primroses, and of the wild rose-bushes display a colorful exuberance of mythically dynamic proportions. At the house Margaret is astonished and even dismayed to find that so many of her family's personal belongings and items which were supposed to have been there only temporarily had been carefully unpacked and arranged. For example, the various items and objects from the library of the Schlegel family house in London have been arrayed in the hall at Howards End. Miss Avery not only asserts her belief that Howards End had been empty for long enough; she even declares that the house is Mrs. Wilcox's, more from a sense of tradition than from a desire to hurt Margaret with the implications of such a statement, and that Mrs. Wilcox would not wish the house to be uninhabited for any longer. Yet, I would say the reasoning of Miss Avery goes even deeper than that. For Miss Avery is, as was implied earlier in the novel, more intelligent than she seems outwardly—and she, as the symbolic spirit of the house after the death of Ruth Wilcox, knows intuitively that Margaret belongs in Howards End. So Miss Avery is trying to do everything she can to promote the presence of Margaret and her family at Howards End.

Margaret, despite her blossoming feeling of attachment to Howards End and despite the illumination of material and spiritual well-being which occurs as more curtains were opened and as more windows were opened to the spring, tries to clarify the situation by explaining to Miss Avery that she and Mr. Wilcox are not planning to reside at Howards End. They have decided instead to build a new home in Sussex which will soon contain Margaret's portion of the Schlegel family furniture. Miss Avery's response to this assertion is noteworthy, for she says with marked certainty and resoluteness to Margaret, calling her Mrs. Wilcox in the process, that she will be coming back to live at Howards End. Miss Avery, who represents a mortal manifestation of the spirit of the house, or one might say a manifestation of the spirit of the house in earthly and mortal form, verbalizes the aspiration, the hope, and the intention of the house. For Howards End, this extraordinary house with its close connection to nature, knows instinctively that Margaret belongs as a presence in it and in its mythical aura and wants to ensure that the world of everyday mortality does not interfere with this destiny. That the furniture of the Schlegels fits so well in Howards End affirms the notion that at least part of the Schlegel family is fated to live in this dwelling overlooking the delightful meadow.

In chapter 37 of *Howards End* when Margaret and Helen meet at the house through Henry's intrigue, Helen is of course disappointed that her sister would have succumbed to such a deception. Nevertheless, Helen is able to make a positive assertion about the house, saying that it feels very alive to her, even more so than when it contained the personal items of the Wilcoxes. As the conversation continues Margaret says to Helen that Howards End seems to have special powers for it "kills what is dreadful and makes what is beautiful live" (314). Helen, who is beginning to feel the enchantment of the place, agrees with her sister.

However, the negative and destructive events of the next several chapters—the painful conversation in chapter 38 in which Margaret asks Henry to allow Helen to sleep in Howards End for one night and his resolute refusal, the death of Leonard Bast at Howards End in chapter 41, the sense in chapter 43 that Helen will leave England and return to Germany and that Margaret will leave Henry—appear to forecast a desolate future for Howards End. Yet, when Charles is sentenced to three years' imprisonment for his role in Leonard's death, Henry Wilcox collapses emotionally—Margaret with her very compassionate heart and soul cannot forsake Henry and decides to take him to Howards End for a period of revitalization.

In chapter 44 Howards End and its aura have created an environment of harmony and peacefulness where the troubled soul can reenergize itself and recuperate from the dissensions and problems of everyday mortality. Fourteen months have passed and Margaret is still at Howards End with Henry—moreover, Helen and her child now seem permanently ensconced at the house. Helen praises Margaret for her heroic life, saying that she was the one who created a new life and a home for her and her child. Both Margaret and Helen have come to love Howards End and believe that it will be their permanent home. The closeness of the house to nature is emphasized in the suggestion that each year the residents of Howards End will appreciate the cyclicality of the surrounding natural environment, for example, the presence of the little red poppies in the wheat every July and the cutting of the wheat every August.

At the end of the novel Henry Wilcox proclaims to his children after a family discussion that he is bequeathing Howards End to his wife Margaret, who at her death will leave the house to her nephew, Helen's child. Through a seemingly errant remark by Dolly, Margaret learns that Ruth Wilcox had originally left her Howards End and that the family had disregarded Ruth's statement because they considered it to be unreliable. Margaret, whose generosity of spirit shines throughout the novel, responds to Henry's query saying that nothing wrong has been done. Destiny, the destiny of a compassionate, sensitive heart, has triumphed over greed and selfishness. Margaret and Helen, through her sisterly bond to Margaret, are fated to be the residents and owners of Howards End. This narrative exemplifies the idea that a house and an individual not initially residing there (but who has an instinctive appreciation for a house of ancestral or historical importance for a family, a house of mythical and transformational possibilities, a house closely connected to its ambience, a house which may illuminate the world around it) can be destined for one another. Even in London Ruth Wilcox sensed Margaret's capacity to appreciate a house such as Howards End. As Ruth Wilcox before her, Margaret not only loves Howards End but also signifies an integral dimension of the spirit of the house, a vital continuation of the spirit of the house, which is so filled with light and harmony and which exists in a resplendent emotional and physical communion with its surrounding natural environment. That Helen's child is seen at the end of the novel as playing congenially in the fields is also important because the child's father, Leonard, had said earlier in the novel that his ancestors were agricultural laborers—it is as if the ancestral voices have been fulfilled and the connection with the land which had previously existed in his family has now been revitalized.

E. M. Forster's *A Room with a View* contains multiple spaces of sanctuary, for example, the delightful house and surrounding land of the Honeychurch family in England and various places in Italy which signify a room or a location of special atmospheric qualities and panorama. The sense of sanctuary in this novel is not hermetic, but more orphic and outward-directed, suggesting an inevitable and potentially constructive connection between a sanctuary-like setting and the immediate environment. The house of the Honeychurch family and the surrounding natural environment appear to exist in a state of perpetually vital union and continuity—at times, especially in the summer, the garden and the property immediately encompassing the house seem to signify an extension of the house into the lovely Surrey landscape.

In Virginia Woolf's *To the Lighthouse* the summer home of the Ramsay family is an architecturally interesting residence which is rather physically isolated and represents a sanctuary in the first part of the novel, "The Window." This is a time of relatively congenial and pleasant events for various members of the family and for several guests. In the second section of the novel, "Time Passes," the sense of sanctuary which had been consistently sustained in the first part, is undermined with the death of Mrs. Ramsay, Andrew, and Prue. Moreover, the summer home falls into decay and is unused for a number of years. In chapter IX of this section of the narrative the house is described as deserted, "left like a shell on a sandhill to fill with dry salt grains now that life had left it" (137). In the third section of the novel, "The Lighthouse," the sanctuary-like atmosphere of the summer home is to some extent restored, although it can never be fully revived, because of the tragic deaths of several members of the Ramsay family in the preceding section. The brushstroke of Lily Briscoe on her canvas at the end of the novel, which signifies the completion of her work, could imply that a goal which had existed in the minds of several individuals present in the first section of the narrative had finally been achieved or it could suggest that the sanctuary-like atmosphere of the summer home has the potential to be revitalized, that artistic creativity may regenerate the soul of this secluded natural setting which has been ravaged by the vicissitudes of mortality.

Edith Wharton's *The Age of Innocence* discusses interesting and fascinating architectural spaces in an urban environment. Mrs. Mingott, who is depicted as governing over one end of Fifth Avenue, created an imposing house which combined family heirlooms with the furniture of the Second Empire. She exemplifies the aspirations of one of the two prominent groups of the New York society of the time, the Mingotts and the Mansons, who were interested primarily in good food, expensive clothes, and money. The house of Mrs. Mingott contrasts notably with other old family houses of the time in University Place and lower Fifth Avenue which contained "a grim harmony of cabbage-rose-garlanded carpets, rosewood consoles, round-arched fireplaces with black marble mantels, and immense glazed bookcases of mahogany" (27). The other group dominating the contemporary New York society was that of the Archer—Newland—van der Luyden families who were typically more interested in aesthetic and intellectual pursuits such as travel, horticulture, and good reading. Mrs. Archer, a widow, lived with her son and daughter in congenial circumstances in West Twenty-eighth Street.

When the Lovell Mingotts sent out invitations to many people in New York society for a "formal dinner" to meet the Countess Olenska, sadly, most refused because of their perception of the questionable status of the countess. The Mingotts, although very disappointed, decided to respond constructively by involving one of the most prominent and aristocratic families in New York. One of the very few aristocratic families in New York society, that is, one of the very few families who could claim a genuine aristocratic origin, was the van der Luydens, who were not only descendants of the first Dutch governor of Manhattan but who were also related to members of the British and French aristocracy. Mr. and Mrs. Van der Luyden spent most of their time at Skuytercliff, their estate along the Hudson, or at Trevenna, their mansion in Maryland, but they also owned an impressive house on Madison Avenue. The solemnity of the interior of this house is symbolized by the "high-ceilinged, white-walled...drawing-room, with the pale brocaded armchairs...and the gauze still veiling the ormolu mantel ornaments and the beautiful old carved frame of Gainsborough's 'Lady Angelica du Lac'" (52). Mr. and Mrs. van der Luyden wield an absolute power and an absolute authority in this New York society—they are depicted as being "the arbiters of fashion, the Court of Last Appeal" (56), although, interestingly, they prefer the solitude of their country estate along the Hudson to the hectic dynamism of the city. One might describe them as possessing such absolute authority without really desiring to use it frequently or domineeringly. The van der Luydens gracefully resolve this current family crisis by saying that they will include the Countess Olenska among their guests to meet their important relative, the Duke of St. Austrey, who is arriving soon. The importance of this event for the Duke is reinforced by the fact that the van der Luydens use their best china and silverware, from the du Lac Sevres and the Trevenna George II plate to the van der Luyden "Lowestoft" and the Dagonet Crown Derby.

Even though Newland Archer marries May Weyland, he preserves a profound love for and attachment to the Countess Olenska. In chapter 18 of the novel Newland and Ellen, the Countess Olenska, reveal their strong feelings for one another. However, Ellen sacrifices her own potential happiness by not interfering with the plans for Newland and May to get married. Ellen even says to Newland that she cannot love him unless she gives him up, suggesting a deep love without physical passion. In chapter 26 it is evident that Newland's emotional and spiritual life is centered around Ellen, although he very rarely sees her. She represents an inner sanctum for him: "...he had built up within himself a kind of sanctuary in which she throned among his secret thoughts and longings. Little by little it became the scene of his real life, of his only rational activities; thither he brought the books he read, the ideas and feelings which nourished him, his judgments and his visions" (262). As this inner sanctum of emotional and intellectual luminescence becomes increasingly important to him, so Newland becomes relatively indifferent to various demands and expectations of the world of everyday mortality. The promise of Ellen's statement in chapter 29, after Newland's expression of his hope that they can leave the current, oppressive society for a world where they can be "the whole of life to each other" (290), that they can only be emotionally near to one another if they remain at a distance from each other is fulfilled at the end of the novel when Newland, sitting on a bench outside the building in Paris where Ellen lives, decides not to go to see her. Newland even says to himself that the interior scene of her apartment is more real to him in the comfort of his vision of it than if he were there in person. This is an ultimate affirmation of the inner life, the inner sanctum of emotional and intellectual hope and possibilities, which he has devoted to Ellen Olenska. Newland and Ellen will always love each other, for they value the integrity and loveliness of their inner beings, of their souls which appreciate art, beauty, and culture, and which feel the allure of the material world of everyday mortality "with all its golden hands" (172) and yet will resist its deceptive and cruel encroachment.

In more contemporary, late twentieth-century literature a house or special architectural space may also generate the aesthetic spirit of and complement the beauty of the surrounding natural environment. For example, in Hugo Walter's "An Edelweiss Castle" the castle is characterized by and infused with an innate dynamism which creates a beautiful ambience:

> Ambrosia-gardens of forsythia-laden, sapphire-astered
> Light scatter silver-acropolis, damask-porcelain clouds
> Across soft-mitred, amaryllis-madrigal winds revealing
> An edelweiss-sibylline, asphodel-burgeoning castle
> Of sunset-eaved, Chatsworth-haloed silences where white-
> Saffron petals of mandolin-vaned repose soar
> Into the afternoon haze in vernal-slender filaments
> Of seraphic-murmuring light, silent menageries of virginal
> Eloquence shaping lily-marrowed, willow-translucent
> Ecstasies of amber-pealing, anemone-glistening rainbows,
> A castle of lilac-moist, Turner-effulgent arbors spilling
> Hyacinth-andromeda diffusions of iris-gloaming,
> Diamond-lintelled light into divine pools
> Of narcissus-blossoming, sunflower-living dreams.

Such a castle estate encompasses various important historical features of garden and landscape design from the Renaissance and the Baroque to the eighteenth century: from Alberti's Renaissance notion, influenced by Vitruvius, that a beautiful form is present when the parts are proportionate to the whole and that the ideal country estate is a place of contemplation and serenity where the lovely aspects of nature can be enjoyed to the delightful and spacious water gardens of the Villa d'Este at Tivoli to the secluded beauty of the Palazzo Farnese, Caprarola; from the expansive Apollonian luminescence of Louis XIV's Versailles to the glorious Schloss Charlottenburg in Berlin to the magnificent English country estates of Blenheim, Stowe with its "picturesque" design, Stourhead, which signifies an Arcadian harmony of the worlds of nature and humankind and exemplifies the aesthetic spirit of a Claude Lorrain painting, typically thought to be *Aeneas on Delos*, and Castle Howard, which, according to Horace Walpole, displayed "the grandest scenes of rural magnificence." As beautiful and extraordinary as such wonderful palaces and great estates are in their architectural magnificence and in their representation of the highest material achievement in the world of everyday mortality, there is also the notion, even implied by some of the more secluded estates and castles, that they signify or symbolize as well landscapes of the mind, castles of luminescent visionary and effulgent imaginative power occasionally or consistently beyond the influence of everyday mortality. The last four lines of the above poem, "An Edelweiss Castle," affirm this point, for the castle disseminates the lovely light into the realm of visions and dreams.

Rainer Maria Rilke's "Sonnet 2, XXI to Orpheus" celebrates the importance of the imagination, poetic vision, and of participating in the glories of a landscape of the mind (which may also affirm a connection to a lovely natural landscape). This sonnet also signifies a vital encouragement to realize the importance of the gardens and of nature and to praise them wholeheartedly so that they become an integral aspect of one's being. The gardens which the "I" of the poem asks the "Thou," the heart, to praise in feeling and in song are beyond the constraints of mortality. By cherishing and participating in this ambience the "I" and the "Thou" experience an aura of timelessness and generate a reciprocal transformation resulting in their integrating themselves into a higher, more emotionally and aesthetically vital existential condition. The affirmational tone of the poem, initiated in the first line with its emphasis on the importance of praising the gardens in song, is preserved throughout and infuses the life of the "I" as well; as long as the "I" maintains his sensitivity for language and for the sensitive heart this strategy of affirmation may continue and blossom. Rilke's "Sonnet 2, XXI to Orpheus" exemplifies his notion that our experiences in life should constantly develop our emotional integrity and vitality and should prepare us to achieve "eine neue Geistesgegenwart," a new and more heightened sensibility of heart, mind, and soul. When the persona of the poem cultivates a close connection to the natural environment, he achieves such a vital sensibility. Such a dynamic connectedness of the individual and the surrounding natural environment is especially manifest in the relation of Max Nansen and his exuberantly colorful and gorgeous garden at Bleekenwarf in Lenz's *Deutschstunde*.

Another interesting thematic consideration, which could be seen as a corollary to the issue of the connectedness between an admired and cherished architectural space and the vision of a luminescent, harmonious sanctuary intimately associated with it, is whether some mansions or splendid architectural creations are or were instinctively destined or fated to be constructed in a particular location. One might wonder whether there exists an innate affinity between a special building and the natural environment in which it is or was created. For example, one might ask whether it is possible that various lovely churches were built in areas which instinctively contain a spiritual aura or ambience or were built on fields of spiritual energy and whether the architect or architects had an intuition that such a site was not just a congenial spot for a congregation but also a location which radiated spiritual power. Or perhaps the architect or designer of a church or chapel even had an intuition that a certain location, whether urban, suburban, or rural would be especially conducive to worship and to the creation of a dynamic spiritual environment. The Vatican in Italy is one such interesting example which has contained structures of religious inclination and vitality for centuries. From a place which contained small tombs and funeral monuments to the location of the church, the Constantine basilica, built by the Emperor Constantine in the third decade of the fourth century over the site of the tomb of St. Peter to the present basilica of St. Peter's which was built between 1506 and 1626, this area has an extended history of buildings generated and preserved by religious and spiritual ardor and motivation. Pope Julius II decided to replace the old basilica built by Constantine with a new monumental structure. The foundation stone for this new church was laid in 1506. The work on this great building has been guided and accomplished by various popes and artists. Numerous important architects such as Bramante, Raphael, Sangallo, G. della Porta, Michelangelo, Maderno, and Bernini contributed to the beauty of the exterior and the interior of the new St. Peter's basilica.

One might also wonder whether such magnificent and spacious palaces and castles as Versailles and Chambord in France, Neuschwanstein, Linderhof, and Charlottenburg in Germany, Schönbrunn in Austria, the Alhambra in Spain, Het Loo in The Netherlands, Karskoe Selo and Peterhof in Russia, the Villa d'Este in Italy, the royal palaces in Norway, Belgium, and Sweden, Rosenborg in Denmark, Balmoral Castle, Drumlanrig Castle, Glamis Castle, Hopetoun House, and Dunrobin Castle in Scotland, and Buckingham Palace, Windsor Castle, Blenheim Palace, Chatsworth, Stourhead, and Castle Howard in England, just to name a few of the many lovely castles and palaces around the world, were built in locations which were natural for them, in which they were destined to be constructed, in which their architectural spirits were fated to blossom, in which their aesthetic souls desired to develop, evolve, and be nurtured, and which would showcase their aesthetic beauty and affirm their connectedness to the surrounding natural ambience. Many of the great castles and palaces in Europe, as well as other architecturally interesting and lovely houses and mansions around the world, seem perfectly suited to their surrounding natural environment as if the site had been chosen by fate or destiny, as if the majestic soul of a special architectural creation had desired to blossom and develop there, as if the architect and perhaps even the landscape architect had been guided not only by their principles and plans and by the owner's aesthetic inclinations, but also by the genius, or mythologically vital spirit, of the place.

Buckingham Palace in England, now an architectural icon of the British monarchy, is an especially interesting example of a royal residence which began its existence simply as a London town house. Buckingham House was originally built in 1703 for the Duke of Buckingham. Perhaps the potential for future architectural development and socioeconomic prominence of this splendid house was already sensed at its inception for it was initially depicted as a "graceful palace" in which the greatest monarch would be content to reside. In 1762 King George III, searching for a residence to replace St. James's Palace, bought the house from the son of the last Duke of Buckingham. From that time to the present Buckingham Palace has signified the official London residence for all British monarchs. Buckingham Palace has been modified considerably through the years. An East Front was added between 1847–53 and a suite of state apartments was constructed in 1854. The East Front of the Palace which is seen today reflects the remodeling which was done in 1913 during the reign of King George V.

This notion of the power of fate or destiny or nature or the instinctive aesthetic sense of the architect or owner as having the capacity to exert a considerable influence on the creation of a splendid house and garden is exemplified in a poem by Annis Stockton about the creation of the garden around her beloved house, Morven, built in the 1750s in Princeton, New Jersey. Morven, named by Annis and Richard Stockton, one of the signers of the Declaration of Independence, after the mythical home of Fingal in Macpherson's *Ossian*, is an eminent example of the style of Georgian architecture developing in the American colonies in the mid-eighteenth century. Georgian architecture reflected the belief in the Age of Enlightenment that the individual could rationally influence and shape the world around him or her—Morven reflects this in the aura of harmony existing between the house and the garden, in the accessibility of the house, and in the harmonious form and symmetry in the garden around Morven. In one of her poems Annis Stockton describes a garden which reflects the aura of the Morven estate and affirms the idea that each part of the design is properly placed with respect to beauty or purpose:

> While fruits and flowers so nicely are displayed,
> As if the powers of order here had made
> Their chosen seat: while usefulness combin'd
> Gives us the portrait of the farmer's mind...
> And in their gardens every lux'ry plac'd
> That nature gives to elegance and taste.

That the "powers of order" might have made or did make "Their chosen seat" in such a lovely place, as Annis Stockton says in her poem, suggests that this location was auspicious for the house and garden, or, one might say that the house and garden of Morven were destined to be created in such a delightful location by the presence of mythically vital forces. One might also view the "powers of order" as being analogous to, comparable to, or synonymous with "the genius of the place" in the spirit of Alexander Pope's use of the phrase in "An Epistle to Lord Burlington" of 1731 in which he emphasizes the importance of consulting the genius of the place "that Paints as you plant, and as you work, Designs." Perhaps not surprisingly, Richard Stockton even visited Pope's garden at Twickenham and was influenced by its design. Morven's history affirms its architectural, socioeconomic, and cultural importance, for after Richard and Annis Stockton it was the home not only of various other Stockton family members such as Commodore Robert Stockton, but also of the governors of the State of New Jersey from 1954 until 1981, before being transformed into a historic house and museum. One might also imagine that other gorgeous historic houses in America such as the Vanderbilt Mansion, Kykuit, and Lyndhurst along the Hudson River, The Breakers and Marble House in Newport, Old Westbury House on Long Island, Nemours Mansion in Delaware, Drumthwacket in New Jersey, and Biltmore in North Carolina were created and nurtured in environments in which they were destined to flourish.

In Thomas Mann's *Buddenbrooks*, *Tonio Kröger*, and *Tristan*, Evelyn Waugh's *Brideshead Revisited*, J. R. R. Tolkien's *The Lord of the Rings*, and Siegfried Lenz's *Deutschstunde*, as in William Wordsworth's Immortality Ode, Joseph von Eichendorff's "Abschied," and Percy Shelley's "Hymn to Intellectual Beauty," the protagonists and personae are able to appease, confront, diminish, and transform the sense of loss which they feel after having been separated, whether temporarily or permanently, from a lovely architectural space of great personal significance for them by developing, nurturing, and preserving a vision of such a space. Such a quietly or vibrantly vital vision, such a landscape of the mind, which sustains them aesthetically, emotionally, and spiritually is motivated by a sense of faith, personal, religious, or aesthetic, or a fusion of all three. In the case of Tony Buddenbrook, it is a faith of personal vitality which is generated by her awareness of her goodness and kindheartedness and by her attachment to her beautiful childhood home—such a sense of faith believes in the perpetual importance of her family heritage, although the socioeconomic prominence of the Buddenbrooks is considerably and publicly diminished by the end of the novel. In the situation of Tonio Kröger, it is a faith in his artistic and literary vitality, in his exceptional capacity to achieve in his creative work the noblest manifestation of the human spirit connected to a faith in and rememberance of glorious youthful days spent in the congenial sanctuary of his childhood home. In the case of Sebastian Flyte, it is a faith of religious piety, a faith that he is quietly fulfilling the expectations of his Catholicism coupled with a faith in aesthetic vitality, generated by and affirmed in his memory and vision of his extraordinary and lovely childhood home, Brideshead Castle. In the case of Siggi Jepsen, it is a faith in art and in his capacity to develop an aesthetic sensibility and to protect the artistic works of such painters as Max Nansen, a faith motivated at least to some extent by his experience of having been a not insignificant presence in the house and studio of the artist at Bleekenwarf. In the case of Max Nansen, it is a faith in the power of art and of aesthetic vitality to triumph over the exigencies and vicissitudes of mortality. In the case of Elrond of Rivendell and in the case of Galadriel of Lothlórien it is a faith in the spirit of their beautiful domains to preserve and recreate a sense of hope for a harmonious and peaceful future isolated from the ravages and vicissitudes of everyday mortality. Elrond knows that he will have to leave Rivendell with his community in the near future, as Galadriel is aware that she will have to leave Lothlórien with the Elves regardless of the outcome of the war of the ring. Yet, Elrond's devotion to Rivendell and Galadriel's devotion to Lothlórien will be forever manifested in their feelings of perpetual connectedness to the beauty and the spirit of these extraordinary and gorgeous places, even when they are physically distant from them. The congenial memories and visions of the beauty, serenity, and aesthetic vitality of Rivendell and Lothlórien respectively which Elrond and Galadriel have and will take with them when they travel to the Grey Havens and beyond will help to sustain them and give them comfort in the future.

The last lines of stanza ten of Wordsworth's Immortality Ode capture perfectly the spirit of the experiences of various protagonists discussed in this book:

> We will grieve not, rather find
> Strength in what remains behind;
> In the primal sympathy
> Which having been must ever be;
> In the soothing thoughts that spring
> Out of human suffering;
> In the faith that looks through death,
> In years that bring the philosophic mind. (179–86)

The persona will find strength in a "timeless" present of things past, things present, and things future. In fusing these qualities in the "faith that looks through death" (186), the persona implies his capacity to participate in and shape an expansive sense of time.

In stanza ten of the Immortality Ode especially Wordsworth's persona attains intimations of immortality not only through the joy of nature, by participating instinctively and vitally in the eternal beauty and dynamic joyousness of nature, but also through his experience of the primal sympathy and the philosophic mind and through his own creativity. In articulating his notion of "the primal sympathy," the poet implies that he is an integral part of the harmonious whole which is the universe. The "soothing thoughts" of this stanza signify not only the poem itself, but also Wordsworth's creativity as an artist. The philosophic mind represents the mature understanding of Nature linked to the visionary sense of faith which is analogous to the "faith in life endless, the sustaining thought / Of human Being, Eternity, and God" (*The Prelude*, 14.204–05). Wordsworth anticipates here the prospect of a perpetually vital future for humanity as eternal as that of God or a divine force in the universe.

Wordsworth's persona says in this poem that he has learned to appreciate and to love Nature even more through his mortality, through his awareness of the inevitable flux of time and animate life, than he did in his earlier, child-like, seemingly immortal state. Only through the passage of time can we develop a series of "spots of time" (as described in stanza nine) to make life meaningful and worthwhile. And only through the passage of time does Wordsworth's persona achieve a mature understanding and vision of Nature, which involves realizing the importance of the spatial permanences of nature, of its beautiful and sacred spaces. By believing in and participating in the eternal cyclicality of such lovely spaces of luminescence, expansiveness, and tranquility which may result in a sensation of "innocent brightness" or in "Thoughts that do often lie too deep for tears" (203), the persona may achieve a dynamic continuity of self. Such a sensitive and perceptive persona not only gains a sense of the expansiveness of space and time but also participates in the radiant vitality of the lovely natural spaces which illuminate and soothe the heart, the mind, and the soul. Each of the protagonists discussed in this book, especially Tony Buddenbrook, Tonio Kröger, Spinell, Hans Castorp, Sebastian Flyte, Frodo Baggins, Elrond, Galadriel, Gandalf, Aragorn, Arwen, Siggi Jepsen, and Max Nansen, share Wordsworth's belief in the importance of such spatial permanences of nature and aspire to achieve a dynamic continuity of self.

The experience of Wordsworth which is described in Book 6 of *The Prelude* is somewhat reminiscent of that of Sebastian Flyte in *Brideshead Revisited*. In Book 6 Wordsworth speaks of his intellectual contemplations at Cambridge leading him to realize the presence of the "one / Supreme Existence" (6.133–34) which is beyond the exigencies of space and time and beyond the vicissitudes of mortality. Wordsworth's meditation on the existence of God gives him a sense of "transcendent peace" (6.139) which prefigures the serene wisdom of the majestic intellect of Book 14. After leaving Cambridge Wordsworth takes a trip to continental Europe where he visits the Convent of Chartreuse. His description of the spatiality of La Grande Chartreuse, the chief monastery of the Carthusian order in the mountains near Grenoble, exemplified by the idea that entering this domain "leaves far behind life's treacherous vanities" (6.453), reveals an aura similar to that of Matthew Arnold's depiction of the Grande Chartreuse in his poem "Stanzas from the Grande Chartreuse" and similar to that of Sebastian's experience of the monastery environment in Morocco.

In Book 14 of *The Prelude* Wordsworth's persona experiences the extraordinary vision on Mt. Snowdon which possesses a dynamic luminescence and an epiphanic vitality—these are qualities which are also essential to Hans Castorp's vision during his perilous adventure in the snow in Mann's *Der Zauberberg*. In *The Prelude* the stream of moonlight combined with "the roar of waters" (14.59) creates a moment of exceptional sensory vitality. This experience of the dynamism and the power of nature suggests to Wordsworth's persona the presence of a "majestic intellect" (14.67), of a mind "that feeds upon infinity" (14.71). The capacity of the majestic intellect to create and to participate in an expansiveness of self, space, and time is affirmed in the lines that stress the significance of the "mind sustained / By recognitions of transcendent power" (14.74–75). In the following line, "In sense conducting to ideal form," the persona implies the potential of the majestic intellect to be an active part of an ambience of spatial expansiveness, an ambience aspiring to encompass ideal forms. Line 77, "In soul of more than mortal privilege," suggests the capacity of the majestic intellect to signify an extraordinary individual and to challenge and transcend mortality. Hans Castorp, Tony Buddenbrook, Thomas Buddenbrook, Tonio Kröger, Sebastian Flyte, Cordelia Flyte, Bilbo Baggins, Frodo Baggins, Gandalf, Galadriel, Aragorn, Legolas, Elrond, Arwen, Siggi Jepsen, and Max Nansen, in particular, of the protagonists discussed in this book, are "souls of more than mortal privilege" who exemplify in varying degrees the emotional generosity, the spiritual expansiveness, the imaginative amplitude, and the transcendent vitality of the majestic intellect.

The magnificent houses and the memories and visions of those houses in the works of Mann, Waugh, Tolkien, and Lenz are all permeated, nurtured, and sustained by an aesthetic sensibility as powerful as that of Tonio Kröger in Mann's *Tonio Kröger*, or of Tony Buddenbrook in Mann's *Buddenbrooks*, or of Sebastian Flyte or Charles Ryder in Waugh's *Brideshead Revisited*, or of Elrond, Gandalf, and Bilbo in *The Lord of the Rings* in their appreciation of Rivendell, or of Galadriel, Aragorn, and Frodo in *The Lord of the Rings* in their appreciation of Lothlórien, or of Max Nansen in *Deutschstunde* in the creation of his delightful and colorful paintings and interpretations of nature, by a glorious radiance as vital as the light in Nansen's painting *Sails Dissolving into Light* which he presents to Doktor Busbeck in gratitude for his support, as mythologically potent as the harmonious light of the landscape-room in the Buddenbrook house in the Meng Strasse, as vibrant as the light of Lothlórien in *The Lord of the Rings*, and as visionary as the effusion of light in the "Snow" episode of Mann's *Der Zauberberg*, by a sense of the spatial expansiveness of the soul as profound and as delightful as the experience of Tonio Kröger in Mann's *Tonio Kröger*, or of Hans Castorp in Mann's *Der Zauberberg*, or of Sebastian Flyte in Waugh's *Brideshead Revisited* during that blissful summer at Brideshead Castle, or of Galadriel in Tolkien's *The Lord of the Rings*, or of Darcy at Pemberley in Austen's *Pride and Prejudice*, or of Anselmus and Serpentina in Hoffmann's *Der goldne Topf*, by the spirit of hope and faith as vibrant and self-perpetuating as that of Tony Buddenbrook in Mann's *Buddenbrooks* despite the financial losses of her family, of Tonio Kröger in Mann's *Tonio Kröger* in his attempt to revitalize his artistic vitality, of Sebastian in Waugh's *Brideshead Revisited* when no one seems to care about him and is interested in helping him, or of Frodo and Sam as they heroically make their way towards Mount Doom, or of Nansen in *Deutschstunde* when he creates his "invisible pictures" during the cruel ban on his work by the authorities, by a sense of tranquility as pure and as strong as that of the Elves, Frodo, Aragorn, and other individuals in Rivendell and in Lothlórien, or of Tonio Kröger in the rich silences of his childhood home, or of Brideshead Castle during the wonderful times when Sebastian can live there in relative privacy, or of the High Lama and Conway in the beautiful ambience of Shangri-La, or of Eichendorff's Taugenichts in the natural ambience of the palace in Vienna, or of the eternally beautiful garden in Shelley's "The Sensitive Plant," and by a devotion to and belief in the power of the light as great as that of the persona in Shelley's "Song of Apollo," or of Asia in *Prometheus Unbound*, or of Lindhorst, Anselmus, and Serpentina in Hoffmann's *Der goldne Topf*, or of Tony Buddenbrook in Mann's *Buddenbrooks* despite the various vagaries of fate which have encroached upon her life, or of Sebastian in *Brideshead Revisited* whose inner light is preserved despite his considerable suffering, or of Elrond in Rivendell and Galadriel in Lothlórien who know intuitively that their beloved domains are extraordinary sanctuaries of cultural, intellectual, and mythological luminescence, or of Max Nansen in Lenz's *Deutschstunde* whose aesthetic sensibility appreciates and values daily the nuances and subtleties of the light of the natural environment. Each of these lovely architectural and natural spaces represents, as Wordsworth says of nature in "Tintern Abbey," the guide and guardian of the heart and soul and a refuge of beautiful radiance, effulgent serenity, and sublime harmony.

Such lovely and splendid mansions and residences as Tonio Kröger's childhood home, Tony Buddenbrook's house on Meng Strasse, Sebastian's Brideshead Castle, Rivendell, Lothlórien, the house of Tom Bombadil and Goldberry, the renewed Minas Tirith under the wise guidance of Aragorn and Arwen, and Nansen's Bleekenwarf possess and perpetually reaffirm a capacity to regenerate and revitalize emotionally, aesthetically, and spiritually the individuals who admire those architectural and natural spaces so deeply and so lovingly that they preserve enduring memories and perpetual visions of them. The beautiful visions of these houses, the remembered images of these mansions, and the images which blossom and evolve creatively through time are not only infused with the aesthetic genius, architectural magnificence, powerful luminescence, profound serenity, devout hope, and spatial expansiveness of these places, and inspired by these places, but are also pervaded by an aura of mythological vitality and by a sense of continuity with ancestral voices of past splendor, affirming that they nurture and preserve as an integral dimension of their being the spirit of the radiance in Shelley's "Hymn to Intellectual Beauty" which alone "Gives grace and truth to life's unquiet dream" (36), of the Apollonian effulgence of Lindhorst's house in Hoffmann's *Der goldne Topf* with its intimate connection to the eternity of Atlantis, of the love which Anselmus and Serpentina share in Atlantis, of the capacity of Asia as the "Life of Life" (II.v.48), the "Child of Light" (II.v.54), and the "Lamp of Earth" (II.v.66) in Shelley's *Prometheus Unbound* to establish and to signify by her presence a sanctuary of light and love, of the admiration which Marie Stahlbaum shows in *Nußknacker und Mausekönig* for the exquisite Marzipan Castle, of the self-regenerating light and effulgent imagination of the majestic intellect of Book 14 of Wordsworth's *The Prelude*, of the architectural beauty and spatial expansiveness of Lindhorst's house in Hoffmann's *Der goldne Topf*, of Pemberley House in Austen's *Pride and Prejudice*, and of Hartfield in Austen's *Emma*, and of the devotion and love which the individuals who truly admire such houses have for them and try to sustain for the duration of their lives, of the loveliness of the "Paradise of vaulted bowers" (II.v.104) in *Prometheus Unbound* which signifies a sanctuary of light, harmony, and serenity beyond the vicissitudes of mortality, of the "healing paradise" (355) in Shelley's "Lines written among the Euganean Hills" which is infused with the radiance of "soft sunshine" (348) and "the light and smell divine / Of all flowers that breathe and shine" (350–51), of the profound hope which Anselmus, Serpentina, Marie Stahlbaum, Jane Eyre, the Taugenichts, and Elinor Dashwood in Austen's *Sense and Sensibility* maintain in their respective narratives despite the anguish and the vagaries of the world of everyday mortality, of the serenity of Ferndean which signifies the focus for the rejuvenated love of Jane and Rochester in Charlotte Brontë's *Jane Eyre*, of the refulgent beauty and tranquility of the palace estate in Vienna where the Taugenichts in Eichendorff's narrative finds a sense of happiness, and of the revitalizing capacity of those "first affections" (148) in Wordsworth's Immortality Ode which represent "the fountain-light of all our day" (151) and the "master-light of all our seeing" (152).

Works Consulted

Abrams, M. H. *The Mirror and the Lamp: Romantic Theory and the Critical Tradition*. New York: Oxford UP, 1953. Print.

———. *Natural Supernaturalism: Tradition and Revolution in Romantic Literature*. New York: W. W. Norton, 1971. Print.

Allison, Alexander W., Arthur J. Carr, and Arthur Eastman, eds. *Masterpieces of the Drama*. New York: Macmillan, 1974. Print.

Alt, Peter-Andre. *Ironie und Krise*. Frankfurt am Main: Peter Lang, 1985. Print.

Anderson, William. *Castles of Europe: from Charlemagne to the Renaissance*. New York: Crown Publishers, 1984. Print.

Apter, T. E. *Thomas Mann: The Devil's Advocate*. London: Macmillan, 1978. Print.

Arnold, Matthew. *Selected Poems and Prose*. Ed. Miriam Allott. London: J. M. Dent, 1978. Print.

Auden, W. H. *The Dyer's Hand*. New York: Random House, 1962. Print.

———. "The Quest Hero." *Tolkien and the Critics: Essays on J. R. R. Tolkien's 'The Lord of the Rings.'* Ed. Neil D. Isaacs and Rose A. Zimbardo. Notre Dame, IN: U of Notre Dame P, 1968. 40–61. Print.

Austen, Jane. *Emma*. Oxford; New York: Oxford UP, 1998. Print.

———. *Persuasion*. Ed. Janet Todd and Antje Blank. Cambridge, UK; New York: Cambridge UP, 2006. Print.

———. *Pride and Prejudice*. Ed. Donald Gray. New York: Norton, 2001. Print.

———. *Sense and Sensibility*. Intro. Mark Schorer. New York: Dell, 1959. Print.

Avery, Gillian. *Nineteenth-Century Children: Heroes and Heroines in English Children's Stories 1780–1900*. London: Hodder & Stoughton, 1965. Print.

Bassmann, Winfried. *Siegfried Lenz. Sein Werk als Beispiel für Weg und Standort der Literatur in der Bundesrepublik Deutschland*. Bonn: Bouvier, 1976, Print.

——. "Zur Erinnerung verurteilt. Siegfried Lenz im Gespräch mit Winfried Bassmann." *Siegfried Lenz: Werk und Wirkung*. Hrsg. Rudolf Wolff. Bonn: Bouvier Verlag Herbert Grundmann, 1985. 78–95. Print.

Baumgart, Reinhart. *Das Ironische und die Ironie in den Werken Thomas Manns*. München: Hanser, 1966. Print.

Beaty, Frederick L. *The Ironic World of Evelyn Waugh: A Study of Eight Novels*. DeKalb: Northern Illinois UP, 1992. Print.

Beddow, Michael. "The Magic Mountain." *The Cambridge Companion to Thomas Mann*. Ed. Ritchie Robertson. Cambridge: Cambridge UP, 2002. 137–50. Print.

Beja, Morris. *Epiphany in the Modern Novel*. Seattle: U of Washington P, 1979. Print.

Berendsohn, Walter E. *Thomas Mann—Artist and Partisan in Troubled Times*. Trans. George C. Buck. University, Alabama: U of Alabama P, 1973. Print.

Beutin, Wolfgang. "*Ein Kriegsende* von Siegfried Lenz. Eine Kritik."*Siegfried Lenz: Werk und Wirkung*. Hrsg. Rudolf Wolff. Bonn: Bouvier Verlag Herbert Grundmann, 1985. 55–77. Print.

Bewley, Marius. "Scott Fitzgerald's Criticism of America." *Modern Critical Interpretations—F. Scott Fitzgerald's The Great Gatsby*. Ed. Harold Bloom. New York: Chelsea House, 1986. 11–27. Print.

Birzer, Bradley. *J. R. R. Tolkien's Sanctifying Myth: Understanding Middle-earth*. Wilmington, Del.: ISI Books, 2002. Print.

Blayac, Alain, ed. *Evelyn Waugh: New Directions*. London: Macmillan, 1992. Print.

Bloom, Harold, ed. *Deconstruction and Criticism*. New York: Continuum, 1979. Print.

——, ed. and intro. *Modern Critical Interpretations—Charlotte Brontë's 'Jane Eyre.'* New York: Chelsea House, 1987. Print.

——, ed. and intro. *Modern Critical Interpretations—F. Scott Fitzgerald's The Great Gatsby*. New York: Chelsea House, 1986. Print.

——. *Shelley's Mythmaking*. New Haven: Yale UP, 1959. Print.

——, ed. *Thomas Mann*. New York: Chelsea House, 1986. Print.

——, ed. *Thomas Mann's 'The Magic Mountain.'* New Haven: Chelsea House, 1986. Print.

——. *The Visionary Company: A Reading of English Romantic Poetry*. Garden City, NY: Doubleday, 1961. Print.

Böll, Heinrich. *Die Ansichten eines Clowns*. München: Deutscher Taschenbuch Verlag, 1967. Print.

——. *Billard um halbzehn*. Cologne: Kiepenheuer & Witsch, 1960. Print.

——. *Billiards at Half-Past Nine*. Trans. Leila Vennewitz. New York: McGraw-Hill, 1962. Print.

Borchers, Klaus. *Mythos und Gnosis im Werk Thomas Manns*. Freiburg: Hochschulverlag, 1980. Print.

Boulby, Mark. *Hermann Hesse: His Mind and Art.* Ithaca: Cornell UP, 1967. Print.

Bradley, Marion Zimmer. "Men, Halflings, and Hero-Worship." *Tolkien and the Critics: Essays on J. R. R. Tolkien's 'The Lord of the Rings.'* Ed. Neil D. Isaacs and Rose A. Zimbardo. Notre Dame, IN: U of Notre Dame P, 1968. 109–27. Print.

Breeze, Ruth. "Places of the Mind: Locating *Brideshead Revisited.*" *Waugh without End: New Trends in Evelyn Waugh Studies.* Ed. Carlos Villar Flor and Robert Murray Davis. Bern: Peter Lang, 2005. 131–45. Print.

Brennan, Joseph G. *Thomas Mann's World.* New York: Columbia UP, 1942. Print.

Brodsky, Claudia. *In the Place of Language: Literature and the Architecture of the Referent.* New York: Fordham UP, 2009. Print.

Brontë, Charlotte. *Jane Eyre.* New York: Signet, 1982. Print.

Bruccoli, Matthew J. *Some Sort of Epic Grandeur: The Life of F. Scott Fitzgerald.* New York: Harcourt Brace Jovanovich, 1981. Print.

Bruford, W. H. "'Bildung' in *The Magic Mountain.*" *Thomas Mann's 'The Magic Mountain.'* Ed. Harold Bloom. New York: Chelsea House, 1986. 67–83. Print.

———. *The German Tradition of Self-Cultivation: 'Bildung' from Humboldt to Thomas Mann.* Cambridge: Cambridge UP, 1975. Print.

Bruhn, Gert E. *Selbstzitat bei Thomas Mann: Untersuchungen zum Verhältnis von Fiktion und Autobiographie in seinem Werk.* New York: Peter Lang, 1992. Print.

Buckley, Jerome H. *The Triumph of Time.* Cambridge, Mass.: Harvard UP, 1966. Print.

Burgess, Gordon J. A. "Pflicht und Verantwortungsgefühl: *Es waren Habichte in der Luft, Deutschstunde, Ein Kriegsende.*" *Siegfried Lenz: Werk und Wirkung.* Hrsg. Rudolf Wolff. Bonn: Bouvier Verlag Herbert Grundmann, 1985. 26–34. Print.

Bürgin, Hans, and Hans-Otto Mayer. *Thomas Mann: Eine Chronik seines Lebens.* Frankfurt am Main: Fischer, 1965. Print.

Burke, Edmund. *Philosophical Enquiry into the Origin of Our Ideas of the Sublime and the Beautiful.* London, 1757. Print.

Burnett, Frances H. *The Secret Garden.* New York: Knopf, 1993. Print.

Caldecott, Stratford, and Thomas Honegger, eds. *Tolkien's 'The Lord of the Rings.' Sources of Inspiration.* Zurich: Walking Tree Publishers, 2008. Print.

Cameron, Kenneth Neill. *The Golden Years.* Cambridge, MA: Harvard UP, 1974. Print.

Campbell, Joseph. *The Hero with a Thousand Faces.* New York: Pantheon, 1949. Print.

Carens, James F., ed. and intro. *Critical Essays on Evelyn Waugh.* Boston: G. K. Hall, 1987. Print.

———. *The Satiric Art of Evelyn Waugh.* Seattle: U of Washington P, 1966. Print.

Carpenter, Humphrey. *The Brideshead Generation: Evelyn Waugh and his Friends.* Boston: Houghton Mifflin, 1990. Print.

———. *The Inklings: C. S. Lewis, J. R. R. Tolkien, Charles Williams, and Their Friends.* Boston: Houghton Mifflin, 1979. Print.

———, ed. *The Letters of J. R. R. Tolkien.* Boston: Houghton Mifflin, 1981. Print.

———. *Tolkien: A Biography*. Boston: Houghton Mifflin, 1977. Print.

Chance, Jane. *The Lord of the Rings: The Mythology of Power*. New York: Twayne, 1992. Print.

———, ed. *Tolkien, the Medievalist*. London: Routledge, 2003. Print.

Chekhov, Anton. *The Cherry Orchard*. New York: Dover, 1991. Print.

Chevalier, Jean-Louis. "Arcadian Minutiae: Notes on *Brideshead Revisited*." *Evelyn Waugh: New Directions*. Ed. Alain Blayac. London: Macmillan, 1992. 35–61. Print.

Clark, George, and Daniel Timmons, eds. *J. R. R. Tolkien and His Literary Resonances: Views of Middle-earth*. Westport, CT: Greenwood P, 2000. Print.

Coignard, Jerome and Marc Walter. *Dream Palaces: The Last Royal Courts of Europe*. New York: Vendome Press, 2004. Print.

Conard, Robert C. *Heinrich Böll*. Boston: Twayne, 1981. Print.

Cook, William J., Jr. *Masks, Modes and Morals: The Art of Evelyn Waugh*. Rutherford, NJ: Fairleigh Dickinson UP, 1971. Print.

Crabbe, Katharyn W. *Evelyn Waugh*. New York: Continuum, 1988. Print.

Craik, W. A. *The Brontë Novels*. London: Methuen, 1968. Print.

Cunningham, Valentine. *British Writers of the Thirties*. New York: Oxford UP, 1989. Print.

Curry, Patrick. *Defending Middle-earth: Tolkien, Myth, and Modernity*. New York: St. Martin's P, 1997. Print.

Curschmann, Michael. *Wort—Bild—Text: Studien zur Medialität des Literarischen in Hochmittelalter und früher Zeit*. Baden-Baden: V. Koerner, 2007. Print.

Daemmrich, Horst S. *The Shattered Self: E. T. A. Hoffmann's Tragic Vision*. Detroit: Wayne State UP, 1973. Print.

Daemmrich, Horst S. and Ingrid G. Daemmrich. *Spirals and Circles*. 2 vols. New York: Peter Lang, 1994. Print.

Davie, M., ed. *The Diaries of Evelyn Waugh*. London; Boston: 1976. Print.

Davis, Robert Murray. *Brideshead Revisited: The Past Redeemed*. Boston: Twayne, 1990. Print.

———. *Evelyn Waugh and the Forms of His Time*. Washington: Catholic UP of America, 1989. Print.

———. "Evelyn Waugh's Audiences." *Waugh without End: New Trends in Evelyn Waugh Studies*. Ed. Carlos Villar Flor and Robert Murray Davis. Bern: Peter Lang, 2005. 71–90. Print.

———. "Imagined Space in *Brideshead Revisited*." *Evelyn Waugh: New Directions*. Ed. Alain Blayac. London: Macmillan, 1992. 22–34. Print.

Davis, Robert Murray, Paul A. Doyle, Donat Gallagher, Charles E. Linck, and Winnifred M. Bogaards, eds. *A Bibliography of Evelyn Waugh*. Troy, N.Y.: Whitston Publishing, 1986. Print.

Demetz, Peter. *Die süsse Anarchie. Deutsche Literatur seit 1945*. Berlin: Propyläen, 1970. Print.

Demetz, Peter, Thomas Greene, and Lowry Nelson, Jr., eds. *Disciplines of Criticism: Essays in Literary Theory, Interpretation, and History*. New Haven: Yale UP, 1968. Print.

Deterding, Klaus. *Hoffmanns Erzählungen: Eine Einführung in das Werk E. T. A. Hoffmanns*. Würzburg: Königshausen & Neumann, 2007. Print.

Dickens, Charles. *David Copperfield*. New York: Penguin, 1985. Print.

Dickerson, Matthew. *Following Gandalf: Epic Battles and Moral Victory in 'The Lord of the Rings.'* Grand Rapids, MI: Brazos P, 2003. Print.

Dickerson, Matthew, and Jonathan Evans. *Ents, Elves, and Eriador: The Environmental Vision of J. R. R. Tolkien.* Lexington, KY: UP of Kentucky, 2006. Print.

Diersen, Inge. *Thomas Mann: Episches Werk, Weltanschauung, Leben.* Berlin; Weimar: Aufbau-Verlag, 1985. Print.

———. *Untersuchungen zu Thomas Mann; Die Bedeutung der Künstlerdarstellung für die Entwicklung des Realismus in seinem erzählerischen Werk.* 5. Auflage. Berlin: Rütten & Loening, 1965.Print.

Dittman, Britta und Hans Wisskirchen. *Das Buddenbrookhaus.* Lübeck: Schmidt-Römhild, 2008. Print.

Dittmann, Ulrich. *Sprachbewusstsein und Redeformen im Werk Thomas Manns.* Stuttgart; Berlin: W. Kohlhammer, 1969. Print.

Donaldson, Frances. *Evelyn Waugh. Portrait of a Country Neighbor.* London: Weidenfeld and Nicolson, 1967. Print.

Doyle, Paul A. *Evelyn Waugh: A Critical Essay.* Grand Rapids, Michigan: William B. Eerdmans, 1969. Print.

———. *A Reader's Companion to the Novels and Short Stories of Evelyn Waugh.* Norman, Okla.: Pilgrim, 1989. Print.

Durbach, Errol. *Ibsen the Romantic: Analogues of Paradise in the Later Plays.* Athens: U of Georgia P, 1982. Print.

Durzak, Manfred. *Der deutsche Roman der Gegenwart.* Stuttgart: 1971. Print.

———. *Gespräche über den Roman. Formbestimmungen und Analysen.* Frankfurt am Main: Suhrkamp, 1976. Print.

———. "Männer mit Frauen. Zu den Kurzgeschichten von Siegfried Lenz." *Siegfried Lenz: Werk und Wirkung.* Hrsg. Rudolf Wolff. Bonn-Bouvier Verlag Herbert Grundmann, 1985. 35–54. Print.

Dyson, A. E. "*The Great Gatsby:* Thirty-Six Years After." *F. Scott Fitzgerald: A Collection of Critical Essays.* Ed. Arthur Mizener. Englewood Cliffs, NJ: Prentice-Hall, 1963. Print.

Eaglestone, Robert, ed. *Reading 'The Lord of the Rings.' New Writings on Tolkien's Classic.* London: Continuum, 2005. Print.

Eagleton, Terry. *Exiles and Emigres: Studies in Modern Literature.* London: Chatto & Windus, 1970. Print.

Echtermeyer, Ernst T. und Benno von Wiese, eds. *Deutsche Gedichte von den Anfängen bis zur Gegenwart.* Düsseldorf: A. Bagel, 1962. Print.

Egner, Robert E. and Lester E. Denonn, eds. *The Basic Writings of Bertrand Russell, 1903–1959.* New York: Simon and Schuster, 1961. Print.

Ehinger, Franziska. *Gesang und Stimme im Erzählwerk von Gottfried Keller, Eduard von Keyserling und Thomas Mann.* Würzburg: Königshausen & Neumann, 2004. Print.

Eliot, George. *Middlemarch.* New York: Bantam, 1985. Print.

Elm, Theo. *Siegfried Lenz—'Deutschstunde.' Engagement und Realismus im Gegenwartsroman.* München: Fink, 1974. Print.

——. "Siegfried Lenz: Zeitgeschichte als moralisches Lehrstück." *Siegfried Lenz: Werk und Wirkung.* Hrsg. Rudolf Wolff. Bonn: Bouvier Verlag Herbert Grundmann, 1985. 98–128. Print.

Emrich, Elke. "Zum 'metaphysischen Bedürfnis' in Thomas Manns *Buddenbrooks* und Heinrich Manns *Im Schlaraffenland.*" *Thomas Manns 'Buddenbrooks' und die Wirkung. 2. Teil.* Hrsg. Rudolf Wolff. Bonn: Bouvier Verlag Herbert Grundmann, 1986. 95–111. Print.

Enge, Torsten Olaf and Carl Friedrich Schröer. *Garden Architecture in Europe (1450–1800).* Köln: Benedikt Taschen, 1992. Print.

Ewbank, Inga-Stina. "The Last Plays." *The Cambridge Companion to Ibsen.* Cambridge: Cambridge UP, 1994. 126–54. Print.

Ezergailis, Inta M., ed. *Critical Essays on Thomas Mann.* Boston: G. K. Hall, 1988. Print.

Fetzer, John F. *Music, Love, Death, and Mann's 'Doctor Faustus.'* Columbia, SC: Camden House, 1990. Print.

Feuerlicht, Ignace. *Thomas Mann.* New York: Twayne, 1968. Print.

Fiedler, H. G., ed. *The Oxford Book of German Verse.* 2nd edition. Oxford: Oxford UP, 1927. Print.

Fitzgerald, F. Scott. *The Great Gatsby.* New York: Scribner, 1995. Print.

Fjelde, Rolf, ed. *Twentieth Century Views on Ibsen.* New York: 1965. Print.

Flieger, Verlyn. "Gilson, Smith, and Baggins." *Tolkien's The Lord of the Rings: Sources of Inspiration.* Ed. Stratford Caldecott and Thomas Honegger. Zurich: Walking Tree Publishers, 2008. 85–95. Print.

——. *A Question of Time: J. R. R. Tolkien's Road to Faerie.* Kent, OH: Kent State UP, 1997. Print.

——. *Splintered Light: Logos and Language in Tolkien's World.* Grand Rapids, MI: Eerdman's, 1983. Print.

Flieger, Verlyn, and Carl F. Hostetter, eds. *Tolkien's Legendarium: Essays on the History of Middle-Earth.* Westport, Conn.: Greenwood P, 2000. Print.

Flor, Carlos Villar and Robert Murray Davis, eds. *Waugh without End: New Trends in Evelyn Waugh Studies.* Bern: Peter Lang, 2005. Print.

Fonstad, Karen Wynn. *The Atlas of Middle-earth.* Boston: Houghton Mifflin, 1981. Print.

Forster, E. M. *Howards End.* New York: Vintage, 1954. Print.

——. *A Room with a View.* New York: Vintage, 1986. Print.

——. *Two Cheers for Democracy.* London: Edward Arnold, 1949. Print.

Foster, Robert. *The Complete Guide to Middle-earth: From 'The Hobbit' to 'The Silmarillion.'* New York: Ballantine, 1979. Print.

Freedman, Ralph. *The Lyrical Novel: Studies in Hermann Hesse, Andre Gide, and Virginia Woolf.* Princeton, N.J.: Princeton UP, 1963. Print.

Frye, Northrop. *Anatomy of Criticism.* Princeton, N.J.: Princeton UP, 1957. Print.

Fussell, Paul. *Abroad: British Literary Traveling Between the Wars.* New York: Oxford UP, 1980. Print.

Gale, Iain. *Waugh's World: A Guide to the Novels of Evelyn Waugh*. London: Sidgwick & Jackson, 1990. Print.

Gallagher, Donat, ed. *The Essays, Articles, and Reviews of Evelyn Waugh*. London: Methuen, 1983. Print.

———. "The Humanizing Factor: Evelyn Waugh's 'Very Personal View of Providence.'" *Waugh without End: New Trends in Evelyn Waugh Studies*. Ed. Carlos Villar Flor and Robert Murray Davis. Bern: Peter Lang, 2005. 21–36. Print.

Garnett, Robert A. *From Grimes to Brideshead: The Early Novels of Evelyn Waugh*. Lewisburg, PA: Bucknell UP, 1990. Print.

Geiser, Christoph. *Naturalismus und Symbolismus im Frühwerk Thomas Manns*. Bern: Francke, 1971. Print.

Giddings, Robert. *J. R. R. Tolkien: This Far Land*. Totowa, N.J.: Barnes and Noble, 1984. Print.

Gilbert, Sandra, and Susan Gubar. "A Dialogue of Self and Soul: Plain Jane's Progress." *Modern Critical Interpretations—Charlotte Brontë's Jane Eyre*. Ed. Harold Bloom. New York: Chelsea House, 1987. 63–96. Print.

Gilbert, Sandra, and Susan Gubar. *The Madwoman in the Attic: The Woman Writer and the Nineteenth-Century Literary Imagination*. New Haven, CT: Yale UP, 1979. Print.

Gill, Richard. *Happy Rural Seat—The English Country House and the Literary Imagination*. New York: 1972. Print.

Gill, Stephen. *William Wordsworth: A Life*. Oxford: Clarendon P, 1989. Print.

Gillispie, Gerald. *Proust, Mann, Joyce in the Modernist Context*. Washington, DC: Catholic U of America P, 2003. Print.

Girouard, Mark. *Life in the English Country House: A Social and Architectural History*. New Haven, CT: Yale UP, 1978. Print.

———. *The Victorian Country House*. Oxford: Clarendon P, 1971. Print.

Gray, Thomas. *The Poems and Letters of Thomas Gray*. Ed. William Mason. London, 1820. Print.

Green, Martin. *Children of the Sun: A Narrative of "Decadence" in England after 1918*. New York: Basic, 1976. Print.

Greenblatt, Stephen J. *Three Modern Satirists: Waugh, Orwell, and Huxley*. New Haven, CT: Yale UP, 1965. Print.

Greene, Donald. "A Partiality for Lords: Evelyn Waugh and Snobbery." *American Scholar* 58 (1989): 444–459. Print.

Greiff, Constance M., Mary W. Gibbons, and Elizabeth G. C. Menzies. *Princeton Architecture—A Pictorial History of Town and Campus*. Princeton, N.J.: Princeton UP, 1967. Print.

Grimm, Wilhelm, and Jacob Grimm. *Grimm's Fairy Tales*. New York: Barnes and Noble, 2003. Print.

———. *Grimm's Fairy Tales*. Intro. John Ruskin. London: Adam & Charles Black, 1911. Print.

———. *Grimm's Fairy Tales*. Ed. Louis and Bryna Untermeyer. New York: Ltd. Editions Club, 1962. Print.

———. *Kindermärchen*. Stuttgart: K. Thienemanns Verlag, 1953. Print.

Gronicka, André von. *Thomas Mann: Profile and Perspectives*. New York: Random House, 1970. Print.

Grotta, Daniel. *J. R. R. Tolkien: Architect of Middle-Earth*. Philadelphia: Running Press, 1992. Print.

Hage, Volcker. *Eine Liebe fürs Leben: Thomas Mann und Travemünde*. Frankfurt: S. Fischer, 2002. Print.

Haldimann, Eva. "Ein masurischer Erdgeist. Zur Figur der Edith im Roman *Heimatmuseum* von Siegfried Lenz." *Siegfried Lenz: Werk und Wirkung*. Hrsg. Rudolf Wolff. Bonn: Bouvier Verlag Herbert Grundmann, 1985. 130–35. Print.

Halverson, Rachel J. *Historiography and Fiction. Siegfried Lenz and the 'Historikerstreit.'* New York: Peter Lang, 1990. Print.

Hamburger, Käte. *Thomas Manns Biblisches Werk*. München: Nymphenburger Verlagshandlung, 1981. Print.

Hamilton, Nigel. *The Brothers Mann*. New Haven, CT: Yale UP, 1979. Print.

Hansen, Volkmar, ed. *Interpretationen: Thomas Mann, Romane und Erzählungen*. Stuttgart: Reclam, 1993. Print.

Hardy, Thomas. *Far from the Madding Crowd*. London: Penguin, 1978. Print.

——. *The Return of the Native*. London: Penguin, 1999. Print.

Hartman, Geoffrey. *The Unremarkable Wordsworth*. Minneapolis: U of Minnesota P, 1987. Print.

Hartsteen, Hans und Peter Henschel, hrsg. *Siegfried Lenz und Emil Nolde*. Kopenhagen, 1977. Print.

Hastings, Selina. *Evelyn Waugh: A Biography*. Boston: Houghton Mifflin, 1994. Print.

Hatfield, Henry. *From The Magic Mountain: Mann's Later Masterpieces*. Ithaca: Cornell UP, 1979. Print.

——. *Thomas Mann*. Norfolk, Conn.: New Directions, 1951. Print.

——, ed. *Thomas Mann: A Collection of Critical Essays*. Englewood Cliffs, N.J.: Prentice-Hall, 1964. Print.

Hawthorne, Nathaniel. *The House of the Seven Gables*. New York: Penguin, 1986. Print.

——. *Selected Tales and Sketches*. Intro. Michael J. Colacurcio. New York: Penguin, 1987. Print.

——. *Young Goodman Brown and Other Short Stories*. New York: Dover, 1992. Print.

Hayman, Ronald. *Thomas Mann: A Biography*. London: Bloomsbury, 1996. Print.

Hazlitt, William. *The Spirit of the Age*. London, 1825. Print.

Heath, Jeffrey. *The Picturesque Prison: Evelyn Waugh and His Writing*. Kingston and Montreal: McGill—Queen's UP, 1982. Print.

Heck, Francis S. "The Domain as a Symbol of a Paradise Lost: *Lost Horizon* and *Brideshead Revisited*." *Nassau Review* 4.3: 24–29. Print.

Heilbut, Anthony. *Thomas Mann: Eros and Literature*. London: Macmillan, 1996. Print.

Heller, Erich. *The Ironic German: A Study of Thomas Mann*. Boston: Little, Brown, 1958. Print.

——. *Thomas Mann—Der ironische Deutsche*. Frankfurt am Main: Suhrkamp, 1959. Print.

Helms, Randel. *Tolkien's World*. Boston: Houghton Mifflin, 1974. Print.

Hesse, Hermann. *My Belief—Essays on Life and Art*. Trans. Denver Lindley. Intro. and Ed. Theodore Ziolkowski. New York: Farrar, Straus and Giroux, 1974. Print.

———. *Siddhartha*. Trans. Hilde Rosner. New York: New Directions, 1951. Print.

———. *Der Steppenwolf*. Frankfurt am Main: Suhrkamp Taschenbuch, 1977. Print.

———. *Steppenwolf*. Trans. Basil Creighton. New York: Bantam, 1969. Print.

Hewett-Thayer, Harvey W. *Hoffmann: Author of the Tales*. Princeton, N.J.: Princeton UP, 1948. Print.

Hilton, James. *Lost Horizon*. New York: William Morrow, 1934. Print.

Hoffmann, E. T. A. *The Nutcracker and The Golden Pot*. New York: Dover, 1993. Print.

———. *Tales of Hoffmann*. Trans. R. J. Hollingdale. New York: Penguin, 2004. Print.

Hoffmann, Gisela E. *Das Motiv des Auserwählten bei Thomas Mann*. Bonn: Bouvier Verlag Herbert Grundmann, 1974. Print.

Hollingdale, R. J. *Thomas Mann—A Critical Study*. London: Rupert Hart-Davis, 1971. Print.

Hollis, Christopher. *Evelyn Waugh*. London: Longmans, 1954. Print.

Holzapfel, Heinrich. *Subversion und Differenz: Das Spiegelmotiv bei Freud, Thomas Mann, Rilke, und Jacques Lacan*. Essen: Blaue Eule, 1986. Print.

Honour, Hugh. *Romanticism*. New York: Harper and Row, 1979. Print.

Houghton, Walter E. and G. Robert Stange. *Victorian Poetry and Poetics*. 2nd ed. Boston: Houghton Mifflin, 1968. Print.

Hungerford, Edward B. *Shores of Darkness*. Cleveland: World Publishing, 1963. Print.

Hutchinson, Peter, ed. *Landmarks in the German Novel*. Bern; Oxford: Peter Lang, 2007. Print.

Ibsen, Henrik. *Four Major Plays (A Doll's House, Ghosts, Hedda Gabler, The Master Builder)*. Trans. James McFarlane. New York: Oxford UP, 1998. Print.

———. *Hedda Gabler and Other Plays (Hedda Gabler, The Pillars of the Community, and The Wild Duck)*. Trans. Una Ellis-Fermor. New York: Penguin, 1961. Print.

———. *Peer Gynt*. Trans. William Archer and Charles Archer. New York: The Heritage Press, 1957. Print.

Isaacs, Neil, and Rose Zimbardo, eds. *Tolkien and the Critics: Essays on J. R. R. Tolkien's 'The Lord of the Rings.'* Notre Dame, IN: U of Notre Dame P, 1968. Print.

———, eds. *Tolkien: New Critical Perspectives*. Lexington, KY: UP of Kentucky, 1981. Print.

James, Henry. *The Turn of the Screw*. Ed. Peter Beidler. Basingstoke: Palgrave Macmillan, 2010. Print.

Janssen, Werner. *Der Rhythmus des Humanen bei Heinrich Böll*. Frankfurt am Main: Peter Lang, 1985. Print.

Johnson, Claudia L. *Jane Austen: Women, Politics, and the Novel*. Chicago: U of Chicago P, 1988. Print.

Johnson, Judith Ann. *J. R. R. Tolkien: Six Decades of Criticism*. Westport, CT: Greenwood P, 1986. Print.

Kahler, Erich. *The Orbit of Thomas Mann*. Princeton, N.J.: Princeton UP, 1969. Print.

Karthaus, Ulrich. "Der Zauberberg—ein Zeitroman."*Deutsche Vierteljahrsschrift* 44 (1970). Print.

Kaufmann, Fritz. *Thomas Mann—The World as Will and Representation*. Boston: Beacon P, 1957. Print.

Keenan, Hugh T. "The Appeal of *The Lord of the Rings*." *Tolkien and the Critics: Essays on J. R. R. Tolkien's 'The Lord of the Rings.'* Ed. Neil D. Isaacs and Rose A. Zimbardo. Notre Dame, IN: U of Notre Dame P, 1968. 62–80. Print.

Kenosian, David. *Puzzles of the Body. The Labyrinth in Mann's 'Zauberberg,' Kafka's 'Prozess,' and Hesse's 'Steppenwolf.'* New York: Peter Lang, 1995. Print.

Kernan, Alvin B. "The Wall and the Jungle: The Early Novels of Evelyn Waugh." *Critical Essays on Evelyn Waugh*. Ed. James F. Carens. Boston: G. K. Hall, 1987. 82–91. Print.

Klugkist, Thomas. *Pessimistische Humanismus*. Würzburg: Königshausen & Neumann, 2002. Print.

Knies, Earl. *The Art of Charlotte Brontë*. Athens: Ohio University P, 1969. Print.

Knight, Richard Payne. *Analytical Inquiry into the Principles of Taste*. London, 1805. Print.

Kocher, Paul H. *Master of Middle-earth: The Fiction of J. R. R. Tolkien*. Boston: Houghton Mifflin, 1972. Print.

Kommer, Björn R. *Das Buddenbrookhaus in Lübeck: Geschichte, Bewohner, Bedeutung*. Lübeck: C. Coleman, 1993. Print.

Kontje, Todd. *The Cambridge Introduction to Thomas Mann*. Cambridge; New York: Cambridge UP, 2011. Print.

———. *The German Bildungsroman: History of a National Genre*. Columbia, S.C.: Camden House, 1993. Print.

Koopmann, Helmut. "*Buddenbrooks*: Die Ambivalenz im Problem des Verfalls." *Thomas Manns 'Buddenbrooks' und die Wirkung.1. Teil*. Hrsg. Rudolf Wolff. Bonn: Bouvier Verlag Herbert Grundmann, 1986. 37–66. Print.

———. *Die Entwicklung des 'Intellektualen Romans' bei Thomas Mann*. Bonn: Bouvier Verlag Herbert Grundmann, 1971. Print.

———. *Thomas Mann: Buddenbrooks*. Frankfurt am Main: M. Diesterweg, 1995. Print.

———. *Thomas Mann*. Göttingen: Vandenhoeck & Ruprecht, 1975. Print.

———. *Thomas Mann—Handbuch*. Stuttgart: Alfred Kröner, 1990. Print.

———. *Thomas Mann—Heinrich Mann: die ungleichen Brüder*. München: Beck, 2005. Print.

Kraske, Bernd M. "Über den Einfluss der Romane Alexander Lange Kiellands auf Thomas Manns *Buddenbrooks*." *Thomas Manns 'Buddenbrooks' und die Wirkung. 2. Teil*. Hrsg. Rudolf Wolff. Bonn: Bouvier Verlag Herbert Grundmann, 1986. 57–71. Print.

Krieger, Peter. "Caspar David Friedrich." *Galerie der Romantik*. Berlin: National Galerie Berlin; Staatliche Museen, 1986. 32–45. Print.

Kroeber, Karl. *Romantic Landscape Vision: Constable and Wordsworth*. Madison: U of Wisconsin P, 1975. Print.

Kurzke, Hermann. *Thomas Mann: Epoche, Werk, Wirkung*. München: C. H. Beck, 1985. Print.

———. *Thomas Mann: Das Leben als Kunstwerk*. München: C. H. Beck, 1999. Print.

———. *Thomas Mann—Ein Porträt für seine Leser*. München: C. H. Beck, 2009. Print.

Lämmert, Eberhard. *Bauformen des Erzählens*. 2. Aufl. Stuttgart: 1967. Print.

Lane, Calvin W. *Evelyn Waugh*. Boston: Twayne, 1981. Print.

Langbaum, Robert. *The Mysteries of Identity*. Oxford: Oxford UP, 1979. Print.

Lange, Victor, Theodore Ziolkowski, and Stanley Corngold, eds. *Thomas Mann*. Princeton, N. J.: Princeton University Library, 1975. Print.

———. *Thomas Mann—Tradition and Experiment*. Davis: U of California P, 1976. Print.

Lehnert, Herbert. *Thomas Mann: Fiktion, Mythos, Religion*. Stuttgart: W. Kohlhammer, 1976. Print.

Lehnert, Herbert and Eva Wessell. *Companion to the Works of Thomas Mann*. Rochester, N.Y.: Camden House, 2004. Print.

Leighton, Angela. *Shelley and the Sublime*. Cambridge: Cambridge UP, 1984. Print.

Lenz, Siegfried. *Deutschstunde*. Hamburg: Hoffmann und Campe, 1968. Print.

———. *Es waren Habichte in der Luft*. Hamburg: Hoffmann und Campe, 1951. Print.

———. "Etwas über Namen. Rede." *Siegfried Lenz: Werk und Wirkung*. Hrsg. Rudolf Wolff. Bonn: Bouvier Verlag Herbert Grundmann, 1985. 14–23. Print.

———. *The German Lesson*. Trans. Ernst Kaiser and Eithne Wilkins. New York: New Directions, 1986. Print.

———. *Heimatmuseum*. Hamburg: Hoffmann und Campe, 1978. Print.

———. *Das serbische Mädchen. Erzählungen*. Hamburg: Hoffmann und Campe, 1987. Print.

———. *So zärtlich war Suleyken. Masurische Geschichten*. Hamburg: Hoffmann und Campe, 1955. Print.

———. "Über Heinrich Böll." *Heinrich Böll: Leben und Schreiben 1917 bis 1985*. Ed. Christian Linder. Köln: Verlag Kiepenheuer & Witsch, 1986. Print.

———. *Das Vorbild*. Hamburg: Hoffmann und Campe, 1973. Print.

Leser, Esther H. *Thomas Mann's Short Fiction*. Rutherford, N.J.: Fairleigh Dickinson UP, 1989. Print.

Letsch, Felicia. *Auseinandersetzungen mit der Vergangenheit als Moment der Gegenwartskritik: Die Romane 'Billard um halb zehn' von Heinrich Böll, 'Hundejahre' von Günter Grass, 'Der Tod in Rom' von Wolfgang Koeppen und 'Deutschstunde' von Siegfried Lenz*. Köln: Pahl-Rugenstein, 1982. Print.

Lewis, C. S. *The Lion, the Witch, and the Wardrobe*. New York: Macmillan, 1955. Print.

Linder, Cynthia. *Romantic Imagery in the Novels of Charlotte Brontë*. London: Macmillan, 1978. Print.

Littlewood, Ian. "Nostalgia." *Critical Essays on Evelyn Waugh*. Ed. James F. Carens. Boston: G.K. Hall, 1987. 168–73. Print.

———. *The Writings of Evelyn Waugh*. Oxford: Blackwell, 1983. Print.

Liu, Alan, ed. Home page. *Voice of the Shuttle*. Dept. of English, U of California, Santa Barbara. Web. 14 May 2010.

Lodge, David. *Evelyn Waugh*. New York: Columbia UP, 1971. Print.

Loecker, Armand de. *Zwischen Atlantis und Frankfurt: Märchendichtung und goldenes Zeitalter bei E. T. A. Hoffmann*. Frankfurt am Main: Peter Lang, 1983. Print.

Long, J. V. "The Consolations of Exile: Evelyn Waugh and Catholicism." *Waugh without End: New Trends in Evelyn Waugh Studies*. Ed. Carlos Villar Flor and Robert Murray Davis. Bern: Peter Lang, 2005. 11–20. Print.

Lukács, Georg. *Thomas Mann*. Berlin: Aufbau-Verlag, 1949. Print.

Lüthi, Hans Jürg. *Hermann Hesse—Natur und Geist*. Stuttgart: W. Kohlhammer Verlag, 1970. Print.

Lützeler, Paul M., hrsg. *Deutsche Romane des 20. Jahrhunderts: neue Interpretationen*. Königstein/ Ts.: Athenäum, 1983. Print.

Lyons, Charles R. *Henrik Ibsen: The Divided Consciousness*. Carbondale: U of Southern Illinois P, 1972. Print.

Maletzke, Erich. *Siegfried Lenz: Eine biographische Annäherung*. Springe: zu Klampen Verlag, 2006. Print.

Mann, Thomas. *Adel des Geistes: Sechzehn Versuche zum Problem der Humanität*. Stockholm: Bermann—Fischer, 1945. Print.

———. *Die Betrachtungen eines Unpolitischen*. Berlin: S. Fischer, 1918. Print.

———. *Briefe*. Hrsg. Erika Mann. Frankfurt am Main: S. Fischer, 1961. Print.

———. *Buddenbrooks*. Trans. H. T. Lowe-Porter. New York: Vintage, 1984. Print.

———. *Buddenbrooks: Verfall einer Familie*. Berlin: S. Fischer, 1901. Print.

———. *Death in Venice and Seven Other Stories*. New York: Vintage, 1989. Print.

———. *Diaries, 1918–1939*. Trans. Richard and Clara Winston. London: Deutsch, 1983. Print.

———. *Doctor Faustus*. Trans. John E. Woods. New York: A. A. Knopf, 1997. Print.

———. *Doktor Faustus: das Leben des deutschen Tonsetzers Adrian Leverkühn erzählt von einem Freunde*. Frankfurt am Main: S. Fischer, 1951. Print.

———. *Essays of Three Decades*. Trans. H.T. Lowe-Porter. New York: A. Knopf, 1971. Print.

———. *Goethe und Tolstoi: zum Problem der Humanität*. Berlin: S. Fischer, 1932. Print.

———. *Joseph and His Brothers*. Trans. John E. Woods. New York: Everyman's Library, 2005. Print.

———. *Königliche Hoheit*. Berlin: Fischer, 1909. Print.

———. *Letters of Thomas Mann, 1889–1955*. Trans. Richard and Clara Winston. New York: A. A. Knopf, 1971. Print.

———. *Lotte in Weimar*. Stockholm: Bermann-Fischer Verlag, 1939. Print.

———. *The Magic Mountain*. New York: Vintage, 1969. Print.

———. *On Myself and Other Princeton Lectures*. Ed. James N. Bade. Frankfurt am Main: Peter Lang, 1997. Print.

———. *Sämtliche Erzählungen*. Frankfurt am Main: S. Fischer, 1971. Print.

———. *Thomas Mann—Heinrich Mann: Briefwechsel, 1900–1949*. Hrsg. Hans Wysling. Frankfurt am Main: S. Fischer, 1968. Print.

————. *Der Tod in Venedig.* Berlin: S. Fischer, 1913. Print.

————. *Tonio Kröger.* Berlin: Fischer, 1921. Print.

————. *Tristan: Sechs Novellen.* Berlin: S. Fischer, 1909. Print.

————. *Wagner und unsere Zeit: Aufsätze, Betrachtungen, Briefe.* Hrsg. Erika Mann. Frankfurt am Main: Fischer, 1963. Print.

————. *Der Zauberberg.* Berlin: S. Fischer, 1925. Print.

Matthias, Klaus. "*Renee Mauperin* und *Buddenbrooks.* Über eine literarische Beziehung im Bereich der Rezeption französischer Literatur durch die Brüder Mann. *Thomas Manns 'Buddenbrooks' und die Wirkung. 1 Teil.* Hrsg. Rudolf Wolff. Bonn: Bouvier Verlag Herbert Grundmann, 1986. 67–115. Print.

du Maurier, Daphne. *Rebecca.* Garden City, NY: Doubleday, 1938. Print.

Mayer, Hans. *Thomas Mann.* Frankfurt am Main: Suhrkamp, 1980. Print.

McCartney, George. *Confused Roaring: Evelyn Waugh and the Modernist Tradition.* Bloomington: Indiana UP, 1987. Print.

————. "Helena in Room 101: The Sum of Truth in Waugh and Orwell." *Waugh without End: New Trends in Evelyn Waugh Studies.* Ed. Carlos Villar Flor and Robert Murray Davis. Bern: Peter Lang, 2005. 59–69. Print.

McDonnell, Jacqueline. *Evelyn Waugh.* London: Macmillan, 1988. Print.

McFarlane, James, ed. *The Cambridge Companion to Ibsen.* Cambridge: Cambridge UP, 1994. Print.

————, ed. *Henrik Ibsen.* London: Penguin, 1970. Print.

————. *Ibsen and Meaning.* Norwich, England: Norwich P, 1989. Print.

McGlathery, James. *E. T. A. Hoffmann.* New York: Twayne, 1997. Print.

Mellor, Anne K. *English Romantic Irony.* Cambridge: Harvard UP, 1980. Print.

Meyerhoff, Hagen. *Die Figur des Alten im Werk von Siegfried Lenz.* Frankfurt am Main: Peter Lang, 1979. Print.

Mileck, Joseph. *Hermann Hesse: Life and Art.* Berkeley: U of California P, 1978. Print.

Mill, John Stuart. *On Liberty.* Ed. Elizabeth Rapaport. New York: Hackett, 1978. Print.

————. *The Spirit of the Age.* Ed. Frederick A. von Hayek. Chicago: U of Chicago P, 1942. Print.

Miller, James E. *F. Scott Fitzgerald: His Art and His Technique.* New York: NYU Press, 1964. Print.

Mizener, Arthur. *The Far Side of Paradise: A Biography of F. Scott Fitzgerald.* Boston: Houghton Mifflin, 1951. Print.

Moglen, Helene. *Charlotte Brontë—The Self-Conceived.* New York: W. W. Norton, 1976. Print.

————. "The End of *Jane Eyre* and the Creation of a Feminist Myth." *Modern Critical Interpretations—Charlotte Brontë's Jane Eyre.* Ed. Harold Bloom. New York: Chelsea House, 1987. 47–62. Print.

Montgomery-Massingberd, Hugh and Christopher S. Sykes. *Great Houses of England and Wales.* New York: Rizzoli International, 1994. Print.

Moorman, Charles. "The Shire, Mordor, and Minas Tirith." *Tolkien and the Critics: Essays on J. R. R. Tolkien's 'The Lord of the Rings.'* Ed. Neil D. Isaacs and Rose A. Zimbardo. Notre Dame, IN: U of Notre Dame P, 1968. 201–17. Print.

Morelli, Marcello, ed. *Royal Palaces*. New York: Barnes & Noble (by arrangement with White Star S. r. l., Italy), 1999. Print.

Moreno, Cristina Flores. "Dialogue between E. Waugh and G. Greene: Two Different Approaches to Art and Religion in *Brideshead Revisited* and *The End of the Affair*." *Waugh without End: New Trends in Evelyn Waugh Studies*. Ed. Carlos Villar Flor and Robert Murray Davis. Bern: Peter Lang, 2005. 181–191. Print.

Morton, Timothy, ed. *The Cambridge Companion to Shelley*. Cambridge; New York: Cambridge UP, 2006. Print.

Moseley, Charles. *J. R. R. Tolkien*. Plymouth (UK): Northcote House, 1997. Print.

Mosley, Charlotte, ed. *The Letters of Nancy Mitford and Evelyn Waugh*. Boston: Houghton Mifflin, 1996. Print.

Myers, William. *Evelyn Waugh and the Problem of Evil*. Boston: Faber, 1991. Print.

Nehring, Wolfgang. *Spätromantiker: Eichendorff und E. T. A. Hoffmann*. Göttingen: Vandenhoeck & Ruprecht, 1997. Print.

Nicholson, Lewis E., ed. *An Anthology of Beowulf Criticism*. Notre Dame, IN: U of Notre Dame P, 1963. Print.

Nicolson, Nigel. *The World of Jane Austen*. London: Weidenfeld and Nicolson, 1991. Print.

Nielen, Manfred. *Frömmigkeit bei Heinrich Böll*. Annweiler: Verlag Thomas Plöger, 1987. Print.

Nietzsche, Friedrich. *Thus Spoke Zarathustra*. Trans. R. J. Hollingdale. Baltimore: Penguin, 1962. Print.

Nitzsche, Jane Chance. *The Genius Figure in Antiquity and the Middle Ages*. New York and London: Columbia UP, 1975. Print.

———. *Tolkien's Art: A Mythology for England*. New York: St. Martin's P, 1979. Print.

Noel, Ruth S. *The Languages of Tolkien's Middle-earth*. Boston: Houghton Mifflin, 1980. Print.

———. *The Mythology of Middle-earth*. Boston: Houghton Mifflin, 1978. Print.

Nordbruch, Claus. *Über die Pflicht: Eine Analyse des Werkes von Siegfried Lenz*. Hildesheim: Georg Olms, 1996. Print.

Northam, John. *Ibsen, A Critical Study*. Cambridge: Cambridge UP, 1973. Print.

Page, Norman. *An Evelyn Waugh Chronology*. New York: St. Martin's, 1997. Print.

Pasternak, Boris. *Doctor Zhivago*. Trans. Max Hayward and Manya Harari. New York: Pantheon, 1958. Print.

Pater, Walter. *The Renaissance*. London: Macmillan, 1925. Print.

Patey, Douglas Lane. *The Life of Evelyn Waugh: A Critical Biography*. Oxford: Blackwell, 1998. Print.

Pätzold, Hartmut. *Theorie und Praxis moderner Schreibweisen am Beispiel von Siegfried Lenz und Helmut Heissenbüttel*. Bonn: Bouvier, 1976. Print.

Paulsen, Wolfgang. *Eichendorff und sein Taugenichts: die innere Problematik des Dichters in seinem Werk*. Bern: Francke Verlag, 1976. Print.

Paulson, Ronald. *Emblem and Expression: Meaning in English Art of the Eighteenth Century*. Cambridge, Mass.: Harvard UP, 1975. Print.

Pearce, Joseph. *Tolkien: Man and Myth*. London and San Francisco: HarperCollins & Ignatius P, 1998. Print.

Perkins, David, ed. *English Romantic Writers*. New York: Harcourt Brace, 1967. Print.

Perosa, Sergio. *The Art of F. Scott Fitzgerald*. Ann Arbor: U of Michigan P, 1965. Print.

Petty, Anne C. *One Ring to Bind Them All: Tolkien's Mythology*. University, AL: U of Alabama P, 1979. Print.

Pfeifer, Martin, Hrsg. *Hermann Hesses weltweite Wirkung*. Frankfurt am Main: Suhrkamp Verlag, 1977. Print.

Phillips, Gene D. *Evelyn Waugh's Officers, Gentlemen and Rogues: The Fact behind His Fiction*. Chicago: Nelson-Hall, 1975. Print.

Prater, Donald A. *Thomas Mann: A Life*. Oxford: Clarendon P, 1995. Print.

Pritzlaff, Christine. *Zahlensymbolik bei Thomas Mann*. Hamburg: Helmut Buske Verlag, 1972. Print.

Prodaniuk, Ihor. *The Imagery in Heinrich Böll's Novels*. Bonn: Bouvier Verlag Herbert Grundmann, 1979. Print.

Pryce-Jones, David, ed. *Evelyn Waugh and His World*. Boston: Little, Brown, 1973. Print.

Purtill, Richard. *J. R. R. Tolkien: Myth, Morality, and Religion*. New York: Harper and Row, 1984. Print.

Pütz, Peter. *Kunst und Künstlerexistenz bei Nietzsche und Thomas Mann. Zum Problem des ästhetischen Perspektivismus in der Moderne*. Bonn: 1963. Print.

Pyle, Forest. *The Ideology of Imagination*. Stanford: Stanford UP, 1995. Print.

Radcliffe, Ann. *The Mysteries of Udolpho*. Oxford; New York: Oxford UP, 1998. Print.

Raddatz, F. J. *ZEIT-Gespräche 2*. Frankfurt am Main: Suhrkamp, 1982. Print.

Reed, T. J. "Mann and History." *The Cambridge Companion to Thomas Mann*. Ed. Ritchie Robertson. Cambridge: Cambridge UP, 2002. 1–21. Print.

———. *Thomas Mann: The Uses of Tradition*. Oxford: Clarendon P, 1996. Print.

Reich-Ranicki, Marcel. *Deutsche Literatur in West und Ost. Prosa seit 1945*. München: Piper, 1963. Print.

———. "Siegfried Lenz: die Ein-Mann-Partei. Eine Jubiläumsrede." *Siegfried Lenz: Werk und Wirkung*. Hrsg. Rudolf Wolff. Bonn: Bouvier Verlag Herbert Grundmann, 1985. 8–13. Print.

Reid, J. H. *Heinrich Böll—A German for His Time*. Oxford: Berg, 1988. Print.

Reiman, Donald H. *Percy Bysshe Shelley*. New York: Twayne, 1969. Print.

Reiman, Donald H. and Neil Fraistat, eds. *Shelley's Poetry and Prose*. 2nd ed. New York: W. W. Norton, 2002. Print.

Reiter, Nikolaus. *Wertstrukturen im erzählerischen Werk von Siegfried Lenz*. Frankfurt am Main: Peter Lang, 1982.

Rickes, Joachim. *Die Romankunst des jungen Thomas Mann: 'Buddenbrooks' und 'Königliche Hoheit.'* Würzburg: Königshausen & Neumann, 2006. Print.

Ridley, Hugh. *Problematic Bourgeois: Twentieth-Century Criticism on Thomas Mann's Buddenbrooks and The Magic Mountain.* Columbia, S.C.: Camden House, 1994. Print.

———. *Thomas Mann: Buddenbrooks.* Cambridge: Cambridge UP, 1987. Print.

Rilke, Rainer Maria. "Thomas Manns *Buddenbrooks.*" *Thomas Manns 'Buddenbrooks' und die Wirkung. 1. Teil.* Hrsg. Rudolf Wolff. Bonn: Bouvier Verlag Herbert Grundmann, 1986. 21–23. Print.

Robertson, Ritchie, ed. *The Cambridge Companion to Thomas Mann.* Cambridge: Cambridge UP, 2002. Print.

———. *The Golden Pot and Other Tales: A New Translation.* New York: Oxford UP, 2009. Print.

Rose, Ernst. *Faith from the Abyss: Hermann Hesse's Way from Romanticism to Modernity.* New York: NYU Press, 1975. Print.

Rosebury, Brian. *Tolkien: A Critical Reassessment.* New York: St. Martin's P, 1992. Print.

Russ, Colin, hrsg. *Der Schriftsteller Siegfried Lenz. Urteile und Standpunkte. 2. Auflage.* Hamburg: Hoffmann und Campe, 1973. Print.

Ryder, Frank, ed. *German Romantic Stories.* New York: Continuum, 1988. Print.

Sale, Roger. *Modern Heroism: Essays on D. H. Lawrence, William Empson, and J. R. R. Tolkien.* Berkeley, Los Angeles, and London: U of California P, 1973. Print.

———. "Tolkien and Frodo Baggins." *Tolkien and the Critics: Essays on J. R. R. Tolkien's 'The Lord of the Rings.'* Ed. Neil D. Isaacs and Rose A. Zimbardo. Notre Dame, IN: U of Notre Dame P, 1968. 247–88. Print.

Sammons, Jeffrey. *Heinrich Heine: A Modern Biography.* Princeton, N.J.: Princeton UP, 1979. Print.

Sandt, Lotti. *Mythos und Symbolik im Zauberberg von Thomas Mann.* Bern: Paul Haupt, 1979. Print.

Sartre, Jean-Paul. "Existentialism and Humanism." *The Humanities in Contemporary Life.* Ed. Robert F. Davidson and Sarah Herndon. New York: Henry Holt, 1960. 423–32. Print.

Saueressig, Heinz. *Die Entstehung des Romans 'Der Zauberberg.'* Biberach an der Riss: 1965. Print.

Scaff, Susan von Rohr. *History, Myth, and Music: Thomas Mann's Timely Fiction.* Columbia, SC: Camden House, 1998. Print.

Scharfschwerdt, Jürgen. *Thomas Mann und der deutsche Bildungsroman.* Stuttgart: W. Kohlhammer, 1967. Print.

Schneider, Wolfgang. *Lebensfreundlichkeit und Pessimismus: Thomas Manns Figurendarstellung.* Frankfurt am Main: Klostermann, 1999. Print.

Schorske, Carl E. *Fin-de-siècle Vienna.* New York: Vintage, 1981. Print.

Schwarz, Egon. *Joseph von Eichendorff.* New York: Twayne, 1972. Print.

Seidlin, Oskar. *Von Goethe zu Thomas Mann.* Göttingen: 1963. Print.

Seiters, Dan. *Image Patterns in the Novels of F. Scott Fitzgerald.* Ann Arbor: U of Michigan Press, 1986. Print.

Shippey, Tom. *J. R. R. Tolkien: Author of the Century.* Boston: Houghton Mifflin, 2000. Print.

———. *The Road to Middle-earth.* Rev. and expanded ed. Boston: Houghton Mifflin, 2003. Print.

Shookman, Ellis. *Thomas Mann's Death in Venice: A Novella and its Critics.* Rochester, N.Y.: Camden House, 2003. Print.

Spacks, Patricia Meyer. "Power and Meaning in *The Lord of the Rings.*" *Tolkien and the Critics: Essays on J. R. R. Tolkien's 'The Lord of the Rings.'* Ed. Neil D. Isaacs and Rose A. Zimbardo. Notre Dame, IN: U of Notre Dame P. 1968. 81–99. Print.

Spender, Stephen. "The World of Evelyn Waugh." *Critical Essays on Evelyn Waugh.* Ed. James F. Carens. Boston: G.K. Hall, 1987. 59–71. Print.

Sprecher, Thomas. *Davos im "Zauberberg": Thomas Manns Roman und sein Schauplatz.* München: Fink, 1996. Print.

Stannard, Martin, ed. *Evelyn Waugh: The Critical Heritage.* London: Routledge and Kegan Paul, 1984. Print.

———. *Evelyn Waugh: The Early Years 1903–1939.* New York: Norton, 1987. Print.

———. *Evelyn Waugh: The Later Years 1939–1966.* New York: Norton, 1992. Print.

Stanton, Michael N. *Hobbits, Elves, and Wizards: Exploring the Wonders and Worlds of J. R. R. Tolkien's 'The Lord of the Rings.'* New York: Palgrave, 2001. Print.

Stavola, T. J. *Scott Fitzgerald: Crisis in an American Identity.* London: Vision Press, 1979. Print.

Stelzig, Eugene L. *Hermann Hesse's Fictions of the Self.* Princeton, N.J.: Princeton UP, 1988. Print.

Stopp, Frederick J. *Evelyn Waugh: Portrait of an Artist.* London: Chapman and Hall, 1958. Print.

Swales, Martin. *Buddenbrooks: Family Life as the Mirror of Social Change.* Boston: Twayne, 1991. Print.

———. *The German Bildungsroman from Wieland to Hesse.* Princeton, N.J.: Princeton UP, 1978. Print.

Sykes, Christopher. *Evelyn Waugh: A Biography.* Boston: Little, Brown, 1975. Print.

Tatar, Maria, ed. *The Classic Fairy Tales.* New York: Norton, 1999. Print.

Thomas, R. Hinton. *Thomas Mann: The Mediation of Art.* Oxford: Oxford UP, 1956. Print.

Tolkien, Christopher, ed. *The Book of Lost Tales, Part One.* Volume 1, *The History of Middle-Earth.* Boston: Houghton Mifflin, 1983. Print.

———, ed. *The Book of Lost Tales, Part Two.* Volume 2, *The History of Middle-Earth.* Boston: Houghton Mifflin, 1984. Print.

———, ed. *The Shaping of Middle-Earth: The Quenta, the Ambarkanta, and the Annals, Together with the Earliest 'Silmarillion' and the First Map.* Volume 4, *The History of Middle-Earth.* Boston: Houghton Mifflin, 1986. Print.

———, ed. *The Return of the Shadow: The History of The Lord of the Rings, Part One.* Volume 6, *The History of Middle-Earth.* Boston: Houghton Mifflin, 1988. Print.

———, ed. *The Treason of Isengard: The History of The Lord of the Rings, Part Two.* Volume 7, *The History of Middle-Earth.* Boston: Houghton Mifflin, 1989. Print.

———, ed. *The War of the Ring: The History of The Lord of the Rings, Part Three.* Volume 8, *The History of Middle-Earth.* Boston: Houghton Mifflin, 1990. Print.

Tolkien, J. R. R. *The Hobbit.* New York: Ballantine, 1966. Print.

———. *The Lord of the Rings* (3 volumes). New York: Ballantine Books, 1965. Print.

———. "On Fairy-Stories." *Tree and Leaf.* London: Unwin Hyman, 1988. 9–73. Print.

———. *The Silmarillion.* Ed. Christopher Tolkien. Boston: Houghton Mifflin, 1977. Print.

——— and E. V. Gordon, eds. *Sir Gawain and the Green Knight.* Oxford: Clarendon P, 1967. Print.

———. *The Tolkien Reader.* New York: Ballantine, 1966. Print.

Tolstoy, Leo. *War and Peace.* Trans. Constance Garnett. New York: Random House, 1994. Print.

Tyler, J. E. A. *The New Tolkien Companion.* New York: St. Martin's P, 1979. Print.

Untermeyer, Louis. *Modern American and Modern British Poetry.* New York: Harcourt Brace, 1955. Print.

Urban, Martin. *Emil Nolde—Flowers and Animals.* Trans. Barbara Berg. New York: Frederick A. Praeger, 1966. Print.

Vaget, Hans Rudolf. *Thomas Mann's 'The Magic Mountain': A Casebook.* New York: Oxford UP, 2008. Print.

Vendler, Helen. "Tintern Abbey: Two Assaults." *Wordsworth in Context.* Ed. Pauline Fletcher and John Murphy. Lewisburg, PA: Bucknell UP, 1992. 173–190. Print.

Vogt, Jochen. *Thomas Mann: Buddenbrooks.* München: Wilhelm Fink, 1983. Print.

Wagener, Hans, hrsg. *Gegenwartsliteratur und Drittes Reich. Deutsche Autoren in der Auseinandersetzung mit der Vergangenheit.* Stuttgart: Reclam, 1977. Print.

———. *Siegfried Lenz.4. Auflage.* München: Beck, 1985. Print.

Walpole, Horace. *The Castle of Otranto.* London: Cassell, 1886. Print.

Walter, Hugo G. *Beautiful Sanctuaries in Nineteenth- and Early-Twentieth-Century European Literature.* New York; Bern: Peter Lang, 2011. Print.

———. *A Purple-Golden Renascence of Eden-Exalting Rainbows.* Santa Barbara, CA: Fithian P, 2001. Print.

———. *Sanctuaries of Light in Nineteenth Century European Literature.* New York; Bern: Peter Lang, 2010. Print.

———. *Space and Time on the Magic Mountain: Studies in Nineteenth- and Early-Twentieth-Century European Literature.* New York; Bern: Peter Lang, 1999. Print.

Wasserman, Earl R. *Shelley: A Critical Reading.* Baltimore: Johns Hopkins UP, 1971. Print.

Waugh, Evelyn. *Brideshead Revisited: The Sacred and Profane Memories of Captain Charles Ryder.* Boston: Little, Brown, 1946. Print.

———. *The Complete Short Stories and Selected Drawings.* Ed. Ann Pasternak Slater. London: Everyman's Library, 1998. Print.

———. *The Diaries of Evelyn Waugh.* Ed. Michael Davie. Boston: Little, Brown, 1976. Print.

———. *The Essays, Articles and Reviews of Evelyn Waugh.* Ed. Donat Gallagher. Boston: Little, Brown, 1983. Print.

———. *The Letters of Evelyn Waugh.* Ed. Mark Amory. New York: Ticknor & Fields, 1980. Print.

———. *Men at Arms.* Boston: Little, Brown, 1952. Print.

————. *Officers and Gentlemen.* Boston: Little, Brown, 1955. Print.

————. *Unconditional Surrender.* London: Chapman & Hall, 1961. Print.

Weber, Albrecht, hrsg. *Siegfried Lenz: Deutschstunde.* München: Oldenbourg, 1973. Print.

Weigand, Hermann J. *The Magic Mountain.* Chapel Hill: U of North Carolina P, 1964. Print.

————. *The Modern Ibsen.* New York: E. P. Dutton, 1960. Print.

West, Richard C. *Tolkien Criticism: An Annotated Checklist.* Kent, OH: Kent State UP, 1981. Print.

Whittingham, Elizabeth A. *The Evolution of Tolkien's Mythology.* Jefferson, NC: McFarland & Company, 2008. Print.

Williams, C. E. "Not an Inn, But an Hospital." *Thomas Mann's 'The Magic Mountain.'* Ed. Harold Bloom. New York: Chelsea House, 1986. 37–51. Print.

Williams, Oscar, ed. *Immortal Poems of the English Language.* New York: Simon and Schuster, 1952. Print.

Williams, Raymond. *Culture and Society: 1780–1950.* New York: Columbia UP, 1960. Print.

Wilson, John Howard. *Evelyn Waugh—A Literary Biography, 1924–1966.* London: Associated University Presses, 2001. Print.

Wilton, Andrew. *Turner and the Sublime.* London: British Museum Publications, 1980. Print.

Winston, Richard. *Thomas Mann: The Making of an Artist.* New York: Alfred A. Knopf, 1978. Print.

Winston, Richard and Clara Winston, trans. *Exceptional Friendship: The Correspondence of Thomas Mann and Erich Kahler.* Ithaca: Cornell UP, 1975. Print.

Wirth, Annette. *The Loss of Traditional Values and the Continuance of Faith in Evelyn Waugh's Novels: A Handful of Dust, Brideshead Revisited* and *Sword of Honour.* New York: Peter Lang, 1990. Print.

Wlecke, Albert O. *Wordsworth and the Sublime.* Berkeley: U of California P, 1973. Print.

Wodehouse, P. G. *Sunset at Blandings.* New York: Simon & Schuster, 1977. Print.

Wolf, Ernest M. "Scheidung und Mischung: Sprache und Gesellschaft in Thomas Manns *Buddenbrooks.*" *Thomas Manns 'Buddenbrooks' und die Wirkung. 2. Teil.* Hrsg. Rudolf Wolff. Bonn: Bouvier Verlag Herbert Grundmann, 1986. 75–94. Print.

Wolff, Rudolf, Hrsg. *Siegfried Lenz: Werk und Wirkung.* Bonn: Bouvier Verlag Herbert Grundmann, 1985. Print.

Wolff, Rudolf, Hrsg. *Thomas Manns 'Buddenbrooks' und die Wirkung. 1. Teil.* Bonn: Bouvier Verlag Herbert Grundmann, 1986. Print.

————, Hrsg. *Thomas Manns 'Buddenbrooks' und die Wirkung. 2. Teil.* Bonn: Bouvier Verlag Herbert Grundmann, 1986. Print.

Woolf, Virginia. *To the Lighthouse.* San Diego: Harcourt Brace, 1981. Print.

Wordsworth, Jonathan, et al. *Wordsworth and the Age of English Romanticism.* New Brunswick, N.J.: Rutgers UP, 1987. Print.

Wordsworth, William. *The Prelude (1799, 1805, 1850).* Ed. Jonathan Wordsworth, M. H. Abrams, and Stephen Gill. New York: W. W. Norton, 1979. Print.

Worm-Kaschuge, Heidrun. *Lenz—Deutschstunde. Untersuchungen zum Roman.* Hollfeld/Ofr.: J. Beyer, 1977. Print.

Wührl, Paul-Wolfgang. *E. T. A. Hoffmann: Der goldene Topf: die Utopie einer ästhetischen Existenz.* Paderborn: F. Schöningh, 1988. Print.

Wykes, David. *Evelyn Waugh: A Literary Life.* New York: St. Martin's, 1999. Print.

Wysling, Hans, and Yvonne Schmidlin, eds. *Thomas Mann: Ein Leben in Bildern.* Zürich: Artemis, 1974. Print.

Yarwood, Doreen. *The Architecture of Europe.* London: Chancellor Press, 1974. Print.

Zeller, Michael. "Seele und Saldo. Ein texttreuer Gang durch *Buddenbrooks*." *Thomas Manns 'Buddenbrooks' und die Wirkung.* 2. *Teil.* Hrsg. Rudolf Wolff. Bonn: Bouvier Verlag Herbert Grundmann, 1986. 9–42. Print.

Zimbardo, Rose A. "Moral Vision in *The Lord of the Rings.*" *Tolkien and the Critics: Essays on J. R. R. Tolkien's 'The Lord of the Rings.'* Ed. Neil D. Isaacs and Rose A. Zimbardo. Notre Dame, IN: U of Notre Dame P, 1968. 100–08. Print.

Zimmermann, Jürg. *Repräsentation und Intimität: zu einem Wertgegensatz bei Thomas Mann, mit besonderer Berücksichtigung der Werke aus den Jahren vor und während des Ersten Weltkriegs.* Zürich; München: Artemis-Verlag, 1975. Print.

Ziolkowski, Theodore. *Dimensions of the Modern Novel.* Princeton, N.J.: Princeton UP, 1969. Print.

———, ed. *Hesse: A Collection of Critical Essays.* Englewood Cliffs, N.J.: Prentice-Hall, 1973. Print.

———. *The Novels of Hermann Hesse: A Study in Theme and Structure.* Princeton, N.J.: Princeton UP, 1965. Print.

Zipes, Jack. *The Brothers Grimm: From Enchanted Forests to the Modern World.* New York: Palgrave Macmillan, 2002. Print.

Index

Studies on Themes and Motifs in Literature

The series is designed to advance the publication of research pertaining to themes and motifs in literature. The studies cover cross-cultural patterns as well as the entire range of national literatures. They trace the development and use of themes and motifs over extended periods, elucidate the significance of specific themes or motifs for the formation of period styles, and analyze the unique structural function of themes and motifs. By examining themes or motifs in the work of an author or period, the studies point to the impulses authors received from literary tradition, the choices made, and the creative transformation of the cultural heritage. The series will include publications of colloquia and theoretical studies that contribute to a greater understanding of literature.

For additional information about this series or for the submission of manuscripts, please contact:

Dr. Heidi Burns
Peter Lang Publishing
P.O. Box 1246
Bel Air, MD 21014-1246

To order other books in this series, please contact our Customer Service Department:

800-770-LANG (within the U.S.)
212-647-7706 (outside the U.S.)
212-647-7707 FAX

Or browse online by series at:

www.peterlang.com